Pea Ridge

Bill Moore

1/19

William L. Shea & Earl J. Hess

The University of North Carolina Press   Chapel Hill & London

Pea Ridge

Civil War Campaign in the West

Library of Congress Cataloging-in-Publication Data

Shea, William L.

  Pea Ridge : Civil War campaign in the West / by William

L. Shea and Earl J. Hess.

    p.   cm.

  Includes bibliographical references and index.

  ISBN 0-8078-2042-3 (acid-free paper)

  1. Pea Ridge, Battle of, 1862.   I. Hess, Earl J.   II. Title.

E473.17.S54   1992

973.7′31 — dc20   92-4465

                          CIP

96 95 94 93 92   5 4 3 2 1

Contents

Maps

Illustrations

Preface

In 1902 while speaking to a National Encampment of the Grand Army of the Republic in Washington, D.C., Grenville M. Dodge recalled the beginning of his Civil War experience forty years before. Dodge had risen to the rank of major general and had participated in many famous operations in Tennessee and Georgia, but he told his audience that he was proudest of what he had accomplished as a young colonel in Missouri and Arkansas in the second year of the war. He declared that during the Pea Ridge campaign the unheralded Army of the Southwest, Samuel R. Curtis commanding, did "more marching and endured more suffering than the great armies I was connected with east of the Mississippi." Dodge accurately expressed the sentiments of many aging Federal veterans of Pea Ridge, one of whom wrote a few years earlier that "for hard fighting, long and weary marches, as well as privations and sufferings endured, no army can show a better record, or one deserving greater credit, than the Army of the Southwest."[1]

This book is the first detailed study of the Pea Ridge campaign, an often overlooked but important Trans-Mississippi operation which had a significant impact on the course of events in the West. It is primarily the story of how the Federal Army of the Southwest triumphed over its nemesis, the Confederate Army of the West, in a desperate two-day battle in northwestern Arkansas in March 1862. In preparing this study, we were discouraged to note how frequently military operations in the Trans-Mississippi are disparaged or even dismissed as irrelevant by historians who should know better. It seems obvious to us that events in Missouri and Arkansas were as much a part of the Civil War as events in Virginia or Georgia and are equally deserving of scholarly and popular attention. True, campaigns west of the great river had only a modest effect on the ultimate outcome of the struggle, but the terrible drama of battle and the devastation wrought by passing armies recognized no geographical barriers. Northerners and southerners fought as desperately in an Arkansas thicket as they did in a Pennsylvania wheatfield.

In attempting to produce a comprehensive account of the Pea Ridge campaign we foraged for unpublished manuscript material in archives from Connecticut to California and from Michigan to Louisiana. We also reconnoitered dozens of big-city and small-town newspapers in search of soldiers' letters published as a public service for the information they contained, a common practice during the Civil War. We uncovered an enormous amount of unpublished and published (but long forgotten) material on the campaign, far more than we expected to find or could possibly use. We came away from this project convinced that the Civil War in the West is fertile ground for pioneering historians.

A one-volume study of a large campaign or battle rarely takes note of tactics below the brigade level, but because Pea Ridge was a medium-sized engagement, we discuss tactics down to the company and battery level and examine leadership, logistics, medical care, ethnic and personal conflicts, and other aspects of Civil War operations often overlooked. And because the story of a campaign does not necessarily end when the last shot has been fired or the last mile has been marched, we also explore the cultural legacy of Pea Ridge and the fate of the battlefield itself, now largely preserved within the boundaries of Pea Ridge National Military Park. We hope that the result will come close to being a complete study of a single Civil War campaign.

At an early stage of this project we realized that we would have to undertake a meticulous examination of the battlefield. It is no exaggeration to say that without this inspection our study of the campaign, and especially of the battle, would have been only half done. Unlike Shiloh, Vicksburg, Chickamauga, and Gettysburg, Pea Ridge National Military Park is not graced (or cursed) with a forest of memorials and markers erected in the postwar decades. The National Park Service has installed only minimal interpretive aids, and these are limited to a handful of sites along the tour road and hiking trails. Fortunately, the sprawling park includes essentially all the ground where maneuvering and fighting took place, and the terrain and vegetation are much as they were in 1862. Intensive exploration of the battlefield over several years proved invaluable; the land often yielded information and insights not found in the written record. Faint traces of forgotten fences and lanes were vital clues to the location of units, the rationale for tactical decisions, and the evolution of the battle. We also struck out from the battlefield and explored the web of roads—nearly all of which still exist in some form—that brought the Army of the Southwest and the Army of the West to their tragic encounter in the northwestern corner of Arkansas.

This particular methodology often took us away from our microfilm readers and word processors and allowed us to enter, at least to some extent, the physical world of 1862. On frosty Ozark days we followed the same winding roads, walked across the same rolling fields, explored the same rugged high lands and deep hollows, and plunged into the same thickets where thousands of cold, hungry, and anxious men had marched, camped, fought, and died more than a century ago. No better way exists to experience faint, fleeting glimpses of another time.

Many archivists, librarians, and historians were extremely helpful during our research trips and exploratory treks. We would like to express our special thanks to William Droessler, Sandra Dupree, and Jacqueline Robinson of the University of Arkansas at Monticello; Michael Dabrishus and Kim Scott of the University of Arkansas at Fayetteville; Chris Marhenke of the Broward County Public Library; John Bradbury, Jr., of the University of Missouri at Rolla; Michael Meier of the National Archives and Records Administration; Michael Mullins of Wayne, New Jersey; Kenneth Winn of the Missouri State Archives; Thomas Graber of Dallas; and the staff of Pea Ridge National Military Park, past and present.

Financial support was provided by the Faculty Development Fund and the Faculty Research Committee of the University of Arkansas at Monticello, the McLaughlin Fund of the History Department of the University of Arkansas at Fayetteville, and the National Endowment for the Humanities.

1 Winter Campaign

By the end of 1861 the struggle for Missouri had reached an impasse. Federal forces firmly held St. Louis and maintained a tenuous grip on the Missouri River Valley, but the secessionist Missouri State Guard defiantly stood its ground near Springfield in the southwest corner of the state. As the opposing forces faced each other across the drab wintry landscape of the Ozark Plateau, developments were taking place that would put thousands of men in motion and shatter the stalemate. Missouri's fate, and the course of the Civil War in the Trans-Mississippi, would be determined early in the new year on a frosty battlefield in northwestern Arkansas.

Brig. Gen. Nathaniel Lyon was primarily responsible for Federal achievements in Missouri during the first year of the war. He seized the initiative in the uncertain weeks following Fort Sumter and, relying heavily on volunteer regiments raised from the loyal German population of St. Louis, drove the secessionist government and its military arm, Maj. Gen. Sterling Price's Missouri State Guard, out of Jefferson City and into the far reaches of southwestern Missouri.

Lyon was not satisfied with this partial victory. He recognized that as long as the state guard remained in being, it posed a threat to Federal authority. In midsummer Lyon boldly marched into southwestern Missouri with a small army and occupied Springfield. This time Lyon's aggressiveness led to disaster. The Federals were outnumbered two to one by the combined forces of Price's state guard and Brig. Gen. Benjamin McCulloch's Confederate army that had crossed into Missouri from northwestern Arkansas. McCulloch believed it was essential to sustain the secessionist cause in Missouri, which still remained in the Union, because the state guard provided a buffer between the Federals and the Confederate states of the Trans-Mississippi. The opposing forces clashed south of Springfield at Wilson's Creek on August 10, 1861. Lyon was killed, and his little army was driven from the field.

While the Federals retreated to Rolla, Price led his triumphant state guard northward to wrench the Missouri River Valley from enemy hands. The Missourians marched without their Confederate allies. McCulloch was prepared to edge across the border into Missouri to help the state guard stay in the field, but he was unwilling to launch a major invasion of a Union state on his own initiative. Moreover, he did not believe such an offensive could succeed given the large number of Federal troops in Missouri and their control of the rivers and railroads. McCulloch's assessment proved correct. Price and the state guard managed to overwhelm an isolated Federal garrison at Lexington on the southern bank of the Missouri River but soon were compelled to fall back toward Springfield.[1]

Maj. Gen. John C. Frémont, Lyon's successor, gathered a sizable Federal force and reoccupied Springfield in late October. Price again called on McCulloch, who responded by massing his troops along the Arkansas-Missouri line. The Federal threat ended in an unexpected manner in early November when President Abraham Lincoln relieved Frémont from command. Maj. Gen. David Hunter promptly abandoned all that Frémont had gained and dispersed his army across Missouri. For the second time in only a few months the Federals had seized and then lost the initiative in Missouri.[2]

McCulloch was satisfied that the Trans-Mississippi Confederacy was secure for the time being and placed his men in winter quarters in Arkansas. Price, ever the opportunist, could not resist advancing northward once again in the wake of the retiring Federals. A bit more cautious this time, Price halted his command on the Osage River near Osceola, sixty miles north of Springfield, and settled down to await developments. While on the Osage, Price learned that Governor Claiborne F. Jackson and a rump session of the Missouri legislature had assembled in Neosho and had approved an ordinance of secession. The legitimacy of this proceeding was dubious, to say the least; but it satisfied the authorities in Richmond, and Missouri added its star to the Confederate flag on November 28. Price hoped his state guardsmen would transfer en masse into Confederate ranks, but he was disappointed. Many Missourians had no desire to serve outside the state or for more than a few months at a time. Officers were especially reluctant to transfer for fear they would lose their commissions or be demoted. By the end of the year only about half of Price's Missourians had enlisted in the Confederate army; the other half remained in the state guard.[3]

While these events were taking place in southwestern Missouri, a notable change in Federal personnel occurred in St. Louis. On November 19 Maj. Gen. Henry W. Halleck replaced the ineffectual Hunter as commander of the Department of the Missouri. Halleck's appointment was the major turning point in the Civil War in the West. The new Federal commander was a military intellectual who was known in the army, somewhat derisively, as "Old Brains." No one yet realized that Halleck also was an exceptionally capable administrator. Few other Union officers had the skills necessary to professionalize the bumbling Union war effort in the Trans-Mississippi, which to this point had been marked by rashness, amateurism, and incompetence. Surveying the wreckage left by his predecessors, Halleck recognized that Price's amalgam of Confederate and state guard troops was much more than a local threat. St. Louis was the primary base of operations for projected offensives on the Mississippi, Tennessee, and Cumberland rivers. Every Federal soldier stationed in Missouri to counter the state guard and protect St. Louis was one less soldier that could be used in the upcoming river campaigns. Brig. Gen. William T. Sherman also saw Halleck's strategic dilemma. Sherman informed his brother, Senator John Sherman, that as soon as Halleck "moves a man from the interior to go to Cairo, Price will return. That is his game. And in that way with a comparatively small force he holds in check five times his number."[4]

The projected river campaigns in Halleck's Department of the Missouri were to be coordinated with overland movements in Maj. Gen. Don Carlos Buell's Department of the Ohio. Buell, supported by Lincoln and Maj. Gen. George B. McClellan in Washington, pressured Halleck to cooperate with him in moving against Confederate positions in Kentucky and Tennessee. But Halleck considered it "madness" to siphon off men for operations outside Missouri so long as a rebel force menaced St. Louis.[5]

This was an intolerable situation. Price's ragtag Missouri army was paralyzing Federal operations from Kentucky to Kansas. Like Lyon and Frémont before him, Halleck realized that he must go on the offensive in Missouri and harry the rebels out of the state as quickly as possible. But unlike his prede-

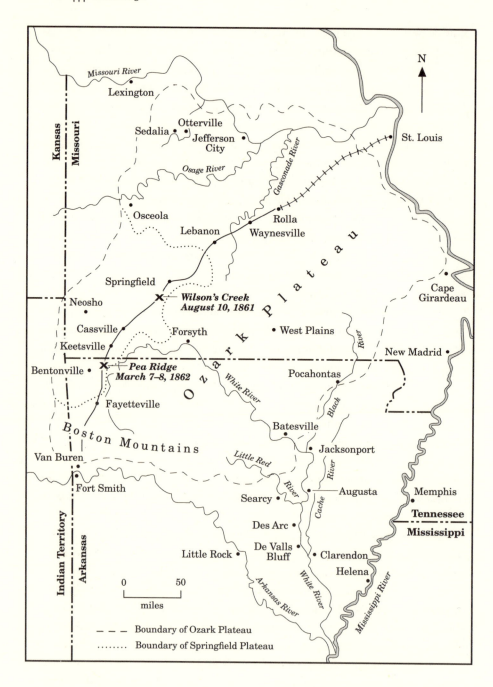

Map 1-1. Southern Missouri and Northern Arkansas

cessors, Halleck would not take the field himself. On December 25 he placed Brig. Gen. Samuel R. Curtis in command of the new Military District of Southwest Missouri, an area which included all of Missouri south of the Osage River and west of the Meramec River. Curtis's mission was simple: to launch an offensive and defeat, disperse, or destroy Price's Missouri army. Once the rebels were neutralized, Halleck could take the troops presently standing idle in garrisons all across Missouri and send them down the Mississippi and up the Tennessee and Cumberland rivers.[6]

Curtis was an 1831 West Point graduate who had served briefly in the Indian Territory. He left the army after only one year and prospered modestly as a civil engineer, attorney, and railroad entrepreneur in Ohio. In 1846 Curtis went to Mexico in command of an Ohio volunteer regiment. He saw no fighting and served as military governor of several occupied cities. He resettled in Keokuk, Iowa, after the war and continued to work as a civil engineer, in both Iowa and Missouri, and as an energetic promoter of a transcontinental railroad. Curtis entered politics and was elected to Congress as a Republican in 1856. He was a supporter of the Lincoln administration and a firm foe of slavery and secession. When the Civil War began, he resigned his seat in Congress and raised the 2nd Iowa. After being promoted to brigadier general, Curtis was assigned to Frémont's headquarters in St. Louis where he supervised military activities in and around the city. Halleck never explained in so many words why he selected Curtis for such a critical assignment, though there is no doubt that he was impressed with Curtis's ability to bring order out of chaos in St. Louis.[7]

A reserved and rather formal Victorian gentleman, Curtis was not the popular image of a dashing military leader. He was fifty-six years of age in 1861, and his much younger soldiers considered him to be a "fine looking old man." An acquaintance described him in more detail as being "tall, finely though heavily formed, with high forehead, large hazel eyes, decidedly grave face[,] . . . in demeanor serious, deliberate, in speech and action undemonstrative." Curtis was fastidious about his dress and carried out his affairs in a precise, methodical fashion. Beneath the stiff, fussy Victorian exterior, however, was an aging West Pointer who deeply desired military distinction but was far too proper to promote himself publicly or privately. Until being picked to command the District of Southwest Missouri, he had labored quietly at his desk in St. Louis, hoping his diligence would be noticed and rewarded by his superiors. The private Curtis was something of a poet as well as a warrior. While campaigning in Mexico and the Confederacy, he

Samuel Ryan Curtis (State Historical Society of Missouri)

often wandered by himself for hours in search of wildflowers and wrote long, rambling letters to his family describing the exotic people and places he had seen. His awkward prose reveals a sensitive and sentimental nature not usually associated with persons in the engineering and military professions. Such was the colorless but complex man who became the most successful Union field commander in the Trans-Mississippi.[8]

Curtis was tremendously excited about his new assignment. He hastened away from St. Louis and established his headquarters at Rolla, a railhead that was the obvious starting point for an offensive into southwestern Missouri. Two divisions belonging to Brig. Gens. Franz Sigel and Alexander S. Asboth occupied the fortifications and camps surrounding the little town. A third division commanded by Col. Jefferson C. Davis lay some distance to the west around Sedalia and Otterville. Curtis arrived in Rolla on December 26 and took lodging in a log building that normally housed railroad engineers. In a cold and sparsely furnished room on the second floor he unpacked and wrote an order assuming command of the district and its military forces, which he called the Army of the Southwest.[9]

The order was immediately challenged by Sigel, who complained that the command rightfully belonged to him and resigned in protest. Sigel was an 1843 graduate of the Karlsruhe military academy who had taken part in the unsuccessful revolutionary movements in Germany in 1849. He fled to the United States with thousands of his countrymen and eventually became director of public schools in St. Louis. Because of his military background, rank, and involvement with the two previous advances to Springfield—and because most of the troops at Rolla also were German immigrants—Sigel believed he should command the new district. The short, slight, myopic officer was enormously popular with fellow Germans, and a nationwide furor erupted over his resignation. Halleck was alarmed at these developments. He recognized Sigel's symbolic importance to the large German population in the North, and he also shared the widespread, if unduly optimistic, belief that a man with Sigel's credentials was a major asset to the Union cause. Determined not to allow Sigel's ego to undermine his plan to rid Missouri of Price, Halleck soothed the German general's wounded feelings. After a few days Sigel withdrew his resignation and agreed to serve under Curtis.[10]

Curtis and Sigel cooperated fairly well after this inauspicious beginning, but their relations never became cordial. The rift between the two highest ranking officers in the Army of the Southwest inevitably led to problems. Supporters of Curtis, mostly Iowans, and supporters of Sigel, mostly Ger-

Franz Sigel (Massachusetts Commandery, U.S. Army Military History Institute)

mans, coalesced into two mutually antagonistic cliques. Sigel seems to have been largely responsible for this development: he encouraged a high degree of personal loyalty among his subordinates and made it clear that he considered himself to be a victim of nativist prejudice. Curtis went out of his way to be courteous to Sigel, but he did not help matters by surrounding himself with a headquarters staff composed largely of fellow Iowans, including a son and a nephew. Partisan sniping between the two factions erupted almost immediately and continued for decades afterward.[11]

Having more or less resolved the matter of Sigel's resignation, Halleck was anxious to get things moving even if it meant campaigning in the midst of winter atop the Ozark Plateau. But now he encountered a different obstacle, one far less amenable to his powers of persuasion. After the Frémont-Hunter fiasco, an exasperated Lincoln had decreed that no offensive operations should take place in southwestern Missouri without permission from McClellan. Halleck did what he could to impress his distant superior with the urgency of the situation in Missouri. "Winter is already upon us," he telegraphed McClellan, "and I fear much longer delay will render it exceedingly difficult to operate, and yet a winter campaign seems absolutely necessary." There was no response from Washington.[12]

It was Price, of all people, who unknowingly set the Federals in motion. A few days before Halleck established the District of Southwest Missouri, Price decided to give up his advanced position on the Osage River. The Missouri army marched back to Springfield and settled into winter quarters. When Halleck learned of this movement, he jumped to the conclusion that Price was falling back into Arkansas to join McCulloch and obtain supplies. He ordered Curtis to harass the retreating rebels. Curtis sent Col. Eugene A. Carr forward with a force of fifteen hundred horsemen. After a few days Carr reported that the rebels had merely returned to their old haunts at Springfield. Halleck nevertheless decided the time had come to move. On January 1, 1862, he advised Curtis to prepare to march on Springfield. Curtis in turn directed Carr to occupy Lebanon, about halfway between Rolla and Springfield, and to keep a close eye on the rebel army.[13]

Halleck now stepped up his correspondence with Washington. He pressed McClellan for permission to unleash Curtis, alternately adopting alarming and assuring tones. Halleck warned that if the Federal troops scattered across the state were not utilized aggressively, Price would "unquestionably return to the Missouri River" and wreak havoc among the isolated garrisons there. On the other hand, if the Federals seized the moment and advanced, they would send Price packing. "I am satisfied that he will retreat the moment I make a move," declared Halleck. A few weeks earlier Lincoln had despaired at Halleck's immobility; now the general was champing at the bit. Despite the confident, even cocky, tone of some of Halleck's messages, McClellan continued to temporize. Two weeks passed without any word from Washington.[14]

Things began to happen on January 13. That day Halleck received a message from Curtis stating erroneously that five thousand rebel cavalrymen were approaching Carr's position at Lebanon and that Carr was falling back to Waynesville where he could be reinforced by a sizable force of infantry and artillery under Col. Peter J. Osterhaus. Halleck's anxiety and frustration boiled over at this news, and he did a very uncharacteristic thing: he authorized Curtis to begin the offensive without permission from Washington. The order to march was followed by a sobering reminder of the stakes involved for both Missouri and the two principal Federal actors. "We must have no failure in this movement against Price," Halleck warned Curtis. "It must be the last."[15]

Neither Halleck nor Curtis had any illusions about the logistical difficulties of conducting a winter campaign in such high, rugged, sparsely settled country. Every step toward Springfield would take the Federals farther from the railhead at Rolla. Most Federal forces operating in the West were transported and supported by steamboats or railroads, but the Army of the Southwest would have to rely on wagons struggling along primitive roads winding through hostile territory. Such a tenuous line of communications would be vulnerable to weather, enemy action, and administrative breakdowns. Even if everything went smoothly, eventually the line would become so long the teams and teamsters would consume the contents of the wagons before they reached their destination. When that happened, at some as yet undetermined distance from Rolla, the Army of the Southwest would reach the end of its tether and advance no more. The rebels' greatest ally in the coming campaign would be the fragility and inelasticity of overland logistical arrangements on the frontier.

Only an exceptional supply officer could keep Curtis's army in the field under such trying circumstances. Halleck assigned the thankless task to Capt. Philip H. Sheridan, an energetic regular officer, who hurried to Rolla and assumed his new position as quartermaster and commissary of the Army of the Southwest. Halleck, Curtis, and Sheridan recognized that the Federals would have to live off the countryside as much as possible in order to ease the strain on their line of communications, but they were uncertain whether foraging would be effective in a frontier area that had been picked over by armies for several months. The necessity of relying on the civilian population for supplies caused Curtis much anxiety at this point in the operation, for he remembered how quickly legitimate foraging had degenerated into wanton plundering in Mexico.[16]

The Army of the Southwest would have to travel light if it was to travel at all. Curtis severely limited the amount of food, fodder, clothing, bedding, and camp equipage permitted on the army's wagons and issued a detailed list of what individuals should carry on their backs. The rules were strictly enforced. "The order to reduce baggage is again renewed," complained a soldier in the 59th Illinois. "We have cut down our baggage three or four times, and the officers still seem to think there is a surplus." Curtis expected his officers to serve as examples for the enlisted men in this matter and allowed no exceptions for them. After considerable grumbling Capt. Henry Curtis, Jr., of the 37th Illinois (no relation to the general) finally got his kit in order. He marched after the rebels with three pairs of socks, one spare shirt, and a change of underwear stuffed in his pack and two blankets strapped on top. At this early stage of the war no other army, Federal or Confederate, began a campaign so lightly burdened.[17]

Logistical problems would be compounded by weather and terrain. The delay in beginning the campaign meant that the Federals would struggle toward Springfield at the worst possible time of the year in a mid-latitude climate. Blasts of snow, sleet, and freezing rain; biting winds; and bitterly cold temperatures alternated with sudden, springlike thaws to make movement excruciatingly difficult from January through March. The primitive dirt roads could be glazed with a sheet of ice one day and dissolve into a sea of mud the next. To make matters even more challenging, the entire campaign would take place atop the Ozark Plateau, a massive limestone uplift that occupied most of southern Missouri and northern Arkansas. The physiography of the plateau ranged from gently rolling tablelands to rocky highlands and narrow valleys. Much of this rugged land was forested, but there were prairies of varying size scattered across the western edge of the plateau.

The main thoroughfare across the Ozark Plateau was Telegraph Road, sometimes called Wire Road. The road was constructed in 1838 to serve as a supply route for frontier forts. It served as a part of the Trail of Tears that carried thousands of Cherokees and other eastern tribes to the Indian Territory. As the years passed, a number of small commercial centers such as

Springfield and Fayetteville grew up along the road. In 1858 entrepreneur John Butterfield signed a government contract to deliver mail twice weekly from St. Louis to San Francisco. He surveyed every possible route across the Ozark Plateau and finally settled on the old military road. Almost overnight a string of inns, taverns, and stables sprang up to service Butterfield's fleet of Overland Mail stagecoaches. A telegraph line strung along the route in 1860 gave the road its common names, though the line was taken down south of Springfield after the outbreak of the war. Telegraph Road was vital to both sides in the early stages of the Civil War in the Trans-Mississippi. It connected Price with friendly (if not always cooperative) Confederate forces to the south, and it provided the Federals with a natural invasion route into southwestern Missouri and northwestern Arkansas.[18]

Telegraph Road was narrow, unpaved, and largely unimproved. A Federal infantryman who marched many a painful mile along that primitive frontier thoroughfare described it in almost poetic terms: "Winding along, up and down, guiltless of art, or fill, or bridge; mere hard and beaten path, or prolonged dust-heap, or lengthened quagmire, according to the sun or rain, the shifting and uncertain elements, stretched the 'Wire road,' a *Via Dolorosa*." In 1862 the road carried thousands of men to their fate.[19]

Curtis began moving men and equipment forward from Rolla to Waynesville after he received the order to proceed on January 13. Once the five thousand rebel horsemen proved to be phantoms, Curtis sent Carr's cavalry and Osterhaus's infantry ahead to Lebanon and joined them there on January 29 after an exhausting three-day ride from Rolla. Curtis decided to make Lebanon his forward staging area. The town was a natural gateway to southwestern Missouri, for it lay near the eastern edge of the Springfield Plateau, a gently rolling section of the larger Ozark Plateau, which extended all the way to Fayetteville and the Boston Mountains in northwestern Arkansas. The country was perfect for campaigning, and Curtis was certain that his army could rapidly cover the fifty miles from Lebanon to Springfield. Getting men, animals, and supplies over the sixty-three miles of rugged hills and valleys that lay between Rolla and Lebanon, however, was a problem.[20]

Inexperience, inclement weather, and shoddy equipment combined with the difficult terrain to hamper the movement of the Federal columns. Asboth's division, for example, required six wearisome days to march from Rolla to Lebanon. The men started off smartly but had to go without food and tents their first night because the divisional train was nowhere to be found. Next morning the cold, hungry soldiers retraced their steps and found the train four miles up the road. The wagons had bogged down in a sea of mud that had frozen solid during the night. The Federals labored for hours chopping the wagon wheels free with axes. After this experience Asboth's men were careful to march only as fast as the wagons could roll. Mud, water, and ice quickly demonstrated the worthlessness of the new shoes issued to several regiments. The soles ripped apart from the uppers, and the hapless soldiers had to hold the shoes together with string and strips of blanket. Sigel's division, plodding along the same road, had a similarly dispiriting experience.[21]

Davis's division was struggling toward Lebanon from Sedalia and Otterville when a snag developed. McClellan belatedly approved of Halleck's fait accompli, but he insisted that Davis's command be held in limbo in case it could be spared by Curtis and used elsewhere. Halleck dutifully halted Davis's division on the ice-choked Osage River and informed Curtis that he could call on Davis for support only if Price made a stand. Curtis pointed out that Davis would not be in supporting distance on the northern bank of the Osage. The issue was resolved a few days later in a curious fashion when Davis ferried his troops across the river and pressed on toward Lebanon. What prompted Davis to advance beyond the Osage is unclear, but apparently, for the second time in two weeks, Halleck decided to ignore McClellan and quietly instructed Davis to push on. All that is known for certain is that Halleck did not interfere or protest as Davis's men slogged through the freezing mud toward Lebanon.[22]

A soldier in the 37th Illinois described the trials and tribulations experienced by the Army of the Southwest at this early stage of the campaign: "For two days and the night intervening everything we possessed, and we in connection, became saturated with the rain that was poured down upon us. . . . All this froze right away, and tents and tent occupants and furniture were like little land ice bergs. Our pantaloons, when we drew them on at reveille, were stiff with ice, so also were shirts, coats, boots, everything. Yet there was no remedy, so we shivered till our animal heat thawed the ice, and wore wet clothes till they dried upon us." Alternately freezing and thawing, the primitive roads degenerated into sloughs. "The mud ancle-deep to men, becomes hub-deep to the heavy army wagons, and the eight yoke wagons ('prairie schooners') that brought up the rear, were almost really schooners, sailing along a gently flowing river of mud." Another soldier in the 59th Illinois was more succinct: he termed the situation "mud without mercy." After only a few days on the march, everyone in blue, from Curtis down to the lowliest private, clearly understood why armies shunned winter campaigns.[23]

While his men and animals recuperated from their ordeal in Lebanon, Curtis celebrated his fifty-seventh birthday on February 3. During this brief lull in the advance, he reorganized the mélange of military units under his command into an operational field army of four undersized divisions: Osterhaus's 1st Division, composed of the 25th, 36th, and 44th Illinois, the 12th and 17th Missouri, and two batteries; Asboth's small 2nd Division, composed of the 2nd, 3rd, and 15th Missouri, the 4th and 5th Missouri Cavalry, and two batteries; Davis's 3rd Division, composed of the 8th, 18th, and 22nd Indiana, the 37th and 59th Illinois, the 1st Missouri Cavalry, and two batteries; and Carr's 4th Division, composed of the 4th and 9th Iowa, the 25th Missouri, the 35th Illinois, the 3rd Illinois Cavalry, and two batteries. The 24th Missouri, the 3rd Iowa Cavalry, the 6th Missouri Cavalry, and Bowen's Missouri Cavalry Battalion formed a contingent of troops under Curtis's direct command.[24]

Curtis named Sigel second-in-command of the army and placed him in charge of the 1st and 2nd Divisions. This move reflected the unusual ethnic makeup of the Army of the Southwest: more than a third of the regiments and batteries were composed wholly or largely of immigrants, overwhelmingly Germans. Curtis assigned these units to the 1st and 2nd Divisions, commanded by a German (Osterhaus) and a Hungarian (Asboth), respectively, with Sigel in overall command. Units composed essentially of native-born troops were assigned to the 3rd and 4th Divisions. The new 4th Division was created for Carr in order to achieve an ethnic balance among divisions and division commanders. As there were fewer foreign-born than native-born troops in the army, the 2nd Division was barely the size of a brigade, but Asboth had led a division since Frémont's abortive fall campaign and could not be denied one now. The kid-glove treatment of Sigel and the creation of undersized ethnic divisions were Curtis's clumsy if well-intentioned response to the uproar that had erupted at Rolla in December.

At Lebanon the Army of the Southwest consisted of roughly 12,100 men (9,600 infantry and 2,500 cavalry) and 50 guns. Hundreds of other troops from various units were posted along the line of communications, and the entire 13th Illinois remained behind to secure the railhead and supply base at Rolla. As Curtis advanced, this "tail" would grow and the "teeth" of his army would shrink accordingly: he would have only 10,250 men and 49 guns at Pea Ridge.[25]

Many of the Missouri soldiers in the Army of the Southwest had a personal stake in the success of the campaign. Since the beginning of the war the secessionists had driven large numbers of unionists from their homes in southwestern Missouri. Thousands of refugees fled to Rolla and huddled in makeshift shelters on the hills surrounding the town. Their suffering was severe, and there were several confirmed instances of starvation. Col. John S. Phelps, a former Democratic congressman from Springfield, secured Lincoln's permission to organize these dispossessed men into Phelps's Independent Missouri Regiment, officially known as the 25th Missouri. By the beginning of the campaign Phelps had filled eight companies with six-month volunteers. The 24th Missouri and Bowen's Missouri Cavalry Battalion also contained substantial numbers of refugees from the southwestern corner of the state. Price's rebels were not the only Missourians who fought to defend—or to recover—hearth and home.[26]

Two journalists also were present at Lebanon, William L. Fayel of the St. Louis *Daily Missouri Democrat* and Thomas W. Knox of the New York *Herald*. Fayel had written detailed articles on Carr's expedition to Lebanon in early January that Curtis thought provided too much information about his strength and intentions. Curtis scolded Fayel and then invited him and Knox to accompany his headquarters staff for the duration of the campaign. This proved to be a mutually profitable arrangement: Curtis exercised some influence over what Fayel and Knox wrote for their newspapers, and the two journalists had access to all the pertinent information they desired. The result was a stream of unusually reliable accounts of the progress of the campaign. Fayel's work was especially accurate and insightful. He stayed with the Army of the Southwest for the duration of the campaign and developed a congenial and mutually respectful relationship with Curtis.[27]

After completing the organization of his little army, Curtis monitored the steady buildup of supplies at Lebanon. Whenever the cold, miserable weather allowed, he rode out to inspect his troops. Returning from one such foray greatly encouraged, he proudly informed his brother that "I have a splendid command." By February 10 Curtis was ready to advance against the rebel army in Springfield. His hopes, and those of his men, were high.[28]

The commanding general of the rebel army in Springfield was an improbable soldier. Despite the handicap of a genteel Virginia upbringing, Sterling Price flourished in Missouri's rough and tumble politics and served as legislator, congressman, and governor. He lacked formal military training but performed satisfactorily in the Mexican War at the battle of Taos Pueblo and as military governor of Chihuahua. His charismatic style of leadership and his uncompromising devotion to the Confederate redemption of Missouri inspired remarkable loyalty among his men, who affectionately dubbed him "Old Pap." Price, now in his fifty-third year, his tall frame crowned by a mane of white hair, had the aura of a man born to command. A Missouri rebel named Ephraim Anderson said of Price that "his figure was portly, striking and noble; the countenance exhibited marked intelligence, and wore a genial expression, while his manner was at once courteous, dignified and impressive." Anderson believed the Missouri general's appearance "came nearer to the portraits of Washington than any I have ever seen."[29]

Price was not a particularly talented administrator or tactician, but he was enough of a strategist to realize that as long as his army remained in the field there was hope that Missouri might be liberated. He maneuvered vigorously in order to keep the Federals off balance and to threaten their hold on the central part of the state, but he engaged in battle only when he felt confident of success. Price had done well thus far, but he knew he could not achieve a meaningful victory against the Federals without the assistance of the Confederate forces stationed in northwestern Arkansas.

The commander of that Arkansas army, Benjamin McCulloch, was a Tennessee frontiersman who had gone to Texas in search of adventure. He missed a chance at immortality when measles prevented him from joining his friend and neighbor David Crockett at the Alamo in 1836, but he missed little else during the next twenty-five years of his remarkable life. He fought as an artilleryman under Sam Houston at San Jacinto, served in the congresses of the Republic of Texas and the United States, mined for gold in California, labored as a peace commissioner in the Mormon War, and gained a well-deserved reputation as an Indian-fighting captain of Texas Rangers. Service in the Mexican War added to his store of practical experience as a small unit commander. McCulloch was untutored in military matters, but he studied military history between clashes with Comanches on the Texas frontier and longed to become an army officer. He was an able administrator, tactician, and strategist who took exceptionally good care of the men under his command. Not surprisingly, "Old Ben" inspired intense loyalty among his troops, especially Texans. Fifty years old, McCulloch was wiry, short, slightly stooped, and balding with a weather-beaten face with crow's-feet radiating from his deepset gray eyes. Despite his small size and reserved manner, McCulloch impressed nearly everyone who met him. "There is no half-way

Sterling Price (Louisiana Historical Association Collection, Howard-Tilton Memorial Library, Tulane University)

Benjamin McCulloch, wearing the black velvet suit in which he was killed (Eugene C. Barker Texas History Center)

ground about him," observed a fellow Texan. "Individuality is strongly marked. He is not a talkative man, and consequently not a very sociable one. He seems to be separate, self-existant, independent, original."[30]

Unfortunately for the Confederate cause in the Trans-Mississippi, Price and McCulloch did not get along with one another. Price saw the war entirely in terms of liberating Missouri; McCulloch's primary concern was the defense of Confederate Arkansas and the Indian Territory in accordance with his orders from Richmond. Price was pompous and overbearing in his dealings with McCulloch, who took an instant dislike to the windy Missouri politician. Moreover, McCulloch considered Price's ill-disciplined Missourians to be more of a mob than an army and was reluctant to cooperate with them except in an emergency. Price eventually became extremely vocal in his denunciations of McCulloch, who replied in kind. Well before the end of 1861 the dispute between the two generals was a public scandal.

After Missouri's admission to the Confederacy, Governor Jackson and the Missouri congressional delegation in Richmond added fuel to the fire by lobbying vigorously and tactlessly for Price's appointment as overall commander in the Trans-Mississippi. President Jefferson Davis resisted this demand but promised to make Price a Confederate major general as soon as enough Missourians enrolled to form a Confederate division, a condition that was not met until the Pea Ridge campaign was over. McCulloch responded to these political machinations by traveling to Richmond in December to tell his side of the story. Before the Texan left northwestern Arkansas, he settled his troops in well-prepared winter quarters, confident that the Federals would make no move while winter weather gripped the Ozark Plateau.[31]

Davis saw the controversy as an opportunity to bring a higher level of professionalism to Confederate operations in the Trans-Mississippi. The Confederate president lacked confidence in both Price and McCulloch because neither had a West Point education, which Davis considered to be an essential qualification for high command. The Trans-Mississippi was part of Gen. Albert S. Johnston's huge Department of the West, but Johnston was far too busy in Tennessee and Kentucky to exercise effective control over affairs west of the great river. Consequently, Davis decided to put the Trans-Mississippi under the command of a professional soldier. Referring to the change from Frémont to Halleck, Davis warned that Union forces in Missouri no longer were commanded by "path-finders and holiday soldiers, but by men of military education and experience in war. The contest is therefore to be on a scale of very different proportions than that of the partisan warfare witnessed during the past summer and fall."[32]

Davis thereupon selected Col. Henry Heth for the command. A West Point graduate and young Virginia officer, Heth's main qualification, other than his education, seems to have been his personal friendship with Davis. Protest immediately swelled from Arkansas and Missouri congressmen who opposed Heth because of his youth, inexperience, and complete unfamiliarity with the Trans-Mississippi. The colonel was anything but eager for the job, and the protests gave him an excuse to refuse gracefully.[33]

The Confederate president turned next to Maj. Gen. Braxton Bragg, a West Pointer and a Mexican War veteran who had demonstrated considerable ability as a departmental commander in Alabama and Florida. Bragg was unenthusiastic to begin with, and Secretary of War Judah P. Benjamin certainly did not help matters when he told Bragg that the Missouri army was a "mere gathering of brave but undisciplined troops, coming and going at pleasure, and needing a master mind to control and reduce it into order and to convert it into a real army." Bragg declined the honor of being that master mind.[34]

The third candidate for the position was Maj. Gen. Earl Van Dorn, a West Point graduate commanding a division in the Confederate Army of the Potomac, as the future Army of Northern Virginia was then styled. Van Dorn was forty-one years old and a product of the planter aristocracy of Port Gibson, Mississippi. He was a close friend of the Confederate president, whose own plantation lay only a few miles north of Port Gibson. Van Dorn invariably was described as handsome and dashing—his rather short, slight frame was topped with wavy, dark blond hair—and he had the slightly unsavory reputation of being a ladies' man. Van Dorn was a romantic warrior, not a military intellectual. The Mexican War had awakened an unquenchable desire for fame in the young Mississippi officer. "I did not know then the fire that was in my heart," he wrote his sister. "It had never been kindled. The hot sigh of death which first passed by me awakened what had always slumbered, and set fire to my ambition. It rages now like a house on fire." Years later the prospect of achieving martial glory in the Civil War electrified Van Dorn, as he made clear to his wife in melodramatic prose bristling with exclamation points. "Who knows but that *yet* out of the storms of revolution . . . I may not be able to catch a spark of the lightning and shine through all time to come, a burning name! I feel a greatness in my soul! . . . I am getting young once more at the thought that my soul shall be awakened again as it was in Mexico."[35]

Earl Van Dorn (Alabama Department of Archives and History)

Van Dorn's romantic martial spirit so impressed his friends, including Davis, that they failed to notice serious flaws in his military character. He was truly in his element only once during his prewar military career, as a leader of small cavalry units on the Texas frontier in the 1850s. Another Confederate general, Richard S. Ewell, remembered that during his own tour of duty in antebellum Texas he had "learned all about commanding fifty United States dragoons, and forgotten everything else." So it was with Van Dorn. His zeal for closing with the enemy was matched by his impatience with reconnaissance, logistics, and staff work of any kind. He never understood that the hell-for-leather methods he employed against bands of Plains Indians were not particularly well suited for conventional warfare in the nineteenth century. Until the day of his death at the hands of a jealous husband in 1863, Van Dorn relied on tried and true frontier tactics: speed and surprise. Perhaps the kindest thing that can be said of his generalship in the Civil War is that he made war by the heart, not by the head.[36]

On January 10, 1862, Davis appointed Van Dorn commander of the new Military District of the Trans-Mississippi, which included Missouri, Arkansas, the Indian Territory, and northern Louisiana. Secretary of War Benjamin was greatly relieved that "the whole of the difficulties in the Western (Trans-Mississippi) Department will now, I trust, be at an end." Van Dorn rushed westward and assumed command at Little Rock on January 29. He then established his headquarters at Pocahontas, a small town in the northeastern corner of Arkansas just south of the Arkansas-Missouri line.[37]

While en route to his new command Van Dorn decided to quell the Price-McCulloch controversy by the simple expedient of combining their two forces into a single army and placing himself at its head. Furthermore, he intended to reverse Confederate fortunes in the Trans-Mississippi by leading that army, reinforced by a host of new recruits, into Missouri. Van Dorn was certain that he could rush his command from Pocahontas to St. Louis and capture the city before the thousands of Federal soldiers scattered across Missouri could react. As always, logistical difficulties and other complications did not enter into his thinking. He simply assumed that his men and animals would find the necessary food and fodder as they dashed northward across the Ozark Plateau and that the Federals would cooperate by remaining inert. Van Dorn told his wife that he intended "to make a reputation and serve my country conspicuously or to fail. I must not, shall not, do the latter. I must have St. Louis—then Huzza!" He planned to launch the campaign as soon as the first signs of spring appeared.[38]

In Pocahontas Van Dorn reviewed the latest information on the two small but formidable armies in his district, armies that he had not yet seen. McCulloch's Arkansas army consisted of an oversized infantry brigade, an oversized cavalry brigade, and four batteries of artillery: 8,700 men and 18 guns. Though not especially large, it was the primary Confederate fighting force in the Trans-Mississippi. The huge infantry brigade, commanded by Col. Louis Hébert, was composed of the 3rd Louisiana, the 4th, 14th, 15th, 16th, and 17th Arkansas, and the dismounted 1st and 2nd Arkansas Mounted Rifles and 4th Texas Cavalry Battalion, a total of 5,700 men. The 3rd Louisiana had seen action earlier at Wilson's Creek and was by all accounts the best Confederate infantry unit ever to serve west of the Mississippi. The Arkansas regiments were untried in battle as units but included numerous veterans of Wilson's Creek. The cavalry brigade, led by Brig. Gen. James M. McIntosh, consisted of about 3,000 hard-riding westerners in the 3rd, 6th, 9th, and 11th Texas Cavalry and the 1st Arkansas and 1st Texas Cavalry battalions. Many of the troopers also had seen action at Wilson's Creek and in the Indian Territory.[39]

Price's Missouri army was quite different from McCulloch's command. It had been created on the run after the Federal capture of Jefferson City the previous summer and was seriously deficient in organization, training, and logistical support. Volunteers who reached Price's fugitive army had to make do with improvised uniforms, equipment, and weapons. The 1st Missouri Brigade, commanded by Col. Henry Little, consisted of the 1st and 3rd Missouri, the 1st Missouri Cavalry, and two artillery batteries. The 2nd Missouri Brigade, led by Col. William Y. Slack, was not yet organized into regiments. The men were placed into temporary battalions, three of infantry, one of cavalry, and two batteries. The 3rd Missouri Brigade, commanded by Col. Colton Greene, was smaller and less well organized than Slack's command. Roughly half of Price's men remained in the Missouri state guard, which consisted of seven skeletal divisions little larger than regiments. At the beginning of 1862 the Missouri army was composed of about eight thousand men and forty-seven guns, some of them obsolete cast-iron weapons. Many of the soldiers were veterans of Wilson's Creek, Lexington, and other small engagements in Missouri.[40]

In addition to these two bodies of more or less regular forces, Van Dorn felt that he could call upon the most unusual troops in the Confederate army: Brig. Gen. Albert Pike's Indians. Pike was a fat, eccentric Arkansas politician without any military experience or ability. At the outset of the war

Albert Pike (Archives and Special Collections, University of Arkansas at Little Rock)

he had negotiated treaties between the Confederacy and the Five Civilized Tribes that authorized the tribes to organize their own home guard units for protection against a possible Federal invasion from Kansas. The result was the formation of the 1st and 2nd Cherokee Mounted Rifles, the 1st Choctaw and Chickasaw Mounted Rifles, the 1st Creek, and assorted battalions and companies. Pike candidly described his 2,500 native soldiers as "entirely undisciplined, mounted chiefly on ponies, and armed very indifferently with common rifles and shotguns." According to the treaties the Indians could not be sent outside the Indian Territory without their consent, but Van Dorn considered the Indian Territory to be no different from any other part of his district and simply ignored the treaties. He ordered Pike to prepare the Indians to participate in the planned invasion of Missouri.[41]

While Van Dorn scanned reports and impatiently waited for spring to arrive, Halleck set his unorthodox winter campaign in motion. Old Brains, the deskbound staff officer, caught Van Dorn, the dashing cavalryman, and all of the other ranking Confederates in the Trans-Mississippi completely off guard. It was Price who first noticed that the Federals in Missouri were stirring. In late January he became aware of the Federal concentration at Lebanon, only fifty miles from Springfield. He surmised what it meant and immediately called upon the Confederates in northwestern Arkansas for help, sending a stream of hysterical but not very informative dispatches to McIntosh in Fort Smith and Hébert in Fayetteville. McIntosh was in command, as McCulloch had not yet returned from Richmond. He shared the general opinion that a Federal offensive atop the Ozark Plateau in midwinter was highly unlikely, but he advised Hébert to be ready to march north toward Springfield just in case.[42]

This halfway measure did not satisfy Price. In melodramatic language he warned McIntosh that unless he was reinforced at once he would have to give up Springfield and fall back toward Arkansas. Price's dispatches to Hébert were even more alarmist than those to McIntosh, probably because the Missouri general hoped to inspire Hébert to act on his own initiative. Price also wrote to Van Dorn in Pocahontas, urging him in the strongest terms to order troops to Springfield before it was too late. The lack of telegraphic contact between Springfield, Fayetteville, and Pocahontas crippled Confederate communications at this critical moment. It took two days for Price's couriers to reach Hébert, and twice as long to reach Van Dorn. As a result, Van Dorn did not even learn that the Federals were on the move until after they had captured Springfield.[43]

McCulloch finally returned to Fort Smith on February 5 in the midst of this flurry of shrill pleas from Price. McCulloch realized that his old antagonist in Springfield was genuinely alarmed by some sort of Federal activity in his vicinity, but he decided that McIntosh had acted correctly in refusing to march. By chance, McCulloch had encountered Van Dorn in Little Rock a few days earlier and had learned of the latter's plan to invade Missouri from northeastern Arkansas in the spring. Because McCulloch knew that Van Dorn intended to shift his army to Pocahontas in the near future, he did not believe he was "authorized to march it to Springfield for the purpose of holding that place." Nevertheless, McCulloch decided that if Price was driven out of Springfield yet again, "I will take the responsibility to march and meet him and by our united strength win a battle."[44]

While Confederate generals in Arkansas tried to understand what was happening in Missouri, Price issued a final plea for help from Springfield on February 9. The message, which as usual contained considerably more emotion than information, was directed to Hébert in Fayetteville. "Colonel, you have said you would respond when I called. I have called. *I call, I call, now.* Be up. *Move,* move night and day. By every consideration dear to the Southern Cause come on and come rapidly. You may be too late."[45]

2 Price's Running Stand

The third and final effort to secure Missouri for the Union began on February 10, 1862. Early that morning the thousands of tents surrounding Lebanon were struck and the Army of the Southwest set out for Springfield in the best nineteenth-century fashion with bands playing and flags flying. Curtis set a steady but unhurried pace across the rolling terrain of the Springfield Plateau. Mercifully, the weather was unseasonably mild and the roads were dry. On the evening of February 12 the Federals reached Pierson's Creek. Springfield lay only eight miles ahead.[1]

Price now was resigned to the fact that Springfield was untenable. He feared that the approaching Federal army was much larger than his own, and he did not want to risk everything "with greatly unequal numbers upon result of one engagement." While the Federals settled in for the night at Pierson's Creek, the Missouri rebels made ready to abandon Springfield for the third time in seven months.[2]

To cover his withdrawal Price sent Col. Elijah Gates's 1st Missouri Cavalry to drive in the Federal pickets. Just after dark Gates's command sallied forth from Springfield and struck a battalion of the 3rd Illinois Cavalry posted a mile and a half forward of the Federal main body. The Illinoisans held their ground and were reinforced by infantry, cavalry, artillery, and a flock of high-ranking officers including Curtis, Sigel, and Davis. When Federal cannons opened fire, the rebels disengaged and fell back to Springfield.[3]

While the skirmish at Pierson's Creek was under way, the Missouri army slipped away from Springfield. Soldiers formed ranks in the darkness and trudged along Telegraph Road to the old battlefield at Wilson's Creek, ten miles to the south. After a brief stop for breakfast the Missourians continued another twelve miles to McCullah's Spring and camped for the night of February 13. Price was deeply depressed over the sudden change in his fortunes and could not decide whether to halt or continue drifting south toward the Arkansas-Missouri line. In his distracted condition he allowed three days to pass before he informed his Confederate allies in Arkansas of the loss of Springfield.[4]

Curtis also was unaware that the Missouri army was in flight. The skirmish at Pierson's Creek reinforced the widespread belief in the Army of the Southwest that the rebels would not give up Springfield without a fight. The next morning the Federals were gripped by a mix of apprehension and excitement as they advanced toward the rebel lair. Five miles east of Springfield the Federals approached a fog-shrouded ravine. Curtis suspected that if Price intended to make a stand, he would do it here. Curtis deployed his entire command into line of battle and sent hundreds of skirmishers toward the ominous ravine.[5]

A particularly adventurous company of skirmishers from the 4th Iowa scrambled in and out of the ravine and advanced all the way to Springfield without encountering a single rebel. The Iowans hastened back to the army on liberated horses and mules to report that the enemy appeared to be altogether gone. Relieved and not a little puzzled by this unexpected turn of events, Curtis ordered an immediate advance. At 10:00 A.M. on February 13 the vanguard of the Army of the Southwest entered Springfield and raised the stars and stripes over the Greene County courthouse amidst "great rejoicing." The flag would remain flying there for the duration of the war.[6]

Most of Springfield's citizens had fled either north or south, and the town was a shambles. A Federal officer wandered through homes and shops cluttered with "straw, bunks, boards, old clothes, fragments of corn bread . . . and other rubbish, the walls defaced with charcoal sketches and rebel rhymes, descriptive of the way in which 'Lien dide and sigiel flu,' at Wilson's Creek, the prospects of France and England interfering with 'Lincoln's war,' and other kindred subjects delightful to a 'secesh' ear." Carcasses and offal littered the streets, and flocks of crows and buzzards hovered overhead. In their rush to escape, the rebels left four hundred invalids, perhaps half as many stragglers, and a number of storehouses only partially emptied of supplies and equipment.[7]

Curtis established his headquarters in the same house Price had used. There the Federals found more evidence of Old Pap's hasty departure: tables heaped with military paperwork, including correspondence from McIntosh and Hébert, and a pantry full of food fit for a commanding general. Curtis considered launching an immediate pursuit of the rebels but decided to stay the night in Springfield to permit his command to rest and regroup. The Federals appropriated whatever accommodations they could find. Soldiers of Asboth's 2nd Division occupied a rebel camp just outside town that contained huts built of boards and roofed with raw beef hides. Correspondent Fayel informed his readers that the rustic accommodations combined "the comfort of a small parlor bed room, with the elegance of a hog pen." Officers and men of the 25th Missouri took advantage of the delay to visit the few friends and relatives who remained in the area.[8]

The Federals were quick to confiscate and consume the stores of food left by the Missouri army. By midafternoon the town square was filled with milling midwesterners feasting on their first spoils of war: beer and gingerbread. Elsewhere in Springfield, troops of the 59th Illinois found a commissary building bulging with stores. One of the Illinoisans noted that "soon there was a string of provisions like an army of ants flowing from it to our quarters."[9]

While his men celebrated in varying ways, Curtis pondered his next move. He did not know whether the Missouri rebels were falling back toward Arkansas or lurking south of town preparing for battle. Nor did he know the present whereabouts and intentions of McCulloch's command, last reported to be in winter quarters in northwestern Arkansas. Despite these uncertainties and a host of distractions, Curtis never lost sight of the fact that his primary objective was the neutralization of Price's army, not the occupation of territory. Indeed, the bloodless triumph at Springfield seems to have invigorated Curtis and convinced him that an aggressive course of action was the only means of assuring the safety of Missouri. He was more determined than ever to pursue Price and bring him to battle at the first opportunity.

That night Curtis met with his division commanders and discussed how best to proceed. Sigel proposed that Curtis and the 3rd and 4th Divisions follow Price down Telegraph Road. While Price's attention was focused on the threat to his rear, Sigel and the 1st and 2nd Divisions would hurry along a network of country roads to the west and reach Telegraph Road at McDowell south of the rebel army. Price would be trapped. Sigel's plan was suitably aggressive but had two glaring weaknesses. The distance from Springfield to McDowell on Telegraph Road was about ten miles shorter than Sigel's round-about route. If Curtis prodded Price too vigorously from the rear or if Price learned that he was in danger of being cut off, he could reach the junction at McDowell ahead of Sigel's column and escape. Even worse, if Price suddenly turned and lashed out at either Curtis or Sigel, the two halves of the Federal army would not be within supporting distance of each other.[10]

Despite the probability of failure and the possibility of disaster, Curtis approved Sigel's plan. He did so primarily because it offered an opportunity to shatter the rebel army but also because it offered his ambitious, disgruntled subordinate an opportunity to act independently. Curtis, like Halleck, had not yet learned that Sigel had an alarming tendency to ignore orders and engage in eccentric maneuvers. At this point in the campaign Curtis was willing to let Sigel go his own way; within a few weeks he would be careful not to let the German general out of his sight.[11]

While Curtis and his lieutenants mulled over their options, a fierce winter storm swept across the Ozark Plateau. An Illinois soldier wrote that February 13 was "the worst night we have yet passed." Most of the Federals were relatively snug in Springfield, but Price's troops were caught in the open at McCullah's Spring. They wrapped themselves in their canvas tents to ward off blasts of sleet and snow and huddled around campfires while the temperature dropped far below freezing. Few got much sleep.[12]

The next morning, February 14, the sun rose "clear and bright upon a glittering sheet of snow and ice" that covered the rolling prairie south and west of Springfield. The Federals set out in pursuit of Price's army shortly after dawn. Sigel and the 1st and 2nd Divisions marched through Little York and Marionville on a primitive road glazed with ice. The German general accompanied the 5th Missouri Cavalry at the head of the column, wearing a fur cap and a large cloak that enveloped his slight frame and nearly covered his small horse as well. Progress was slow, and the intense cold caused eighteen horsemen, including Sigel, to suffer slightly frostbitten feet. The only incident of note occurred when the 5th Missouri Cavalry surprised and captured a large foraging party and fifteen wagons filled with supplies for the rebel army.[13]

Curtis and the 3rd and 4th Divisions followed Telegraph Road across a stretch of prairie cut by numerous watercourses. The Federals approached each declivity with caution but invariably found only broken-down wagons and rebel stragglers seeking shelter from the biting wind. Around midmorn-

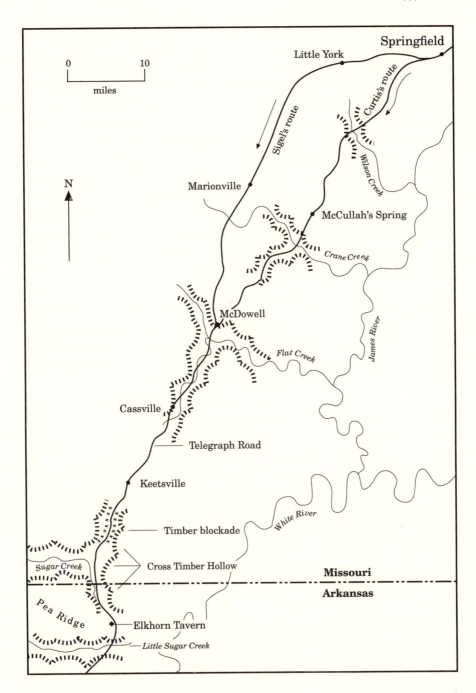

Map 2-1. Springfield to Little Sugar Creek

ing the blue column reached Wilson's Creek. Some Federals were certain Price would make a stand on the site of his hard-fought victory over Lyon, but there was no sign of the Missouri army. "We got up and started this morning after Price," wrote a perplexed Iowa soldier, "but no Price was there." As the Federals marched across the battlefield, they discovered that animals and floods had exposed the skeletal remains of men hastily buried six months earlier. "A *bad, bad* sight," wrote a shaken Illinois officer.[14]

Pursuers and pursued finally made contact at the end of the day about thirty miles south of Springfield. Price and his weary, half-frozen command left McCullah's Spring that morning and continued south on Telegraph Road. There was no sense of urgency among the Missourians, for none expected the Federals to pursue under such difficult conditions. After struggling along the icy road for eight miles, the column stumbled to a halt in Crane Creek Valley. Price decided to bivouac there for a few days and see what the yankees would do next. The rebels were laying out their encampment and preparing their evening meals when they were interrupted by the crash of artillery and the shriek of incoming projectiles. The shells landed amongst the soldiers of Little's 1st Missouri Brigade, the Confederate rear guard. Little's troops hastily fell into line on the low bluffs north of Crane Creek, shivering in the bitter cold, and awaited an attack that never came. The Federal cannons abruptly ceased firing and were not heard from again that night.[15]

The brief bombardment was the work of the vanguard of Curtis's column. All that day Col. Calvin A. Ellis had advanced well ahead of the 3rd and 4th Divisions with his own 1st Missouri Cavalry and Maj. William D. Bowen's Missouri Cavalry battalion, the latter equipped with four twelve-pounder mountain howitzers. Somehow Ellis had gotten the idea from Curtis that he was to harass the rebels, though this was the very thing Curtis wanted to avoid. Just after sunset the Federal cavalrymen crested a hill and looked down into Crane Creek Valley, sparkling with hundreds of campfires in the twilight. Excited at having finally caught up with the enemy, Ellis directed Bowen's gunners to shell the valley with their mountain howitzers. When dusk faded into darkness a few minutes later, Ellis halted the firing and led his force back up Telegraph Road. The cavalrymen rejoined the 3rd and 4th Divisions at McCullah's Spring, where Curtis had halted for the night.[16]

This minor affair at Crane Creek had major consequences. Price was greatly alarmed at the presence of Federal troops with artillery so far south of Springfield. Convinced that Curtis must be in pursuit in overwhelming strength, Price abandoned any thought of observing the enemy and concentrated all his energy on getting away. From this point Old Pap drove his army south toward Arkansas with feverish haste, pausing only occasionally to allow his men a few hours of sleep on the frozen ground. The rebels unknowingly surged ahead of Sigel's flanking column, which was plodding along several miles to the west, and escaped being cut off at McDowell.

During the retreat the Missouri army was burdened with an overabundance of stores, surely a rare if not unique occurrence in Confederate military history. The rebel force lacked institutionalized logistical support and literally had to haul around its base of supplies. While at Springfield, Quartermaster Maj. James Harding had worked diligently to gather food, forage, and equipment. Price was determined to take as much of this as he could. The result was spectacular. The countless numbers of wagons that followed the Missouri army down Telegraph Road constituted "the most *multitudinous* and *variegated* wagon-train ever concentrated on the continent," according to one veteran. "Every species of wheel vehicle, from the jolting old ox-cart to the most fantastically-painted stage-coach, rolled along the road." With the Federals apparently in pursuit, the safety of the huge train was of paramount importance. Price ordered the road cleared south of Crane Creek and sent the train ahead of the army. As the wagons creaked and rumbled past his immobilized troops for hours on end during the night of February 14–15, even Price was surprised at the number of vehicles. At one point he turned to Harding and asked, "Is there no end to the train?" It was nearly dawn before the troops were able to get onto the road and follow the train south.[17]

Meanwhile, back at McCullah's Spring, Curtis was so angry over Ellis's blunder at Crane Creek he almost had the Missouri colonel arrested for disobedience of orders. Curtis assumed that Price would accelerate the pace of his retreat. Casting about for some way to prevent the rebels from getting away, Curtis decided to attack the rear of the Missouri army the next day with his two divisions in a risky attempt to salvage the original plan. If the Missourians stopped to fend off their pursuers, Sigel's two divisions might be able to cut off the rebel column or attack its flank at McDowell. Curtis sent a message to Sigel explaining the situation and urging him to push forward as rapidly as possible.[18]

Early on the morning of February 15 Curtis and the 3rd and 4th Divisions advanced from McCullah's Spring as rapidly as the frozen road would permit. At Crane Creek they found abandoned wagons, discarded equipment, and "meet on the fire in kettles cooking" but no rebels save for the usual collection of forlorn stragglers. Curtis sent a chastened Ellis trotting after the retreating foe. When Ellis and his cavalry force reached the junction at McDowell, there was no sign of either Price or Sigel. The rebels had moved too fast, and the trap had failed to close. Disappointed but determined to finish what he had started, Curtis pressed on after the fleeing rebels.[19]

While all this frenzied activity was taking place on Telegraph Road, Sigel and the 1st and 2nd Divisions proceeded along the Marionville detour at an unhurried pace. It is not known whether Sigel failed to receive Curtis's request for additional haste or chose to ignore it. On February 16 Sigel finally reached McDowell only to learn that Price had passed by the previous day with Curtis close behind. Mortified by his failure to cut off the enemy, Sigel turned his command onto Telegraph Road and joined the race south toward Arkansas.[20]

Now the pursuit began in earnest. The rebels hurried over the fifty miles from Crane Creek in Missouri to Little Sugar Creek in Arkansas in less than thirty-six hours. Weather, fatigue, hunger, and demoralization took a severe toll. Everyone became "foot-sore and tired from marching over the hard and frozen ground." Exhaustion was a critical problem because the Missourians had not had a full night of sleep since February 11 in Springfield. Whenever the column halted for a few moments, men in the ranks dozed while leaning against one another. Soldiers even fell asleep while marching. "I saw men walking with gun on shoulder—fast asleep—then stumble and wake—only to repeat the process," recalled one rebel. By the time the Missourians crossed the Arkansas-Missouri line on February 16, they were approaching the limits of human endurance: "We were tired of retreating, completely broken down, weary and footsore, almost under an absolute necessity of sleeping at least for a short time."[21]

The bitterly cold weather made matters worse. "I felt like I was dying, I was so chilled," recalled a state guardsman named Samuel McDaniel. "The snow was all over us, and our clothes frozen on our bodies." One morning McDaniel's feet were so swollen he could barely stand up. He called out: "O, God, Colonel, shoot me, if you will, but don't tell me to fall in, I'm nearly dead and cannot walk for the life of me." He was placed atop a passing caisson that carried him south to Arkansas. Hundreds of other Missouri rebels were less fortunate than McDaniel and fell out along the road where they either died of exposure or were gathered up by the pursuing Federals.[22]

The campaign was difficult for the Federals as well, but they seemed to bear up better. Despite their stopping to camp each night, Curtis's men steadily gained ground on the reeling Missourians. The Federals had rested

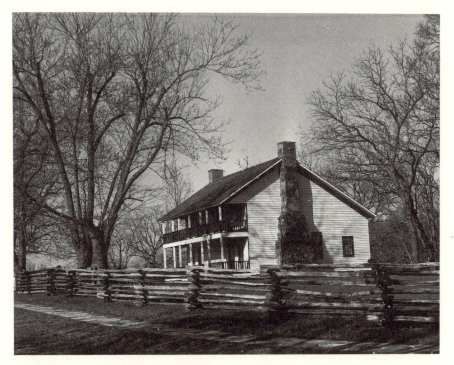

Elkhorn Tavern (authors' collection)

well in Springfield on February 13 and had the psychological advantage of knowing that the enemy was on the run. Evidence of a desperate flight was unmistakable. The wake of the Missouri army was marked by "crippled and demolished wagons, pots, pans, skillets, camp trumpery, dead and dying horses and mules, together with all manner of goods and chattels." Also cluttering the road were those rebels who were unable or unwilling to go any farther. By the third day of the pursuit Curtis informed Halleck that "more straggling prisoners are being taken than I know what to do with."[23]

The Federals nevertheless experienced their share of hardships. They often outpaced their supply wagons and went to bed hungry, and rations were sometimes doled out on the run. A loyal Missouri soldier recalled that, during the pursuit, his regiment stopped and opened ranks to either side of the road in order to let a supply wagon pass. Every thirty yards or so a box of hardtack was thrown off the back of the wagon. The troops broke open the boxes with bayonets and filled their pockets with the dense crackers, which they ate while trudging along. When hardtack was not available, the men were issued flour or cornmeal and left to their own devices. Soldiers in the 9th Iowa subsisted for days on flour and water hurriedly cooked into "indigestible" flapjacks. Rations were so short that Curtis placed guards over the corn and oats reserved for the army's horses and mules.[24]

The Federals foraged vigorously to supplement their meager rations but quickly discovered that the sparsely settled Ozark highlands were a far cry from the bountiful prairies of the Midwest. A disgusted Iowan wrote that the land along Telegraph Road was "not mutch setled, nor good for any thing but to raise Punkins." The hardscrabble homesteads the Federals encountered usually were abandoned because the settlers had been told by the rebels that the "terrible Sigel" and his minions would slaughter helpless civilians. Curtis's men failed to live up (or down) to their reputation, but they did ransack houses and outbuildings for anything edible. In some instances they found tables set for a meal with food cooking in a fireplace. But such pleasant surprises, however welcome to a fortunate and enterprising few, did little to assuage the army's hunger.[25]

Despite these privations Federal morale soared as the Army of the Southwest approached the Arkansas-Missouri line. An Illinois infantryman proudly trumpeted that "the march of this army has no parallel in American history." Each day rumors passed along the blue column that somewhere up ahead "Price's pedestrians" had made a stand. But the rumors invariably proved false, and a Federal soldier concluded that the Missouri army was making only "a walking stand and double quick at that."[26]

Ellis and his cavalrymen finally caught up with the Confederate rear guard on the afternoon of February 15 near Flat Creek. After the scare at Crane Creek, Little was careful to secure every likely defensive point in order to delay the Federals and prevent them from making another dash at the retreating column. This tactic compelled Ellis to proceed with caution. Whenever he encountered a body of rebels, he ordered Bowen's mountain howitzers to open fire and called for infantry support. But while the Federal foot soldiers came up at the double-quick and deployed from column into line of battle, the Confederate rear guard invariably beat a hasty retreat to the next ravine or bend in the road. So it went for the final twenty-four hours of the chase.[27]

Three miles south of Keetsville, Telegraph Road enters a deep, narrow gorge nearly eight miles long. When Frémont's army threatened to move south from Springfield in November 1861, McCulloch's soldiers blocked the road by cutting down thousands of trees inside the gorge. The timber barrier

Telegraph Road, a narrow, unpaved thoroughfare which crawled up and down the ravines of the Ozark Plateau. Many stretches of the road, such as this one in Pea Ridge National Military Park, have been authentically preserved. (authors' collection)

extended for about four miles. When the Federal threat receded, the soldiers took up saws and axes once again and cleared a winding passage barely wide enough for a wagon through the felled trees. By the beginning of 1862 local inhabitants were calling the gorge Cross Timber Hollow.[28]

The Missouri army trudged through Cross Timber Hollow on February 16. Late in the afternoon Ellis and his cavalrymen warily approached the northern end of the gorge and commenced "boring through" the narrow passage. After proceeding two or three miles they encountered a detachment of Gates's 1st Missouri Cavalry and a two-gun section of Capt. Churchill Clark's Missouri Battery positioned at a bend in the gorge. Ellis called for support and waited to see if the rebels would fall back without a fight. True to form, the Confederates disappeared around the bend just as the leading elements of Davis's 3rd Division arrived on the scene. Frustrated by Little's game, Davis ordered Ellis to pursue the rebels at once and run them down before

they could find another place to stand. Hundreds of Federal horsemen galloped forward in column along the winding road and suddenly emerged from
the southern end of the timber blockade into the relatively spacious valley of
Big Sugar Creek. The Confederate rear guard was visible just ahead.[29]

Ellis led his men forward without a halt. Just south of the creek the head
of the loyal 1st Missouri Cavalry plowed into the rear of the rebel 1st Missouri Cavalry. A melee ensued in which the two groups of Missourians swung,
slashed, and shot at one another as they careened down Telegraph Road.
The moving mass enveloped Clark's Missouri Battery, and the artillerymen
joined the fray with ramrods and whatever else was handy. When Little realized what was happening at the rear of his column, he ordered his infantry
to countermarch. One rebel recalled that the exhausted soldiers "could
scarcely move one foot before the other and yet they went back to fight." At
this point Ellis prudently disengaged and fell back to Big Sugar Creek to
await the rest of the army. Federal casualties were remarkably light: one man
killed and five wounded. The Missourians lost sixteen killed and "many men"
wounded. The Federals settled down for the night of February 16 at the
intersection of Cross Timber Hollow and Big Sugar Creek Valley. They were
only one mile from Arkansas.[30]

On February 14 the shops and streets of Fayetteville were alive with rumors
that the Federals had captured Springfield. Hébert passed the information
to McCulloch in Fort Smith, who directed him to be ready "to take the field
very shortly with your entire force and probably march with it to Springfield."
Hébert made what preparations he could and waited anxiously for some
reliable news from Missouri. The suspense ended early on the morning of
February 16 with the arrival of a message from Price, written in haste as he
passed through Keetsville. In the message Old Pap belatedly informed Hébert
that Springfield had fallen three days earlier and that the Missouri army was
fast approaching the Arkansas-Missouri line with the Federals close behind.[31]

Astounded, Hébert immediately informed McCulloch and prepared to
march at once to Price's relief. Couriers raced out of Fayetteville with urgent
messages for Confederate infantry regiments scattered in winter quarters
across northwestern Arkansas. Hébert instructed some units to rendezvous
at Cross Hollow, a large Confederate cantonment on Telegraph Road sixteen
miles north of Fayetteville, and directed others to hurry forward to meet
Price. As Hébert's troops marched north on Telegraph Road, they encountered the Missouri army's train, now somewhat reduced by the rigors of the

retreat, and a pathetic swarm of civilian refugees fleeing all manner of imagined yankee horrors. It was, said a Louisiana soldier, "a scene that beggared description."[32]

In the afternoon of February 16 a portion of Hébert's command made contact with the Missouri army near a hostelry called Elkhorn Tavern, about three miles south of the Arkansas-Missouri line. As Price's weary men emerged from the southern end of Cross Timber Hollow, they raised a ragged cheer at the sight of the long-awaited reinforcements. Hébert's men stepped aside to let the long column shuffle past and then took up the position of rear guard. The Missourians plodded another three miles and halted in Little Sugar Creek Valley, where they enjoyed their first good night's sleep since leaving Springfield.[33]

The next morning, February 17, the Army of the Southwest marched through Cross Timber Hollow with the 1st Missouri Cavalry and Bowen's Missouri Cavalry Battalion once again in the van. When the Federals crossed the state line into Arkansas, they sent up cheer after cheer for the Union as bands played "The Arkansas Traveler," "Yankee Doodle," and other patriotic tunes. "Such yelling and whooping, it was glorious," wrote an Illinois officer. Curtis, riding near the head of the column on this auspicious day, congratulated his men for restoring the Stars and Stripes to the "virgin soil" of Arkansas. Before pushing on into the Confederacy, he paused to savor the moment and composed a brief but triumphant message for Halleck: "The flag of our Union again floats in Arkansas."[34]

A little after 1:00 P.M. Ellis and his cavalrymen emerged from Cross Timber Hollow, clattered past Elkhorn Tavern, and reached the bluffs overlooking Little Sugar Creek. The Missouri army had marched out of the valley hours earlier, but a considerable force of rebel infantry and artillery was visible atop the bluffs on the opposite side. Ellis jumped to the conclusion that the enemy finally was making a stand and sent a courier racing back to apprise Curtis of the situation.[35]

When Curtis learned that the enemy was in sight, he galloped forward at the head of a column composed of Maj. Clark Wright's battalion of the 6th Missouri Cavalry, Maj. John McConnell's battalion of the 3rd Illinois Cavalry, and Capt. Mortimer M. Hayden's 3rd Iowa Battery. By the time this force reached Ellis's position, the rebels had disappeared. Curtis directed his artillery to fire into the woods where the enemy had last been seen. When there was no response to this challenge, Curtis left Bowen's battalion with the artillery and personally led the rest of the cavalry down into the valley and

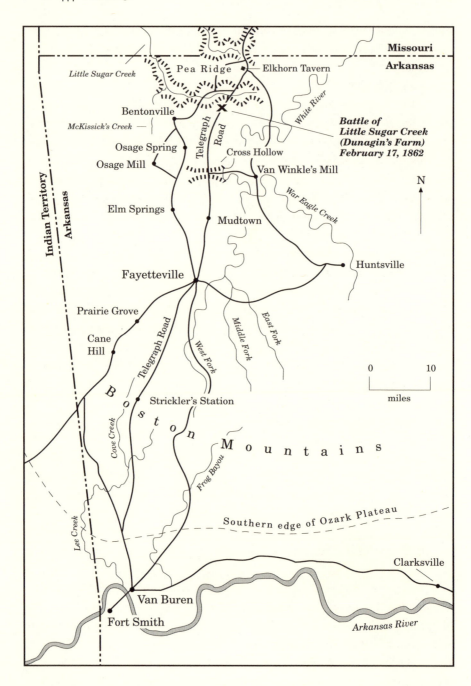

Map 2-2. Northwestern Arkansas

across the creek. At the foot of the southern bluffs Curtis seemed to remember that leading a reconnaissance in force was not the business of an army commander. He turned over command of the column to Ellis and ordered him to advance and to regain contact with the enemy.[36]

Though Curtis did not realize it, the Confederate troops encountered at Little Sugar Creek were part of McCulloch's Arkansas army, not Price's Missouri army. Hébert had arrived at Little Sugar Creek early that morning to meet with Price and to discuss how best to stop the yankees. Much to Hébert's surprise, Price brushed aside all talk of making a stand and insisted on continuing the retreat to Cross Hollow, twelve miles to the south. Vexed at Price's erratic behavior, Hébert nevertheless decided to remain behind with the 3rd Louisiana and the 4th and 15th Arkansas and cover the withdrawal of the Missouri army. Price detached Clark's Missouri Battery to support Hébert and then set out toward Cross Hollow with the rest of his command. Hébert's force was modest but his position was immensely strong. Little Sugar Creek Valley was nearly half a mile wide at this point and was bordered by limestone bluffs almost one hundred feet high. Unlike Cross Timber Hollow, which ran roughly north and south, Little Sugar Creek Valley ran east and west directly across the route of Telegraph Road. It was a natural moat of gigantic proportions.[37]

When Ellis's cavalry force appeared on the bluffs north of Little Sugar Creek in the early afternoon, Hébert made certain the Federals could see his line of infantry and artillery posted on the opposite bluffs. Satisfied that the enemy would think long and hard before assaulting such a strong position, Hébert quietly withdrew his troops and proceeded toward Cross Hollow in the wake of Price's column. As the rebels marched away on Telegraph Road, the boom of Federal artillery echoed across the frigid landscape.[38]

Hébert had not experienced the dogged Federal pursuit from Springfield and was surprised to learn that a strong force of enemy cavalry had crossed Little Sugar Creek Valley. Unable to return to his imposing position on the bluffs, Hébert had no choice but to stand and fight where he was. He sent a courier dashing after Little's 1st Missouri Brigade, which turned about and soon reached the field of action. Hébert placed his three regiments on the eastern side of Telegraph Road, Little's infantry on the western side, and Clark's battery in the center, all facing north. The Confederate line was located along the southern edge of a large field belonging to a farmer named James Dunagin. Dismounted horsemen of the 1st Missouri Cavalry were scattered through the woods as skirmishers four hundred yards in front of the infantry and artillery. Shortly after the deployment was complete, the rebels saw the Federals advancing "as if determined to bring us to a regular engagement."[39]

When Ellis reached the top of the southern bluffs, he spotted Confederate stragglers hurrying away to the south. Fleeing rebels were a familiar sight to Ellis, and he followed at a gallop without waiting for infantry or artillery support. After advancing about half a mile the Federals blundered headlong into the Confederate position on Dunagin's farm. Clark's battery opened the engagement with a "heavy fire of ball and shell" straight down Telegraph Road. The first salvo shrieked just over the heads of the oncoming yankees. Ellis immediately ordered the 1st Missouri Cavalry off the road to left and right. Taking their cue from Ellis, Wright swung his battalion of the 6th Missouri Cavalry into the woods to the right of the road while McConnell led his battalion of the 3rd Illinois Cavalry to the left. Telegraph Road soon was empty except for the leading battalion of the 1st Missouri Cavalry, led by Maj. James M. Hubbard, which advanced at a dead run directly toward the rebel position. Hubbard was well out in front and apparently failed to hear Ellis's order to get off the road.[40]

At this moment a number of mounted rebels dashed out of the woods and fled down Telegraph Road. They were overtaken by Hubbard's onrushing battalion, and the intermingled mass of horsemen swept into Dunagin's field directly in front of the main line of Confederate infantry and artillery. It was almost a reprise of what had occurred the day before in Cross Timber Hollow. The Federals turned about and fled in wild disorder through a hail of Confederate small arms fire. A rebel observed that the Federals "found themselves in a hornet's nest and got out the best they could." Hubbard and most of the loyal Missourians managed to escape in the smoke and confusion, but the field was dotted with blue-clad bodies and dead and dying horses.[41]

While Hubbard's battalion was the center of attention, the rest of the Federals pushed through the woods on either side of the road, trading shots with dismounted skirmishers of Gates's 1st Missouri Cavalry. The Federals finally reached the northern edge of Dunagin's field and saw the solid line of enemy infantry and artillery on the far side. Ellis knew this was more than his command could handle and ordered a withdrawal.[42]

Back on the northern side of Little Sugar Creek, Curtis was rushing reinforcements forward from Carr's 4th Division, which was leading the main body of the Army of the Southwest that day. Col. William Vandever's 2nd Brigade, which included the 9th Iowa and 25th Missouri, crossed the valley and ascended the southern bluffs in Ellis's rear. The Iowa and Missouri infantrymen were so exhausted by the rapid march and the sprint up the bluffs that at least half of them fell out along the road. Around 3:00 P.M. Vandever reached Ellis's position and deployed his depleted brigade into line of battle, the Iowans on the right and the Missourians on the left. Hayden's 3rd Iowa Battery came up and occupied the center on the road. The Iowa gunners went into action against Clark's Missouri cannoneers half a mile to the south. The infantry closest to the two dueling batteries had a bad time. "They was poring the shells and balls into us," wrote a member of the 9th Iowa, but the Iowans lay on the ground and came through unscathed. The Confederate regiments on either side of Clark's battery were not so fortunate; several projectiles cut down men standing in the rebel ranks.[43]

While the two batteries dueled, Curtis hurried additional reinforcements toward the sound of the fighting. Col. Grenville M. Dodge's 2nd Brigade of the 4th Division, consisting of the 4th Iowa, 35th Illinois, and 1st Iowa Battery, crossed the valley at the double-quick. Like most green troops they were anxious to get into the fight; an Iowa officer recalled that "the roar of the cannon was loud and frequent and was very exciting." Dodge's men pulled off their coats and tossed their packs aside as they struggled up the bluffs, but by the time they reached Vandever's line, the fight was over.[44]

Around 4:00 P.M. Hébert decided that his men had done enough and disengaged. Curtis chose not to follow. Night was coming, and the Federal army was stretched out all the way back to Keetsville. The rebels got away safely and trudged across the darkening landscape toward Cross Hollow. A Louisiana soldier remembered that they were "tired, hungry, and shivering with cold" by the time they reached the Confederate cantonment. The Federals camped in the valley and on the battlefield.[45]

Little Sugar Creek, the name given to the engagement on Dunagin's farm, was the first battle of the Civil War in Arkansas. Federal casualties included thirteen killed and about twenty wounded, half or more of them from Hubbard's battalion of the 1st Missouri Cavalry. As many as forty-six Federal cavalry mounts also were killed. Confederate casualties are not known, though Federal soldiers claimed that up to twenty-six enemy dead were left on the field.[46]

Curtis's men carried the wounded to Enoch Trott's store in Little Sugar Creek Valley, buried the dead, and gawked at the shattered trees and telegraph poles, the patches of blood on the frozen ground, and the dozens of dead horses lying about. "For the first time [I] saw men [who] were killed in battle and it was a nasty sight," George A. Cummins of the 36th Illinois scribbled in his diary. "I hope to see but few of such."[47]

Reactions to the engagement varied. At one extreme, Colonel Dodge gloried in having participated, however marginally, in an actual battle. He thought the fight was "sharp and short" and added, with a touch of bravado, that "bullets flew like hail but the men stood firm as rocks." At the other extreme, Lt. George E. Currie of the 59th Illinois considered February 17 the day he lost the innocence of an untried soldier. Currie arrived on the field after the fighting was over and chanced upon an ambulance hauling bodies: "The heads covered with blood were hanging out at the back end of the ambulance, the tail gate not being closed, jarring and knocking with every jerk of the wagon. A ghastly sight. I followed it and when it stopped went up and saw a soldier's burial on the battlefield. Two men were digging a trench about three by seven feet, and into this side by side with an army blanket under and one over them, the soldiers were placed and the dirt, which was being removed for graves for the next dead comrades, covered them from sight forever."[48]

The Confederates generally were less impressed. They viewed Little Sugar Creek as nothing more than an unusually large rear guard action, "a right brisk skirmish" as one Arkansan put it. Some rebels had fired at Hubbard's horsemen or traded shots with the Federals in the woods, but most had not been engaged at all. "I never thought it was much of a battle," wrote a Missourian after the war, "but I have talked with some Federal soldiers, since, who claimed it was a stunner." Little Sugar Creek raised Confederate morale a bit, not only because the Federals had been bloodied, but because for the first time since Wilson's Creek portions of the Missouri and Arkansas armies fought side by side against the common foe. Little Sugar Creek also was the first time the new Confederate battle flag was unfurled in action in the Trans-Mississippi, though none of the Federals seem to have noticed the distinctive crossed red banner flying above the line of the 3rd Louisiana.[49]

That night Curtis sat alone in his tent and pondered his situation. He now faced the two largest rebel armies west of the Mississippi River, armies that had not been able to cooperate effectively for months until he had literally driven them together. Nathaniel Lyon had come to grief at the hands of those combined armies the previous summer at Wilson's Creek, but Curtis was undeterred. The Army of the Southwest would continue to advance.[50]

3 The Hunter and the Hunted

C urtis had no detailed section maps of northwestern Arkansas, but there were numerous soldiers in the Army of the Southwest who were familiar with the area. The gently rolling upland of the Springfield Plateau is dotted with occasional hills and ridges and covered by a mix of woods and prairies. It extends south from Missouri to the Boston Mountains and west into the Indian Territory. In 1862 roads were primitive and population was sparse, but it was one of the few places on the Ozark Plateau where armies could be maneuvered as if on a map.

The Federal commander intended to take full advantage of the relatively level terrain. Since leaving Springfield he had received reports that the Confederate cantonment in Cross Hollow was heavily fortified against an assault from the north. The reports were exaggerated, but Curtis had no way of knowing this. He decided against a direct advance down Telegraph Road and cast about for an alternative approach. On February 18, the day after the clash at Little Sugar Creek, Curtis sent scouts fanning across the countryside west of Telegraph Road to see if Cross Hollow could be outflanked in that direction.[1]

He also sent a reconnaissance in force toward Bentonville, a small town nine miles west of the Federal position at Little Sugar Creek. Sigel's half of the army had finally arrived, and Curtis chose Asboth to lead this expedition. Asboth, a former Hungarian nobleman, had no formal military training and had gained only a modicum of military experience in the failed

Hungarian revolution of 1848, but in the first year of the war in Missouri he demonstrated considerable competence as a cavalry leader. He set out on this expedition with portions of the 4th and 5th Missouri Cavalry and the 1st Missouri Flying Battery and reached Bentonville at noon on February 18. The Federals captured about thirty men from the 17th Arkansas who were gathering baggage left behind when Hébert called the regiment out from winter quarters. After confiscating the regimental flag flying atop the Benton County courthouse and administering the oath of allegiance to all civilians who presented themselves, Asboth and his command returned to Little Sugar Creek. The operation had a bizarre and tragic ending. A trooper of the 5th Missouri Cavalry rode back into town to fill his canteen with whiskey. He never returned to his regiment. A search party found his body stashed in an outhouse and burned much of Bentonville in retribution.[2]

By sunset on February 18 Curtis knew with reasonable certainty that the area west of Telegraph Road was empty of enemy troops and that he was free to maneuver as he wished. He decided to shift his command to his right and outflank the "great trap" at Cross Hollow. Confident that he soon would have the rebels on the run once again, the old soldier turned in for the night. As he slept, another winter storm howled out of the northwest and pelted Federals and Confederates with more freezing rain, sleet, and snow.[3]

Curtis did not know, however, that McCulloch also had concluded that Cross Hollow was untenable. The Texas general reached Cross Hollow that night and found everyone in line of battle awaiting an attack from the Federals at Little Sugar Creek. When McCulloch rode among the shivering soldiers, he triggered a tremendous demonstration. At the sight of their long-absent commander, the troops of the Arkansas army cheered wildly and tossed their hats into the air. McCulloch was so moved by this display of affection that tears came to his eyes. As he reached the center of each regiment, he shouted in his laconic fashion: "Men, I am glad to see you!" The response was deafening.[4]

The joyous reunion turned to sour debate as soon as McCulloch walked into Price's headquarters tent. A heated discussion erupted over the proper course of action. Price had regained his nerve and announced that the combined armies should stand fast in Cross Hollow and wait for Curtis to attack. McCulloch, aware that Cross Hollow was no place to make a stand, argued for a retreat to the Boston Mountains thirty miles to the south along the rugged southern edge of the Ozark Plateau. McCulloch pointed out that drawing the Federals deeper into Arkansas—and farther from supplies and

Alexander S. Asboth (Massachusetts Commandery, U.S. Military History Institute)

reinforcements—was the most effective strategy the Confederates could adopt. When the senior officers of both armies were polled, two-thirds agreed with McCulloch, but Price was unmoved. The conference broke up in disagreement.[5]

Later that night McCulloch received information that confirmed the wisdom of a withdrawal. A stalwart civilian made his way through the storm to report that the Federals had reached Bentonville and were heading toward Elm Springs, twelve miles south of Bentonville and ten miles southwest of Cross Hollow. The report was exaggerated—the Federal force was Asboth's cavalry expedition—but it accurately predicted Curtis's next move around the Confederate left flank. In the morning Price bowed to the inevitable, and the retreat from Springfield resumed. The weather was horrid. Freezing precipitation glazed Telegraph Road and coated beards and uniforms with a layer of ice. As the last infantrymen tramped out of Cross Hollow, the 6th Texas Cavalry torched the hundreds of stout wooden huts and storehouses in the cantonment. A spreading pillar of flame and smoke hung over the retreating column.[6]

The next day, February 20, the rebels reached Fayetteville, the major forward supply depot for the Arkansas army. The provisions and other supplies stored in the town could not be moved because of a shortage of transportation. Nearly all of the army's draft animals, along with most cavalry mounts, were wintering fifty miles to the south in the Arkansas River Valley, where forage was more plentiful. Determined to save what he could, McCulloch ordered that everything in Fayetteville be made available to the passing troops. The doors to warehouses were opened wide, and hundreds of tons of meat and flour were literally dumped in the streets. The hungry Confederates took full advantage of this unexpected cornucopia and filled their packs, pockets, and arms with anything edible or portable. A Missouri soldier said that "nearly every man in the regiment got a ham or a shoulder or a side of bacon, ran his bayonet through them and carried it to camp." He added that "it was a novel sight to see so much meat on the march." One company of Missouri infantry staggered out of town with over seven hundred pounds of meat. There was so much food that the men even burned piles of bacon to provide heat.[7]

The chaotic method of distribution degenerated into looting as many rebels ignored the distinction between military stores and private property. Homes and businesses were ransacked, and ragged soldiers made off with bonnets, dresses, mirrors, baby rattles, artificial flowers, and schoolbooks.

Confederate officers were unable to restore order. Surgeon Washington L. Gammage of the 4th Arkansas was appalled at the riotous behavior of his compatriots and called the sack of Fayetteville "one of the most disgraceful scenes that I ever saw."[8]

As the last of the troops passed through Fayetteville the following day, McCulloch ordered all remaining supplies put to the torch. Soldiers burned several storehouses and then set fire to the Female Institute, which had been used as an arsenal and cartridge factory. Condemned shells stored in the building exploded and sprayed flaming debris in every direction. No one was injured by this barrage, but several city blocks burned to the ground. South of town the retreating soldiers stopped and looked back at the melancholy sight. An officer in the 3rd Louisiana always remembered how the smoke from Fayetteville "rose like a cloud in the heavens."[9]

All that day and the next the Confederates plodded along Telegraph Road deeper into the Boston Mountains. The column lengthened as McIntosh's cavalry regiments dribbled in from their winter encampments in the Arkansas River Valley. McCulloch finally called a halt at Strickler's Station seventeen miles south of Fayetteville. The long retreat was over.

Strickler's Station was the last Butterfield Overland Mail stop atop the Ozark Plateau before Telegraph Road plunged down toward the Arkansas River. It lay in a little valley carved by a stream rather grandly called the Illinois River. Two miles to the west, over a limestone ridge topped with oak and hickory, lay a similar valley created by Cove Creek. McCulloch's men bivouacked along the Illinois River; Price's troops crossed the ridge and camped along Cove Creek. This arrangement made for less crowding and meant that the two antagonistic generals would not have to associate with each other any more than necessary.[10]

Relations between McCulloch and Price had deteriorated badly. After leaving Cross Hollow, Old Pap behaved like a child. He refused to speak or even to write to McCulloch. All but one of Price's letters during this period were written in the first person and signed by the Missouri general. The exception was a formal message to McCulloch, written in the third person and signed by Price's chief of staff, which imperiously summoned the Texan to Price's headquarters on Cove Creek. Price also continued his campaign to undermine or usurp McCulloch's authority. He sent a letter to Van Dorn complaining that "General McCulloch refuses to co-operate" and another to Pike claiming that Van Dorn had given Price command over all forces in the Indian Territory. In the latter communication Price demonstrated his flair for creative writing. After ordering Pike to proceed at once to Cove Creek, an order Pike properly ignored, Price declared that "I have for four or five days been fighting the enemy on my retreat from Springfield with great success."[11]

While Price alternately pouted and boasted, his troops gradually recuperated from their ordeal. Quartermaster Harding streamlined the army's train and distributed some of the clothing, equipment, and food carted so laboriously from Springfield. Soldiers of the 1st Missouri Brigade received jackets and pants made of undyed and unwashed wool. The whitish cloth smelled strongly of sheep but was warm and nicely set off by large wooden buttons and black belts. It was the first uniform of sorts that any Missouri soldiers had received.[12]

At Cove Creek the Missourians resumed the transfer of men from the state guard to Confederate service. Price ordered all guardsmen whose enlistment expired and who did not enter Confederate ranks to "leave the army *and leave it at once*." He also announced that guardsmen who did not join the Confederate army would have their names recorded so "future times may know who were willing to stand firm and aid the Cause of Southern Independence." Despite such heavy-handed tactics many disillusioned guardsmen shouldered their meager belongings and started the long walk home. These defections, combined with straggling during the retreat, reduced the Missouri army from about eight thousand to fewer than sixty-eight hundred troops in less than two weeks.[13]

On February 19 Curtis launched his flanking maneuver against Cross Hollow by extending his right from Little Sugar Creek toward Osage Spring, a point about halfway between Bentonville and Elm Springs. The weather made movement slow and difficult. The next morning Curtis learned from local Arkansas unionists, whom he came to depend on for reliable information, that the enemy had abandoned Cross Hollow and was falling back to Fayetteville. Surprised, Curtis halted the movement toward Osage Spring and ordered an immediate advance down Telegraph Road toward Cross Hollow. The thawing road was in terrible condition, but the Army of the Southwest reached the abandoned Confederate cantonment that afternoon. Asboth's cavalry slogged ahead another four miles to the aptly named hamlet of Mudtown and gathered up the usual gaggle of stragglers. Asboth urged that the Federals push on to Fayetteville, but Curtis decided to halt for a day or two at Cross Hollow. His men and animals needed time to rest, and he needed time to assess the situation.[14]

Curtis was ecstatic that he had taken Cross Hollow so easily. Most of the cantonment was a wasteland of smoldering ruins, but a pair of mills and a few storehouses had survived the conflagration. "It looked as if a Small Town had been burnt," wrote an Iowa infantryman. Some Federals strolled about like tourists; others scavenged for anything of value or interest. A company of midwestern farmboys found two hundred roosters and ate most of them before a more cosmopolitan officer identified the fowl as gamecocks, apparently left behind by the 3rd Louisiana. The rest of the cocks were saved and named after rebel generals so the soldiers could enjoy watching Beauregard and Price and Johnston battle it out. Not everyone had the energy for such frivolities. Many men were so worn out by the relentless pursuit that they spent their time in Cross Hollow "getting *slept up*."[15]

On February 22 a pair of runaway slaves made their way to Cross Hollow with the news that the Confederates had passed through Fayetteville and gone on toward the Boston Mountains. For the first time since leaving Springfield Curtis declined to follow the foe. The headlong Confederate retreat had drawn the Army of the Southwest much farther south than he or Halleck had expected. The Federals were now over two hundred miles from the railhead at Rolla, and even the hard-driving Sheridan was barely able to keep supplies moving over such a vast distance in the middle of winter. It was more important than ever that the Federals supplement their meager rations with local foodstuffs. The men of the 59th Illinois, for instance, foraged "by regiment, by company, by platoon, squad and by individual—to find something to eat in the adjoining country." What they found was not always of the most desirable quality or quantity, for the area between Springfield and Fayetteville had been picked over by the Confederates for months. The surgeon of the 18th Indiana noted that "what beef we get it takes two men to hold up while one knocks them down." He worried that "it looks like starving if we do not save rations."[16]

Once the excitement of the chase wore off, the toll taken by the strenuous campaign from Rolla became evident. Nearly a thousand horses and mules had broken down. Hundreds of infantrymen were barefoot in the wintry weather, and hundreds more would be in the same condition within a few weeks. Additional hats, coats, pants, gloves, socks, and underwear were sorely needed. "Standing around our camp fires, hungry and chilled, our faces became sooty and black, and we were anything in appearance but dress parade soldiers," recalled one veteran. To alleviate the logistical crisis, Curtis could do little more than encourage Sheridan to greater efforts.[17]

Curtis faced a strategic dilemma as a result of his success in clearing the rebels out of southwestern Missouri and a large part of northwestern Arkansas. Price and McCulloch had joined forces and had moved just out of his reach into the Boston Mountains thirty miles to the south. The Federal commander had three options, none of them attractive. First, he could advance into the Boston Mountains and risk the loss of his army either in battle or through starvation. Second, he could fall back toward Springfield in order to improve his supply situation and risk encouraging Price to return to his old mischief in Missouri. Third, he could attempt to hold his ground in northwestern Arkansas and keep the enemy at bay.

Curtis reluctantly settled on the third option as the only feasible course of action. He knew that as soon as the Federals assumed the strategic defensive, the initiative would pass to the enemy, but he felt that he had no other choice. After dropping off detachments along the road from Rolla, the Army of the Southwest was down to about 10,500 men. Curtis was uncertain whether his small, isolated command could handle the combined Arkansas and Missouri armies if they launched a bold counterattack. He informed Halleck of his decision to halt the pursuit and to hold his position. For the first time he asked for reinforcements: 7,000 infantry, 3,000 cavalry, 4 batteries, 1,000 replacement cavalry mounts, and 10,000 pairs of pants. Halleck replied that he could send the pants but nothing else. The message from St. Louis was clear: the Army of the Southwest was on its own.[18]

Curtis spread out his forces to facilitate foraging but kept them within a dozen miles or so of Little Sugar Creek Valley. He decided that in the event of a Confederate counteroffensive the Federals would hasten to the high bluffs on the northern side of the stream and dig in. Curtis had been impressed by the valley's defensive properties during his stay there on February 17–19. He later told his brother that it was the place "where I knew I could make the best fight."[19]

If the rebels stormed out of the Boston Mountains, they would have to advance north from Fayetteville toward Little Sugar Creek on either Telegraph Road or Elm Springs Road, so Curtis placed half of his army near each road. As the roads were six to eight miles apart, this disposition created a sizable gap between the two wings of the army. To minimize the possibility of a nasty surprise, Curtis established a screen of advanced pickets and patrols across his entire front. "Shall be on the alert, holding as securely as possible," he assured his anxious superior in St. Louis.[20]

By the beginning of March the various units of the Army of the Southwest had moved to their assigned positions. Carr's 4th Division remained in Cross Hollow, forming the Federal left. Osterhaus's 1st Division and Asboth's 2nd Division, both commanded by Sigel, were sprawled along the banks of McKissick's Creek four miles southwest of Bentonville, forming the Federal right. Davis's 3rd Division, originally stationed in Cross Hollow, was back in Little Sugar Creek Valley preparing defensive works in case of an emergency. Advanced cavalry pickets were in position on Telegraph and Elm Springs roads: at Mudtown in front of Cross Hollow and at Elm Springs in front of Bentonville. Finally, to protect facilities needed for grinding grain, two isolated infantry outposts were established beyond the army's flanks: the 2nd Missouri guarded Osage Mill (also called Smith's Mill) about five miles south of McKissick's Creek, and the 4th Iowa occupied Blackburn's Mill (also called War Eagle Mill) on War Eagle Creek sixteen miles east of Cross Hollow. Curtis kept his headquarters in Cross Hollow with the 4th Division and its large contingent of Iowa troops.[21]

Halleck approved the defensive posture Curtis assumed in northwestern Arkansas. In early February a combined naval and military expedition led by Brig. Gen. Ulysses S. Grant had sailed up the Tennessee and Cumberland rivers and had broken the back of rebel resistance in western Tennessee at Forts Henry and Donelson. This was the first of the long-awaited river offensives that Halleck, Buell, and McClellan had wrangled over for months and that Curtis's difficult overland offensive was helping to make possible. As long as the Army of the Southwest kept the rebels out of Missouri, Halleck could use all of his limited resources elsewhere. Halleck was optimistic that a forthcoming Federal offensive down the Mississippi River would reach the Arkansas River and compel the rebels facing Curtis to withdraw into Louisiana. Until then, he told Curtis, hold your ground and remain alert.[22]

Curtis was unwilling to give up the initiative altogether and tried to keep the rebels off balance with a series of raids and expeditions. The first of these operations was a reconnaissance in force down Telegraph Road to Fayetteville on February 22. Asboth left Mudtown at the head of the 3rd Illinois Cavalry, the 3rd Iowa Cavalry, portions of the 1st, 4th, and 5th Missouri Cavalry, and the 1st Missouri Flying Battery, about twelve hundred men in all. Upon reaching Fayetteville Asboth personally led a charge into town that netted around thirty rebel stragglers. While his men picked their way past smoking ruins and aromatic piles of charred bacon, Asboth rode back to the edge of town and apologized to Jonas M. Tebbetts for the damage done to his lawn and garden by the charging horsemen. Tebbetts was an outspoken Arkansas unionist and invited Asboth to stay for dinner and use his house as headquarters. Asboth accepted on the condition that York, his huge St. Bernard, be allowed to sit at the table and share his food. Little Marion Tebbetts, the youngest child in the family, was fascinated by the tall, gaunt soldier who spoke accented English and sported an enormous mustache. Half a century later she still recalled how her mother was upset with Asboth for eating the Tebbetts's last jar of jelly all by himself.[23]

The Federals occupied Fayetteville for three days, much to the delight of unionist residents such as Tebbetts who had remained rather than flee south with the Arkansas and Missouri armies. Asboth wanted to hold the town permanently, but Curtis refused and directed him to withdraw on February 26. Curtis saw no advantage in maintaining an exposed outpost sixteen miles in advance of his infantry at Cross Hollow. Asboth's column trotted away and left Fayetteville in a no-man's-land between the opposing armies, visited occasionally by cavalry patrols and foraging parties garbed in butternut or blue.[24]

The Achilles' heel of the Army of the Southwest was its long and vulnerable line of communications. Curtis did what he could to protect the line by establishing posts at Marshfield, Springfield, Cassville, and Keetsville. To keep trains rolling safely along the line, the army had to patrol as often as possible or, as one Federal officer put it, to give "the neighborhood a good scouring." The Federals assigned to these garrisons rarely saw any state guard or Confederate troops but occasionally engaged in vicious little fights with gangs of desperadoes, later romanticized as Confederate guerillas, who stole supplies from anyone they could victimize.[25]

Despite a tremendous advantage in cavalry, the Confederates attempted to interdict the Federal line of communications only once. Shortly after arriving in the Boston Mountains, McCulloch dispatched Maj. Lawrence "Sul" Ross and the 6th Texas Cavalry on a raid behind the Army of the Southwest. The Texans passed well to the west of Sigel's position and on February 25 reached Keetsville, where they discovered five sutlers' wagons parked for the night. They easily drove off the outnumbered garrison, destroyed the wagons, and got away with sixty horses and mules. The Federals suffered two killed and one missing; the Confederates, two wounded and one or two missing. Ross and his men returned to the Boston Mountains on March 1 after an arduous trek through the rugged terrain east of the White River. The latter stage of the raid had the unintended effect of causing the Federals to abandon their easternmost outpost at Blackburn's Mill on War Eagle

Creek. Colonel Dodge was alarmed by the passage of a large rebel force so close to his isolated command and withdrew across the White River to Cross Hollow.[26]

McCulloch had tried to explain to Price at Cross Hollow that the attenuated Federal line of communications was vulnerable to cavalry raids. The damage done at Keetsville, however minimal, proved his point. Had the Confederates initiated a sustained and vigorous interdiction effort, it is possible that they would have compelled Curtis to withdraw to Springfield. But after the Keetsville raid McCulloch limited his horsemen to harassing Federal foraging parties and ascertaining the location of Federal camps. The reason for McCulloch's uncharacteristic passivity was an urgent telegram from Van Dorn in Pocahontas.

Van Dorn was as surprised as anyone by the Federal winter offensive and the headlong retreat of Price's army. He first received word of the loss of Springfield on February 22, about the time the Missourians reached Cove Creek in the Boston Mountains. Van Dorn impulsively decided to leave Pocahontas for the Boston Mountains that very day and to launch an immediate counteroffensive. He informed his superiors in Virginia and Tennessee that he would take personal command of Confederate forces in the field and engage the Federal army at the first opportunity. "I have no doubt of the result," he declared. "If I succeed I shall push on." Van Dorn now envisioned northwestern rather than northeastern Arkansas as the starting point for his drive on St. Louis. He instructed McCulloch to prepare to march as soon as he arrived.[27]

Van Dorn traveled by steamboat down the Black River to Jacksonport then set out on horseback to Van Buren, about two hundred miles to the west. He was accompanied by his chief of staff, Col. Dabney H. Maury, his nephew and aide, Lt. Clement Sullivane, two slaves named Milton and Jem, and a "stupid, hulking fellow" who acted as guide. On the second day the party attempted to cross the Little Red River in a dugout canoe. The clumsy guide capsized the boat and pitched Van Dorn into the frigid stream. Van Dorn, ever the romantic, emerged from the river quoting Cassius through chattering teeth:

> Once upon a raw and gusty day
> The troubled Tiber chafed within her shores;
> Accoutered as I was, I plunged in,
> The torrent roared, and I did buffet it
> With lusty sinews.

Van Dorn pressed on across the wintry landscape without stopping to change clothes. That night he developed a severe fever that would plague him throughout the Pea Ridge campaign. The next day the party providentially found an ambulance along the route and commandeered it for the ailing general.[28]

When Van Dorn arrived in Van Buren on the evening of March 1, he received a telegram from McCulloch at Strickler's Station: "I have ordered the command to be ready to march as soon as you arrive... and will notify General Price to be ready also. We await your arrival anxiously. We now have force enough to whip the enemy." Van Dorn responded immediately: "I thank you for anticipating me in regard to getting in readiness to move forward. We must do it without delay." After another feverish and restless night, the Confederate commander climbed into his ambulance and set out toward the Boston Mountains thirty miles to the north.[29]

Van Dorn and his companions struggled uphill all day in the teeth of a bitter cold wind. Upon reaching the top of the Ozark Plateau, they turned onto Cove Creek Road and made their way to Price's headquarters. There Van Dorn received an enthusiastic welcome that included a salute of twelve guns and a starlight serenade in a frosty mountain meadow. A sumptuous dinner was followed the next morning by an elaborate breakfast that included kidneys stewed in sherry.[30]

Van Dorn stayed with Price that Sunday night in John Morrow's house, each general snug under a pile of buffalo robes. The following morning, March 3, Van Dorn and Price crossed the ridge separating the two armies and reached Strickler's Station on Telegraph Road. McCulloch quietly welcomed his visitors to his spartan headquarters and immediately got down to business. The stark contrast between the feuding generals impressed Maury, who recognized in McCulloch and his staff "the stern seriousness of soldiers trained to arms."[31]

McCulloch informed Van Dorn that the Federals had ceased offensive operations and had settled into two widely separated encampments, one in Cross Hollow and the other along McKissick's Creek southwest of Bentonville. When Van Dorn learned of the inviting manner in which Curtis had divided his forces, he "resolved to attack him at once." If he could destroy the Federal army in detail, he might yet open the road to St. Louis and glory. Orders were drawn up for a northward movement the next morning. What Van Dorn now proclaimed to be the Army of the West would march rapidly to Bentonville, interpose itself between the two wings of the Federal army, and deal with each in turn.[32]

The hastily formulated plan was simplicity itself. McIntosh's brigade of 3,000 Texas and Arkansas cavalrymen would advance up Telegraph Road beyond Fayetteville to demonstrate against the Federal left wing at Cross Hollow and screen the advance of the main Confederate force toward the Federal right wing near Bentonville. While McIntosh distracted the enemy, Price's division of 6,800 Missourians and 47 guns and Hébert's brigade of about 5,700 Arkansas, Louisiana, and Texas infantrymen (many of them actually dismounted cavalrymen) and 18 guns would hurry to Bentonville on Elm Springs Road, west of and parallel to Telegraph Road. McIntosh and his horsemen would rejoin the main body on Elm Springs Road. If all went well, the Confederates would reach Bentonville before Curtis realized what was happening, cut off and destroy the right wing of the Federal army, then turn and destroy the Federal left.[33]

During the conference at Strickler's Station Van Dorn demonstrated his inability to rise above his experience on the Texas plains. He expected the Army of the West to travel light, move fast, and strike the enemy without warning, that is, to operate essentially as a cavalry squadron stalking a band of irregulars. He also demonstrated his marked tendency to act impulsively. He was without a staff of his own other than Maury and Sullivane. He was unfamiliar with the capabilities and personalities of his new subordinates, some of whom had little military training or experience. He knew nothing of the two very different military organizations awkwardly joined under his command or of the supply systems that kept them in the field. He was ignorant of the primitive frontier roads he must use and the rugged terrain he must traverse, and he ignored the obvious fact that winter weather still gripped the Ozark Plateau. Finally, he was tired and unwell. Yet he insisted on marching the next morning. Had Van Dorn spent a week in the Boston Mountains preparing himself and his men for the ordeal ahead, things might have turned out differently.

Word of the imminent forward movement electrified the army. Price's refugee warriors were especially thrilled at the news. "The boys were eager to get into a battle with Curtis," recalled John Smith of the 2nd Missouri Brigade, "thinking that they would drive him back and then we could return to Missouri again." Instead of resting for the rigorous march scheduled to begin after only a few hours, most soldiers stayed up late cleaning weapons, drawing ammunition, and cooking rations. An Arkansan wrote prophetically to his fiancée of coming events: "Just wait now to hear of the Dutch and Yankees being run to St. Louis. Otherwise you'll see us coming on the double-quick through Van Buren."[34]

At least the men would not be burdened with a heavy load. Van Dorn ordered that each soldier carry only his weapons, forty rounds of ammunition, three days' rations, and a single blanket. Tents, bedding, extra clothing, and cooking utensils were to be left behind in the camps. McCulloch's and Price's divisions—as the two armies were now styled—each were to have an ammunition train and an abbreviated supply train carrying only one day's emergency rations. Van Dorn intended his troops to subsist on the supplies left behind by the fleeing yankees and gave no serious thought to alternate means of supply. He was taking an enormous risk. The scanty issue of rations, barely enough to sustain an active man for forty-eight hours, would be exhausted by the time the Confederates made contact with the Federals. In the forthcoming operation the Army of the West must conquer or starve.[35]

Determined to give his command every possible advantage in this all-or-nothing enterprise, Van Dorn even called upon Pike's ragtag forces in the Indian Territory. He ordered Pike to lead his native troops into Arkansas and rendezvous with the Army of the West at Elm Springs two days hence on March 5. Pike was not at all surprised to discover that many Indians cited the terms of the recently concluded treaties with the Confederacy and adamantly refused to leave the Indian Territory. Others agreed to go only if they received an advance on their salaries. After patiently doling out Confederate dollars for two days, the rotund Arkansas general finally led the undersized 1st and 2nd Cherokee Mounted Rifles and two companies of Texas cavalry —perhaps nine hundred men in all—into northwestern Arkansas.[36]

Van Dorn left no stone unturned in his search for additional manpower. On February 17 McCulloch had issued a desperate proclamation calling upon able-bodied Arkansans to "turn out and form companies, and rally to meet the advancing enemy." Hundreds of citizens made their way to the encampments in the Boston Mountains. When Van Dorn learned of the existence of several unattached companies of these "emergency men," he added them to the ranks of Hébert's brigade and directed that they be kept under "constant instruction" even as the army prepared to advance.[37]

Late in the afternoon of March 3 two brand new regiments of Confederate infantry trudged up Telegraph Road from Van Buren and presented themselves at Strickler's Station. Van Dorn's enthusiasm over the unexpected arrival of the 19th and 20th Arkansas was dampened somewhat when he discovered that the raw recruits were untrained and practically unarmed. After conferring with Price he sent them over the ridge to Cove Creek Valley, where they were issued castoff weapons and other equipment left over from the reorganization of the Missouri State Guard. The Arkansans struggled for thirty-six hours to put some of their arms in working order. They were unable to accompany the Army of the West when it moved out the next morning and would not participate in the battle except in a marginal way.[38]

Van Dorn would begin his offensive on March 4 with at least sixteen thousand men and sixty-five guns. Had he waited a few days, he could have added the 19th and 20th Arkansas to his ranks. As it was, the Army of the West had a three-to-two advantage in manpower and a four-to-three advantage in artillery over the Army of the Southwest. Never did a Confederate army march off to battle with greater numerical superiority.

On March 3, the day Van Dorn conferred with McCulloch and Price at Strickler's Station, Curtis reluctantly decided to fall back and concentrate his army at Little Sugar Creek without waiting for the Confederates to strike. He directed Sigel to put his 1st and 2nd Divisions on the road and to join Davis's 3rd Division as soon as possible. Sigel requested permission to remain at McKissick's Creek a short time in order to exhaust his dwindling store of forage. Curtis approved a brief delay but politely reminded Sigel not to tarry too long: "I hope I meet you soon, say in two or three days, in position on [Little] Sugar Creek where we must entrench ourselves to await the progress of our comrades on our flanks." Carr's 4th Division, and Curtis himself, would remain in a blocking position at Cross Hollow until the other three divisions were secure in the new camp.[39]

Curtis made the decision to concentrate at Little Sugar Creek, not because he sensed the Confederates were up to something, but for a much more mundane reason: the difficulty of obtaining forage from the barren countryside for the army's horses and mules. The Federals, like the Confederates before them, had discovered that the Ozark Plateau in winter simply could not support large numbers of grazing animals. Curtis feared that if his draft animals grew much weaker the scattered Federal divisions would have to remain where they were until spring, an extremely dangerous prospect with the enemy so close. Better to move now than not be able to move at all later.

While the Federals prepared to fall back to the imposing bluffs along Little Sugar Creek, Curtis remained alert to the possibility of a Confederate counteroffensive. As yet, however, he had not the slightest hint that the rebels were stirring. On March 3 a battalion of the 3rd Iowa Cavalry patrolled to within five miles of Fayetteville. The Iowans found no sign of enemy activity except a curious report from unionist citizens that the rebels had fired a dozen cannons the previous night in the Boston Mountains. It struck some listeners as a salute of some kind, but for whom or what no one could guess.[40]

The next day, March 4, yet another winter storm swept across the Ozark Plateau. Huddled in his tent in Cross Hollow, Capt. Henry Cummings of the 4th Iowa informed his wife that the howling wind was "spitting snow." The normally vigilant Federals let down their guard and curtailed patrolling, confident that few rebels would be out and about in such weather. Federal vigilance was reduced even more when Sigel chose this moment to withdraw the cavalry picket from Elm Springs. Sigel's inexplicable action left Elm Springs Road between Fayetteville and Bentonville unguarded. The only Federal force south of Sigel's encampment on McKissick's Creek now was the isolated 2nd Missouri at Osage Mill. Col. Frederick Schaefer, commanding the 2nd Missouri, was understandably anxious about the yawning gap on his left caused by the withdrawal of the cavalry. On his own initiative he stretched his infantry picket line eastward to cover Elm Springs Road. Schaefer's move would have significant consequences.[41]

At the same time Sigel sent an expedition to his rear. He ordered Maj. Joseph Conrad to proceed to Maysville in extreme northwestern Arkansas and to prevent Missourians from sneaking southward to join Price's army. Conrad took with him two companies of the 17th Missouri; one company each from the 3rd, 12th, and 15th Missouri, the 36th Illinois, and the 4th and 5th Missouri Cavalry; and two guns from Welfley's Independent Missouri Battery, about 360 men in all. The heterogeneous force set out on the morning of March 4 despite the near-blizzard conditions. Late the next day Sigel reinforced Conrad with two companies of the 4th Missouri Cavalry commanded by Maj. Emeric Meszaros.[42]

Carr also dispatched an expedition from Cross Hollow. Early on March 4 Colonel Vandever marched into the dismal weather with portions of the 9th Iowa, the 25th Missouri, the 3rd Illinois Cavalry, and the 3rd Iowa Battery, a total of about seven hundred men. The column headed for Huntsville, a small town thirty-five miles southeast of Cross Hollow on the eastern side of the White River, which was reputed to be a gathering place for secessionists. The Federals reached Huntsville at noon the next day and rounded up a few suspicious characters. Disappointed at this meager catch, Vandever decided to spend the night in the town and return to Cross Hollow in the morning.[43]

By the beginning of March the strategic initiative in the Trans-Mississippi had dramatically changed hands. After completing a highly successful winter campaign, the Army of the Southwest was practically immobilized at the end of a long and vulnerable supply line and was facing a combined enemy force of uncertain size and intentions. Unable to advance or retreat without potentially dire consequences, Curtis reluctantly assumed a defensive posture. Van Dorn, meanwhile, was leaping recklessly to the offensive. The hunter had become the hunted.

4 Rush to Glory

The campaign to liberate Missouri and retrieve the honor of Confederate arms in the West began in the Boston Mountains on Tuesday, March 4. Shortly after dawn the soldiers of the Army of the West formed up on Telegraph Road and moved briskly to the north through a curtain of falling snow. Despite the cold, gloomy weather the rebels were in good spirits. A Texan recalled that the signal to advance "was hailed with enthusiastic shouts, and other demonstrations of joy."[1]

At Strickler's Station Van Dorn shakily mounted a horse and rode along the length of Hébert's infantry brigade until he reached the gray-clad 3rd Louisiana. "The snow was falling fast," remembered Maury, "and we did not feel very bright, until we were struck by the splendid appearance of a large regiment we were passing. It halted as we came upon its flank, faced to the front and presented arms, and as General Van Dorn reached its center, three rousing cheers rang out upon the morning air, and made us feel we were with soldiers." Van Dorn was delighted by this little ceremony and responded with a brief, fiery speech, but within an hour he felt so weak he was compelled to retire to his ambulance.[2]

McIntosh's cavalry brigade took the lead, followed by Price's division, Hébert's brigade, and the small ammunition and supply trains. Forage was in extremely short supply in the Boston Mountains, and most of what was available had gone to the cavalry and artillery horses. Because of the sorry condition of the draft animals, keeping the trains closed up proved impossible, and within a few hours the line of wagons was "stretched out seemingly with no end to it." This was the first indication that the offensive would not go as planned.[3]

The rigors of the march soon began to tell on the men as well. McCulloch's troops had been in winter quarters for months, and the strain of rapid marching was too much for some of them. The men in the recently dismounted cavalry regiments had a particularly difficult time keeping up. Winded soldiers with blistered feet littered Telegraph Road before noon. Van Dorn made matters worse by forcing a killing pace. Jolting along at a brisk gait in his ambulance, the feverish Confederate commander failed to see what was happening to his troops. "We were being rushed upon the foe like a thunderbolt," said an officer in the 3rd Louisiana. "It seemed as if General Van Dorn imagined the men were made of cast-steel, with the strength and powers and endurance of a horse, whose mettle he was testing to its utmost capacity and tension. Scarcely time was given the men to prepare food and snatch a little rest." As the hours passed, enthusiasm gave way to discontent. One Missourian remarked sarcastically that Van Dorn "had forgotten he was riding and we were walking." In his rush to glory, Van Dorn was his own worst enemy.[4]

Worsening weather aggravated the situation. As the Army of the West emerged from the shelter of the Boston Mountains onto the Springfield Plateau, a blizzard struck. Men and animals trudged into the howling wind, heads down, struggling to keep their footing on the icy roads. Late in the afternoon Van Dorn finally called a halt at Fayetteville. Having marched without tents, the soldiers wrapped themselves in their blankets and huddled together for warmth in the snow. Van Dorn and some other high-ranking officers rested comfortably in Fayetteville that night, but for most of the thousands of shivering Confederates bivouacked around the town "anything like sleep was out of the question."[5]

On Wednesday, March 5, the northward movement continued through intermittent showers of snow. McIntosh's cavalry brigade rode up Telegraph Road and halted several miles north of Fayetteville. From there McIntosh sent Col. B. Warren Stone's 6th Texas Cavalry forward to demonstrate against the Federal outpost at Mudtown. This diversion was intended to focus Curtis's attention on Telegraph Road while the main body of the Confederate army advanced on Elm Springs Road. The Texans captured a yankee foraging party of forty men and ten wagons and exchanged a few shots with the pickets at Mudtown before falling back to Fayetteville as directed.[6]

After sending Stone on his way, McIntosh led the main body of his brigade west across the rolling landscape to Elm Springs Road. The cavalrymen reached the road a considerable distance ahead of the toiling column of infantry. McIntosh directed Col. Elkanah Greer to take his 3rd Texas Cavalry and clear the way toward Bentonville, being very careful not to alert or alarm the yankees. All went well at first. Greer's horsemen fanned out and swept the countryside clean of Federal scouts and patrols. Then, as evening came on and snow flurries reduced visibility to a few yards, the Texans stumbled blindly into a Federal outpost north of Elm Springs. The pickets belonged to Colonel Schaefer's loyal 2nd Missouri, which was stationed several miles to the northwest at Osage Mill. The Federal infantrymen defended themselves ably and kept the rebel horsemen at bay. After a prolonged skirmish the two sides disengaged in the gathering darkness. The Missourians fell back to Osage Mill, the Texans to Elm Springs. The failure of the Confederate cavalrymen to avoid or capture the Federals would prove to be a costly error.[7]

As the Confederate cavalry carried out its assignments with varying degrees of success, the infantry plodded north from Fayetteville toward Bentonville across a frozen landscape. Progress was slow, and the long column staggered into Elm Springs after a march of only twelve miles. The cheerless camp provided few comforts. "I will never forget that night," wrote a man in the 1st Missouri Brigade. "It had turned bitter cold and was snowing a regular March blizzard. We had no tents and only one blanket to each man. We built log heaps and set them afire to warm the ground to have a place on which to lie, and I remember well the next day there were several holes burned in my uniform by sparks left on the ground." The men were so utterly exhausted that most of them fell into a fitful sleep despite the cold.[8]

After marching for two days under extremely difficult conditions, the Army of the West was bivouacked only twelve miles south of the vital junction at Bentonville. There still were no signs that the Federals realized what was happening, but Van Dorn fretted over the clash between the 3rd Texas Cavalry and the detachment of Federal infantry north of Elm Springs. Near midnight he made a decision: McIntosh's cavalry brigade would proceed to Osage Mill in the morning and capture whatever Federal force was there before pushing on to Bentonville. This change in plans was a mistake on Van Dorn's part, for it meant that the lunge toward Bentonville would have to be carried out by the exhausted and footsore infantry.[9]

The troops awoke well before dawn the next morning, Thursday, March 6, and ate the last of their rations. At first light McIntosh's brigade moved off toward Osage Mill, probing warily for the feisty pickets encountered the previous evening. Price's division and Hébert's brigade advanced directly on Bentonville but encountered an unexpected obstacle in Osage Creek, which twisted back and forth across the line of march. The column ground to a halt every few miles as the infantrymen dragged logs across the icy stream and trickled over in single file. Van Dorn now learned that neither of the two divisions of the Army of the West had a pioneer corps to build bridges and clear away obstacles. It was a discovery that would return to haunt him again and again during the next twenty-four hours.[10]

Despite these delays Van Dorn still hoped to reach the junction at Bentonville before the enemy learned of his approach. Around 9:00 A.M. he received word from McIntosh that the Federal garrison at Osage Mill had departed for Bentonville in the middle of the night. An hour later firing broke out ahead on Elm Springs Road as Price's division collided with a detachment of Federal cavalry at Osage Spring (not to be confused with Osage Mill) four miles southeast of Bentonville.[11]

Van Dorn knew his approach was no longer a secret. The success of the operation depended on getting some horsemen to Bentonville to hold the junction until the infantry could arrive. He directed Price to send forward whatever Missouri cavalry was at hand. Colonel Gates soon was on his way toward Bentonville at the head of his own 1st Missouri Cavalry, Lt. Col. James T. Cearnal's Missouri Cavalry Battalion, and Capt. Joseph Shelby's unattached Missouri State Guard company. The two columns of cavalry commanded by McIntosh and Gates met at the junction of Elm Springs and Osage Mill roads just south of Bentonville.[12]

Shortly after 10:00 A.M. a phalanx of Confederate horsemen from Arkansas, Texas, and Missouri emerged onto the glistening white expanse of the Osage Prairie. Visible two miles away across the level terrain was Bentonville. Billows of dark smoke were rising from the town.

The frosty morning of March 5 passed uneventfully at Cross Hollow except for a brief outbreak of firing in the direction of Mudtown. Curtis was in his tent writing when an Arkansas unionist rode up through the swirling snow with startling news. The Arkansan—identified only as a citizen of Fayetteville —told Curtis that a short time earlier he had fallen in with the 6th Texas Cavalry on Telegraph Road between Fayetteville and Mudtown. Pretending to be a secessionist, the Arkansan asked the Texans what they were doing so far from their camps in the Boston Mountains. The Texans replied that the combined Arkansas and Missouri armies were no longer in the Boston Mountains but were on their way north to whip the yankees. Shocked by this revelation, the Arkansan slipped away at the first opportunity and turned his horse toward Cross Hollow. (There is no truth to the oft-repeated story that James "Wild Bill" Hickock was a scout for the Army of the Southwest and that it was he who warned Curtis of the Confederate advance. Hickock played no role in the Pea Ridge campaign.)[13]

Curtis listened carefully, asked a few questions, and then thanked the Arkansan for his patriotism. He did not waste time attempting to verify the unofficial report but decided to concentrate his scattered divisions at Little Sugar Creek immediately. He informed Sigel of the probable Confederate approach and added, "This may be only a feint, but we had better unite our forces at Sugar Creek, and be ready for any occasion." At the end of the message Curtis repeated himself more emphatically to make sure Sigel got the point: "Our stand must be at Sugar Creek, where I hope to join you tomorrow."[14]

That evening a rebel deserter was brought to the general's tent in Cross Hollow. The "deserter" was William B. Miller, a Missouri-born member of the 3rd Iowa Cavalry, who had been sent ahead two weeks earlier to join the rebels. Miller had slipped away from Price's division north of Fayetteville on Elm Springs Road. He confirmed everything the Arkansas unionist had reported and provided the additional information that the Confederates, now commanded by Van Dorn, were advancing on Bentonville with the intent of cutting off the 1st and 2nd Divisions. Curtis rushed a second message to Sigel summarizing Miller's report: "They are coming sure, he says. Make a night march, if need be, so as to join me at Sugar Creek early tomorrow." Curtis thanked Miller and sent him back to the rebel army to gather additional information. Later in the evening, amidst a frenzy of staff work, Curtis scribbled a terse message to Halleck: the rebels were on their way, and he intended to "give them the best reception possible."[15]

By 10:00 P.M. on March 5 Curtis was on his way from Cross Hollow to Little Sugar Creek. Carr's 4th Division followed two hours later. "It was now our turn to run," observed a Federal artilleryman. The withdrawal from Cross Hollow was excruciatingly difficult. A corporal in the 9th Iowa described how "artillery, cavalry, wagon trains and infantry floundered along in the mud and darkness, now a complete jam and blockade and then a rapid rush ahead until another blockade was encountered." Men remembered that frigid march for the rest of their days. "It was snowing and most intensely cold," recalled

Capt. Henry Cummings of the 4th Iowa. "I never suffered so much in my life." Deserted buildings along Telegraph Road were set afire to light the way. Bonfires once again lit the sky over Cross Hollow as the rear guard destroyed piles of equipment and personal baggage that could not be removed because of a shortage of wagons.[16]

Thirty-five miles southeast of Cross Hollow, Vandever and his seven hundred men from Carr's division were settling in for the night at Huntsville. The Federals were uneasy because the secessionist inhabitants of the little town were abuzz with rumors that the Confederate army was on the move. Vandever, unable to sleep, considered the matter for several hours. At 3:00 A.M. on March 6 he awoke his men and put them on the road toward Cross Hollow. The Federals covered only a few miles before they met couriers from Curtis, Carr, and Davis hastening to warn them of the enemy advance. Vandever received new orders to hurry to Little Sugar Creek as fast as his men could walk.[17]

Certain that he was in danger of being cut off, Vandever set a punishing pace. "It was a long and weary day, hour after hour passed away, and still that straining silent column struggled on," remembered a loyal Missouri infantryman. The Federals forded the icy White River and trudged across the snow-covered landscape eating whatever food they had in their pockets. After covering forty-two difficult miles in sixteen hours, Vandever and every one of his men reached Little Sugar Creek at 8:00 P.M. on March 6. Not a single straggler was left behind. It was one of the memorable marches of the war.[18]

The 3rd Division had been camped in Little Sugar Creek Valley for several days, but Davis and his men had done little to prepare the position for a fight. Curtis arrived in the early morning of March 6 and ordered Davis to move his command to the top of the steep bluffs on the northern side of the creek. Despite evidence that the rebels were advancing on Elm Springs Road several miles to the west, Curtis still believed Telegraph Road to be a likely avenue of approach to his new position. He personally laid out a line of fortifications facing south. When Curtis was done, Davis's men attacked the rocky soil with picks and shovels. They constructed two blufftop redoubts for artillery on either side of Telegraph Road, an advanced line of rifle pits partway down the slope in front of the redoubts, and a main line of rifle pits atop the bluffs. The Federals cut down hundreds of trees along the face of the bluffs and in the valley below to obtain a clear field of fire. They also burned Enoch Trott's store to deny the enemy even that modest bit of cover.[19]

Davis placed Col. Thomas Pattison's 1st Brigade to the west of Telegraph

Road on three prominent bluffs or headlands, each separated by a deep ravine. Col. Julius White's 2nd Brigade occupied a similar position to the east of Telegraph Road. Carr's 4th Division, minus Vandever's command, arrived at Little Sugar Creek at dawn and filed into place to the east of White's brigade. By noon on March 6 the bulk of the work was done. Curtis was impressed and later told Halleck that "breastworks of considerable strength were erected by the troops . . . as if by magic." The soldiers agreed. "We had a fine place," wrote an Indiana infantryman of his trench sixty feet above the valley floor, "the best Position any wheres along the road."[20]

While the troops perfected their defenses, Curtis scouted the terrain behind the bluffs and busied himself with administrative matters. He established his headquarters at Samuel Pratt's store on Telegraph Road two miles north of Little Sugar Creek. Another mile or so farther north was Elkhorn Tavern and the head of Cross Timber Hollow. The rolling tableland between Little Sugar Creek Valley and Cross Timber Hollow was known locally as Pea Ridge, a name not yet familiar to the officers and men of the Army of the Southwest. Curtis directed that the army's trains be parked in some large fields between the store and the tavern where they would be out of the line of fire. To protect the trains and the army's rear from bushwhackers, he posted Maj. Eli Weston's battalion-sized 24th Missouri and a few cavalry companies at the tavern. Preparations for a fight at Little Sugar Creek were going smoothly, but only half the army was present. Where was Sigel?

After receiving the two warnings from Curtis on March 5, Sigel prepared to move his command from McKissick's Creek to Little Sugar Creek in a deliberate, unhurried manner. Sigel's lack of urgency is curious; he seemed to doubt that the Confederates were coming. Between 10:00 and 11:00 P.M., however, Curtis's warning was confirmed by a dispatch from Colonel Schaefer at Osage Mill. Schaefer reported that just before dark his pickets had engaged in a brisk skirmish with a large body of enemy cavalry near Elm Springs.[21]

Schaefer's message jolted Sigel out of his complacency. He ordered his entire command, including Schaefer's 2nd Missouri, to withdraw immediately to Little Sugar Creek. He also rushed a cavalry company to Osage Spring on Elm Springs Road to observe the approach of the enemy, and he sent couriers chasing after Conrad and Meszaros with new instructions to head for the rendezvous site at Little Sugar Creek. In accordance with Sigel's frantic orders the ponderous trains of the 1st and 2nd Divisions began rumbling from McKissick's Creek shortly before dawn on March 6, followed by long columns of cavalry, artillery, and infantry. Despite a series of delays in getting under way, and a considerable amount of confusion as thousands of men and animals stumbled about in the freezing darkness, the evacuation of the Federal encampment was successful. By midmorning nearly all of Sigel's command was safely past the crucial junction at Bentonville.[22]

Now began one of the most controversial episodes of the campaign. While Asboth and Osterhaus led the 1st and 2nd Divisions toward Little Sugar Creek, Sigel inexplicably remained behind in Bentonville with the rear guard. In his official report Sigel stated that he was waiting for communications from the cavalry detachment at Osage Spring and that, at any rate, he did not wish the rear guard to be "too close to the train," which by this time was at least five miles to the east. Years later he changed his story, explaining that he tarried in Bentonville "with the intention of finding out whether the enemy was approaching in strong force" and whether he was advancing via Osage Mill or Osage Spring. Sigel's explanations are unconvincing. Since the 1st and 2nd Divisions were safely past Bentonville, the route of the rebels was unimportant, and Sigel's actions of the previous ten hours demonstrated that he believed they were advancing on Elm Springs Road. Moreover, if Sigel was interested only in observation, a few cavalry regiments unburdened by slow-moving infantry would have been more appropriate to the task. It is worth noting that Sigel fashioned the rear guard in the form of a "legion," a small all-arms force theoretically capable of independent action. All things considered, it seems likely that he deliberately lagged behind in order to meet the enemy with his miniature army and demonstrate his capacity for independent command.[23]

Sigel's force in the Bentonville town square consisted of eight companies of Maj. Hugo Wangelin's 12th Missouri, half of Col. Joseph Nemett's 5th Missouri Cavalry, two cavalry companies of the 36th Illinois, and four twelve-pounder James rifles and two twelve-pounder howitzers of Capt. Gustavus Elbert's 1st Missouri Flying Battery—a little over six hundred men in all. When the 2nd Missouri arrived from Osage Mill, it would double the size of the rear guard. The cavalrymen at Osage Spring had not yet made contact with the enemy, so Sigel strolled over to the Eagle House, a hotel near the southwestern corner of the square, and ate a breakfast of ham and eggs. The soldiers in the square did not enjoy the privileges of rank; they stacked their arms and tried to make themselves as comfortable as possible. The temperature was below freezing but the sun was shining for the first time in days. "No one sensed danger," remembered an officer, "we built a big camp fire on the Court House plaza, and sat around it, sleeping most of the time." So many bonfires were set that the clearing sky above Bentonville soon was smudged with smoke.[24]

About 9:30 A.M. Schaefer and the 2nd Missouri arrived from Osage Mill. Schaefer was unaware that he was supposed to join the rear guard and led his Missourians on toward Little Sugar Creek. When Sigel emerged from the Eagle House thirty minutes later, he learned that the 2nd Missouri had come and gone. His angry recriminations were cut short by the sound of gunfire to the south. The cavalry company posted at Osage Spring raced into Bentonville to report, quite unnecessarily, that the enemy was approaching on Elm Springs Road. Sigel rode to the edge of town to see for himself. For several minutes the myopic general peered intently through his field glasses at "dense masses of men" about two miles away across the snow-covered Osage Prairie. Satisfied that the rebels had arrived in force, Sigel galloped back into Bentonville. His capacity for command was about to be tested.[25]

On the opposite side of the Osage Prairie, McIntosh halted his command and rode forward a short distance to study the situation in Bentonville. Everything he saw indicated that the Federals had escaped the trap and left a detachment behind to destroy excess supplies in the town. After the strenuous efforts of the past two days this was a disheartening moment for McIntosh, but he hoped he still might be able to bag the laggards and gain a partial victory.[26]

McIntosh was an 1849 West Point graduate who had served for years on the frontier but had failed to develop the skills necessary for high command. Impulsive, reckless, and courageous to a fault, McIntosh liked nothing better than plunging headlong into a fight. At Bentonville he was true to his nature and immediately launched a poorly conceived three-pronged attack designed to surround and overwhelm the Federal contingent in his front. In so doing McIntosh made several basic errors: he divided his command in the presence of an enemy force of unknown size, failed to reconnoiter the ground over which the various detachments would advance, and neglected to take into account the poor condition of his men and horses. Had he simply led the entire Confederate cavalry force to the east across the Osage Prairie, which afforded a superb approach for mounted forces, he could have blocked Bentonville Road quickly and effectively and cut Sigel off from any hope of escape or succor.[27]

After issuing orders to his subordinates, McIntosh sped away at the head

James M. McIntosh (Archives and Special Collections, University of Arkansas at Little Rock)

of his powerful mounted brigade. He intended to swing completely around Bentonville in a clockwise fashion and strike the Federal escape route, Bentonville Road, from the north. The Confederates trotted across the Osage Prairie west of Bentonville in column of battalions. Immediately north of town the prairie gave way to a dense forest of oak and hickory, and the impressive advance halted abruptly. Amidst considerable confusion the tightly packed rebels redeployed into column of fours and funneled into a narrow road that continued in a northerly direction. Unable to find a road, lane, or path branching off to the east, McIntosh led his brigade away from the scene of action.[28]

Three miles north of Bentonville McIntosh's brigade descended into Little Sugar Creek Valley and turned east on a road that ran along the valley floor. Precious time had been lost, but at last the Confederates were moving in the right direction. Yet now the rigors of the march and the bitterly cold weather caused another unexpected delay as horses and riders began to break down. The mounts were exhausted by the furious pace of the advance that morning. The soldiers had been in the saddle since long before dawn, and their hands and feet were in serious condition. "I was so benumbed with cold that I could not cap my pistols," said a young Texan. "I tried ever so hard to do so, but had my life depended upon it I could not have succeeded." Progress literally slowed to a walk as the chilled riders dismounted and led their jaded horses along the road. While McIntosh cursed his luck, the rumble of artillery fire could be heard to the southeast.[29]

As McIntosh's brigade rode north, the assorted Missouri cavalry units moved east across the prairie and halted about two miles southeast of Bentonville. Gates's mission was to cooperate with McIntosh's brigade when it reappeared on the far side of Bentonville Road. Gates waited for fifteen minutes for some sign of McIntosh's approach. When he saw Sigel's rear guard emerge from the town and head in his direction on Bentonville Road, Gates decided to act with or without McIntosh. His Missourians had fended off Federal pursuers during the long running fight from Springfield; now the tables were turned, and they would have a chance to harry a retreating foe. About a mile east of Bentonville the road passes over a knoll and turns northeast into a wooded area. Gates sent the 1st Missouri Cavalry into the timber to block the road and readied the rest of his command to attack the oncoming enemy in flank and rear.[30]

As soon as he was clear of Bentonville, Sigel deployed his meager resources to protect the six guns of the 1st Missouri Flying Battery. Two companies of

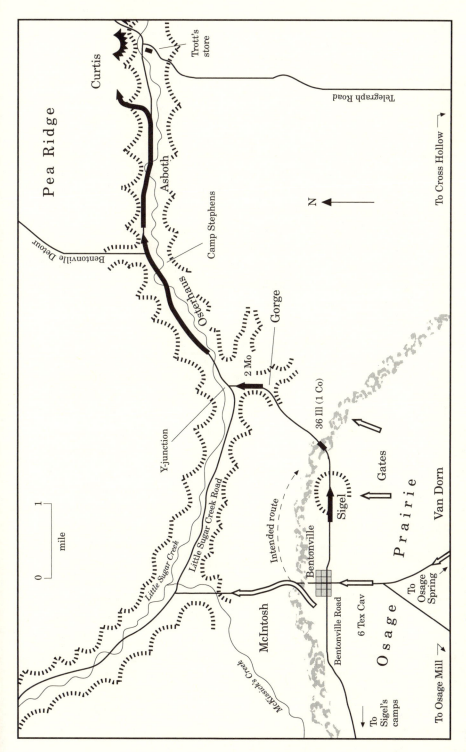

Map 4-1. *Bentonville: McIntosh Attempts to Intercept Sigel*

the 12th Missouri marched in advance of the artillery as skirmishers, two companies marched on either side as flank guards, and the remaining four companies followed behind the guns. Two companies of the 5th Missouri Cavalry trotted along as extended flank guards while the rest brought up the rear.[31]

Only minutes after Sigel's command marched out of Bentonville, Stone's 6th Texas Cavalry charged noisily into town from the south, as McIntosh had instructed, in order to flush the Federals into the trap east of town. The Texans captured a dozen Federal stragglers, but when they ventured out on Bentonville Road, they were challenged by Federal horsemen and withdrew into town. Lacking instructions from the absent McIntosh and all but immobilized by their exhausted mounts, the 6th Texas Cavalry took no further part in the pursuit of the Federal rear guard.[32]

Sigel halted atop the knoll to assess the situation. He saw Gates's Missourians advancing across the prairie in his direction and moving into the woods just ahead. Sigel was noticeably agitated at this development. He muttered to himself in German, repeatedly pounded his fist into his palm, and blurted out to Albert Jenks of the 36th Illinois: "Captain Jenks, we are surrounded; the enemy is on all sides of us; but we must go through; we must cut our way through; we will go through."[33]

Having convinced himself that escape was possible, Sigel directed Major Wangelin of the 12th Missouri to take three of his four trailing companies and use them to reinforce the skirmishers spread out along the front and flanks of the artillery column. While Wangelin continued toward Little Sugar Creek with the infantry and four of the guns, Sigel remained behind with the two James rifles and the cavalry to direct a delaying action. He deployed his modest force atop the knoll and opened fire on the rebels approaching across the prairie. The first shells exploded directly in front of the Missourians and caused them to scatter in all directions "with telegraphic speed." After a dozen rounds had been expended with like effect, the Federal cavalry charged a short distance after the fleeing rebels to give the artillerymen time to limber up their guns and withdraw. The plan worked successfully, and Sigel and his little band soon rejoined the rear guard.[34]

While Sigel's successful delaying action was in progress, the Missourians scored an unexpected coup about half a mile up Bentonville Road. Earlier that morning an ammunition wagon belonging to the 36th Illinois had broken down during the withdrawal to Little Sugar Creek. A company of sixty men was detailed to remain and guard the wagon while it was repaired. The

Illinoisans stacked their arms and milled around in the narrow road trying to keep warm. Suddenly they were surrounded by several hundred horsemen of the 1st Missouri Cavalry, the men Gates had sent ahead to block the road. "We thought it prudent to surrender," said one Illinois soldier, and so they did.[35]

The elated Confederates were sorting out the prisoners and collecting their weapons when Sigel's rear guard arrived on the scene with the 12th Missouri marching in the van. Startled Missourians of both persuasions exchanged a fusillade of wildly aimed shots that caused only a few casualties. In the confusion about thirty-five of the disarmed Illinoisans dashed headlong into the timber on either side of the road and escaped from their captors. The rebels of the 1st Missouri Cavalry disappeared almost as quickly and soon rejoined Gates on the Osage Prairie. Having failed to block the road as instructed, Gates regrouped his men and set out in pursuit of Sigel's rear guard on the narrow road, wondering what had happened to McIntosh.[36]

Sigel incorporated into his rear guard as many of the orphaned Illinoisans as could be found, abandoned the ammunition wagon (but inexplicably failed to destroy it), and continued along the road at a measured pace. A Federal officer observed that the German general "seemed determined not to be hurried in his passage along the public highways." One of the James rifles broke down twice during this phase of the retreat and fell some distance behind the rest of the rear guard. The Confederates tried several times to capture this trailing gun, but the Federals "stood their ground bravely" and parried each rebel thrust.[37]

About a mile northeast of the knoll Bentonville Road turns east then north as it descends into a gorge bordered by steep bluffs over 150 feet high. Here Sigel was forced to call in his skirmishers and flank guards and proceed in a regular column. While the Federals halted to re-form, the Confederates rushed forward and occupied the high ground on the west side of the gorge directly above the road. They dismounted and fired on the head of the Federal column. Sigel and his men were in a critical situation. "It now meant do or die," said a German officer with little exaggeration.[38]

Instead of trying to push through the gorge under a hail of rebel gunfire, Sigel sent the 12th Missouri and one of the twelve-pounder howitzers up a ravine to the top of the bluff. Lt. Henry Voelkner hauled his howitzer all the way up only to have the ammunition chest on the limber tumble back down the ravine. Undaunted, he advanced the useless cannon along with the infantry, hoping its presence might demoralize the enemy. A confused firefight took place atop the bluff as the rebel cavalrymen sought to counter this unforeseen development. With the enemy distracted, Sigel sent the remaining guns of the 1st Missouri Flying Battery on a wild dash through the gorge. Once the artillerymen reached the level floor of Little Sugar Creek Valley, they wheeled their guns and blasted the rebel position with shell and case shot. It was too much for Gates, who by now was completely baffled by McIntosh's disappearance. He ordered his Missourians to withdraw from the bluff and end their pursuit of Sigel's force. Miraculously, no Federal soldiers were killed or seriously wounded in the affair. Confederate casualties are not known.[39]

Sigel and his men regrouped in Little Sugar Creek Valley near a Y-shaped junction where Bentonville Road intersected Little Sugar Creek Road. The Federals turned east at the junction and proceeded up the valley, blissfully unaware that they barely had escaped being cut off by McIntosh's brigade, which was no more than a mile away down the valley. Had Gates been able to delay the Federals for another thirty minutes, McIntosh would have reached the junction first and slammed the trap shut.[40]

The Federals marched less than a mile up the narrowing valley before scouts rushed in reporting a large cavalry force approaching from the rear. Sigel halted and quickly deployed his command so that the Confederates would have to make a frontal assault. He placed his artillery and cavalry in a patch of woods on the valley floor and spread his infantry up the rocky bluffs on either side. He then sent a squad of cavalry down toward the junction to observe the enemy.[41]

McIntosh was a short distance ahead of his brigade when he saw the squad of Federal horsemen at the junction. When they turned and galloped away, he impulsively set out in pursuit and bellowed for his leading regiment to charge. The 3rd Texas Cavalry was thrown into total disarray by the unexpected and irregular command. The forward portion of the regiment under Lt. Col. Walter Lane thundered after McIntosh in column of fours while the remainder deployed for a conventional attack on a broad front, a difficult undertaking in the confined valley. The rest of the brigade was strung for miles along the narrow road and had no idea what was happening up front. Many of the men still were walking their horses.[42]

McIntosh's force passed through the junction and blundered headlong into Sigel's line. "We all raised the Texas war whoop and rushed ahead," recalled B. P. Hollinsworth of the 3rd Texas Cavalry, "but soon a most galling fire of small arms, followed by the thunder of artillery, opened our eyes and closed our mouths." McIntosh and Lane survived the initial blast of bullets and canister but found themselves almost alone in the open barely sixty yards from the Federal guns. Dead and wounded horses and men lay sprawled around them. McIntosh reached down and picked up the regimental flag, waved it above his head, and called upon the stunned Texans to rally for another assault; but his dramatic appeal was spoiled by Lane, who galloped back down the road yelling, "Fall back or you will all be murdered!" The Texans chose to heed Lane's advice and retreated in a confused mass with McIntosh reluctantly following. Ten dead men and twice that number of dead horses were left behind; another twenty or more men were wounded. The survivors were shaken by their first experience with artillery at close range. "Why they did not kill all of Company A and B of our regiment the Lord only knows," wondered the dazed regimental bugler.[43]

The remainder of the 3rd Texas Cavalry now reached the scene. Surveying the carnage and confusion directly ahead, the Texans swerved to the right into Brush Creek Hollow. As the trailing regiments came up one by one, they too veered off to right or left to seek shelter from the Federal artillery firing straight down Little Sugar Creek Valley. McIntosh abandoned the idea of another frontal assault and decided to dislodge the enemy by outflanking them. He ordered his men to dismount and seize the bluffs on either side of the valley. But once again McIntosh was too late. While his skirmishers scrambed up the bluffs, a column of Federal infantry, cavalry, and artillery reached Sigel's position from the east.[44]

Asboth arrived at the fortified rendezvous point along Little Sugar Creek shortly after 10:00 A.M. with the cavalry and trains of the 1st and 2nd Divisions. Between 1:00 and 2:00 P.M. Osterhaus came up leading a column of infantry and artillery that stretched for miles down the valley. By this time both officers were alarmed over the sound of artillery fire coming from the direction of Bentonville. Rumors swept along the blue column that the rear guard was in trouble.[45]

Sometime after 2:00 P.M. Asboth and Osterhaus received a message from Sigel directing them to "advance in haste" to his relief. They notified Curtis of Sigel's plight and ordered the regiments and batteries still on the road in Little Sugar Creek Valley to countermarch at the double-quick. For good measure, Curtis directed a portion of his headquarters cavalry force, the 3rd Iowa Cavalry, to move down the valley at "full speed" and provide additional support.[46]

Four regiments and a battery from the 1st Division and two regiments from the 2nd Division reached the embattled rear guard around 3:30 P.M. Sigel, more exhausted than exhilarated, congratulated the officers and men of his small command on their "miraculous escape" from the pursuing rebels. He then delegated tactical command of the situation to Osterhaus and rode up the valley with Asboth. Sigel's role in this affair was central and paradoxical. He was primarily responsible for extricating the rear guard from a perilous situation, but he was also primarily responsible for creating that situation in the first place. All things considered, however, the little German general handled himself and his troops well on March 6. The fighting retreat from Bentonville was one of the few bright moments in his military career.[47]

The long pursuit from Osage Mill and Bentonville was over. The Federals slowly withdrew up Little Sugar Creek Valley toward their fortified position, but McIntosh made no attempt to follow. Over the next few hours various far-flung detachments from the 1st and 2nd Divisions made their way past or through the Confederates to safety. Meszaros and four companies of the 4th and 5th Missouri Cavalry and a twelve-pounder howitzer of Welfley's Independent Missouri Battery picked their way up Little Sugar Creek Valley in the darkness. Bundled up in heavy coats and all manner of scarves and headgear, the Federals rode through the Confederate army without being challenged. Conrad and his infantrymen were far to the northwest and set out for Keetsville; they would not arrive at Little Sugar Creek in time for the battle. Curtis and his lieutenants successfully concentrated the dispersed elements of the Army of the Southwest, with the lone exception of Conrad's detachment, within twenty-four hours at the predetermined defensive position.[48]

Van Dorn, riding in his ambulance, arrived in Bentonville about an hour behind the Confederate cavalry. He stated in his report that the Confederate infantry "moved so very slowly" that the head of Price's division did not reach the town until 11:00 A.M. "We had the mortification to see Sigel's division, 7,000 strong, leaving it as we entered. Had we been one hour sooner we should have cut him off with his whole force, and certainly have beaten the enemy the next day."[49]

If "we" refers to Van Dorn, his claim that he saw Sigel's command leaving Bentonville was untrue. Moreover, his assertion that, had his infantry moved only a little faster, he would have intercepted Sigel's half of the Federal army was incorrect. Asboth, Osterhaus, and the bulk of the 1st and 2nd Divisions were safe in Little Sugar Creek Valley long before any Confederates reached

Bentonville, and Sigel and the rear guard were long gone from the town before Van Dorn arrived. Van Dorn's version of events may reflect a genuine misunderstanding of what took place at Bentonville, but he might also have deliberately misrepresented matters in order to obscure his own reckless planning and inept handling of the operation. In any event, Van Dorn's shameless attempt to blame his cold, hungry, and exhausted infantrymen for the slow pace of the advance on March 6 reveals much about his character. By emphasizing how close his gambit came to success despite the substandard performance of his men, he deftly shifted blame for the failure onto other shoulders.

Desperately unhappy, Van Dorn drove the infantry ahead in the hope that McIntosh's horsemen could find a way to delay the enemy and bring him to battle. Regiment after regiment of Confederate infantry crossed the Osage Prairie encouraged by a band playing "The Bonny Blue Flag." A soldier in the 3rd Louisiana noticed that "the army looked splendidly as the long line marched across the open prairie with their flags fluttering in the breeze."[50]

Around 4:00 P.M. McIntosh informed Van Dorn that the yankees had escaped and were digging in at the Telegraph Road crossing of Little Sugar Creek. No longer was there any need to hurry. Weary Confederate infantrymen shuffled into Little Sugar Creek Valley and bivouacked east of the Y-shaped junction in the general area where the final skirmish with Sigel's rear guard had taken place. This section of the valley had been occupied by some of McCulloch's troops the previous summer. They had christened the site Camp Stephens after Alexander Stephens, vice-president of the Confederacy.[51]

As daylight faded on March 6, the Confederates found themselves in a critical situation. After three days of arduous toil men and animals were in pitiful condition, straggling was epidemic, and food and forage were gone. "Such a worn-out set of men I never saw," exclaimed a Confederate soldier of his colleagues. "They had not one single mouthful of food to eat." Despite this perilous state of affairs Van Dorn never considered returning to the Boston Mountains. He believed that the Federals had barely escaped annihilation and were on the run; he intended to pursue them into Missouri as far as possible, perhaps all the way to St. Louis. Van Dorn's resolve was strengthened by the arrival late in the day of Pike's command from the Indian Territory: the battalion-sized 1st and 2nd Cherokee Mounted Rifles and a squadron of Texas cavalry. Pike's understrength brigade was assigned to McCulloch's division and took its place at the rear of the column.[52]

The northern bluff of Little Sugar Creek, from Telegraph Road near the site of Trott's store. If Van Dorn had elected to attack Curtis's fortifications, his men would have assaulted this height. (authors' collection)

Van Dorn met with Price, McCulloch, and McIntosh around 5:00 P.M. to discuss their next move. McCulloch was quite familiar with the area. During Frémont's abortive campaign the previous fall McCulloch's headquarters had been located at Twelve Corner Church, a Baptist meetinghouse about five miles northeast of Camp Stephens on the Bentonville Detour. McCulloch stated that the Federal position along Little Sugar Creek was extremely strong and recommended against an attack. He suggested instead that the Army of the West attempt to get around the enemy's right flank via the Bentonville Detour. This "good gravelly road" branched from Little Sugar Creek Road at Camp Stephens and proceeded in a rough northeasterly arc for about eight miles across Pea Ridge. It intersected Telegraph Road in Cross Timber Hollow five miles north of the Federal entrenchments. Van Dorn seized McCulloch's suggestion and decided to set the army in motion that very night.[53]

McCulloch was aghast at the thought of a night march. He asked Van Dorn "for God sake to let the poor, worn-out and hungry soldiers rest and sleep that night ... and then attack the next morning." But Van Dorn was adamant: the army would move immediately. Another point of contention was the

Remains of trenches the Federals constructed atop the northern bluff of Little Sugar Creek. They were simple earthworks, with no traverses to the rear, retrenchments on the flanks, or obstructions in front, but they made an already strong position even stronger. (authors' collection)

nature of the coming operation. McCulloch proposed a limited maneuver around the Federal right flank to compel Curtis to abandon his fortifications and fall back into Missouri. In a rare moment of agreement, Price vigorously supported McCulloch's plan. But after Van Dorn learned that the Bentonville Detour extended all the way to Telegraph Road, he envisaged something grander and more decisive than a flanking movement. Van Dorn immediately seized the opportunity to envelop rather than to outflank his foe: the Confederates would march over the Bentonville Detour to Cross Timber Hollow and block Telegraph Road deep in the Federal rear. With the Army of the West firmly astride the Federal escape route to Missouri, Curtis would have no choice but to surrender. The victory would be complete and, even better, would open wide the road to St. Louis and glory.[54]

There is no evidence that Van Dorn gave any serious thought to the difficulties and risks inherent in his plan. While an envelopment clearly offered the possibility of a more spectacular triumph than a flanking movement, it meant that the exhausted Confederates would have to march nearly twice as far and still achieve tactical surprise. Moreover, the maneuver was exceptionally dangerous. If Van Dorn placed his entire army in the Federal rear, he also effectively placed the entire Federal army in his own rear.

Van Dorn's analysis of the situation contained a fatal flaw: he failed to see that Curtis was concentrating for a fight, not running away from one. Major Ross of the 6th Texas Cavalry, a former Texas Ranger who had served with Van Dorn on the frontier, saw into his commander's mind with uncanny accuracy: "The truth of the whole matter was, General Van Dorn did not believe the Federals would fight him, but rather, *that they would get away from him.*" Undeterred by his lack of success thus far, unconcerned by misgivings of his two principal lieutenants, and indifferent to the deteriorating condition of his forces, Van Dorn set his envelopment in motion.[55]

Three miles to the east the Federals made their own preparations for the morrow. On the bluffs above Little Sugar Creek the 1st and 2nd Divisions filed into place on the right of the 3rd Division. Curtis was relieved by the successful concentration of his army, but the presence of an enemy force of undetermined size at Camp Stephens made him anxious about his right flank. He placed Asboth's small 2nd Division behind a deep ravine so that it faced west, giving the overall Federal position the shape of an elongated L lying on its side. While the new arrivals cleared fields of fire and piled up breastworks of branches and logs, Curtis considered the unwelcome possibility that his little army might be outflanked on the right and would have to abandon its works and fight in the open. He made certain that the narrow roads immediately behind his position were kept clear for rapid troop movements and checked to see that his staff had everything well in hand. When an anxious officer asked Curtis what would happen next, the general replied tersely, "I will either fight them tomorrow or they me."[56]

Around sunset Colonel Dodge, commanding the 1st Brigade of the 4th Division, suggested to Curtis that the Bentonville Detour be blockaded to prevent or delay any rebel movement around the Federal right flank the next morning. Curtis had been considering such a move, and he offhandedly told Dodge to "go and do it." As darkness fell, the future Union Pacific railroad tycoon trooped off to the north on Telegraph Road with six companies of the 4th Iowa and one company of the 3rd Illinois Cavalry in tow.[57]

By 9:00 P.M. Dodge's small command was well along the Bentonville Detour. In a deep ravine about a mile east of Twelve Corner Church the Federals felled trees across the narrow road "with efficiency and dispatch." The result

Grenville M. Dodge (State Historical Society of Iowa, Des Moines)

was an impressive tangle of branches and trunks. After about two hours the men withdrew closer to Cross Timber Hollow and created a second, smaller blockade. Around midnight Dodge became edgy when his pickets reported hearing a good deal of noise on the far side of the first blockade. He collected his exhausted woodcutters and trudged back to the encampment above Little Sugar Creek. At 2:00 A.M. on March 7 Dodge reported to Curtis at Pratt's store. Much to his surprise the commanding general did not seem alarmed at his account of suspected enemy activity on the Bentonville Detour.[58]

Curtis assumed Dodge had encountered a Confederate scouting party and nothing more. He believed the enemy would stay the night at Camp Stephens, where Federal scouts reported hundreds of campfires were burning brightly, and offer battle the next day in the form of either a frontal assault or a flanking maneuver, or some combination of the two. Sigel and the division commanders apparently were of the same mind. But many of the men in the ranks on the Federal right knew better. They were convinced that the rebels were on the move because "the rumbling of there artillery was plain to be herd all knight." For some unaccountable reason this vital information never reached the higher echelons of the Army of the Southwest.[59]

The failure to detect the Confederate march on the Bentonville Detour might have had disastrous consequences for the Federals but for the initiative of an Iowa colonel. Dodge and his men garnered more blisters than glory for their labor that night, but without firing a shot they changed the course of the battle.

Van Dorn, Price, McCulloch, and McIntosh ended their conference at Camp Stephens around 6:00 P.M. on March 6. The envelopment was scheduled to begin two hours later. If all went well, the Army of the West would reach Telegraph Road in Cross Timber Hollow before dawn on March 7. The troops built up their campfires in order to fool Federal scouts into thinking they were bivouacking for the night at Camp Stephens. Van Dorn wanted McIntosh's brigade in the lead, but when the cavalry attempted to move up Little Sugar Creek Valley to the Bentonville Detour, they found their way blocked by a crush of men and equipment. Because of poor staff work the infantry and artillery had formed up ahead of the cavalry. General McCulloch "urged us to be in haste in order that we might have the road clear before us," recalled a disgusted Major Ross. "We were very prompt in starting and had gone but about one-half mile when we were halted and just there we stood until two o'clock in the morning, and it was bitter cold." It was ironic that in his first major battle Van Dorn, a cavalryman to the core of his being, advanced against the foe with most of his mounted arm trapped behind a slow-moving mass of infantry and artillery.[60]

Disorganization and confusion combined with plummeting temperatures to make that night miserable for everyone in the Army of the West. By 8:00 P.M. all of the regiments were in column in the road, but few were going anywhere. The initial delay was caused by the absence of a bridge across Little Sugar Creek near the Bentonville Detour. As they had done earlier that morning at Osage Creek, Price's infantrymen wrestled a few logs into place across the icy stream. Hours of precious time were lost as thousands of men broke ranks, filed across the logs, and re-formed on the other side. The long wait was agonizing. The surgeon of the 4th Arkansas, far down the nearly immobile line of shivering men and animals, wrote that "the night was one of intense severity and the men suffered immeasurably more whilst standing still than they possibly could had they been moving, however fast. For my own part I shall retain a lively and an unpleasant recollection of my suffering on that wretched night, for my whole natural lifetime."[61]

McCulloch was dismayed but did his best to rally the troops. At one point during the night he stopped to chat with a group of Louisiana soldiers who had broken ranks to stand around a blazing pile of fence rails. He explained the situation and then added, "I tell you, men, the army that is defeated in this fight will get a hell of a whipping!" McCulloch may have betrayed his own uneasiness. "The men all remarked how different he seemed from his usual manner," recalled a soldier. "He was unusually reticent, and spoke in a quiet, subdued voice, so unlike his customary energetic, determined actions and speech." An hour before midnight the last of Price's Missourians dribbled over the makeshift bridge and trudged out of the valley on the Bentonville Detour. For the next three hours Hébert's infantrymen took their turn. McIntosh's cavalrymen began to splash across the creek about 2:00 A.M., and Pike's Indians did not cross until after dawn.[62]

Little Sugar Creek was not the last obstacle the Confederates encountered that night. About midnight the head of Price's column discovered a maze of felled trees blocking the Bentonville Detour. The column halted as the Missourians struggled to clear the road. After about two hours the advance began again, only to encounter a second tangle of felled trees before dawn. Another halt, another two hours lost. At sunrise, when Van Dorn had hoped to be astride Telegraph Road in full force, the head of his attenuated column had not yet reached Cross Timber Hollow, and the tail was not yet across Little Sugar Creek.[63]

The Army of the West was not only falling behind, it was falling apart. Soldiers were collapsing in droves. "Every half mile I saw the Infantry in squads of fifty and sixty, and even more lieing on the roadside, asleep, and overcome with hunger and fatigue," wrote a Texas cavalry officer bringing up the rear. "Then it was my spirits began to fail and I trembled with fear at the result of an Engagement . . . when our best men—those upon whom we must rely in battle—were lieing exhausted on the roadside, unable to reach the battle field." Brig. Gen. Daniel M. Frost, commanding the 7th and 9th Divisions of the Missouri State Guard, estimated that "unremitting marching and fasting" en route to Pea Ridge caused at least one-third of his men to fall by the wayside. Other state guard and Confederate officers also reported serious loss of manpower. As the hours and miles passed, Van Dorn's numerical superiority continued to erode.[64]

It was nearly 7:00 A.M. on March 7 before Missouri cavalrymen trotted into Cross Timber Hollow and cautiously probed Telegraph Road in both directions. Not a yankee was in sight. Van Dorn arrived an hour later at the head of Price's division. The commanding general emerged a bit unsteadily from his ambulance, well wrapped against the morning chill, and mounted his horse in triumph. For Van Dorn it was the supreme moment of his military career. Despite his lingering illness, despite all the difficulties and missed opportunities of the past few days, he had enveloped the enemy. But Van Dorn could not long savor his success. His army was so strung out that the trailing units would not reach Cross Timber Hollow before afternoon. It was essential that the Confederates concentrate more rapidly.[65]

After consulting local guides Van Dorn decided to risk dividing the Army of the West into its two major components for a few hours. Price's division would turn south onto Telegraph Road and drive toward Elkhorn Tavern, about two and a half miles away. McCulloch's division would leave the Bentonville Detour at Twelve Corner Church and turn south on Ford Road. This nondescript country road passed around the western end of a rocky ridge called Big Mountain, turned east, and eventually intersected Telegraph Road just south of Elkhorn Tavern. By taking this shortcut McCulloch's division would march only about three and a half miles, rather than six or seven miles via Cross Timber Hollow. The two halves of the army would be separated for a short time by Big Mountain, but Van Dorn was confident that the yankees had not yet stirred from their trenches along Little Sugar Creek. He was equally confident that by the time they did, the Army of the West would be reunited near Elkhorn Tavern and ready for battle.[66]

McCulloch received his new orders after the head of his division had passed Twelve Corner Church, so he ordered a countermarch, a difficult and time-consuming maneuver on a narrow road. As the Texas general passed back down the long column of weary, shuffling soldiers, he greeted perplexed officers with the casual remark: "We are going to take 'em on the other wing." It was past midmorning when McCulloch's division finally turned south on Ford Road. There had been some picket firing in the vicinity just after sunrise, but all was quiet now. A little before noon the head of McCulloch's division rounded Big Mountain and turned east. Elkhorn Tavern was only two and a half miles ahead. In an hour the Army of the West would be reunited and arrayed for battle.[67]

5 Death of a Texan

Friday, March 7, was a cold, clear, windless day. The temperature remained below freezing all morning, and patches of snow covered the ground. Thousands of Federal soldiers awoke stiff and chilled in their camps overlooking Little Sugar Creek and stamped around their campfires drinking scalding coffee. At Pratt's store Curtis ate a spartan breakfast in his headquarters tent and reviewed matters with his staff. He was annoyed because he had no information about the occasional crackle of gunfire coming from the vicinity of Big Mountain to the north. About 8:00 A.M. Curtis looked up in surprise to find Maj. Eli Weston standing at the entrance to his tent.

As provost marshal of the Army of the Southwest, Weston was responsible for securing the Federal rear, among other things. The previous day Curtis had posted Weston at Elkhorn Tavern, one mile north of Pratt's store, with six companies of his own 24th Missouri and two companies of horsemen from the 1st Missouri Cavalry and 3rd Illinois Cavalry. During the night Weston had placed small cavalry pickets to the north of the tavern at the junction of Telegraph Road and the Bentonville Detour, to the west on Ford Road, and to the east on Huntsville Road. Other than the passage to and fro of Dodge's woodcutters, the night had been uneventful. Dawn brought a flurry of activity. About 5:00 A.M. the picket on Telegraph Road reported a brush with a small party of rebel horsemen who had emerged from the Bentonville Detour. Moments later the picket on Ford Road reported a sizable band of mounted rebels south of Big Mountain.[1]

The Confederates on Ford Road were dangerously close to the army's trains, so Weston dispatched a company of the 24th Missouri and the two cavalry companies in that direction. The Federals encountered the rebels about one mile west of the tavern just as dawn was breaking and pushed them back in a noisy but bloodless skirmish—the first shots of the battle of Pea Ridge. Weston's men continued moving west on Ford Road until they reached the gentle western slope of Big Mountain. There they were brought to an abrupt halt by the sight of a solid column of butternut infantry and cavalry moving eastward along the Bentonville Detour.[2]

The Federals turned and hurriedly retraced their steps toward Elkhorn Tavern. When Capt. Barbour Lewis of the 1st Missouri Cavalry, the senior officer in the detachment, learned that Weston had gone to see Curtis at Pratt's store, he galloped after him. Lewis arrived while Weston was briefing Curtis on the initial reports he had received from his pickets. The captain entered Curtis's tent and told of sighting a large enemy force on the Bentonville Detour at Twelve Corner Church. Curtis thanked both officers and sent them back to Elkhorn Tavern, instructing Weston to find out as much as possible about the movements of the enemy. As the two men sped away, Curtis ordered a meeting of his division and brigade commanders at 9:00 A.M.[3]

While awaiting the arrival of his lieutenants Curtis pondered the information he had just received. The Confederates had managed to get a strong force around his right flank during the night without being detected. (It may have crossed his mind that Dodge had been correct when he had reported enemy activity on the Bentonville Detour six hours earlier.) Curtis assumed that the rebels were attempting to maneuver him out of the Little Sugar Creek fortifications by turning his right flank. Nevertheless, he remained alert to the danger that the turning movement was a diversion and the rebels were preparing to launch an attack against those fortifications. As yet he gave little serious thought to the possibility that the Confederate column on the Bentonville Detour was moving toward Cross Timber Hollow, and he failed to consider the improbable notion that the entire Confederate army was heading in that direction. For the next two hours Curtis acted on the reasonable but incorrect assumption that he was confronting two enemy forces: one in Little Sugar Creek Valley opposite his fortifications and another near Twelve Corner Church moving around his right flank.

Around 9:00 A.M. the Federal division and brigade commanders assembled at Pratt's store for a council of war. Curtis informed everyone of the Confederate movement on the Bentonville Detour and asked for their opinions as to what he should do. Osterhaus, Davis, and Dodge declared that the army should stand and fight; the other officers either were noncommittal or took the orthodox position that if the army's flank had been turned, a withdrawal was both necessary and proper. Like most councils of war this one failed to achieve a consensus, much less endorse an aggressive course of action.[4]

Perhaps Curtis expected as much. He listened without comment and then announced that he intended to stay and fight. That decision made, Curtis acted at once to regain the tactical initiative. He ordered Osterhaus to assemble a division-sized force of cavalry, artillery, and infantry and to move northwest toward Twelve Corner Church. Osterhaus called his assignment a "demonstration," but it might better be described as a cross between a reconnaissance in force and a spoiling attack. Curtis wanted Osterhaus to locate the enemy force on the Bentonville Detour, ascertain its strength and intentions, and if possible, engage it.[5]

Osterhaus was a good choice for such a critical assignment. He was steady and reliable and could draw on a modest amount of military experience in his native Germany. After receiving his instructions Osterhaus hastened from the council of war with Cols. Cyrus Bussey and Nicholas Greusel. He directed Bussey to take his own 3rd Iowa Cavalry, assorted companies of the 1st, 4th, and 5th Missouri Cavalry, and half of the 1st Missouri Flying Battery and proceed at once to Leetown and from there to Twelve Corner Church. Greusel would follow as quickly as possible with the infantry: Greusel's own 2nd Brigade of the 1st Division, consisting of the 36th Illinois and the 12th Missouri, along with the 22nd Indiana, the 4th Ohio Battery, and half of Welfley's Independent Missouri Battery. Osterhaus's force combined fragmented elements of the 1st and 3rd Divisions and Curtis's headquarters units, a clumsy technique that Curtis and his subordinates used throughout the campaign.[6]

While Osterhaus, Bussey, and Greusel rushed to Little Sugar Creek to assemble the task force and get it moving, Curtis and the rest of his officers continued to discuss the situation. In the middle of this discussion, around 10:30 A.M., a startling message arrived from Weston: there was a column of Confederate cavalry and infantry on Telegraph Road in Cross Timber Hollow only one mile north of Elkhorn Tavern. Curtis was disconcerted by this latest information. He stepped outside the tent into the bright sunshine, perhaps

Peter J. Osterhaus (Missouri Historical Society)

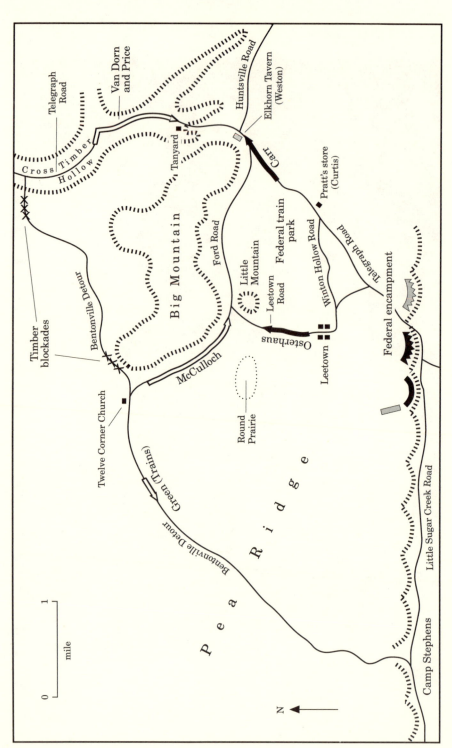

Map 5-1. *Pea Ridge: Midday, March 7*

intending to ride to the tavern and see for himself if this improbable report could be true.[7]

Curtis was brought up short by the sight of a substantial body of infantry, cavalry, and artillery standing in Telegraph Road a few yards away, nearly two miles north of the Little Sugar Creek fortifications. "Whose troops are those?" he asked in surprise. Dodge answered that they were his: the 1st Brigade of the 4th Division, consisting of the 4th Iowa, the 35th Illinois, the 3rd Illinois Cavalry, and the 1st Iowa Battery. After his experience on the Bentonville Detour the previous night, Dodge was convinced the rebels were moving against the Federal right and rear. On his own initiative Dodge pulled his brigade from its assigned place in the fortifications and brought it to the council of war at Pratt's store, certain that it would be needed somewhere to the north. Curtis chose to ignore Dodge's amazingly cavalier action, undoubtedly because he was relieved to have so many soldiers close at hand. He turned to Carr, Dodge's immediate superior as commander of the 4th Division, and instructed him to take Dodge's brigade to Elkhorn Tavern at once and hold that point. Curtis then terminated the council of war and sent everyone else back to their commands to await orders.[8]

By 11:00 A.M. roughly one-third of the Army of the Southwest was in motion: Osterhaus was hurrying northwest through Leetown toward Twelve Corner Church, and Carr was marching northeast up Telegraph Road toward Elkhorn Tavern. Despite launching these two offensive countermoves Curtis was compelled to keep most of his troops in a defensive posture along Little Sugar Creek. His primary problem during the morning and early afternoon of March 7 was a lack of information. Were most of the rebels still lurking near Camp Stephens preparing to storm the Little Sugar Creek fortifications? Were they moving around the Federal right flank via Twelve Corner Church? Or were they attempting to cut off the Federals by seizing Telegraph Road? Or were they up to some combination of all three? If so, what were the relative strengths of the three enemy detachments? As long as Confederate intentions remained unclear, Curtis had to temper his natural aggressiveness with caution.

Pea Ridge is a broad plateau or tableland that slopes gently toward Little Sugar Creek. The northern edge of the plateau is dominated by Big Mountain, a sandstone ridge three miles long that extends from Telegraph Road on the east to Twelve Corner Church on the west. A much smaller, cone-shaped feature, Little Mountain, lies immediately south of Big Mountain. A low rise or saddle connects the two heights. In 1862 most of the plateau was covered with a dense forest of post oak, blackjack oak, white oak, hickory, red cedar, poplar, elm, and all manner of briers and vines. The only natural break in this scrubby, hardwood thicket was the Round Prairie, a small grassland dotted with trees half a mile west of Little Mountain.

Settlers had altered the natural landscape of Pea Ridge by cutting roads, building homes, and clearing fields for cultivation and pasture. About midway between Little Sugar Creek and Big Mountain was the hamlet of Leetown, an unimpressive collection of a dozen log buildings. Several adjacent cornfields owned by Samuel Oberson, Wix Mayfield, George Lee, and other Leetowners comprised a rectangular cultivated area north of Leetown. For the sake of convenience, this area is known as Oberson's field. A belt of trees four hundred yards deep separated Oberson's field from farms owned by Wiley Foster and George Sturdy, which were located between Little Mountain and the Round Prairie. East of Oberson's field lay a densely wooded thicket owned in large part by Elizabeth Morgan.[9]

Four roads on this section of Pea Ridge formed a rough parallelogram and linked the battlefields at Leetown and Elkhorn Tavern. On the eastern side of the parallelogram Telegraph Road connected Elkhorn Tavern, Pratt's store, and Little Sugar Creek. On the northern side Ford Road ran across the southern and western slopes of Big Mountain and connected Elkhorn Tavern and Twelve Corner Church. On the southern side the Winton Hollow Road connected Pratt's store and Leetown. Leetown Road completed the western side of the parallelogram. The latter road began in Leetown, separated Oberson's field from Morgan's woods, and intersected Ford Road between Little Mountain and Sturdy's farm. A network of smaller roads and lanes snaked through the woods and provided alternate but less accessible routes across the plateau.

Osterhaus's "demonstration" was well under way by 11:30 A.M. Bussey's six hundred cavalrymen and three artillery pieces passed through Leetown and headed north on Leetown Road. Above the jingle of bridles and sabers and the clatter of hooves the Federal horsemen could hear the boom of artillery fire from the direction of Elkhorn Tavern where Carr and Dodge had gone into action against the rebels in Cross Timber Hollow. They passed along the eastern edge of Oberson's field and then turned west into Foster's lane. This narrow track ran along the northern edge of the field for about three hundred yards and then turned north through the belt of trees to Foster's farm.[10]

Osterhaus, who caught up with the blue column north of Leetown, was concerned because he still had "no knowledge whatever of the whereabouts of the enemy." As he trotted past Oberson's field, he made a fateful decision: he and Bussey's cavalry would press on toward Twelve Corner Church in accordance with Curtis's instructions, but Greusel's infantry would deploy in Oberson's field as a precautionary measure. Should they encounter the enemy in overwhelming force, as seemed entirely possible, the cavalry would fall back to Oberson's field in good order and support the infantry. The large cornfield was the best defensive position in the area. It offered an open field of fire more than four hundred yards deep and eight hundred yards wide. More important, the field commanded Leetown Road, the only north-south road in the vicinity.[11]

Osterhaus left a staff officer behind to inform Greusel of his new assignment and then rode forward through the belt of trees. On the southern edge of Foster's farm, near a modest collection of log structures comprising the Foster homestead, Osterhaus reined in his horse and stared at a sight that took his breath away. Six hundred yards to the north across a wheatfield was McCulloch's division: regiment after regiment of Confederate infantry and cavalry, flags flying and weapons gleaming in the noonday sun, was marching steadily east on Ford Road. The tail of the enemy formation extended back into the woods toward Twelve Corner Church; the head was approaching the rise or saddle between Big Mountain and Little Mountain.[12]

Osterhaus needed a few moments to get his bearings. Then he realized with a shock that on the far side of the rise was Elkhorn Tavern, Telegraph Road, Pratt's store, and the army's trains. The Confederates had gotten around the Federal right flank and were advancing directly into the undefended Federal rear. "Notwithstanding my command was entirely inadequate to the overwhelming masses opposed to me," reported Osterhaus without exaggeration, "I could not hesitate in my course of action. The safety of our position was dependent upon the securing of our right flank and the keeping back of the enemy until I was reinforced." Unfortunately, there was no time to wait for reinforcements; Bussey had to attack at once regardless of the impossible odds. Osterhaus's decision was in keeping with the spirit of Curtis's instructions and proved to be a turning point in the developing battle.[13]

At Osterhaus's command, Bussey quickly deployed his artillery and cavalry and prepared to engage the enemy. Captain Elbert unlimbered his three twelve-pounder James rifles of the 1st Missouri Flying Artillery in the southwestern corner of the wheatfield. One company of Colonel Ellis's 1st Missouri Cavalry deployed on either side of the artillery. The five companies of the 3rd Iowa Cavalry and the four companies of Colonel Nemett's 5th Missouri Cavalry formed in echelon behind and to the right of the artillery. The two companies of the 4th Missouri Cavalry were still passing through the belt of trees and had not yet reached Foster's farm. The small Federal force faced northeast toward the head of the massive Confederate column.[14]

At the last minute Bussey sent Lt. Col. Henry H. Trimble with two companies of the 3rd Iowa Cavalry north on Foster's lane to attack the enemy closer to Twelve Corner Church. He probably hoped to cause as much confusion as possible by striking the head and tail of the enemy column simultaneously. Bussey's decision to divide his slim force was unwise and reduced the number of Federals on Foster's farm to roughly five hundred men.[15]

Shortly before noon Elbert's three cannons crashed into action and opened the battle of Leetown. Osterhaus surveyed the effect of the three rounds of solid shot on the Confederate column and was encouraged by the apparent confusion. He ordered Bussey to prepare to advance with the 3rd Iowa Cavalry and the 5th Missouri Cavalry. But before anything could be done, the small Federal force on Foster's farm was swept away by a rebel whirlwind.[16]

Around midmorning McCulloch informed Van Dorn by courier that he had finally turned his division around on the Bentonville Detour and was proceeding "as fast as his men could walk," which was probably little better than a shuffle at that point. McCulloch added that "everything looked favorable" for a reunion of the two Confederate divisions at Elkhorn Tavern around noon. He did not mention the severe attrition his command had suffered since leaving the Boston Mountains, particularly during the past twenty-four hours. His division had shrunk from 8,700 to around 7,000 cold, hungry, and inexpressibly weary men. Losses were especially severe among Hébert's infantrymen and dismounted cavalrymen.[17]

When the sound of distant gunfire reached McCulloch, he correctly assumed that Price's division was encountering resistance along Telegraph Road. McCulloch now prepared for the possibility that he might have to fight his way through to the Missourians. He halted Hébert's infantry brigade on Ford Road and brought McIntosh's cavalry brigade to the immediate right of the road. The open woods along the northern fringe of the Round Prairie permitted relatively easy movement of cavalry. The Confederate horsemen were arranged in five parallel columns of fours by regiment. From right to left the broad formation was composed of the 3rd, 6th, 9th, and 11th Texas Cavalry, the 1st Arkansas Cavalry Battalion, and the 1st Texas Cavalry Battalion. Pike's Indians and Texans followed.[18]

An hour elapsed before McCulloch's division resumed its advance, the infantrymen trudging along Ford Road, the cavalrymen on their famished horses threading their way through the scattered trees alongside. As the Confederates crossed the northern edge of Foster's wheatfield, the Federal force commanded by Osterhaus and Bussey emerged from the belt of trees onto the southern part of the field and opened fire. McCulloch was taken completely by surprise. He was concentrating on the growing roar of battle two miles ahead at Elkhorn Tavern; the last thing he expected was an attack from his right rear.

Six salvos of Federal artillery fire—eighteen rounds of rifled solid shot —struck the massed rebel columns broadside during the next few minutes. The shots killed at least ten cavalrymen and wounded several times that number. Tom Coleman of the 11th Texas Cavalry had the scare of his life when a shot smashed into the horse next to his, toppling the rider and splattering Coleman's mare with blood and gore. The three Federal cannons were difficult to see in the bright sunlight because they were shaded by two large oak trees. Newton Keen of the 6th Texas Cavalry had the bizarre impression that the oaks were belching flames and smoke and flinging projectiles at him. One such shot struck the ground directly in front of the young Texan, "ploughed out a terrible ditch in the earth and came bounding about twenty feet above my head and went singing on its way." The Confederates stopped in their tracks. McCulloch was among the first to recover from the shock. He ordered Hébert to hurry his infantry from the enemy guns and toward the rise between Big and Little Mountains.[19]

Shortly after the Federal artillery crashed into action, Capt. John J. Good pulled his Texas battery out of the long infantry column on his own initiative and rolled forward. McCulloch saw the cannons approaching and shouted to Good: "Wheel that battery into line!" The Texans turned to the right and unlimbered their six cannons on Sturdy's farm. They managed to shoot only one round, however, before their field of fire was blocked by a mass of mounted Confederates.[20]

While the Texas cannoneers struggled to ready their weapons, McCulloch told McIntosh to attack the Federal battery with his brigade. Relatively little maneuvering was required. McIntosh simply wheeled his horsemen to the right by fours, thereby changing formation from parallel columns to parallel

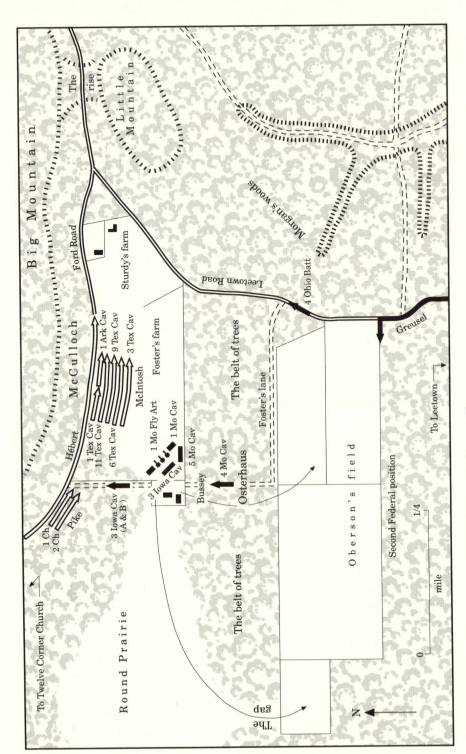

Map 5-2. Leetown: Osterhaus Engages McCulloch on Foster's Farm

lines facing southwest toward the Federals. McIntosh gloried in leading mounted charges, as he had demonstrated the previous day in Little Sugar Creek Valley, but this time he remembered his place and delegated the responsibility to Lieutenant Colonel Lane of the 3rd Texas Cavalry, the regiment closest to the enemy.[21]

Lane called for the regimental bugler, Charles Watts. "Come here, Charley, and blow the charge until you are black in the face." Just then McCulloch had second thoughts and ordered the 3rd Texas Cavalry to stay behind and cover Good's battery. Lane and Watts remained with the brigade, but their disappointed comrades in the 3rd Texas Cavalry trotted out of the way and took a position behind the artillerymen on Sturdy's farm. Meanwhile the Federal cannoneers on Foster's farm continued to send solid shot tearing through the immobile rebel ranks. One Texas cavalryman recalled that during those anxious moments "it suited a good many of us [to] draw our necks in as far into our shoulders as [we] could get them."[22]

McIntosh finally gave the word and Watts blew the charge. The ringing call was picked up by the other regimental buglers, and the attack commenced. Col. Warren Stone's 6th Texas Cavalry, Col. William B. Sims's 9th Texas Cavalry, Col. William C. Young's 11th Texas Cavalry, Maj. Phillip Crump's 1st Texas Cavalry Battalion, and Maj. William H. Brooks's 1st Arkansas Cavalry Battalion surged forward in one of the Civil War's most colorful cavalry charges. Shrieking the Comanche war whoop and other frontier versions of the rebel yell and brandishing sabers, pistols, carbines, shotguns, and the odd Bowie knife and hatchet, three thousand mounted Confederates in a tightly packed mass rushed across the wheatfield toward the Federal position.[23]

Bussey's command in the immediate vicinity of the Foster homestead, outnumbered six to one, was unable to withstand the shock of an assault by such a large number of horsemen. The Missouri cannoneers managed to fire one or two final rounds before being overrun by the "wild, numerous, and irregular throng" of rebels. Moments after the bugles sounded, the color bearer of the 9th Texas Cavalry and dozens of madly yelling Texans were amongst the Federal guns, firing, slashing, and flailing about. Masses of rebels drove the two companies of the 1st Missouri Cavalry back onto the 3rd Iowa Cavalry and 5th Missouri Cavalry in a scene of utter confusion.[24]

The Federal cavalrymen fought back with carbines, revolvers, and sabers, but their ranks were quickly "broken and disordered." Pressed back against the belt of trees, Bussey's command disintegrated in a swirling maelstrom of hand-to-hand combat. "I have read in history of and seen depicted the hor-

Foster's farm, looking northeast from the approximate location of Elbert's battery. McIntosh's cavalry attack began near the treeline in the center of this view. (authors' collection)

rors of battle where foe measured arms with foe in mortal combat," wrote Henry Dysart of the 3rd Iowa Cavalry in his diary that night, "but here my own eyes witnessed them. In every direction I could see my comrades falling. Horses frencied and riderless, ran to and fro. Men and horses ran in collision crushing each other to the ground. Dismounted troopers ran in every direction. Officers tried to rally their men but order gave way to confusion. The scene baffles description."[25]

Osterhaus recognized that the situation was hopeless. He shouted to Bussey to hold on as long as possible; then he spurred his horse down Foster's lane toward Oberson's field. Osterhaus realized that the sight of the retreating cavalry might unnerve Greusel's infantry and lead to disaster. As he hurried to prepare Greusel for the worst, the chaotic sounds of battle on Foster's farm reached a climax and then died away.[26]

Despite Bussey's best efforts Federal resistance quickly collapsed. Those Missouri artillerymen who were not shot down either surrendered or fled. Louis Voelkner abandoned his gun and somehow picked his way through hundreds of clashing cavalrymen. He found a riderless horse and raced back to the Little Sugar Creek fortifications. His brother Henry, who had remained in camp with the other half of the 1st Missouri Flying Artillery, described his terrified, exhausted sibling: "He looked a fright, sweat streaming down his brow. He told me later that when he got to the horse he could not have run another ten feet." Hundreds of Iowa and Missouri cavalrymen, mounted and afoot, also attempted to escape down Foster's lane. When the narrow track became jammed with fleeing troops, the only other line of retreat was west across the Round Prairie.[27]

While McIntosh's cavalry overran the main body of Bussey's command, Trimble's two companies of the 3rd Iowa Cavalry were routed in a separate encounter with Pike's troops. Col. John Drew's 1st Cherokee Mounted Rifles, Col. Stand Watie's 2nd Cherokee Mounted Rifles, and Capt. Otis G. Welch's Texas Cavalry Squadron were following McIntosh's brigade through the woods to the right of Ford Road. McCulloch had instructed Pike to conform with McIntosh's brigade, and when the engagement began and McIntosh faced his cavalrymen to the right, Pike dutifully followed suit. He could see nothing of the enemy because of the trees and brush. Concerned about who or what might be lurking beyond his field of vision, Pike dismounted the 2nd Cherokee Mounted Rifles and advanced the regiment a short distance into the woods. When McIntosh sent his brigade storming across the wheatfield toward the 1st Missouri Flying Artillery, Pike ordered his Cherokees and Texans forward.[28]

Contrary to legend, the Indians—half of whom were on foot—did not participate in the spectacular mounted charge against the Federal guns. They pushed through the open woods west of the wheatfield and struck the head and right flank of Trimble's short column on Foster's lane about three hundred yards north of Bussey's position. Trimble faced his troopers to the right and gamely attempted to stand and fight, but the badly outnumbered Iowans did not last long. Dozens of soldiers and horses tumbled to the ground in the first minutes of the unequal engagement. Trimble suffered a severe wound when a bullet penetrated his right cheek and came out below his right ear. With Trimble incapacitated and Maj. Carlton H. Perry nowhere to be found, the remnants of the two companies broke and fled back down the lane.[29]

All ran except Pvt. Albert Powers. The young Iowan spurred his horse up the lane to rescue a dismounted comrade; then he turned and galloped away through a hail of enemy gunfire. This selfless act earned Powers one of four Medals of Honor awarded for gallantry at Pea Ridge. Powers joined the stream of Iowa and Missouri cavalrymen—Bussey, Ellis, and Nemett among them —flowing west across the Round Prairie.[30]

Amidst the swirling chaos of a cavalry engagement only one Confederate officer had the presence of mind to pursue the routed enemy. "I put in right after the [Federal] cavalry," wrote Major Ross of the 6th Texas Cavalry, "thinking I would have an excellent thing all to myself, as they were running I would have no trouble in killing them like Ants." About four hundred yards west of Foster's lane the Federals turned south into Oberson's field through a gap in the belt of trees. Ross and his battalion of Texans followed as fast as their jaded horses could move. In the northwestern corner of Oberson's field Ross halted at the sight of a line of Federal infantry interspersed with artillery. It was Greusel's command filing into place on the southern side of the field just as Osterhaus had intended. While Ross considered his options, a Federal battery sent a salvo of shot and shell screeching over the heads of the Confederate horsemen. Ross prudently turned his battalion around and headed back through the gap to safety. *"I did not run,"* he confided to a friend, *"but I walked very fast."*[31]

When Ross returned to Foster's farm, he realized why his was the only pursuit. Confederate cavalrymen from every regiment milled around the captured artillery pieces gawking at dead and wounded Federals, rounding up prisoners and captured mounts, or excitedly telling one another of their exploits during the charge. The bedlam worsened when hundreds of Cherokees joined the celebration after routing Trimble's detachment of the 3rd Iowa Cavalry. An unknown number of Indians had gone on a rampage of murder and mutilation in the woods north of the Round Prairie. Some, perhaps all, of Trimble's wounded Iowans were murdered and at least eight were scalped. Even those Cherokees who had not unsheathed their knives were in a frenzy. According to one amazed Confederate officer, "the Indians swarmed around the guns like bees, in great confusion, jabbering and yelling at a furious rate." Pike acknowledged that his Cherokees wandered around "in the utmost confusion, all talking, riding this way and that, and listening to no orders from anyone," including Pike.[32]

Ross made his way through the mob and informed McCulloch of the presence of several thousand yankees beyond the belt of trees. This was a critical moment in the developing battle: McCulloch could not continue to Elkhorn Tavern and leave a sizable Federal force in his rear. After taking a hard look at the disorderly state of affairs on Foster's farm, where McIntosh was trying without much immediate success to re-form his brigade, McCulloch sent a courier after Hébert with orders to turn around and bring up the infantry. Thus the fateful decision was made to fight at Leetown. That decision would have fatal consequences for McCulloch personally and for the Confederates generally, because McCulloch unaccountably neglected to inform Van Dorn that the reunion of the Army of the West at Elkhorn Tavern would be delayed.[33]

The brief affair on Foster's farm was costly for both sides. The Federals suffered as many as 30 killed, 36 wounded, and 20 missing. Roughly 60 percent of the casualties came from the ranks of the 3rd Iowa Cavalry, which endured 24 killed, 17 wounded, and 9 missing, or slightly over 20 percent of the 235 Iowa troopers engaged. Confederate losses, as always, were problematical. McCulloch's division and Pike's brigade suffered a minimum of 20 killed, 17 wounded, and 3 missing. The most important single casualty was Colonel Sims of the 9th Texas Cavalry, who suffered a crippling arm wound; command of the regiment passed to Lt. Col. William Quayle. The three James rifles of the 1st Missouri Flying Battery, with their limbers, caissons, and nearly full ammunition chests, fell into Confederate hands intact. The Missouri cannoneers failed to spike the guns or explode the ammunition chests, but by riding off on those horses that had not been killed, they deprived the rebels of any convenient means of moving the weapons. Both sides lost several cavalry mounts.[34]

The charge of McIntosh's brigade inspired grandiose images among the thousands present at Foster's farm. An exhilarated Texan called it "one of the most sublime and gallant charges that Mars ever feasted eyes upon," and an admiring officer in the 3rd Louisiana exclaimed that "Napoleon's Life Guards never swept upon a foe with more impetuosity and gallantry than did our cavalry in this charge." Amidst the flurry of hyperbole no one seemed to have thought it ironic that one of the last Napoleonic cavalry charges on American soil was carried out by rawboned Texas and Arkansas frontiersmen only thirty miles from the Indian Territory.[35]

The Federal infantry arrived at Oberson's field about the time the cavalry gave way on Foster's farm. Greusel encountered Osterhaus's staff officer, who directed him to deploy his command along the southern edge of the cornfield. The leading troops had just turned west into the field when they were struck by the panicked effluvia of Bussey's luckless command. "Look out for the cavalry!" was the cry as a dozen riderless horses stampeded down Leetown Road. The animals raced along either side of the infantry column, some of them with blood-spattered saddles hanging upside down below their bellies. Large numbers of mounted cavalrymen "without hats or arms, in the utmost confusion and dismay," followed the riderless steeds. A few of them shouted as they raced past: "Turn back! Turn back! They'll give you hell!"[36]

The sights and sounds of the routed cavalrymen caused the "greatest consternation" imaginable in the blue column. "It was one of the most wild and exciting scenes that I have ever beheld," said an Illinois infantryman. "I tell you it was well calculated to cause another Bully running stampede."[37]

Greusel thought so, too. At this critical moment he stood in his stirrups and bellowed to his troops: "Officers and men, you have it in your power to make or prevent another Bull Run affair. I want every man to stand to his post." The reference to the shameful debacle outside Washington seven months earlier—still fresh in every Federal soldier's mind—may have boosted everyone's resolve. Minutes later Osterhaus arrived at a full gallop, fresh from the disaster on Foster's farm, to find Greusel calmly supervising the deployment of his troops in Oberson's field. Osterhaus was impressed by the businesslike scene and informed Curtis that the Illinois, Missouri, and Indiana troops "had stood without flinching" despite their unnerving reception. For his part Greusel proudly reported that in the midst of the rout "my command stood like veteran soldiers."[38]

The hastily formed Federal line stretched nearly the length of Oberson's field. It consisted, from left to right, of Greusel's own 36th Illinois, two twelve-pounder howitzers and four twelve-pounder James rifles of Capt. Louis Hoffman's 4th Ohio Battery, Maj. Hugo Wangelin's 12th Missouri, three twelve-pounder howitzers of Capt. Martin Welfley's Independent Missouri battery, and Lt. Col. John A. Hendricks's 22nd Indiana, whose right flank rested on Leetown Road. All but the 22nd Indiana belonged to Osterhaus's 1st Division. The three regiments contained approximately 1,600 infantrymen: 830 men in the 36th Illinois, 360 in the 12th Missouri, and 410 in the 22nd Indiana. The infantry were posted behind the rail fence on the southern side of the field; the artillery pieces were deployed in the field a few yards in front of the fence.[39]

The decision to hold Greusel's command in Oberson's field now appeared to have been a stroke of genius, but Osterhaus realized that the thin blue line was terribly vulnerable. Both flanks were exposed and there were no reserves. Osterhaus informed Curtis by courier that he had engaged the reported enemy force south of Twelve Corner Church and was in dire need

of substantial reinforcements. As it would be an hour or more before reinforcements arrived, if any arrived at all, Osterhaus sent his aides to round up
the scattered cavalry and bring them to the support of the infantry.[40]

In the brushy woods south of Oberson's field Bussey, Ellis, and Nemett
were trying to do exactly that. They successfully re-formed the detachments
of the 1st, 4th, and 5th Missouri Cavalry but could not find most of the 3rd
Iowa Cavalry. Major Perry, who had disappeared minutes before the debacle
on Foster's farm, magically reappeared after the 3rd Iowa Cavalry reached
the safety of Greusel's line. Perry ordered the regiment to escort the
wounded Trimble back to camp. As the five companies of Iowans clattered
eastward on Winton Hollow Road, they met none other than Franz Sigel.
Since the beginning of the battle Curtis had dealt directly with his four
division commanders, bypassing Sigel entirely, and the exasperated German
general was wandering around in search of something to do. Sigel stopped
the regiment. When he realized what Perry was up to, he relieved him on the
spot and sent the Iowans back to Leetown. Bussey placed his battered cavalry command in Oberson's field to the west of the 36th Illinois.[41]

Only the two artillery batteries of Greusel's command saw any action
while deploying. Hoffman's 4th Ohio Battery had just wheeled into position
and unlimbered when Ross's battalion of the 6th Texas appeared in the
northwestern corner of Oberson's field. The Ohio gunners traversed their
pieces to the left and opened a "brisk fire" on the rebels, who quickly
retired.[42]

Welfley's Independent Missouri Battery had a more exciting time. Upon
reaching Oberson's field Greusel sent Welfley's three howitzers ahead to bol-
ster Bussey's command at Foster's farm. The Missouri cannoneers were passing through the belt of trees on Foster's lane when the rout commenced.
Several Missourians were run down by the stampeding cavalry mounts, but
the others somehow managed to turn around. At the angle in the lane one of
the horses pulling the rearmost howitzer fell and broke the tongue of the
limber. Surrounded by a flood of panic-stricken cavalrymen, many screaming
that the rebels were close behind, the Missourians cut the surviving horses
loose and abandoned the howitzer. Welfley led the two remaining howitzers
around to the southern side of Oberson's field and wheeled them into position between the 12th Missouri and the 22nd Indiana.[43]

The crippled howitzer was visible to the Federals across Oberson's field,
but it was hidden from the Confederates by the belt of trees. After thirty
minutes Osterhaus sent the Missouri artillerymen, supported by two compa-

Nicholas Greusel, in a postwar portrait (Illinois State Historical Library)

nies of the 12th Missouri, across the cornfield to recover the howitzer. Welfley's men carried out their assignment without incident.[44]

While Bussey's shaken cavalrymen trickled into place on the Federal left and Welfley's artillerymen retrieved their howitzer on the right, Osterhaus and Greusel rode slowly along the line encouraging their officers and men. After the commotion of the past hour the field had become oddly quiet, and everyone could hear the sound of battle at Elkhorn Tavern.

The prolonged lull made Greusel uneasy. He wanted to do something to distract the rebels and disrupt whatever preparations they might be making for an assault. With Osterhaus's permission he instructed Captains Hoffman and Welfley to begin lobbing twelve-pound shells over the belt of trees toward Foster's farm. The Ohio and Missouri cannoneers went into action with their five stubby howitzers. Shortly afterward someone called Greusel's attention to the crest of Little Mountain, where some mounted Confederates, apparently a group of scouts, were visible. Two howitzers of Welfley's battery shifted their fire toward this new target and the rebel horsemen quickly disappeared.[45]

As the gunners went about their work, Greusel rode to the left and sent two companies of the 36th Illinois across Oberson's field to establish a skirmish line east of the gap in the trees where the rebel cavalry had appeared. Capt. Silas Miller's Company B and Capt. Irving Parkhurst's Company G hurried forward and spread out along the rail fence that bordered the northern edge of the field. When the rebels advanced through the belt of trees, the Illinois skirmishers would be the first to see them.[46]

Greusel's harassing artillery fire was more effective than he could have imagined. The first salvo of shells from the Federal howitzers exploded on Foster's farm and terrified the Cherokees, who fled back into the woods where they had ambushed Trimble's Iowans. The Indians were of little use to the Confederate cause for the rest of the battle. Other shells crashed into Little Mountain and scattered the handful of rebel horsemen there. Still others sailed over the hill and exploded above Hébert's infantrymen, who were trudging up the western slope of the rise between Big and Little mountains. Instead of hurrying his men over the rise and down the opposite slope toward Elkhorn Tavern, Hébert directed them to halt and seek shelter in the woods on either side of the road. Not long afterward Hébert received McCulloch's orders to return to Foster's farm.[47]

McCulloch deployed Hébert's four thousand infantry into an interrupted

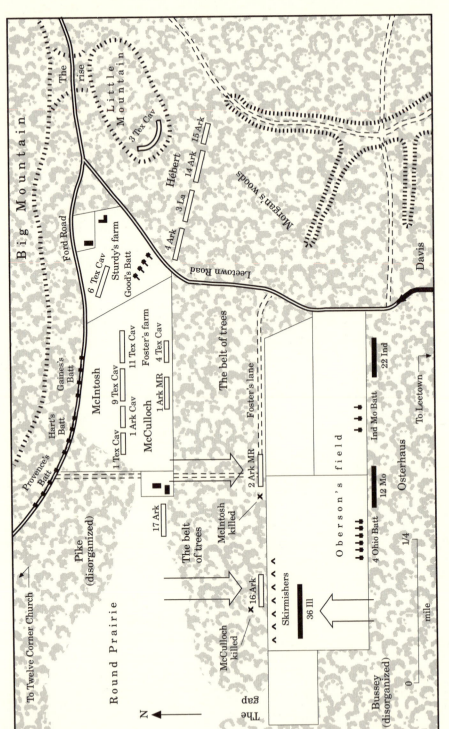

Map 5-3. Leetown: McCulloch and McIntosh Are Killed

line of battle extending from Little Mountain to just short of the gap in the belt of trees. The regiments and battalions west of Leetown Road were deployed in the open immediately north of the belt of trees. From west to east were the 16th and 17th Arkansas, the 2nd and 1st Arkansas Mounted Rifles, and the 4th Texas Cavalry Battalion. The regiments east of Leetown Road were deployed in Morgan's woods and their formation angled slightly to the southeast. From west to east they were the 4th Arkansas, 3rd Louisiana, and 15th and 14th Arkansas. Meanwhile the random barrage of howitzer shells continued, and the number of casualties mounted. To the men in the rebel ranks it seemed as though the yankees had the exact range. In fact the Federal gunners were firing blindly; they could not see any of the Confederate units because of the thick woods.[48]

While the infantry slowly filed into place, McIntosh established a shorter second line a few hundred yards to the north. It was composed of the 9th and 11th Texas Cavalry and the 1st Arkansas and 1st Texas Cavalry battalions. The 6th Texas Cavalry stayed near Good's Texas Battery, which provided a modicum of artillery support by firing blindly over the belt of trees in the general direction of the Federals. Hart's, Provence's, and Gaines's Arkansas batteries remained in column on Ford Road, as McCulloch did not think they would be needed. The 3rd Texas Cavalry dismounted and scrambled partway up the rocky slope of Little Mountain, taking care not to draw Federal artillery fire.[49]

McCulloch intended to launch a frontal assault against the Federal force Ross had seen south of the belt of trees. He assumed command of the five regiments and battalions of Hébert's brigade west of Leetown Road; Hébert retained command of the four regiments east of the road. Despite his fatigue and his misgivings about the progress of the campaign, McCulloch appeared confident that his men would make short work of the Federals. "In one hour they will be ours," he remarked.[50]

Before committing his division to an all-out attack, McCulloch decided to take a few minutes to see for himself what the Confederates were facing. It was characteristic of the former Texas Ranger to carry out his own reconnaissance whenever possible, and despite his elevation to high command he had not abandoned that habit. Ross had seen the Federals by passing through the gap in the belt of trees to the west, so McCulloch rode in that direction along the line of Confederate infantry. Just before setting out he sent instructions to Hébert to advance his half of the brigade when he heard sustained firing west of Leetown Road.[51]

McCulloch rode west a short distance beyond the right flank of the 16th Arkansas. He may have intended to ride all the way to the gap, but he stopped when he spotted a brushy area in the belt of trees that seemed easily passable on horseback. "I will ride forward a little and reconnoiter the enemy's position," he informed his staff. "You boys remain here; your gray horses will attract the fire of the sharpshooters."[52]

McCulloch took what seemed to be adequate precautions. He directed Col. John F. Hill to advance two companies of the 16th Arkansas as skirmishers and to follow with the remainder of the regiment if the skirmishers encountered any Federals. The two companies of Arkansans stepped forward and soon disappeared into the woods; McCulloch followed a short distance to the right where the trees were not so thick.[53]

As McCulloch rode away, Maj. John H. Brown, a close friend and a member of his staff, observed that the normally lean Texan was "in fuller flesh than I ever saw him," probably a result of the general's recent visit to cosmopolitan Richmond. McCulloch had fought in three wars without once donning a uniform or brandishing a sword. At Pea Ridge he wore a black velvet suit, a brown hat with a narrow brim, and high boots covered with woolen netting. His favorite Maynard rifle was slung over his shoulder. He was mounted on a tall, handsome red sorrel that blended into the dead leaves still clinging to the scrub oaks. Brown was not alone in considering McCulloch to be "the personification of splendid manhood."[54]

On the opposite side of the belt of trees the two companies of skirmishers from the 36th Illinois waited nervously behind the rail fence running along the northern edge of Oberson's field. Around 1:30 P.M. the men of Captain Miller's Company B, located closest to the gap, spied a lone horseman wending his way in their direction through the mix of brush and trees. The ground rose slightly in the middle of the belt of trees, and McCulloch, clad in black atop his tall horse, was sharply outlined against the cloudless blue sky. The Federals steadied their rifles on the fence rails. When the rider was about seventy yards away, Miller shouted "Fire!" and Company B loosed a ragged volley.[55]

The crackle of dozens of muskets echoed across the frigid landscape and McCulloch toppled to the ground, killed instantly by a bullet in the heart. His sorrel received four wounds and fled from the scene. The startled Arkansas skirmishers, in front of and to the left of McCulloch, dove for cover at the blast of Federal musketry, and none noticed him fall. The fatal episode occurred only a few hundred yards in front of the stationary Confederate line of battle. "But for the brush, thousands of our men could have seen it all," noted Major Brown.[56]

The first people to reach McCulloch were those who had killed him. The men of Company B scrambled over the fence and drove the Arkansas skirmishers deep into the belt of trees. When the firing died down, several yankees ran to the spot where the rebel officer had fallen. Pvt. Peter Pelican was the first to reach McCulloch's body. He grabbed the general's gold watch and began tugging at his boots. Other Federals came up and joined in the scavenging.[57]

This sordid scene was cut short by the appearance of the entire 16th Arkansas. At the sound of gunfire to his right front Colonel Hill advanced his regiment as instructed by McCulloch. The Arkansans moved obliquely to the right and then pushed straight ahead through the belt of trees, retrieving the two companies of skirmishers along the way. At the first sight of the oncoming Confederates the Illinoisans collected their booty and hastily rejoined their comrades of Company G along the fence. When the opposing forces were about one hundred yards apart, a firefight erupted. Advancing, halting to fire and reload, then advancing again, the right wing of the 16th Arkansas passed directly over McCulloch's body without noticing the fallen general.[58]

After a few minutes the Arkansas regimental colors drew the attention of Federal howitzer crews on the far side of Oberson's field. Glad to have a visible target at last, the Federals lowered their sights and blasted the belt of trees with twelve-pound shells. Hill halted his regiment and told color bearer Joseph M. Bailey to case the flag. The static firefight with the Illinois skirmishers continued while a puzzled Hill awaited further orders from McCulloch, who seemed to have disappeared into thin air. In the meantime Bailey rather casually decided to visit his brother on the right of the regiment. There he found everyone in a commotion: a straggling soldier had stumbled upon McCulloch's body in the brush a few yards behind the Arkansas line. Bailey ran over and gazed upon the fallen general. "He was lying full length on his back," remembered Bailey. "The calm, placid expression of his face indicated that death was instantaneous and that he died without a struggle." McCulloch still had his boots and pistol but his watch, rifle, and field glasses were gone.[59]

Just then another soldier came up and exclaimed, "My God! Its poor old Ben!" This prompted Lt. Benjamin Pixley, adjutant of the 16th Arkansas, to cover the general's body with his coat. "We must not let the men know that

General McCulloch is killed," he cautioned before running to tell Hill of the tragic discovery. Pixley's attitude was shared by the members of McCulloch's staff: during the next few hours they suppressed the news of the Texan's death in order to prevent demoralization in the ranks. Most regimental commanders were kept in the dark along with their men—an error that would have serious consequences. At this critical moment with the division fully deployed for battle, command passed quietly, almost secretly, to McIntosh.[60]

Osterhaus's demonstration was a success despite the setback on Foster's farm. The unexpected appearance of a sizable Federal force north of Leetown derailed Van Dorn's plan to unite the Army of the West at Elkhorn Tavern. But while McCulloch's division had been diverted from its primary objective and had suffered the loss of its famed commander, it had not been defeated. The fighting at Leetown was only just beginning.

6 Battle in the Brush

When McIntosh was informed of McCulloch's death, he told his cavalry commanders on Foster's farm to stay and "wait for orders." Without another word he trotted forward and joined his old regiment, Col. Benjamin T. Embry's 2nd Arkansas Mounted Rifles, which was dismounted and serving as infantry. He immediately ordered the general advance that McCulloch had prepared, but without the coordination that McCulloch had intended. McIntosh did not even wait for his order to be transmitted along the long line of infantry. No sooner had the couriers sped away then he drew his sword and led the 2nd Arkansas Mounted Rifles forward into the belt of trees.[1]

McIntosh should have remained in the rear on Foster's farm. There he could have consulted with Major Brown and other members of McCulloch's staff, informed Hébert of what had happened, and put the finishing touches on the plan of attack. Instead, he reverted to the role of regimental commander in order to be in the thick of the fight. McIntosh's impulsive, irresponsible actions accelerated the disastrous breakdown of command that doomed the Confederate effort at Leetown.

Meanwhile, on the other side of the belt of trees, the two companies of skirmishers from the 36th Illinois—the men who had killed McCulloch—were trying to get out of a tight spot. After trading shots for several minutes with the stationary 16th Arkansas, Captain Miller decided to disengage and fall back to the Federal line on the southern side of Oberson's field. The broad field offered no cover other than rotting stumps and withered cornstalks, but Miller gambled that his men could dash across before the rebels could react.[2]

The Illinoisans turned from the fence and trotted across the furrowed field at the double-quick, but they did not even reach the halfway point before the Arkansans rushed forward to the fence and opened fire. Miller realized his gamble had failed and shouted for everyone to lie down. The well-drilled Federals responded so quickly their alarmed comrades on the southern side of the field thought they "had all been *shot* down."[3]

A soldier in the 36th Illinois melodramatically described the rail fence on the northern side of Oberson's field as "actually fringed with fire; every length of it concealed a score of sharpshooters, safely protected behind rails and logs, and able to select their living target, take deliberate aim and send their shot with fatal effect." Sharpshooters or not, the rebels clearly had an advantage over Miller's two companies. The Federal infantry on the southern side of the field could not fire at all for fear of hitting the skirmishers, and while the Federal cannoneers continued to rake the belt of trees with shell and case shot, their projectiles generally flew well over the heads of the Arkansans. Within minutes twenty of Miller's men were wounded.[4]

From Greusel's position it seemed the skirmishers were being killed off one by one where they lay. If the skirmishers could not come back to their regiment, Greusel decided the regiment must go to them. He ordered the 36th Illinois forward. Seven hundred blue-coated infantrymen scrambled over the fence and advanced across Oberson's field in parade ground formation, not a man "flinching or falling out of line." At midfield the 36th Illinois halted and loosed a crashing volley toward the smaller 16th Arkansas. With the rebels staggered by the hail of bullets, Miller ordered everyone to run. The skirmishers jumped to their feet and sprinted through the ranks of the Illinois regiment, dragging or carrying their wounded to safety. The 36th Illinois continued to advance beyond midfield and fired several more volleys at the Arkansans, who replied only weakly to the Federal challenge.[5]

While this was taking place, McIntosh and the 2nd Arkansas Mounted Rifles were making their way through the belt of trees. Progress was slow because of the thick woods and the pitiful condition of the men, most of whom had limped all the way from the Boston Mountains in high-heeled riding boots. "Our regiment was nearly all broke down when we went into the fight, but done the best we could," recalled one rebel. Seething with impatience, McIntosh left his relatively secure position with Embry behind the center of the ragged Confederate line and rode around the right flank. When Greusel saw the 2nd Arkansas Mounted Rifles emerge from the belt of trees to the east of the 16th Arkansas, he directed the right companies of the 36th Illinois to shift their fire to counter this new threat. McIntosh, several yards ahead and to the right of his old regiment, reached the rail fence just as hundreds of Federal muskets swung in his direction and fired. As the echoes of the volley died, McIntosh fell from his horse, struck in the heart by a Federal bullet.[6]

McIntosh died in full view of his old comrades in the 2nd Arkansas Mounted Rifles, who quickly carried his body to the rear. Without orders and with his dismounted cavalrymen under fire not only from the 36th Illinois but also from the two Federal batteries across the field, Embry chose to abandon the attack and follow his fallen commander. The 2nd Arkansas Mounted Rifles faced about and marched back through the belt of trees toward Foster's farm. Hill had been relieved to see Embry's troops come up, thinking that support had arrived at last, but when they inexplicably withdrew, he ordered his 16th Arkansas to retire as well.[7]

As the two demoralized Arkansas regiments drifted back to the north, they encountered Col. Frank A. Rector's 17th Arkansas, Col. Thomas J. Churchill's 1st Arkansas Mounted Rifles, and Maj. John W. Whitfield's 4th Texas Cavalry Battalion belatedly advancing through the belt of trees. The five regimental and battalion commanders held a singularly dismal conference in the woods. At this critical moment none of the exhausted officers demonstrated any leadership or initiative; all were content to discontinue the attack and wait for Hébert to arrive and tell them what to do. By 2:00 P.M. the Confederate units were back where they had started on the northern side of the belt of trees. The ill-fated and ill-managed infantry assault west of Leetown Road was over.

Casualties on both sides were moderate considering the amount of ammunition expended: the Federals endured two or three men killed and about thirty wounded, all from the 36th Illinois; the Confederates suffered at least two men killed—both generals—and an unknown number wounded. The noise of musketry and artillery sputtered as the Federals in Oberson's field gradually realized the enemy had disappeared back into the woods. Greusel kept the 36th Illinois in its advanced position for a short time longer, unsure of what the rebels were up to, and then led the regiment back to its place in the Federal line on the southern side of the field. The Ohio and Missouri cannoneers, sweating despite the chilly temperature, once again elevated the barrels of their howitzers and resumed firing blindly over the belt of trees toward Foster's and Sturdy's farms.[8]

Thus ended the brief but fateful fighting west of Leetown Road and with it any realistic chance that McCulloch's division would sweep the outnumbered Federals off the field and march on to Elkhorn Tavern.

The only remaining hope for a Confederate victory at Leetown lay in Morgan's woods east of Leetown Road, where Hébert moved back and forth along his section of the Confederate line of battle speaking encouraging words to his soldiers in English and French. The bilingual Acadian colonel had graduated third in his West Point class of 1845 but had left the army to tend to his family's sugar cane plantation near Breaux Bridge on Bayou Teche. Hébert was a capable and popular officer. When he passed along the front of his old regiment, the crack 3rd Louisiana, the troops asked him to stay near them in the coming fight. Flattered and touched by their request, Hébert declared: "I will not leave you, my men, this day." Shortly after this, small arms and artillery fire erupted to the west across Leetown Road. This was the onset of the disastrous clash between the 36th Illinois and the 16th Arkansas and 2nd Arkansas Mounted Rifles. Unable to see anything from his position in the woods, Hébert assumed that the gunfire was the signal for the general advance indicated earlier by McCulloch. A little before 2:00 P.M. he ordered his four regiments forward. Because the soldiers had been slightly misaligned in the woods, they proceeded in a southwesterly direction.[9]

Hébert's command consisted of Col. Evander McNair's 4th Arkansas on the right near Leetown Road, Maj. Will F. Tunnard's 3rd Louisiana in the center, and Col. W. C. Mitchell's 14th Arkansas and Col. Dandridge McRae's battalion-sized 15th Arkansas on the left, a total of about two thousand men. Most of the Arkansans were green, officers and men alike, but they made up in determination what they lacked in experience. A soldier in the 4th Arkansas, the largest and probably the best of the Arkansas units at Pea Ridge, wrote proudly that "our men went in with all the vim and courage that regulars could have displayed."[10]

Hébert did not know that McCulloch and McIntosh were dead and that he was now in command of the division. Nor did he know that his attack was entirely unsupported by the other units of his brigade, which were falling back from the fatal fence along the northern side of Oberson's field. By the time officers from the staffs of the two fallen generals crossed Leetown Road in search of Hébert, he was out of reach, advancing south with his com-

Louis Hébert (Library of Congress)

mand. This was a calamity for the Confederates. Hébert possessed many of the skills McIntosh lacked. Had he assumed command of McCulloch's division at this moment, the battle might have turned out differently. Ironically, Hébert led the only effective Confederate infantry assault at Leetown, but in so doing he unknowingly left the rest of the division leaderless and paralyzed.[11]

Morgan's woods in 1862 was a dense tangle of trees, vines, and brush that limited vision to less than one hundred yards. Dozens of fallen trees, victims of a recent tornado, added to the clutter. The relatively level terrain is cut by two ravines that drain eastward into Winton Springs Hollow. The northern ravine is about ten feet deep and runs from northwest to southeast, or diagonally across the path of the Confederate advance. The southern ravine runs from west to east about two hundred yards farther along.[12]

After advancing only a short distance through the woods, the Confederate line of battle began to unravel. The 14th and 15th Arkansas fell behind and drifted to the right, assuming an *en echelon* position behind the left flank of the 3rd Louisiana. When Hébert realized what was happening, he halted to realign the ranks. During the halt the Federal gunners in Oberson's field turned their attention to the rebel activity in Morgan's woods. Shells and solid shot smashed into the trees, spraying metal fragments and wooden splinters in all directions and inflicting the first casualties on Hébert's command.[13]

The situation worsened when the Confederates resumed their skewed advance. The right flank of the 4th Arkansas emerged from the trees onto Leetown Road and drew a barrage of fire from the Federal cannoneers. McNair quickly moved his regiment obliquely to the left to bring his exposed soldiers back into the cover of the woods. The emergency maneuver played havoc with the Confederate formation. The right of the 3rd Louisiana cut through the left of the 4th Arkansas and separated two and a half companies from the rest of the regiment. "Louisianans and Arkansians intermixed, without regard to Captains or Colonels," said Capt. Rufus K. Garland of the 4th Arkansas, and officers "were never able to form them again into their proper companies or regiments." More jumbled than ever, Hébert's rump brigade pushed on through the woods.[14]

Had the entire Confederate infantry force advanced in concert on both sides of Leetown Road, as McCulloch had intended and as Hébert thought was actually happening, Osterhaus's much smaller command very likely would have been overwhelmed. Even now, with only a fraction of McCulloch's division in action, Hébert still had a chance to strike the Federals a severe blow. His four disordered, overlapping regiments were blindly bearing down on Osterhaus's unsupported right flank on the western side of Leetown Road. Osterhaus had no reserves; every available man was in line facing the belt of trees across Oberson's field. He had asked Curtis for reinforcements an hour earlier. His fate at Leetown now depended on whether help arrived before Hébert.

After terminating the council of war Curtis spent the next hour at his headquarters at Pratt's store listening to the growing roar of battle a mile to the northeast at Elkhorn Tavern. By 11:30 A.M. he could contain himself no longer and rode up Telegraph Road to see how Carr was faring. The swelling volume of Confederate artillery fire in Cross Timber Hollow surprised the Federal commander; the enemy was making a more vigorous attack along Telegraph Road than he had expected.[15]

Curtis returned to Pratt's store, mulling things over in his methodical fashion. What he had seen and heard convinced him that a substantial body of rebels, well supplied with artillery, had marched all the way around Big Mountain to Telegraph Road and was driving into the Federal rear. Since Osterhaus had not yet reported meeting serious opposition south of Twelve Corner Church, Curtis decided that his immediate priority was to secure his line of communications. At 12:30 P.M. he dispatched a courier to Davis with instructions to pull most of his 3rd Division out of the Little Sugar Creek fortifications and march to Carr's support at once. He specified that Davis leave the 8th Indiana and the 1st Indiana Battery behind to guard the Telegraph Road crossing of Little Sugar Creek. Curtis was not ready to discount entirely the possibility of a delayed Confederate thrust in that quarter.[16]

The courier had hardly passed out of sight when an alarming message arrived from Osterhaus, telling of the debacle on Foster's farm and urgently requesting reinforcements. This came as a complete surprise to Curtis, for the tremendous racket at Elkhorn Tavern had masked the more distant sound of battle on Foster's farm. Faced with such unsettling news from Osterhaus, one of the most dependable senior officers in the army, Curtis reevaluated the situation. He was more unsure than ever whether the enemy was present in greater force at Leetown or at Elkhorn Tavern. If Leetown offered a greater threat, as Osterhaus's message and common sense seemed to indicate, then the attack at Elkhorn Tavern, so distant from the enemy's encampment in Little Sugar Creek, was only a noisy diversion. Even if Elkhorn Tavern proved to be something more than a diversion, Carr should be able to hold the high ground at the tavern for some time without additional support. Curtis now reversed himself: "I considered the affair so imminent that I changed my order to Colonel Davis." A second courier went pounding after Davis with instructions to hasten to Leetown instead of Elkhorn Tavern.[17]

Van Dorn's snap decision to divide his forces on either side of Big Mountain continued to have the unintended effect of obscuring his actual intentions and confusing Curtis. All things considered, however, the Federal commander responded appropriately to an uncertain threat in a highly fluid situation. Later, some members of the 4th Division privately criticized Curtis for failing to rush reinforcements to Elkhorn Tavern. Curtis learned of this criticism by his fellow Iowans and was stung by it. Several weeks after the battle he insisted to Halleck that "I did not err in sending Colonel Davis to [Leetown], although Colonel Carr, on the right, also needed re-enforcements."[18]

The old engineer was reluctant to abandon his blufftop fortifications along Little Sugar Creek prematurely, but he could not ignore the presence of dangerously large enemy forces behind his right flank and on his line of communications. As the day wore on, Curtis incrementally shifted the infantry, cavalry, and artillery of all four divisions north from Little Sugar Creek to the broad plateau of Pea Ridge. At the same time, and on the same narrow, clogged roads, he transferred trains, stores, hospitals, and other rear echelon facilities in the opposite direction. The result was a landmark achievement in American military history. Six hours after the start of the battle the Army of the Southwest faced north instead of south, a remarkable 180-degree change of front unparalleled in the Civil War.

About 2:00 P.M. Davis reached Osterhaus's position with 1,400 fresh troops of his 3rd Division. The band marching at the head of the blue column entered Oberson's field and broke into a spirited rendition of "Dixie," a selection that may have struck many in the ranks as incongruous. Just behind the musicians was Col. Julius White's 2nd Brigade: about 950 men in the 37th and 59th Illinois and Battery A, 2nd Illinois Light Artillery, generally known as the Peoria Battery. Close behind came a portion of Col. Thomas Pattison's 1st Brigade: around 450 soldiers of the 18th Indiana.[19]

Osterhaus briefed Davis on the course of the battle and urged him to extend the Federal line into Morgan's woods east of Leetown Road. Davis agreed. He began placing his troops in the path of Hébert's oncoming force while Osterhaus rode back into Oberson's field to oversee his own command.

The deployment of the 3rd Division proceeded rapidly because the troops had shed their coats, packs, and other baggage as they passed through Leetown.[20]

Davis was a regular officer in the prewar army with two decades of military experience from Mexico to Fort Sumter. He was quiet, competent, and supremely self-confident. Despite being the senior Federal officer present at Leetown, Davis declined to assume overall command. Perhaps after the uproar at Rolla he was reluctant to give orders to a "German" division nominally under Sigel's control. For the duration of the fight at Leetown each of the two Federal division commanders handled his own forces independently, cooperating as the situation required. This odd arrangement was fraught with potential danger but turned out satisfactorily.

Capt. John D. Crabtree of Bowen's Missouri Cavalry Battalion rode up while Osterhaus and Davis were conferring. Curtis, apparently having second thoughts about his decision to divert the 3rd Division to Leetown, sent Crabtree to observe the situation there and to determine if any troops could be spared for Carr at Elkhorn Tavern. After listening to Osterhaus's account, Crabtree concluded that Osterhaus and Davis had all the enemy they could handle and trotted off to inform Curtis.[21]

Davis placed Capt. Peter Davidson's Peoria Battery in the southeastern corner of Oberson's field adjacent to Leetown Road. The gunners unlimbered and began shelling Morgan's woods with their two twelve-pounder howitzers, two six-pounder guns, and two six-pounder James rifles, adding their weight to the rain of projectiles coming from the 4th Ohio Battery and Welfley's Independent Missouri Battery. Davis then directed White to deploy his 2nd Brigade to the east of the road about one hundred yards north of Osterhaus's line. White was unable to exercise effective tactical control of his brigade in the woods, and each of the two Illinois regiments fought largely on its own.[22]

After filing into the tangle of trees and brush, Lt. Col. Myron S. Barnes halted his 37th Illinois and faced left. The regimental left flank was just inside the trees bordering Leetown Road; the right was near the northern ravine. At Barnes's command his five hundred Illinoisans moved forward. The troops on the right advanced more rapidly, causing the regiment to present a skewed front to the Confederates.[23]

The Illinoisans pushed ahead only a short distance before they glimpsed dark-clad figures directly ahead. A few soldiers made ready to fire, but an officer cried out: "Don't shoot they are our own men!" No sooner had this

Jefferson C. Davis
(Massachusetts Commandery, U.S. Army Military History Institute)

man closed his mouth than the 37th Illinois received a searing volley at close range from the mysterious figures. "The brush being so heavy we couldn't see very much, but smoke and flashes of fire," said Henry Ketzle. The Illinoisans responded with a volley of their own. The men in Company A on the right flank and Company K on the left were armed with Colt revolving rifles. They opened fire with a sustained roar, or as one soldier put it, they "threw the throttle valve wide open and 'let her go Gallagher.'"[24]

Lt. Col. Calvin H. Frederick's 59th Illinois filed into Morgan's woods behind

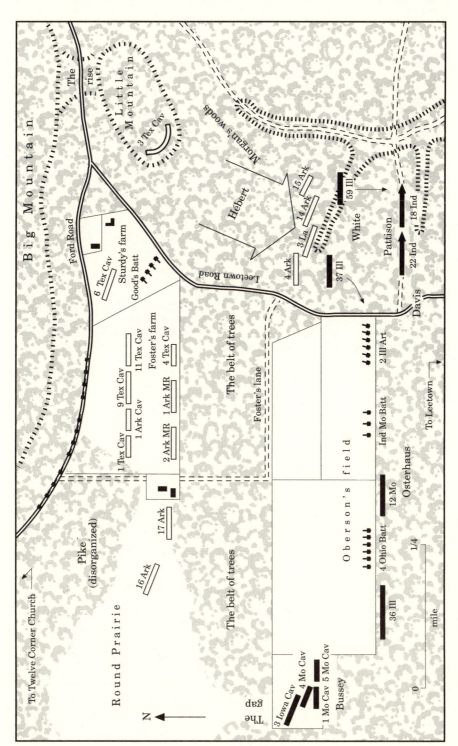

Map 6-1. Leetown: Hébert Advances against Davis

Morgan's woods, east of Leetown Road. On this spot the 37th Illinois deployed and advanced forward—only seventy-five yards ahead were Hébert's rebels. (authors' collection)

the 37th Illinois and crossed to the far side of the northern ravine. Frederick wanted to make certain that his command cleared the right flank of the 37th Illinois, but he went too far to the east and opened a gap between the two Illinois regiments. The men of the 59th finally halted, faced left, and began to push blindly ahead. One soldier wrote that "the underbrush was so dense and thick that we could scarcely make our way through it."[25]

After thrashing through the woods for perhaps fifty yards Frederick's troops were startled by an eruption of musketry to their left front—their comrades in the 37th Illinois had found the enemy. At this point, recalled a soldier, a small number of enlisted men and one or two junior officers "failed to share the honors of the battle, by being dilatory about going in." Soon the soldiers of the 59th Illinois, minus the fainthearted, detected dim figures in the woods ahead. Frederick hesitated—were they rebels or members of the 37th Illinois? Maj. Philip S. Post volunteered to find out and rode forward. There was a spattering of shots and Post came back clutching a bloody shoulder. Frederick shouted "Fire!" and four hundred Federal muskets flamed into action.[26]

Neither side had deployed skirmishers, and the opposing lines of infantry practically collided before sighting and opening fire. The shock was terrific. "Suddenly something like a tremendous peal of thunder opened all along our front," wrote a Louisiana soldier, "and a ridge of fire and smoke appeared close before us, and the trees round us and over our heads rattled with the bullets, as if in a heavy hail-storm." The Louisianans had a particularly harrowing experience. Dozens of emergency men—the poorly trained civilians who had answered McCulloch's call for volunteers or who had joined the marching column during the past three days—were in the ranks of the 14th and 15th Arkansas. Several of them nervously began shooting as soon as they heard the opening volleys of musketry. At least two Louisiana soldiers were hit from behind.[27]

For nearly an hour Hébert's four regiments and White's two regiments flailed at each other in the only sustained fighting at Leetown. The firing, intensified by the rapid blasts of the Colt repeaters, was "cyclonic in sound and effect" to the troops engaged. A soldier in the 36th Illinois, a few hundred yards to the west in Oberson's field, later wrote that the clash in Morgan's woods produced "such a crackling of musketry, I cannot describe it." Confederates half a mile to the north on Foster's farm described the noise as a "deep sullen roar."[28]

Some of the men in blue fired wildly and rapidly; others, more deliberately. Herschel Felton and David Ash of the 37th Illinois each got off only eight shots during the engagement, about one every five minutes. Although less than one hundred yards apart, the Federals and Confederates caught only fleeting glimpses of one another through the withered foliage and billowing smoke. "The pictures in *Harper's Weekly* are mere fancy sketches," complained Capt. Henry Curtis, Jr., after reviewing newspaper reports of the battle. "The brush was so thick we couldn't half the time see who we were fighting, and those pictures show a clear field." Many Federals believed that the vegetation saved their lives; one man wrote that the trees "stopt a great many of the secesh bullets." They stopped many Federal bullets as well.[29]

Despite the limited protection afforded by the scrubby oaks, the Federals found themselves on the receiving end of "a perfect hail-storm of lead." To an Illinois soldier the air "seemed literally filled with leaden hail. Balls would whiz by our ears, cut off bushes closely, and even cut our clothes." Both Barnes and Frederick ordered their men to fight from a prone position. The Federals obeyed with alacrity; David Ash told his fiancée that "we fell down

Julius White (Massachusetts Commandery, U.S. Army Military History Institute)

as flat as we could." Trunks, branches, leaves, and brush all around the huddled soldiers rattled with the impact of bullets, balls, and buckshot. It "sounded for all the world like beans or peas thrown by handfulls among us," wrote an Illinois officer. Another officer was convinced the men of his company "would have been utterly annihilated" had he not "fought them flat on their bellies on the ground." One lucky Federal soldier felt three bullets rip through the crown of his hat as he lay sprawled on the cold, damp ground.[30]

Lying down offered only a modest degree of protection from the deadly projectiles flying in all directions. Albert Hilliard of the 37th Illinois was struck in the forehead while on the ground. He turned to his friend David Ash and cried out, "Oh Dave I am shot." Hilliard miraculously survived his disfiguring head wound, but the soldier on his left, James Lee, did not. The unfortunate Lee was shot in the back of the head by a soldier in his own regiment.[31]

The ranking officers of the 2nd Brigade took their share of punishment. Both White and Barnes were thrown to the ground when their horses were killed. Frederick was stunned by the concussion of an exploding shell from Good's Texas Battery, which fired randomly at the Federals throughout the engagement. Maj. John C. Black of the 37th Illinois, who boldly threw the folds of his cape over his shoulder to expose the red lining, also lost his horse due to rebel fire and then was severely wounded in the arm while rallying his men. Black refused to leave the field, despite being twice ordered to do so by White, until he was eventually incapacitated by loss of blood. Major Post of the 59th Illinois, wounded in the shoulder at the outset of the fight, wept when the regimental surgeon sternly ordered him to the rear.[32]

Company officers suffered as well. Capt. Eugene B. Payne of the 37th Illinois was struck three times: one bullet sliced across his neck; another grazed his leg, "tearing away my pants and drawers"; and a third cut the flesh on his little finger to the bone. "It amounts to nothing," he told his wife. Captain Curtis of the same regiment was less fortunate. He was hit in the right shoulder at the first exchange of fire and then hit again in the side while sprawled in the dirt with his men. White's two Illinois regiments had run into a buzzsaw. Would they hold their ground or be forced back by sheer weight of numbers?[33]

While the battle in the brush raged with mounting fury, Davis sat on his horse in Leetown Road near the Peoria Battery. He could see almost nothing of the fighting, but he could certainly hear the "increasing and excessive fire" of Hébert's troops as they pressed forward against the two Illinois regi-

ments. As Federal casualties began trickling out of the woods, Davis grew
concerned about White's ability to hold his position. He turned to Pattison
and committed the 1st Brigade to the fight.[34]

One of Pattison's regiments, the 22nd Indiana, had reached Oberson's field
earlier as part of Greusel's command but had not been engaged except as an
unwilling target for Confederate artillery fire. Early in the fight a twelve-
pound case shot from Good's Texas Battery decapitated a corporal standing
in the front rank, "passed through the neck and shoulders of his cousin, a
private in the rear rank, and, without exploding, buried itself in the breast of
Lt. Watts, of Company K, killing all three instantly." Colonel Hendricks immediately ordered his men to lie down. This probably was Good's most
significant contribution to the Confederate effort at Leetown; even the Indiana soldier who described the incident in such gory detail acknowledged
that the occasional Confederate artillery projectile was "more demoralizing
than destructive."[35]

When the 3rd Division arrived on the battlefield, Pattison resumed command of the 22nd Indiana and placed the 18th Indiana in line on its right.
This extended the Federal line across Leetown Road. The newly arrived
Hoosiers hardly had time to dress their ranks before Davis ordered the
reunited 1st Brigade to move out at the double-quick in support of the faltering Illinoisans. Pattison hurried his men along a lane leading east from
Leetown Road into Morgan's woods. Pattison's mission was to relieve the
pressure on White's hard-pressed men by striking the Confederate left
flank.[36]

Davis's concern for White's brigade was well founded: the Confederates
were driving the Federals back. "Close in upon them, boys—forward!"
shouted Hébert, leading his old regiment forward through the smoky woods.
By accident rather than by design the 3rd Louisiana pushed into the gap
between the two Federal regiments, slowly but inexorably forcing back the
right wing of the 37th Illinois and the left wing of the 59th Illinois.[37]

The outnumbered Federals gamely tried to hold their ground. "We all fell
back a few Rods and loaded and went up in to them again," wrote a soldier in
the 37th Illinois. "We fired into them again and they returned the fire." But
the Confederates kept coming and soon stumbled across bodies in blue uniforms, grisly evidence that the Federals were giving way. As the flanks on
either side of the gap bent under the pressure of the Confederate advance,
the two Illinois regiments retired in an undulating manner. Individual companies retreated, advanced, and retreated again. Some companies struggled

back and forth across the northern ravine three or four times. These unorthodox maneuvers were uncoordinated; the 37th and 59th Illinois were losing cohesion above the company level in the noisy, smoky wilderness.[38]

The lack of effective brigade or regimental control on the Federal side nearly led to disaster during this fluid phase of the engagement. At one point Captain Payne of the 37th Illinois was startled to discover that the companies on either side of his had pulled back. With the rebels barely fifty yards away Payne ordered his men to fire a last shot and then beat a hasty retreat to locate the rest of the regiment. On the other side of the gap Lt. George Currie of the 59th Illinois had a similar shock when he realized that his company was alone. After firing a parting volley from a kneeling position, the men of Currie's company turned and scrambled "like gophers" to the rear.[39]

As the Federal line of battle swung back and forth, so did the color bearer of the 37th Illinois, a veteran English soldier named Benjamin Manning. An officer shouted at Manning that the erratic movements of the colors were having a bad effect on the men and that he should stay put and serve as a rallying point. Manning felt that his courage had been impugned. When the color company advanced a few moments later, he placed himself a good ten yards ahead of the infantry and squatted to avoid being shot from behind.[40]

This was not precisely what his superior had intended, but Manning was determined to demonstrate his mettle. While bullets from both sides whizzed around him, Manning held the flagstaff erect with his left hand and fired a revolver toward the enemy with his right. It took only a moment for the inevitable to happen. Bullets shredded the flag, splintered the staff, took off Manning's left forefinger, and struck him in the chest. He fell forward on his face, apparently dead. Another member of the color guard retrieved the tattered flag and hastily retired, leaving Manning sprawled in the leaves. That evening Manning appeared at a hospital at Leetown to have his hand bandaged. The spent bullet that struck him in the chest had only knocked him unconscious. When complimented by White for his dramatic, if foolhardy, gesture, Manning replied, "Colonel, I always try to do my duty."[41]

After forty-five minutes of desperate fighting Davis decided to disengage the hard-pressed 37th and 59th Illinois before they disintegrated. Apparently undisturbed by the ungodly racket and the constant traffic swirling around him, Davis had a rather novel idea for retrieving the situation. White would wheel or pivot his 2nd Brigade backward and to the left like a swinging door, changing front from north to east. This maneuver would relieve the pressure on the Illinoisans but would still enable them to cover Leetown Road, the Peoria Battery, and Greusel's exposed right flank. Davis surmised that the Confederates would conform and follow, having no other point of reference in the woods other than the flaming muzzles of the Federals. As they did so, Pattison would wheel his 1st Brigade forward and to the left, changing front from north to west, and strike the rebels in the flank and rear. In effect, the two Federal brigades would pirouette until they were facing each other with the enemy caught in the middle.[42]

White botched the reverse wheeling movement. He failed to exercise effective control over the 2nd Brigade or even to inform Barnes and Frederick of precisely what was expected of them. The 37th Illinois made a disorderly withdrawal to the southwest, more or less as Davis wanted. Some of the troops ended up among the guns of the Peoria Battery west of Leetown Road; others remained in the woods just east of the road. With his men so scattered and disorganized Barnes was unable to establish a coherent line of battle. The 59th Illinois retreated south in a hasty and confused fashion. The soldiers forced their way through the tail of the 22nd Indiana, which was still trudging along the lane, and continued on a short distance to the southern ravine. There Frederick and his officers labored to bring order out of chaos.[43]

The two Illinois regiments fell back as they had fought, each company largely on its own. When word came to retreat, Lieutenant Currie's company of the 59th Illinois dashed through the woods without regard for military formation. Currie himself led the way: "You would not have wagered much on my winning in that hurry! skurry! pell-mell! every man looking out for himself race." He was burdened with a heavy saber and a musket and cartridge box that he had taken from a wounded man. "I was doing fairly well, however, until somehow the sabre twisted itself between my legs and threw me flat on my face. I knew the adjutant of our regiment, who was riding a white horse, was right behind me and turning over on my side I saw the big eyed animal looking down on me as sober as a judge, as if about to pass sentence upon me for such awkwardness. I rolled over out of the way, sprung to my feet, and scampered off making up for lost time."[44]

Davis expected White's brigade to make an orderly fighting withdrawal and change of front, to trade space for time. But the maneuver was not executed as planned and the Confederates now had a golden opportunity to breach the Federal line in the vicinity of Leetown Road. Unfortunately for Hébert, his men were almost as disorganized as the Federals. The rebels had suffered heavy casualties, including dozens of men who had collapsed from

Oberson's field, looking northwest from the site of Davidson's battery. McCulloch fell on the far side of the field at a spot to the left of this view, and McIntosh fell near the left center of this view. (authors' collection)

exhaustion, and they were badly disoriented by the thick smoke that hung motionless in the woods and reduced visibility to only a few yards. When the Federals disengaged and disappeared, seemingly falling back in all directions, Hébert brought his ragged regiments to a halt to assess the situation.

During this brief lull in the fighting the Confederates on the far right were staggered by the discharge of Federal artillery in Oberson's field. The Peoria Battery had been banging away for most of the Confederate attack, but the noise had mingled with the general bombardment and the exchange of musketry at close range in the dense vegetation. Now the other batteries and the muskets were silent, and Hébert's men were across Leetown Road from the battery. Several hundred soldiers from the 4th Arkansas and 3rd Louisiana, loosely under Colonel McNair's command, commenced a very disorderly right wheel and then "rushed forward on the guns."[45]

The Confederates poured out of the woods, crossed Leetown Road, and scrambled over the rail fence into Oberson's field. Davidson's gunners had no infantry support other than two or three companies of the 37th Illinois, which had retreated across the road a few minutes earlier. For a time the

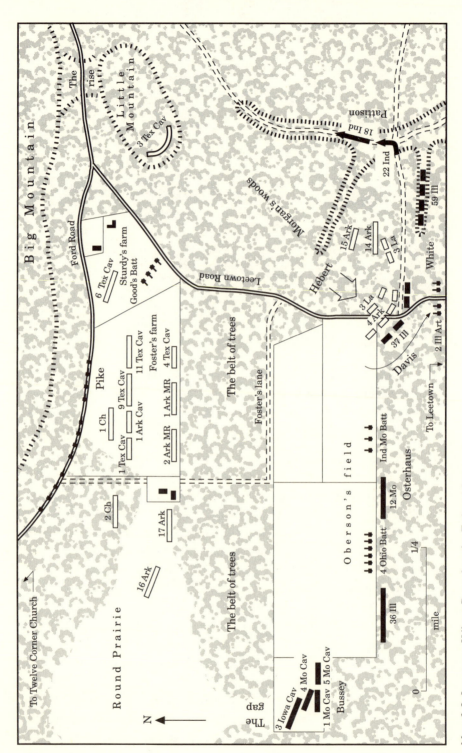

Map 6-2. Leetown: Hébert Breaches the Federal Line

heavily outnumbered Illinois troops stood their ground and sprayed the oncoming rebels with musket and revolving rifle fire. In the midst of the melee Capt. William P. Black of the 37th Illinois picked up a Colt rifle and singlehandedly held off a rebel charge before going down with a bullet in the side, an act that earned him a Medal of Honor. Much "Desperate Fighting" took place before a group of Confederates led by Capt. John M. Simpson of the 4th Arkansas reached the battery. Simpson climbed atop one of the Illinois cannons and exhorted his men to "Push Forward" before a Federal bullet knocked him to the ground, mortally wounded.[46]

For a few moments confusion reigned in the southeastern corner of Oberson's field as the Federals scrambled for cover and the Confederates sorted themselves. Davis abandoned his exposed position and dashed into Morgan's woods. Davidson's artillerymen lost the two cannons nearest Leetown Road but managed to save the other four. The Illinoisans retired about two hundred yards down the road then unlimbered and opened fire on their former position with canister. When the Confederates responded with a "shower of bullets" that struck down several Illinois gunners, Davidson ordered the remainder of his battery to fall back another hundred yards to the northern edge of Leetown. One of the cannons broke down and was left in the road.[47]

Hébert's exhausted, disorganized Confederates had achieved a limited but impressive tactical victory. They had broken up a small Federal brigade, captured part of a Federal battery, and breached the Federal line at its weakest point. Whether they could exploit that breach or even maintain their position without support from the rest of McCulloch's division remained to be seen. Whatever they decided, the Confederates would have to move quickly. In the woods to the east Pattison was leading his brigade around Hébert's unprotected left flank, and in Oberson's field to the west Osterhaus was wheeling his entire command toward Hébert's right flank.

7 A Battle Half Won

Hébert's four Confederate regiments had breached the thin Federal line in the vicinity of Leetown Road, but the Arkansas and Louisiana troops were disorganized and exhausted, the legacy of the desperate labors of the past four days. McNair realized that the rebel soldiers milling around the two cannons in the southeastern corner of Oberson's field were in a precarious situation. They were coming under renewed fire from the 37th Illinois and from the remaining cannons of Davidson's Peoria Battery. Even more alarming to McNair was the sight of fresh Federal infantry and artillery swinging into the field several hundred yards to the west. The Arkansas colonel ordered everyone to abandon the cannons and fall back across Leetown Road into the protection of Morgan's woods. As the rebels streamed away, they let out a ragged, spontaneous cheer. The men of the 37th Illinois responded with what one Louisiana soldier called a "still louder cheer of defiance," though the Federals were more likely yelling in triumph at the sight of the backs of their enemies.[1]

In the smoky thicket McNair and other officers of the 4th Arkansas and 3rd Louisiana attempted to re-form their muddled ranks amidst the crash of renewed Federal artillery fire. The disorganized attack on the battery and the disorderly withdrawal into the woods had transformed the right wing of Hébert's command into an armed mob. Capt. W. L. Gunnells of the 3rd Louisiana tried to re-form the troops in his vicinity, but they paid him little attention. William Watson, also of the 3rd Louisiana, reported that the men of his company were "in considerable confusion or mixed up, and there did not seem to be any movement towards forming us into order again." Watson was correct in sensing that something was amiss with the 3rd Louisiana. Maj. Will Tunnard, the popular and able regimental commander, had fallen victim to exhaustion. At some point during the firefight with White's 2nd Brigade he had sunk quietly to the leafy forest floor and had been left behind. Only now was his absence noticed and felt. Tunnard was not an isolated case. Numerous other Confederates were so utterly worn out that they collapsed or wandered aimlessly about in a dazed condition.[2]

The situation was somewhat better on the Confederate left. The troops there had not been so heavily engaged, and they still maintained reasonably coherent formations. Hébert was near the left flank of the 3rd Louisiana vainly trying to bring the lagging 14th and 15th Arkansas into proper alignment with the Louisianans. During the course of the advance, he had sent away his staff officers, one after the other, in a fruitless effort to contact McCulloch and bring up supporting units. Hébert now had only one officer by his side, and that man had lost his horse and was crippled with a broken arm. Hébert's own horse had been hit so many times that it "was hardly able to stand up," and he had abandoned it. Despite heroic exertions the Louisiana colonel was losing control of his command.[3]

Amid the general breakdown of order and discipline Confederate enlisted men loudly expressed their opinions and offered suggestions to their officers. Some announced that the only proper course was to stand firm and sell their lives as dearly as possible, while others proposed falling back toward Little Mountain. Overcome with frustration a Louisiana captain cried, "Would to God it was night or reinforcements would come."[4]

Unfortunately for the Confederates, neither would happen. Three hours of daylight remained, and fully two-thirds of McCulloch's division—twelve regiments and battalions of infantry and cavalry—remained immobile half a mile to the north awaiting orders that never came. The failure to support Hébert's attack sealed the fate of the Confederates at Leetown.[5]

McNair and his troops returned to the cover of Morgan's woods just as four companies of the 4th Missouri Cavalry launched a halfhearted charge in their direction. This odd episode in the battle occurred, at least indirectly, because of Franz Sigel. After sending the 3rd Iowa Cavalry back to Leetown, Sigel had gone to the section of the Little Sugar Creek fortifications manned by units of the 1st and 2nd Divisions with Asboth in overall command. After ascertaining that Asboth's front was quiet, Sigel directed Maj. Emeric Meszaros to take his battalion of the 4th Missouri Cavalry and the remaining two twelve-pounder howitzers of the 1st Missouri Flying Battery at once to Leetown to support Osterhaus. When Sigel learned that Davis's 3rd Division was marching to Leetown, he instructed Meszaros to send the cannons back to Little Sugar Creek but to continue with his horsemen. At Leetown Meszaros waited for the men and guns of the 3rd Division to pass and then followed in their wake up Leetown Road. He halted his command a short distance south of Oberson's field without reporting to Osterhaus.[6]

The troopers in the 4th Missouri Cavalry believed Meszaros to be an officer of "courage and experience," but the major demonstrated his true colors when White's 2nd Brigade went into action in the thicket. He was unnerved by the sight of Federal casualties streaming down the road toward the hospitals in Leetown. An officer in the battalion recalled that "the noise of arms came nearer, paused a moment, then opened almost by our side." Overwhelmed, Meszaros ordered his battalion back toward Leetown. One of Davis's staff officers saw the retreat and rushed down the road with drawn saber, shouting for the cavalrymen to halt. Most did so, and only about twenty-five troopers followed Meszaros all the way into the village. After a while the major seemed to recover his nerve and rode back to the head of the battalion.[7]

By this time the Confederates had taken and abandoned Davidson's two cannons and were falling back into Morgan's woods east of Leetown Road. Davis hoped that the retreat might be turned into a rout with one good push. He rashly directed Meszaros to attack directly up the road, ignoring the obvious facts that the cavalry would have to advance in column and would not be able to pursue the enemy into the thicket. Meszaros gave the order to charge and then, true to form, "fell back and disappeared from our sight."[8]

The 250 leaderless Missourians drew their sabers and moved forward on the narrow road in column of fours. They made their way around the remaining guns of the Peoria Battery and across the front of the 37th Illinois, forcing both the artillery and the infantry to cease firing. As the Federal cavalrymen neared the corner of Oberson's field, they changed from a trot to a gallop. The surprised Confederates opened fire. Suddenly the "'ping, zip, zip' of the bullets was like a hailstorm," recalled Lt. William A. Burns. "I had never heard them before, and at first did not know what the sound was, but when I did realize it, I thought how pleasant a 'furlough' would be just now."[9]

The attack quickly fell apart. Burns and six enlisted men at the head of the column actually came within a few yards of the rebel infantrymen before breaking off to the west and dashing to safety across Oberson's field. Burns had a particularly memorable ride: "I found my sabre useless, as I could not get near a rebel, on account of the plunging and rearing of 'Genero,' and in the excitement of the moment, I threw it down, and drew my revolver, my cap flew off, my foot came out of the stirrup, and 'Genero' was plunging at such a rate, I could not catch the stirrup, so I leaned over and took the strap in my hand and inserted my foot again, wondering all the time why one of those singing bullets did not strike me."[10]

Most of the Missouri cavalry veered into the brush on either side of the road south of the field. They forced their way through the lines of the 37th Illinois and retreated in complete disorder to Leetown. There Meszaros reappeared and led his command back toward Little Sugar Creek. The 4th Missouri Cavalry suffered five killed, eight wounded, and three missing at Pea Ridge, probably all in this senseless attack.[11]

The abortive charge by the 4th Missouri Cavalry coincided roughly with the start of Pattison's attack against the Confederate left. Deep in Morgan's woods, five or six hundred yards east of Leetown Road, Pattison's 1st Brigade turned north on another of the lanes that crisscrossed Pea Ridge. Trees and brush concealed the Federals and preserved the element of surprise. By about 3:00 P.M. the Hoosiers were facing west with Lt. Col. Henry D. Washburn's 18th Indiana on the right and Lt. Col. John A. Hendricks's 22nd Indiana on the left. Pattison gave the word to advance, and the troops thrashed through the thicket toward the foe. The unsuspecting Confederates did not realize they were under attack until the Federals approached to within fifty yards and opened fire. Hébert's left flank was thrown into total confusion, and for several minutes the yankees were in control. "They were in a thick brushwood and we could not see them, only occasionally," remarked E. E. Johnson of the 18th Indiana, but "we peppered them down as fast as we could see them."[12]

This part of Davis's impromptu plan worked perfectly, and Pattison's 1st Brigade was on the verge of a textbook tactical success. The Federals were heading directly toward Hébert's left and left rear; the 18th Indiana's right flank actually extended north of the Confederate position. If the Federals continued advancing westward, they would roll up the disorganized Confederate line and win a stunning victory. Unfortunately, in the dense woods Pattison did not realize what an opportunity lay before him. Moreover, his command numbered fewer than a thousand men who had very little combat experience. The Federals gradually ground to a halt as they encountered mounting opposition from a dimly seen foe in a tangled thicket. The advance degenerated into a stationary exchange of fire after Washburn ordered his 18th Indiana to lie down and fight from a prone position.[13]

When Pattison's 1st Brigade suddenly appeared with muskets blazing, many rebels in the 14th and 15th Arkansas broke and fled northward in complete disorder, but others stood their ground and fought back. Hébert, Mitchell, and McRae responded to this crisis by changing front to the east with the 14th and 15th Arkansas and several companies of the 3rd Louisiana, essentially every available soldier who had not taken part in the assault on the Peoria Battery. The result of these frantic maneuvers in the thick woods was an irregular but nonetheless formidable line of battle that slowed and then stopped the Federals.[14]

Like McCulloch and McIntosh before him, Hébert personally led some of his troops in a blind thrust toward the enemy. The rebel counterattack consisted of troops from the 3rd Louisiana and 14th Arkansas and struck the unsupported left flank of the 22nd Indiana at an angle. When the flank gave way, the entire regiment fell back, company by company. A similar fate had befallen White's two Illinois regiments earlier in the fight. The blind, desperate encounter was terribly unnerving to the inexperienced Federals. An Indiana officer wrote that "a sheet of fire, volumes of smoke and the incessant roar of musketry, almost stifled our senses and shut out the light of the sun."[15]

Hendricks sent an aide, Randolph Marshall, to inform Pattison of the pressure on his left and ask for help. As Marshall dashed along the line, he turned and saw that Hendricks was "closely observing every movement, looking well to his lines and delivering his orders in person, exhorting his men to be deliberate and courageous." It was the last time he saw Hendricks alive. Marshall reached Pattison a few minutes later and found the brigade commander trying to observe what he could through the smoke and brush.[16]

Pattison offered only encouragement to Marshall: "Tell Col. Hendricks to hold his position—to move only as the 18th moves, and to act in conjunction with it." Managing to keep his head despite the hellish din and ghastly scenes of battle, Marshall was on his way back to the 22nd Indiana when he met Hendricks's orderly stumbling toward him with terrible news: Hendricks had received a fatal wound in the chest from an old-fashioned musket ball.[17]

With Hendricks dead and Maj. David W. Daily serving on Pattison's staff,

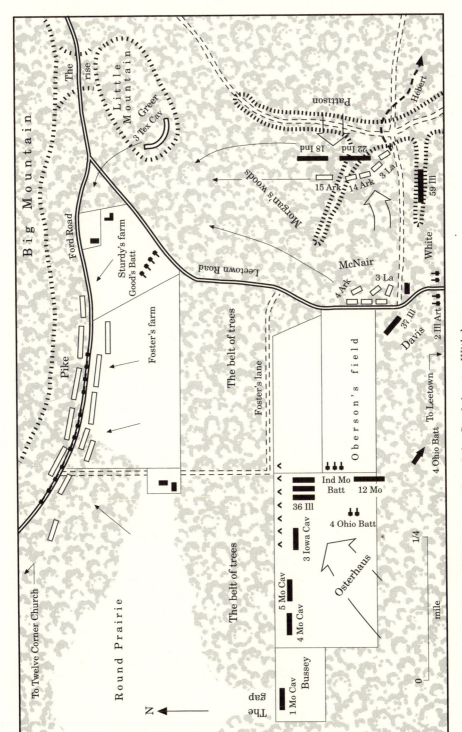

Map 7-1. Leetown: The Federals Counterattack and the Confederates Withdraw

the 22nd Indiana was leaderless. Company officers did their best but could not stop the regiment from drifting back. The Confederates felt the enemy giving way and pressed ahead. "At the flash of the enemy's guns," wrote Capt. Jerome Gilmore of the 3rd Louisiana, "the men would rush madly on them, routing them from behind logs, stumps and trees, shooting them at almost every step." The 18th Indiana remained in place while the 22nd Indiana fell back, opening a sizable gap between the two regiments.[18]

Hundreds of Confederates blindly pushed into the gap and passed behind the 18th Indiana. Faced with a bizarre situation not covered in any infantry manual, Washburn coolly ordered his men to stay on the ground and worm around to fire on any rebels who presented themselves in the regiment's rear. The leaderless rebels were more interested in escaping than fighting. They drifted in a northeasterly direction until they emerged from the woods northwest of Little Mountain. Not long afterward McRae arrived with hundreds more dazed, exhausted survivors from his 15th Arkansas and other regiments. As the senior officer, he sorted the men into their proper units and awaited further orders from Hébert.[19]

Such orders would not be forthcoming. While most of the charging Confederates pushed through the gap between the two Hoosier regiments, a smaller group led by Hébert, which included Colonel Mitchell of the 14th Arkansas, became disoriented in the smoky thicket and drifted to the southeast around the crumpled left flank of the 22nd Indiana. Every step took the rebels deeper into the woods and farther from their comrades. Hébert wandered from McCulloch's division without ever realizing that it was his to command.[20]

The brief, savage encounter deep in Morgan's woods was another disaster for the Confederates. Hébert was knocked out of the fight, and the left wing of his command was shattered. The Federals recovered fairly quickly from the confused spasm of fighting. Major Daily assumed command of the 22nd Indiana and brought the regiment back into line with the 18th Indiana. Shortly thereafter the 1st Brigade resumed its advance toward Leetown Road without meeting any significant opposition. Although the two Indiana regiments failed to exploit their initial advantage and were roughly handled by the spirited rebel counterattack, they had dealt Hébert's command a fatal blow.[21]

While Pattison's troops crashed into the Confederates in Morgan's woods, Osterhaus wheeled Greusel's command into Oberson's field and changed front from north to east. This maneuver would not have been possible had the Confederate forces in the belt of trees west of Leetown Road remained in place and continued to threaten Greusel's command. When those forces fell back to Foster's farm after the deaths of McCulloch and McIntosh, Osterhaus was free to maneuver as he wished. Thus Hébert's command was boxed in from three directions: east, south, and west.

The artillerymen of Welfley's Independent Missouri Battery moved their three twelve-pounder howitzers to the middle of Oberson's field. They drew a bead on the Confederate position in Morgan's woods, less than four hundred yards to the east, and opened fire with every type of shot and shell in their ammunition chests.[22]

The 12th Missouri changed front at the same time. The move was anticipated by Sgt. Henry A. Kircher, in temporary command of Company A on the extreme right of the regiment. When the rebels overran the Peoria Battery, Kircher re-fused his company so that it faced east at a right angle to the rest of the regiment. Kircher thought the move was proper under the circumstances, but he anxiously peered down the line to see if Colonel Wangelin would approve of his initiative. He saw Osterhaus and Wangelin together on horseback near the left of the regiment. Osterhaus pointed repeatedly toward the rebels then rode away. Wangelin turned and shouted a series of commands. The 12th Missouri scrambled over the fence and carried out a perfect right wheel until the entire regiment was facing east in line with Kircher's Company A and Welfley's Independent Missouri Battery. Kircher later proudly informed his mother that he had taken the lead and the rest of the regiment had conformed to his movement: "*I* did it and saved the day." The 12th Missouri opened a "raging fire" on Morgan's woods, and Kircher reported that "the secesh were strangled by our bullets," though in fact the rebels probably suffered few casualties from this blast of long-range musketry.[23]

Osterhaus directed Hoffman to withdraw the four brass rifled guns of the 4th Ohio Battery and place them in reserve in Leetown and to wheel the two twelve-pounder howitzers into the field behind the 12th Missouri. Osterhaus did this to shore up the sagging Federal center—more precisely, the left of Davis's 3rd Division—and to allow Greusel more room to maneuver in Oberson's field.[24]

On the left of Osterhaus's new line, as before, was the 36th Illinois. Greusel marched his large regiment across the field and deployed it in column of battalions facing east. The Illinoisans joined the Missourians in spraying the thicket with "a terrific shower of lead." Nervous about being so close to the belt of trees, Greusel fell back on a tried-and-true procedure and placed several companies of skirmishers along the fence on the northern side of Oberson's field. Osterhaus, too, was edgy. To provide additional protection for the left and left rear of Greusel's command, which was now perpendicular to its original position, he advanced Bussey's reconstituted cavalry force, giving the overall Federal formation in Oberson's field the shape of an inverted L.[25]

The rebels along the edge of Morgan's woods were dismayed by the sight of this solid line of infantry and artillery alive from one end to another with flaming muzzles. McNair, nearly numb with fatigue, concluded that there were at least five thousand fresh Federal troops in the field and that the rebels could only retreat or risk being cut off. Unable to locate Hébert or any other officer above the rank of captain, McNair assumed command of the troops in his vicinity and told them it was time to go. "Stick to me and I will take you out or freeze," he shouted as the withdrawal began—appropriate words considering the weather. McNair and his men hurried north through the woods as fast as their weary legs would permit, shoulders hunched against the hail of metal and splinters. Hébert's attack was over; the thin blue line had held.[26]

As the Confederates streamed away toward Ford Road, the two Indiana regiments of Pattison's 1st Brigade resumed their advance through the smoky woods. The Federals encountered an unexpected hazard as they slowly pushed west toward Leetown Road: rifle and artillery fire from their compatriots in Oberson's field. The color guard of the 18th Indiana held their tattered national and regimental colors aloft through breaks in the foliage and frantically waved them back and forth. The rifles and cannons in the field fell silent one by one as the colors were recognized, and Osterhaus reported that the "emblem of our country was hailed with enthusiastic cheers by the brave men around me." White's re-formed 2nd Brigade finally advanced as well. The two Illinois regiments swept northward behind the Hoosiers until they reached the place where they had gone into action three hours earlier. There was no Confederate resistance.[27]

The Confederate cavalry north of the belt of trees endured an agonizing afternoon awaiting orders, as instructed by McIntosh just before he rode to his death. Those orders never came. The cavalrymen were mystified when the infantry regiments west of Leetown Road emerged from the belt of trees, halted for a time in their original positions, and then fell back across Foster's farm toward Ford Road. "We knew from the way the army was moving that something was wrong but had no idea we had lost both of our Generals," wrote a Texas horseman. Of all the confusion that resulted from the deaths of McCulloch and McIntosh, nothing was more devastating to Confederate fortunes at Leetown than the fact that so many regiments, battalions, and batteries stood idle all or part of the afternoon.[28]

The experience of the 6th Texas Cavalry was typical. The regiment's only action on March 7 was the initial attack against Bussey's force on Foster's farm. "No one seemed to know from that time on what we were there for," complained a soldier. Another Texan believed he knew the answer and called to his company commander, "Captain, let's charge them; that's what we are out for." The eager young soldier probably spoke for everyone in the regiment, including Colonel Stone, but without orders to move, the regiment was immobilized. As the minutes stretched into hours, Stone sent his aides to "every part of the field for orders," but they could not find anyone in authority. By midafternoon Stone and his Texans were "in the most perplexed condition and mental anguish."[29]

Pike was the ranking Confederate officer on the Leetown battlefield at this point, but he was not part of McCulloch's division or privy to Van Dorn's plans. Moreover, he was an inept amateur soldier who could not even control his two Indian regiments. Discipline had broken down among the Cherokees during and after the initial action on Foster's farm, and the howitzer fire from Greusel's line had driven them back into the woods north of the Round Prairie. From this location in the rear, according to one irate rebel, the Indians fired indiscriminately "at every one having on a blue coat, whether friend or foe." This was a considerable danger in an army in which a number of soldiers, including Van Dorn, were wearing blue. Pike managed to stop the shooting, but when he first attempted to recover Elbert's three cannons, he "could not induce a single man to assist in doing so." After haranguing the Cherokees for the better part of an hour Pike finally managed to get enough volunteers to drag the cannons up Foster's lane into the woods.[30]

Around 2:00 P.M. Pike and most of the 1st Cherokee Mounted Rifles left the woods and formed in the rear of the 9th and 11th Texas Cavalry and 1st Arkansas and 1st Texas Cavalry battalions on Foster's farm. Less than an hour later the entire force fell back to Ford Road and joined the 6th Texas Cavalry and the troops who had performed so poorly west of Leetown Road: the 16th and 17th Arkansas, the 1st and 2nd Arkansas Mounted Rifles, and the 4th Texas Cavalry Battalion.[31]

With so many Confederate staff and line officers in one place, word of McCulloch's death no longer could be kept secret. The shocking news passed from officer to officer and rippled through the ranks of the enlisted men. A stunned rebel wrote that the information "went from one to another in a low, mournful voice, scarcely above a whisper, *'McCulloch is dead!'*" After learning that McIntosh also was dead and that Hébert could not be found, Pike finally assumed nominal command around 3:00 P.M. and sent an Indian staff officer galloping off to tell Van Dorn. Stone, perhaps lacking confidence in Pike or his courier, dispatched the redoubtable Major Ross on a similar mission to inform Van Dorn "of the true condition of our end of the field." Of the two officers only Ross reached Elkhorn Tavern and delivered his message.[32]

Pike's brief period of command at Leetown was inglorious. He made no effort to resume the offensive or to support Hébert's command, which was being hammered by Federal counterattacks in Morgan's woods, and he abandoned an attempt to form a defensive line along Ford Road when someone pointed out that the position could be flanked on either side. Pike soon concluded that all was lost at Leetown and the only sensible move was to carry out the original plan and join forces with Price's division at Elkhorn Tavern. Between 3:30 and 4:00 P.M. he gathered some—but not all—of the units immediately at hand and led them north toward Twelve Corner Church. At the church most of the column turned east on the Bentonville Detour and proceeded slowly around Big Mountain to Cross Timber Hollow. About two thousand men went east with Pike: the 16th and 17th Arkansas, the 1st Arkansas Mounted Rifles, the 4th Texas Cavalry Battalion, the 2nd Cherokee Mounted Rifles, and Good's Texas Battery. Another twelve hundred men went in the opposite direction: the 6th Texas Cavalry, the 1st Texas Cavalry Battalion, the 1st Cherokee Mounted Rifles, and Provence's Arkansas Battery turned west at Twelve Corner Church and headed toward the army's trains at Camp Stephens. The commanders of the 9th and 11th Texas Cavalry, the 2nd Arkansas Mounted Rifles, the 1st Arkansas Cavalry Battalion, and Gaines's and Hart's Arkansas batteries refused to obey Pike's order to withdraw and kept their units on Ford Road.[33]

Disobedience of a superior officer might be excused in this instance because Pike's behavior at Leetown verged on the incredible: while Hébert's unsupported command in Morgan's woods was fighting desperately to stave off disaster, Pike casually marched away from the battlefield with seven regiments and battalions and two batteries.

Meanwhile, half a mile to the east, Greer's 3rd Texas Cavalry waited on

Little Mountain. During their three hours on the hill the Texans became increasingly anxious—and not merely because of the harassing artillery fire from the Federal batteries in Oberson's field. "We knew that something was wrong because we were idle too long," wrote Douglas Cater. Greer, like Stone, repeatedly sent couriers in search of McCulloch and McIntosh, but to no avail. Around 3:00 P.M. Capt. William R. Bradfute, McCulloch's adjutant, made an appearance on Little Mountain but failed to inform Greer that McCulloch and McIntosh were dead. Bradfute's silence on this point is inexplicable: Greer was the second-ranking officer in the cavalry brigade after McIntosh and the fourth-ranking officer in the division after Hébert.[34]

Greer and Bradfute watched Arkansas and Louisiana infantrymen stream from Morgan's woods immediately to their right, dramatic evidence that Hébert's command was in trouble. Greer was alarmed by the sight and asked what McCulloch wanted him to do. According to Greer, Bradfute evasively replied that "if the troops on the right did not do better than they had done for the last few moments I had best move my command." Bradfute rode away after making this cryptic remark. Shortly afterward McRae rode up Little Mountain to warn Greer that Hébert's attack had collapsed and that a large force of Federals was counterattacking. Greer decided to pull back with the infantry and join the rest of the division. Sometime after 4:00 P.M. the men of the 3rd Texas Cavalry scurried down the rocky hill, mounted their horses, and retired in the wake of Hébert's beaten soldiers. They were the last Confederate regiment to fall back from the initial line of deployment.[35]

When Greer reached Ford Road and encountered the troops who had refused to depart with Pike, the Texas colonel finally learned that McCulloch and McIntosh were dead, that Hébert was missing and presumed dead, that Pike was gone with a large part of the division, and that he was the senior surviving officer of the division and the ranking officer on the field. The news must have been quite a shock.[36]

Greer assumed command and sent a staff officer galloping toward the Bentonville Detour "to halt and bring back" the errant units of McCulloch's division. But like so many Confederate messengers at Pea Ridge, this one also seems to have vanished without a trace. Though Greer had never commanded anything larger than his own regiment, he did what he could to retrieve the situation. He gathered together the survivors of the 4th, 14th, and 15th Arkansas, the 3rd Louisiana, and the 2nd Arkansas Mounted Rifles of Hébert's brigade; the 3rd, 9th, and 11th Texas Cavalry and the 1st Arkansas Cavalry Battalion of McIntosh's brigade; and Gaines's and Hart's Arkansas batteries, a total of about thirty-five hundred soldiers. Most of the units were "mere skeletons" whose men and animals were "exhausted with fatigue and the want of good food and water." Greer chose not to carry off the three Federal cannons captured on Foster's farm and ordered them disabled. Soldiers piled brush and fence rails around the cannons and set their carriages afire. Upon receiving a garbled report that the trains were threatened, Greer sent the 1st Arkansas Cavalry Battalion toward Camp Stephens, unaware that several regiments and a battery already were heading in that direction.[37]

The Confederates could not resume the offensive and could hardly maintain their present position. As late afternoon shadows crept across Foster's farm, Greer made the difficult but ultimately correct decision to leave the field. He led his tattered command north on Ford Road toward Twelve Corner Church. Between 5:00 and 6:00 P.M. Ross returned from Elkhorn Tavern with an order from Van Dorn for Greer "to hold his position at all hazards." It was too late; the battle of Leetown was over.[38]

After dispatching the 3rd Division to Leetown around midday, Curtis spent the next two hours at Pratt's store supervising his staff and pondering Van Dorn's peculiar tactics. Sometime after 2:00 P.M. a staff officer, Capt. Jason M. Adams, returned to headquarters from an inspection tour of the westernmost section of the Little Sugar Creek fortifications occupied by the 1st and 2nd Divisions. Adams reported that Sigel and Asboth had not seen any Confederates in Little Sugar Creek Valley since early morning. Curtis finally realized that he had underestimated the audacity of his opponent, and he was sure that the entire Confederate army had slipped around the Federal right flank during the night and was now engaged in a two-pronged attack on either side of Big Mountain. After reviewing the disposition of his troops and the overall tactical situation, Curtis concluded that Osterhaus, heavily reinforced by Davis, was strong enough to repel the enemy force near Leetown. But what about Carr at Elkhorn Tavern? Curtis stepped away from the crowd around his headquarters tent and listened intently to the sound of battle in Cross Timber Hollow. The crashing waves of noise seemed much louder than before, as if the fighting was moving closer to Pratt's store. Curtis returned to his headquarters and informed his staff that the time for cautious half-measures was over; he would concentrate his reserves against the "gathering hordes" of rebels on Telegraph Road.[39]

Then Curtis did something that belied his bold words. He mounted his horse and hurried off to visit Sigel. When Curtis reached the bluffs above

Little Sugar Creek, he found, to his immense relief, that the situation was just as Adams had reported: "All was quiet, and the men, not having been under fire [were] fresh and anxious to participate in the fight." Was Curtis mistrustful of Sigel after the events of the past few weeks, or was he simply in need of that extra bit of reassurance that only a personal reconnaissance could provide? Whatever the reason, the hurried trip to Little Sugar Creek seemed to restore the Federal commander's confidence in his own judgment.[40]

Curtis directed Sigel to take the bulk of the troops in the fortifications and proceed to Leetown as rapidly as possible. If Osterhaus and Davis needed help, he was to provide it, but his primary mission was "to press on to re-enforce Carr" at Elkhorn Tavern via Ford Road. This roundabout movement would take some time, particularly with the dilatory German in charge, so Curtis ordered the more dashing Asboth to take four companies of the 2nd Missouri and four six-pounder guns of the 2nd Ohio Battery and head directly for Elkhorn Tavern via Pratt's store. It was a very small command for a brigadier general, but this was no time to stand on military protocol. Curtis accompanied Asboth's little column, setting a brisk pace and "moving forward some straggling commands" that he encountered along the way. One of those "straggling commands" was Meszaros's hapless 4th Missouri Cavalry, which Curtis ordered to Carr's support.[41]

Despite the urgency of the situation, Sigel prepared carefully and deliberately for his first assignment of the day. He divided his troops into four detachments. Maj. August Poten of the 17th Missouri was put in charge of a force consisting of his own regiment, two companies of the 3rd Missouri and two of the 15th Missouri, two companies of the 5th Missouri Cavalry, and two twelve-pounder howitzers, all that remained of Elbert's 1st Missouri Flying Battery. Poten would advance down Little Sugar Creek Valley toward Camp Stephens. His mission was to "demonstrate against the rear of the enemy" and make absolutely certain that no rebel force was lurking down the valley waiting for the Federals to abandon the bluffs.[42]

In case Poten's force encountered more lurking rebels than it could handle, a second contingent consisting of the remaining six companies of the 2nd Missouri and two twelve-pounder howitzers of the 2nd Ohio Battery would stay atop the bluffs to hold the Federal rear and secure the camps of the 1st and 2nd Divisions. Capt. John Russell of the 44th Illinois would take a third contingent, two companies of the 44th Illinois and one cavalry company of the 36th Illinois, and scour the heavily wooded area between Leetown and Little Sugar Creek for infiltrators, by which Sigel apparently meant Indians. All of the remaining troops, the 15th Missouri, the 25th and 44th Illinois, and two twelve-pounder guns of Welfley's Independent Missouri Battery, would march directly toward Leetown under Sigel's personal direction.[43]

By 4:00 P.M. the various detachments of Sigel's command were in motion. After hours of unrelieved boredom on the bluffs many of the soldiers actually felt a "stern joy" at the prospect of going into battle.[44]

Major Poten and his small force proceeded cautiously down Little Sugar Creek Valley toward Camp Stephens. Unknown to the Federals, Camp Stephens was occupied by the Confederate ordnance and supply trains and an escorting force. The fate of these trains is one of the most curious aspects of the battle of Pea Ridge. The trains had fallen well behind the Army of the West during the difficult advance from the Boston Mountains and did not reach Camp Stephens until late morning on March 7, long after the last troops had set out on the Bentonville Detour. Brig. Gen. Martin E. Green of the Missouri State Guard, in command of the trains and the escort, was uncertain what to do or where to go. He followed in the army's wake on the Bentonville Detour for several miles and then returned to Camp Stephens about the time fighting erupted at Leetown. There he deployed his forces —his own 2nd Missouri State Guard Division and Capt. James W. Kneisley's Missouri Battery of five ancient cast-iron guns of varying size—and awaited orders. Instead of orders he received a stream of unexpected reinforcements. First to arrive was the 19th Arkansas, which had remained in the Boston Mountains when the rest of the army marched north. The Arkansans reached Camp Stephens in a state of total exhaustion after an almost non-stop march from Cove Creek.[45]

It was these untried Arkansans who first detected Poten's command moving down Little Sugar Creek Valley. Green spread his small contingent of troops across the valley and prepared to receive a Federal attack. Poten, however, was anything but aggressive. He advanced two companies of the 5th Missouri Cavalry on the valley floor and several companies of the 17th Missouri atop the northern bluffs. The two detachments probed toward the Confederate position but were halted by artillery fire from Kneisley's battery. Convinced that he was outgunned and outnumbered, Poten disengaged and retired to the fortifications without unlimbering his artillery or using more than a fraction of his infantry.[46]

Soon after this episode Green received additional reinforcements. The 20th Arkansas, another green regiment, followed in the wake of the 19th

Arkansas and arrived late in the afternoon. Then the 6th Texas Cavalry, the 1st Texas Cavalry Battalion, the 1st Cherokee Mounted Rifles, and Provence's Arkansas Battery drifted in from the debacle at Leetown, followed by the 1st Arkansas Cavalry Battalion. By nightfall Green's rear guard consisted of a heterogeneous collection of about three thousand men—nearly a fourth of the entire Confederate force at Pea Ridge. The trains were now exceedingly well protected, but they remained inert at Camp Stephens, dangerously distant from the rest of the Army of the West.[47]

While Poten and Green sparred in Little Sugar Creek Valley, Captain Russell's small force of Illinois infantry and cavalry beat the bushes ahead of Sigel's marching column in search of Cherokees and Choctaws. Southeast of the Leetown battlefield the Federals captured about thirty Confederates in Winton Springs Hollow. The catch included Colonels Hébert and Mitchell and other exhausted refugees from the confused fighting with Pattison's brigade in Morgan's woods. Capt. Henry Smith of the 36th Illinois later claimed that his company of horsemen could have captured hundreds more wandering rebels had they been allowed to continue searching, but Sigel ordered Smith to take the thirty prisoners to Pratt's store.[48]

By the time Sigel's command reached Leetown, it was after 4:30 P.M., and the firing north of the village had stopped. To the northeast, however, the roar of Carr's struggle at Elkhorn Tavern continued to reverberate across the woods and fields. While Sigel pondered his next move, Capt. Thomas I. McKenny of Curtis's staff galloped up and urgently requested more troops for Carr. Sigel promptly dispatched half of the 25th Illinois from his relief force along with the two howitzers of the 4th Ohio Battery. The small column moved off on Winton Hollow Road toward the sound of the guns.[49]

Sigel continued to the Leetown battlefield. He reached Oberson's field around 5:00 P.M. and congratulated Osterhaus and Davis on their victory. Command now passed to Sigel, who arranged for two covering moves to screen his march to Elkhorn Tavern. The 44th Illinois and the 15th Missouri swept through Morgan's woods toward Little Mountain. The nervous troops met no resistance but blasted away at any sign of movement in the darkening woods. Major Tunnard of the 3rd Louisiana, still too weak to walk, nearly became a victim of the skittish Federals. "On discovering me, one company fired a volley at me, the balls striking all around me, but fortunately none hitting my person," stated Tunnard. "I at once waved my handkerchief in token of my helpless condition." Tunnard was relieved of his sword and Colt revolver and sent to join his fellow Louisianans in captivity at Pratt's store.[50]

West of Leetown Road the 59th Illinois and the 18th and 22nd Indiana advanced through the belt of trees and across Foster's farm to Ford Road. Lieutenant Currie's company of the 59th Illinois encountered two badly wounded Confederates who begged the yankees not to bayonet them. Currie was shocked that the rebels would think him capable of such a crime. He provided them with water and sent for an ambulance. The Federals also flushed out a number of unwounded Confederate stragglers but met no resistance. The Leetown battlefield was secure, and Sigel was free to press on to Elkhorn Tavern. The battle of Pea Ridge was half won.[51]

8 Clash in Cross Timber Hollow

The fighting near Leetown on March 7 was only one part of the battle of Pea Ridge. Two miles to the east at Elkhorn Tavern a far more intense and costly struggle raged all that day and much of the next for control of Telegraph Road. There the outcome of the battle was decided.

Early on that decisive Friday, hours before the deaths of McCulloch and McIntosh and the repulse of Hébert's brigade at Leetown, the chain of events leading to the fighting at Elkhorn Tavern was set in motion. At about 10:30 A.M., during the council of war at Pratt's store, Curtis learned from Major Weston at Elkhorn Tavern that Confederate infantry was on Telegraph Road in Cross Timber Hollow. The news arrived less than an hour after Curtis had dispatched Osterhaus on the demonstration toward Twelve Corner Church. When Curtis discovered Dodge's 1st Brigade of the 4th Division standing in the road, he immediately instructed Carr to take the brigade and intercept the enemy force in Cross Timber Hollow.

Curtis sent Carr on his way with the cheery prediction that he would "clean out that hollow in a very short time." Carr was a West Point graduate and a regular army officer. During a decade of frontier service he had gained a reputation as an irascible subordinate—his superiors invariably described him as gloomy and argumentative—and a pugnacious fighter. Carr joined Dodge at the head of the blue column and set out toward Elkhorn Tavern, a little over a mile to the northeast.

Dodge's brigade consisted of the 3rd Illinois Cavalry, the 4th Iowa and the 35th Illinois, and the 1st Iowa Battery, around fourteen hundred men in all. The troops had been standing in the cold for over an hour and probably welcomed the chance to move; they maintained a brisk pace despite having to march up a slight incline most of the way to the tavern. With every step the sound of gunfire grew louder.[1]

Carr trotted ahead of the column to familiarize himself with the lay of the land. On this part of Pea Ridge the plateau is slightly more eroded and inclines more steeply toward Little Sugar Creek than is the case north of Leetown. The dominant feature is Big Mountain, whose rocky eastern face rises 170 feet above the plateau and 1,610 feet above sea level. At the time of the battle most of the plateau was covered with the familiar scrubby forest of hardwoods, brush, and vines.

The most prominent structure in the area was Elkhorn Tavern, a white, two-story hostelry named for the huge set of antlers fixed atop its roof. The tavern and its outbuildings were located in a sizable clearing on Telegraph Road near two important junctions. Directly in front of the tavern was the western terminus of Huntsville Road, which extended southeast toward the distant seat of Madison County. A quarter of a mile south was the eastern terminus of Ford Road. The intersection of Telegraph and Ford roads is the northeastern corner of the rough parallelogram of roads linking various points on the battlefield.[2]

A large irregular open area lay between Elkhorn Tavern and Pratt's store, most of it west of Telegraph Road. The clearing was composed of a dozen adjacent fields belonging to Benjamin Ruddick, Jesse Cox, George Ford, and other local inhabitants. On the morning of March 7 these broad fields were covered with hundreds of wagons and thousands of draft animals—the vital trains that just barely kept the Army of the Southwest supplied. Rufus Clemon's modest farm occupied a small clearing east of the tavern on Huntsville Road. All else was forest.

Immediately north of the tavern the Pea Ridge plateau ends and the ground descends nearly three hundred feet to the floor of Cross Timber Hollow. The forested slope below the edge is deeply cut by a fanlike series of ravines that come together to form the upper end of the hollow. At the mouth of the deepest of these ravines in 1862 was a small tanyard. Between the ravines are descending ridges of limestone. The ridges vary in width but are similar in profile. At their upper ends they slope gently downward from the edge of the plateau for about two hundred yards in a northerly direction. A

Eugene A. Carr
(Massachusetts Commandery, U.S. Army Military History Institute)

fairly level bench extends northward for another two hundred yards, and then the ridges descend precipitously to the floor of the hollow. Telegraph Road runs between the tavern and the tanyard along the top of one of these formations, Narrow Ridge. A short distance to the east is Broad Ridge, a considerably larger formation. The ravines that define these two principal ridges are, from west to east, Tanyard Ravine, Middle Ravine, and Williams Hollow. The first of these ravines is deep, rugged, and steep-sided; the latter two are somewhat less difficult of passage. The vegetation on the ridges and in the ravines was, and is today, timber and vines with relatively little underbrush.[3]

At Elkhorn Tavern Carr surveyed the surrounding terrain with the practiced eye of a regular soldier and realized that there was no better place on Pea Ridge to fight a defensive battle. This discovery determined his tactics: he would make no rash attempt to clean out Cross Timber Hollow, as Curtis had suggested, but would deploy Dodge's brigade along the northern edge of the plateau and await the rebels. His troops would have the high ground, would be able to move laterally along level terrain, and would have a direct line of communication with Curtis and the rest of the army via Telegraph Road.

Major Weston briefed Carr on the situation. Not long after meeting with Curtis earlier that morning, Weston learned that a column of rebel cavalry was in Cross Timber Hollow. He promptly sent Capt. Robert W. Fyan's company of the 24th Missouri into the hollow to stop the southerners. Near the tanyard the Federals spotted dark-clad horsemen approaching along Telegraph Road. Fyan hesitated, fearing that the riders might be a Federal patrol from Keetsville, but a blast of shotgun and pistol fire convinced him that he was in the presence of the enemy. Pvt. John Franklin of the 24th Missouri fell wounded immediately, the first known casualty of the battle. As the two sides scrambled for cover, Fyan called for reinforcements. Weston ordered four more companies of the 24th Missouri to Fyan's relief, and in less than an hour a sizable firefight was in progress at the base of the hill.[4]

A little after 10:00 A.M. another runner from Fyan came panting up the hill with the ominous news that Confederate infantry was approaching. Now thoroughly alarmed, Weston sent a courier racing to warn Curtis that the rebel army, or a good part of it, was in the Federal rear on Telegraph Road. This was the message that caused Curtis to break up the council of war at Pratt's store and send Carr to Elkhorn Tavern.[5]

After alerting Curtis to the presence of rebel infantry, Weston sent the

Tanyard Ravine, looking northward down the slope that forms the head of this ravine (authors' collection)

24th Missouri's supply wagons and forty prisoners of war to the relative safety of Pratt's store. The Missouri major did not have the authority to order the army's trains from the broad fields south of Big Mountain or to begin removing the tons of supplies stored in the tavern and its outbuildings, but his decision to send the stores and noncombatants under his immediate command southward was correct. Soon a much larger exodus would be under way as the Army of the Southwest carried out its extraordinary change of front.[6]

While Weston was relating this information to Carr, the picket on Huntsville Road reported rebel cavalry moving up Williams Hollow about a mile east of the tavern. Carr's first order of business clearly was to establish his defensive line and stretch it as far east as possible. When the head of the 1st Brigade reached Elkhorn Tavern, Carr directed Dodge to turn right onto Huntsville Road and form an interrupted line of battle facing north.[7]

By 11:30 A.M. Dodge had deployed his 950 infantrymen and 310 cavalry-men along the edge of the plateau just north of Huntsville Road. Col. Gusta-

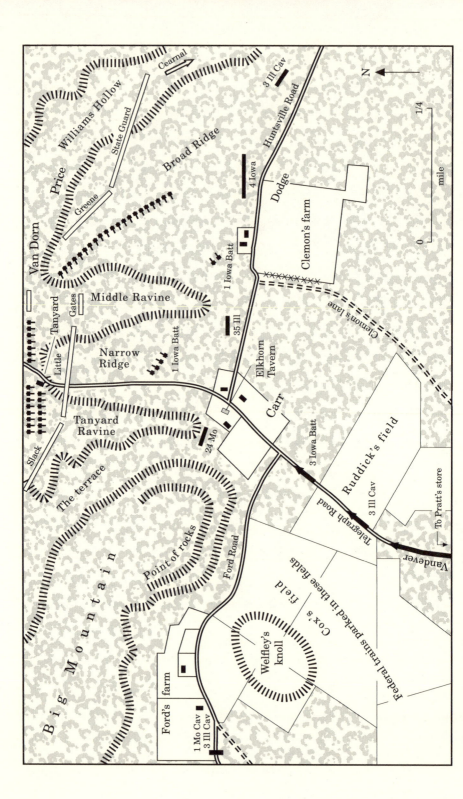

Map 8-1. Elkhorn Tavern: Van Dorn and Carr Deploy

vus A. Smith's battalion-sized 35th Illinois was on the left between Telegraph Road and Middle Ravine; Lt. Col. John Galligan's larger 4th Iowa was on the right to the east of Clemon's log cabin. The two regiments were separated by a gap of at least two hundred yards. Two six-pounder guns of Capt. Junius A. Jones's 1st Iowa Battery unlimbered near the center of the Iowa line and commenced shelling Williams Hollow where the rebel cavalry had been sighted. This was the artillery fire that Bussey's men heard as they rode toward Foster's farm. The two battalions of Maj. John J. McConnell's 3rd Illinois Cavalry were posted farther out along Huntsville Road near the head of Williams Hollow to protect the vulnerable flank and report on rebel activity in that direction. While Dodge's brigade filed into place, Carr ordered Fyan to disengage and hurry back up the hill to the tavern with his battalion of the 24th Missouri. Carr placed the Missourians and one company of the 4th Iowa west of Telegraph Road across the head of Tanyard Ravine. The remaining two six-pounder guns and two twelve-pounder howitzers of the 1st Iowa Battery were held in reserve near the tavern.[8]

After the deployment was complete, Carr could see that even with the advantage of high ground his force was wholly inadequate to the task at hand. If Fyan's report of Confederate infantry was accurate, one slim Federal brigade would not be enough to hold the rebels in check, much less send them packing. Carr sent a message to Curtis explaining the situation and asking for the other half of the 4th Division. Curtis agreed with Carr's assessment and called up Col. William Vandever's 2nd Brigade from the fortifications overlooking Little Sugar Creek.[9]

Carr estimated that it would take at least an hour for the 2nd Brigade to arrive, enough time for the Confederates to assault and possibly sweep away the sketchy Federal line at the tavern. Reasoning that a bold spoiling attack might well catch the rebels off balance and throw them into confusion, Carr decided to abandon his passive stance and carry the fight to the enemy. This move was much more in keeping both with Carr's combative nature and with the aggressive spirit of Curtis's instructions and was essentially identical to what Osterhaus was doing on Foster's farm two miles to the west. Carr personally led two six-pounder guns of the 1st Iowa Battery into the hollow on Telegraph Road. He placed the guns just east of the road on the relatively level bench on Narrow Ridge about three hundred yards forward of the edge of the plateau.[10]

From his advanced position Carr saw line after line of infantry trudging up the forested slope. Any lingering doubts he might have had about the size or

Huntsville Road, looking west toward Elkhorn Tavern. Along this section of the road, the 35th Illinois desperately held on against Price's attacks from the north, or right, of this view. (authors' collection)

seriousness of the Confederate attack were put to rest. Carr sent for the two remaining artillery pieces and ordered Dodge to advance with his entire brigade as soon as possible. Then he told his Iowa cannoneers to select their targets and to open fire. The preliminary skirmishing was over; the first phase of the battle for control of Telegraph Road was under way.[11]

Everything had gone smoothly for the Confederates after reaching Telegraph Road earlier that cold, clear morning. Price's weary Missourians pushed south in Cross Timber Hollow for nearly two miles without encountering any Federals other than a bewildered foraging party that was quickly captured and sent to the rear. It seemed almost too good to be true. They were marching unseen and unmolested into the Federal rear in broad daylight. Van Dorn, ever the optimist, managed to convince himself that his army was "not expected in that quarter, and that the promise was fair for a complete surprise."[12]

The first inkling that the Federals were aware of the Confederate presence came near the tanyard at the foot of the slope that led up to Elkhorn

Tavern. Troopers of Cearnal's Missouri Cavalry Battalion, riding well ahead of the infantry, rounded a bend and collided with Fyan's company of the 24th Missouri, which Weston had dispatched to block the road. The rebel horsemen in the front ranks did not expect to find a line of infantry in their path, but they recovered quickly and blasted away with pistols and shotguns. The Federals responded with a sharp volley of rifle fire that wounded Cearnal and drove his cavalrymen into the protective cover of the thick woods lining the road. The sudden burst of gunfire brought Gates's 1st Missouri Cavalry and Shelby's company of state guard cavalry galloping up in support, but the whizzing bullets caused them to abandon the road and join Cearnal's men in the trees.[13]

Van Dorn, riding with Price at the head of the Missouri infantry, reached the tanyard sometime after 10:00 A.M. The Confederate position three hundred feet down in the rocky depths of Cross Timber Hollow was very much like being at the bottom of a well. Van Dorn could not see what was happening atop Pea Ridge and had no way of knowing that Federal reinforcements —Dodge's brigade—were marching up Telegraph Road toward Elkhorn Tavern. At this critical moment the Confederate commander, heretofore obsessed with speed, became unnerved by his blindness and made a fateful decision. Instead of continuing to advance toward Elkhorn Tavern and the expected rendezvous with McCulloch's division, Van Dorn directed Price to halt, deploy his entire division in line of battle, and "move forward cautiously." It probably was the most uncharacteristic order he ever issued, and it gave the Federals the one thing they needed most—time.[14]

What Old Pap thought of this is not known. He told Colonel Little of the 1st Missouri Brigade to form a line of battle centered on Telegraph Road. Col. Benjamin A. Rives's 3rd Missouri marched right up the road onto Narrow Ridge while Col. John Q. Burbridge's 2nd Missouri moved into the V-shaped canyon of Tanyard Ravine just to the right. Gates's 1st Missouri Cavalry filed into Middle Ravine to the left. As there seemed to be no need for artillery, Little kept his two batteries in reserve on the road near the tanyard. The Confederate deployment had barely begun when the Federal infantry withdrew up the hill.[15]

Price instructed Col. William Y. Slack to place his 2nd Missouri Brigade on Little's right. Slack formed his three infantry battalions into a ragged line of battle in the rugged terrain west of Tanyard Ravine. These were, from left to right, Maj. Robert S. Bevier's 3rd Missouri Battalion, Col. Thomas H. Rosser's 1st Missouri Battalion, and Col. John T. Hughes's 2nd Missouri Battalion.

Henry Little (Chicago Historical Society)

Slack also kept his two artillery batteries, along with his cavalry battalion, in reserve on the road.[16]

The Missouri general rode to the left up Williams Hollow and supervised the deployment of the remainder of his forces, primarily the state guard. Col. Colton Greene's unorganized 3rd Missouri Brigade, Brig. Gen. Daniel M. Frost's 7th and 9th State Guard divisions, Brig. Gen. James S. Rains's 8th State Guard Division, and Col. John B. Clark's 3rd State Guard Division moved into line to Little's left on Broad Ridge. Into Williams Hollow on the extreme left marched Col. James P. Saunders's 5th State Guard Division. Cearnal's Missouri Cavalry Battalion, now commanded by Maj. D. Todd Samuels, and Shelby's company advanced up Williams Hollow and probed toward Huntsville Road before being driven back by Federal artillery. Price kept Maj. D. Herndon Lindsay's tiny 6th State Guard Division in reserve near the tanyard. There appeared to be no need for the five state guard batteries on the left and no easy way of moving them forward except on the road, so they remained at the tanyard with the four Confederate batteries.[17]

The impressive array of divisions, brigades, regiments, battalions, and batteries obscured how severely Price's division, like McCulloch's, had been depleted by the rigors of the march. As best as can be determined, there were no more than five thousand desperately weary Missourians in Cross Timber Hollow on March 7.

While Price sorted his ragtag troops on the left, Little and Slack ordered their Missouri Confederates forward on the right. The tired, hungry soldiers had not encountered an incline so steep since leaving the Boston Mountains three days earlier, and they trudged ahead at a snail's pace. Men stumbled over loose fragments of flint covering Narrow Ridge, plowed through patches of snow on the shadowed slopes, and slipped on ice-covered rocks in the ravines on either side.

About three hundred yards from their starting point near the tanyard the Confederates were surprised to see a small Federal force descending Telegraph Road. It was Carr and the two cannons of the 1st Iowa Battery, well in front of the rest of Dodge's brigade. When the Federal gunners unlimbered and opened fire, Little and Slack halted their brigades and ordered their men to lie down to escape the blasts of solid and case shot that tore through the trees, showering everyone with bark, twigs, and leaves. Unused to firing downhill, the Iowans aimed too high and inflicted few casualties, but they halted the sluggish Confederate advance.[18]

Van Dorn, too, was surprised—perhaps even alarmed—at the presence of Federal artillery at Elkhorn Tavern. When the two yankee guns went into action on Narrow Ridge, he sent an aide to bring up the first battery he could find. Encountering a mass of guns and caissons at the tanyard, the flustered aide shouted, "Van Dorn wants a battery." On the basis of that rather informal order, Capt. Henry Guibor and his state guard battery followed the aide to the foot of Broad Ridge, where they enlisted the assistance of nearby infantrymen and wrestled their weapons up the slope until they reached "a very commanding position" slightly higher than the Iowans and barely three hundred yards to the northeast.[19]

This activity naturally attracted the attention of the Federal gunners. Hunt P. Wilson remembered how the Missourians struggled to deploy their two six-pounder guns and two twelve-pounder howitzers while the Iowans were "pouring in a well-directed fire, knocking off limbs of trees and tearing up the ground in fine style." Van Dorn himself rode up to Guibor, pointed toward the enemy cannons, and said that he wanted them silenced. Guibor responded with a soldierly, "Very well, sir. I will do the best I can." His four pieces soon went into action, and Van Dorn retired down the slope to his proper place in the rear, apparently satisfied with his contribution to the battle.[20]

Little also saw the need for quick action and called up his own artillery. After watching Guibor's cannons successfully ascend the ridge, Little ordered Capt. Churchill Clark's battery of four six-pounder guns and Capt. William Wade's battery of four twelve-pounder howitzers and two six-pounder guns to do the same. Clark and Wade manhandled their ten weapons into position to Guibor's left and joined the artillery duel.[21]

The curving line of Missouri artillery began "pouring its concentric shot and shell upon us with terrible effect," wrote Sam Black of the 1st Iowa Battery. "Any reply we could make seemed but feeble resistance." The odds evened slightly when Captain Jones, commander of the 1st Iowa Battery, arrived on the scene with the two twelve-pounder howitzers Carr had called up from the tavern. Jones was dismayed to find that the rebels had his Iowans "in perfect range of grape, shell, and shrapnel." Soon one of the Federal guns became disabled with a shell jammed halfway down the barrel and was withdrawn.[22]

Despite the loss of a cannon, Carr remained determined to hold his exposed position as long as possible. He knew Dodge's 1st Brigade was coming down the hill and would pitch in at any moment, and somewhere on this side of Little Sugar Creek Vandever's 2nd Brigade was marching toward the sound of the guns. "Give them hell boys," he shouted to the Iowans above the din. "Don't let them have it all their own way, give them hell."[23]

The barrage of Confederate fire soon took a severe toll on the 1st Iowa Battery. Guibor noticed that his gunners were shooting at the rising smoke from the enemy cannons and ordered his men to aim lower. The result of this rudimentary adjustment was spectacular. The ammunition chests on a Federal caisson exploded with a tremendous roar, creating an enormous cloud of smoke and dust and pelting the stunned Federals with debris. Moments later there was a second explosion as Guibor's gunners claimed the ammunition chest on a limber. Terrified horses bolted and dragged away another caisson, which tumbled into Tanyard Ravine. Everyone in blue was knocked flat by the blasts, but, miraculously, no one was killed. The Iowa gunners staggered to their feet and groped about in the murky twilight created by the smoke while the three Missouri batteries continued "pounding away with clocklike regularity." One by one the Federals were struck down by what Carr called a "perfect storm" of solid shot, case shot, grapeshot, shell, splinters, and rocks. Carr received three glancing but painful blows in the wrist, neck, and ankle; Captain Jones was disabled by a spent solid shot that hit him in the leg; and so many of his men were killed or wounded that the guns could not be served properly and the rate of fire decreased.[24]

Though it hardly seemed possible to the embattled Federals, the hail of projectiles increased as two more state guard batteries deployed on Broad Ridge: Capt. Emmett MacDonald's small battery of one six-pounder gun and two twelve-pounder howitzers and Lt. Charles W. Higgins's battery (also called Bledsoe's battery) of four twelve-pounder howitzers. Now the Missourians had twenty-one guns in action against three Federal guns. The advanced position of the 1st Iowa Battery had become untenable.[25]

"We stood in that tempest of death" for what seemed to be hours, said Sam Black. "I believe every man at the guns had made up his mind to die there, for it did not seem possible any of us could get out alive." Black himself had a narrow escape. A six-pound solid shot sailed out of the smoke, bounced twice, and headed directly toward him. "I saw it, and tried to dodge it, but was too slow motioned to escape." As Black twisted to the right, the ball struck him a glancing blow that broke his left ankle. The injured cannoneer crawled most of the way back to the tavern, desperately trying to keep the trees between himself and the deadly missiles.[26]

With his men and horses dropping on all sides and his ammunition nearly exhausted, Jones fixed prolonges and prepared to withdraw the moment

Carr gave the word. Just before leaving the field to seek medical attention, he ordered the ammunition chests on the overturned caisson in the ravine blown up. The exultant rebel cannoneers naturally believed this explosion, too, was the result of their handiwork and cheered mightily as the new pillar of flame and smoke rose through the trees.[27]

The soldiers of the 1st and 2nd Missouri brigades, huddled behind trees and rock ledges on both sides of Telegraph Road, had an uncomfortably close view of the proceedings. "We could distinctly see the red-shirted Federal cannoniers as they worked with a hearty will" at the outset of the engagement, recalled a member of Burbridge's regiment. A number of men directly between the dueling cannons were struck by errant shots and falling branches. For many of the Missourians this encounter was their first taste of the mind-numbing roar and fury of battle. One described how "some of our boys would laugh and mock the shells, and others were as pale as death, while still others had great drops of sweat on their faces." Even the greenest soldiers crouched on that hillside knew that sooner or later they would be called upon to stand and go forward into the flames and smoke and flying metal.[28]

The still, frigid air in Cross Timber Hollow failed to dissipate the smoke. A Missouri soldier noticed that the thick smoke forced the gunners of both sides into a peculiar rhythm. "At times there were more than twenty discharges of artillery within the space of one minute," he wrote, "and it would continue for some time and then there would be a cessation for a time, as the smoke would become so dense that all would be enveloped in darkness." As the fighting raged, the gray billows filled the gorge and then spilled over onto the plateau. "The smoke from the guns settled like a cloud upon the field," wrote a fascinated Federal observer, "and an hour after the beginning of the engagement the position of the enemy's cannon was oftentimes only to be ascertained by the dull red flash at the moment of discharge. As the day advanced this cloud grew more and more dense, and long before nightfall the contending masses of infantry were unable to discern each other, except at very short range." By all accounts the atmospheric and topographical conditions in Cross Timber Hollow combined to produce one of the murkiest battlefields of the Civil War.[29]

When the Federal gunners shifted their attention to Guibor's battery on the ridge, Little decided to act. Rather than advance directly ahead and expose his brigade to renewed artillery fire, he chose to outflank the unsupported Federal battery. Gates's 1st Missouri Cavalry was sheltered in Middle

Ravine two hundred yards east of the road. Little ordered Gates to proceed up the ravine to the top of the hill and either capture or force a hasty withdrawal of the enemy cannons. To cover the advance of the dismounted horsemen, Little ordered his infantry regiments to open fire on the Federal battery, or at least to shoot into the cloud where the battery had last been seen. Supported by a "terrific" blast of musketry, Gates's troopers ascended the ravine in a loose column, trailing their horses behind them. Soon they disappeared into the dense smoke to the left of the Federal battery and suffered the dangerous indignity of coming under fire from their comrades in the rear.[30]

Hastening forward through the twilight to escape from their misguided comrades, Gates and his men blundered into a line of blue infantry coming directly toward them. Some of the Missourians panicked and spread a fearful commotion along the length of the column. Within moments terrified men and animals were fleeing headlong back down the ravine. "The horses came galloping down the hill in riderless yet regular order, as if guided by unseen hands," observed Hunt Wilson from his artillery position. Not seeing a single man among the mounts, a shocked cannoneer exclaimed, "My God! They have all been killed!" He was proved wrong moments later when Gates and his men came tumbling down in a disorganized mass. Their unceremonious return accompanied by crackling volleys of rifle fire from up the slope demonstrated in the most dramatic fashion possible that the Federal cannoneers no longer were alone. The rest of Dodge's brigade had arrived.[31]

When Dodge ordered his line forward, he could only guess what he was getting into. Cross Timber Hollow was wooded and filling with smoke from the artillery exchange. Though the Iowa colonel could not see a thing, the tremendous racket below indicated that Carr had stirred up a sizable number of rebels. Dodge's uncertainties were compounded by an insoluble tactical problem. He had unknowingly deployed his two infantry regiments on different fingers of land, the 35th Illinois on Narrow Ridge and the 4th Iowa on Broad Ridge. As the Federals advanced, the regiments were forced farther and farther apart by Middle Ravine. Dodge could do little about this unforeseen development except to stretch a company of the 4th Iowa across the widening gap and hope for the best.[32]

The Illinois and Iowa troops pushed downhill at a slow but steady pace, struggling to stay aligned in the woods and to keep their footing on the snowy, flinty surface. They soon drove in rebel skirmishers across a broad front. Price was still on the left arranging his state guard forces and erroneously assumed the Federals were attacking in force on both sides of Telegraph Road. He directed some of his batteries to shift their fire to the oncoming enemy line of battle, dimly visible here and there through the haze, then ordered his entire division to close ranks and prepare to repel what he assumed to be a substantial Federal assault.[33]

Price thus played directly into Carr's hands. By abandoning the initiative and going over to the tactical defensive while still in Cross Timber Hollow, the Confederates lost whatever chance they might have had to reach Pea Ridge without a lengthy and costly struggle. Long after the campaign was over, they still failed to see their error and continued to boast that the rebel line "did not yield an inch of ground" to the imagined yankee onslaught.[34]

But there was no Federal attack. Dodge marched his command about a third of the way down the slope, halted more or less in line with Carr's position, and fired two or three volleys in the general direction of the enemy. Then he ordered his men to lie down and pick their targets more carefully, an optimistic directive, considering the murky conditions in the hollow. For roughly half an hour Dodge's stationary command skirmished heavily with the Missourians and endured a considerable artillery bombardment. "Grape and shell whistled over our heads pretty thick," wrote Capt. Henry Cummings of the 4th Iowa to his wife. Capt. William H. Kinsman of the same regiment described the action more colorfully: "The thunder of the artillery was terrific, and the shot and shell hissed and screamed through the air like flying devils, while the infantry with their rifles, shotguns, and muskets, kept a perfect hurricane of death howling through the woods." The Iowans on Broad Ridge suffered few casualties, however, because of the relatively long range and the protection afforded by the smoke and the trees.[35]

The situation was different on Narrow Ridge. Coming up behind and to the right of Carr's advanced position on Telegraph Road, the 35th Illinois walked into the hail of artillery fire and musketry directed at the 1st Iowa Battery. The fate of Colonel Smith, commanding the regiment, vividly illustrated what the Federal infantry endured on that portion of the field. Shortly after ordering his regiment to open fire, Smith's horse was killed under him, his sword was knocked from his hand, and his belt and scabbard were shot away. While waiting for a new mount, he was hit in the shoulder by a bullet and struck in the head by a shell fragment that fractured his skull. The colonel was carried back toward the tavern, bleeding profusely from his lacerated scalp. Command passed to Lt. Col. William P. Chandler.[36]

With most of the infantry and artillery on both sides now fully engaged, the noise in the rocky hollow was almost unendurable. "I never heard any-thing to equal it in any other battle," said one veteran after the war. "The incessant crash of musketry and roar of artillery, amid curtains of rising smoke, appeared both to sight and sound as if two wrathful clouds had descended to the earth, rushing together in hideous battle with all their lightning and thunder." This continued for perhaps half an hour, the Feder-als clearly getting the worst of it but holding the Missourians in check.[37]

Throughout March 7 Curtis maintained a confident demeanor "as if he felt an assurance of victory." In fact, the Federal commander was a bundle of nerves. He later described his true feelings in the oddly formal prose he always used in letters to his wife, Belinda. "The responsibilities resting on me caused me great anxiety, but at no time any emotion of terror or fright, and I felt conscious that I would be sustained by my friends under the cir-cumstances if I did my best without any exhibition of cowardice. But the terrible consequences to my troops, to Missouri, to the peace of Arkansas and our whole country, was constantly before me and augmented the bur-den of my cares more perhaps than at any other period of an eventful life." Curtis added a revealing personal detail in a letter to his older brother, Henry: "The three days were intensely interesting and anxious—I watched the minute hand of my watch a thousand times."[38]

Shortly after the fighting began, someone at the Federal headquarters pointed out that the battle as yet had no name. Various suggestions were made, such as Leetown, Sugar Creek, and Ozark Mountain, but Curtis con-sidered each of these unsatisfactory for one reason or another. During a lull in the discussion a Benton County unionist serving as a guide for the Fed-eral army offered his opinion: "Whatever you call it, the people here will call it the battle of Pea Ridge, for that is the name by which the ridge is known all through the country." After a moment's reflection Curtis made up his mind: "Better call it Pea Ridge then." The staff officers groaned at the homely appellation, thinking it lacked a suitably Napoleonic ring, but the undemon-strative Federal commander was satisfied. In fact, Curtis found the plain toponym appealing. "I like it," he said. "It is something new." And so Pea Ridge it would be, though no one thought to record the identity of the loyal Arkansan who christened one of the largest battles fought west of the Mis-sissippi River.[39]

With that pressing matter out of the way Curtis turned his attention back to the battle itself. Around 11:30 A.M. he became concerned over the increasing roar of artillery fire in Cross Timber Hollow and hurried up Telegraph Road to see how Carr was faring. Near Elkhorn Tavern an errant rebel shell screeched overhead, and some members of the general's cavalry escort ducked their heads. Curtis smiled grimly and said, "Boys you dodged too late."[40]

At the tavern Curtis learned that Carr was down in Cross Timber Hollow personally supervising the 1st Iowa Battery. To the consternation and admiration of his staff, the Federal commander trotted ahead "as cool and unconcerned as if on dress parade." Curtis later told Halleck that he found Carr "under a brisk fire of shot and shell, coolly locating and directing the deployment" of his limited forces. Exactly what the two officers shouted to each other over the tremendous din is not known, though Carr surely told Curtis that he was hard pressed, and Curtis just as surely urged him to hang on. Following this brief exchange Curtis sat on his horse on Telegraph Road and studied the dimly visible rebel line, unaware that he was facing his nemesis. At this hour Van Dorn was directly opposite Curtis about four hundred yards down Narrow Ridge. This might have been the closest the two generals came to each other during the battle. After a moment Curtis turned and ascended the hill.[41]

On the way back to Pratt's store Curtis seemed to notice the army's trains in Ruddick's field for the first time. Rebel gunners in Cross Timber Hollow were occasionally overshooting their marks and dropping shot and shell among the wagons and teams. The army's rear no longer was safe for the trains. Weston had sent his own wagons along with a batch of prisoners to Pratt's store two hours earlier. Curtis decided that the same thing had to be done on a vastly larger scale. He explained the situation to Assistant Quartermaster Capt. Byron O. Carr (the colonel's younger brother) and directed him to move the trains and the stores at the tavern away from the fighting.[42]

As Curtis rode away, Captain Carr grappled with the daunting logistics involved in turning the army around. As more and more artillery projectiles landed amidst the trains, men and beasts "were several times in iminent danger of stampeding and scattering in every direction." Carr eventually got the clumsy wagons and balky teams filing south on Telegraph Road. There were no large fields between Pratt's store and Little Sugar Creek, so Carr parked the trains in the roads and lanes, squeezing the wagons to one side to permit the passage of troops and artillery. While the trains inched away, Carr and a detachment of men and wagons hurried to retrieve the supplies stored in Elkhorn Tavern and its outbuildings.[43]

As Curtis approached Pratt's store, he encountered Vandever's 2nd Brigade marching up Telegraph Road to Carr's support. The appearance of Vandever's command meant that the 4th Division would be reunited within half an hour, doubling the number of Federal men and guns at Elkhorn Tavern. Still, if the volume of artillery fire was any indication of enemy strength in Cross Timber Hollow, Carr was up against a surprisingly large Confederate force. At this time, as related earlier, Curtis ordered Davis's 3rd Division to Elkhorn Tavern, only to rescind the order moments later when Osterhaus's urgent plea for help arrived from Leetown.

Van Dorn's attempt to seize the high ground at Elkhorn Tavern by stealth failed because of the rapid, pugnacious Federal response that brought Price's division to a halt just short of its goal. The Confederates now faced the difficult task of fighting their way out of Cross Timber Hollow against Carr's 4th Division, which would prove itself to be the most battleworthy unit in the Army of the Southwest. From the Federal perspective it was vital that Carr's command hold off the rebel onslaught as long as possible, for Curtis had sent the only readily available reinforcements to Leetown. For the time being, the troops at Elkhorn Tavern were on their own.

9 Perseverance beside a Tavern

The first Federal reinforcements to reach Elkhorn Tavern arrived around 12:30 P.M. The leading element of Vandever's 2nd Brigade was Capt. Mortimer M. Hayden's 3rd Iowa Battery. Hayden's unit was popularly known as the Dubuque Battery and consisted of four six-pounder guns and two twelve-pounder howitzers. When the little column of artillery rumbled up to the tavern, it was met by one of Carr's staff officers. He instructed Hayden to proceed down into Cross Timber Hollow and plant his cannons on Narrow Ridge a little above the churning cauldron marking the 1st Iowa Battery's advanced position.[1]

But before Hayden could move, Franz Sigel, of all people, commandeered two of his guns. Sigel was restless with nothing to do, and around midday he journeyed up Telegraph Road "to see how matters stood" at Elkhorn Tavern. He did not visit Carr but simply watched the fight for a time from the road in front of the tavern. When the 3rd Iowa Battery came up and halted practically by his side, Sigel saw his chance to make a contribution. He led two cannons around the tavern to the head of Tanyard Ravine and directed the artillerymen to open fire. He later made the pathetic claim that "after a few shots the fire of the enemy opposite our position became weaker, and I sent the two pieces forward to join their battery." Sigel then departed and traveled across Pea Ridge to join Asboth and elements of the 1st and 2nd Divisions on the bluffs above

Little Sugar Creek. Along the way he halted the unauthorized withdrawal of the 3rd Iowa Cavalry, as noted earlier.[2]

Hayden reported to Carr while his gunners unlimbered their weapons on Narrow Ridge. He informed Carr that the rest of Vandever's brigade was fast approaching. With relief finally at hand, Carr ordered the 1st Iowa Battery to pull out of the fight and replenish its depleted supply of ammunition. Jones's grimy cannoneers climbed out of Cross Timber Hollow, leaving their former position littered with dead horses and shattered equipment. Carr then instructed the 35th Illinois to fall back and establish a new line in support of the 3rd Iowa Battery. Next, he sent a message to Dodge to move the portion of the 1st Brigade on Broad Ridge back to its original position near Huntsville Road. Obscured by the smoke and shielded by the trees, the Federal units retired in good order and with few casualties through the barrage of enemy fire. After spending an hour with his artillerymen at the most exposed Federal position in the hollow, a gallant if foolhardy act that earned him a Medal of Honor, Carr followed his men back to the edge of the plateau and established a more suitable division command post in the tavern yard.[3]

The Missouri artillerymen on Broad Ridge turned their attention to the muzzle flashes marking the position of the 3rd Iowa Battery. The slightly increased range offered Captain Hayden and his men little protection, and they soon experienced the fate of the 1st Iowa Battery. This second artillery duel had barely begun when the "unearthful howl" of Confederate projectiles was punctuated by a terrific blast as an ammunition chest on a limber blew up. Correspondents Fayel and Knox rode up to the tavern at that moment. They felt the "tremendous concussion" and dramatically informed (or misinformed) their readers that "amid the cloud of smoke we imagined we saw the bodies of horses and men dropping down from the air." In fact, no one was killed or seriously injured in the explosion, but the battery soon lost a third of its firepower when solid shot smashed the carriages of a twelve-pounder howitzer and a six-pounder gun. As the crippled cannons were withdrawn, the Iowans continued to battle against impossible odds.[4]

Because the Confederates fired uphill at the 3rd Iowa Battery, a number of rounds sailed out of the hollow and landed on the plateau in the Federal rear. Fayel and Knox remained in front of the tavern during the height of the barrage, thereby gaining the distinction of being among the very few Civil War journalists to come under sustained enemy fire. The two men stoically sat on their horses at the junction of Telegraph and Huntsville roads and tried to absorb the chaotic scene, mustering all their will power to avoid ducking and dodging the misguided rebel fire. Years later Fayel still recalled with a shudder how projectiles of all sorts "screamed past, cutting the limbs in the grove behind us next to the tavern." Knox was busily jotting down impressions in a notebook when a shell shrieked just over his head and exploded a few yards away. He subsequently acknowledged that the blast "rendered my notes of that moment somewhat difficult to decipher."[5]

Elkhorn Tavern and its outbuildings were directly in the line of Confederate fire, but only one projectile is known to have struck the tavern, which by this time had been converted into a hospital. A solid shot crashed into a second-story bedroom and angled downward, without hurting anyone, until it came to rest in the hearth on the southern side of the building. After that close call Carr ordered the wounded in the tavern removed to a safer place. Ambulances hurried from the tavern and picked their way through dozens of spent artillery projectiles "scattered like turnips" across Telegraph Road and adjacent fields. Half a mile south of the tavern the dolorous caravan turned east into Ruddick's cornfield, where the surgeons established what was quite literally a field hospital. The open-air site was beyond the range of enemy artillery fire at this point in the battle, and the ambulances busily shuttled back and forth with their grim cargoes.[6]

The only persons left at the battered hostelry, in addition to a few unfortunate Federal soldiers too severely wounded to be moved, were members of the Cox family, owners of the tavern and among the more prosperous inhabitants of that hardscrabble region. Jesse Cox was away on business, but his wife, Polly; son Joseph and daughter-in-law Lucinda; and two younger sons huddled in the cellar for two days. They survived the storm unscathed, but the same cannot be said of the Federal soldiers caught outside in the hail of misguided fire. In the few minutes that Fayel and Knox were on the scene, a shell exploded among a company of infantrymen passing around the tavern, a solid shot smashed the leg of a quartermaster sergeant struggling to remove stores from the barn, and other missiles struck down horses and mules and splintered wagons and fences. Their yearning for a glimpse of the battle fully satisfied, the two correspondents turned about and headed toward Curtis's headquarters at a brisk trot.[7]

They left just as the third battalion of the 3rd Illinois Cavalry clattered up to Elkhorn Tavern and reported to Carr. The other two battalions of the 3rd Illinois were with Dodge nearly a mile to the east, guarding the Federal right flank, so Carr sent this battalion to help Weston's 24th Missouri secure the Federal left. The Illinois cavalrymen crossed the head of Tanyard Ravine, passed around Weston's left flank, and proceeded along a level terrace—an extension of the edge of the plateau—that ran along the northern side of Big Mountain. Several hundred yards beyond Weston's position the 160 horsemen inexplicably left the terrace and headed down the slope west of Tanyard Ravine directly toward the right flank of Price's division.[8]

Soldiers in Slack's 2nd Missouri Brigade soon glimpsed cavalrymen slowly approaching their position. The Missourians cautiously held their fire until the unidentified horsemen were less than two hundred yards away. At that point a Confederate officer rode forward and hallooed at the oncoming riders. In response, noted a laconic rebel, "about a hundred feds began to pop at him with their Sharp's carbines." Wheeling about, the officer raced his horse down the treacherous incline, yelling frantically, "It's them, it's them, it's them!" The Missourians opened fire and drove the 3rd Illinois Cavalry back up the hill in complete disorder. The fight—actually a one-sided burst of fire—lasted only minutes.[9]

The Confederates on this part of the field reported with great exaggeration that they had repulsed a major assault, noting that the Federals left "several of their men and horses dead on the field, and overcoats, knapsacks, caps, hats, guns, and sabers strewn on the ground." The Illinois cavalrymen had indeed blundered and suffered unnecessary casualties in the shadow of Big Mountain, but the tactical situation there and everywhere else in Cross Timber Hollow remained unaltered. Each Federal thrust, however limited or unintentional, kept the rebels on the defensive and fixed in place.[10]

Meanwhile, Vandever arrived at the tavern with his two footsore infantry regiments: his own 9th Iowa, commanded by Lt. Col. Francis J. Herron, and Col. John S. Phelps's battalion-sized 25th Missouri. Most of these men had staggered into camp at 8:00 P.M. the night before, exhausted by the forced march of forty-two miles from Huntsville. Capt. Robert Mathews described his loyal Missourians that morning as "about as worn out a lot of fellows as ever sat around a camp fire," but when duty called, they stepped out briskly enough along Telegraph Road. At Pratt's store the column passed through a swarm of mounted couriers, orderlies, and aides "dashing hither and thither" with messages to and from Curtis. Carr greeted Vandever at the tavern and instructed him to engage the enemy force that had just routed the 3rd Illinois cavalry somewhere beyond the Federal left.[11]

Vandever deployed the 840 men of his 2nd Brigade into line of battle in the tavern orchard on the western side of Telegraph Road, the 25th Missouri on the left and the 9th Iowa on the right, and prepared to launch another

Left to right: *Francis J. Herron, William Vandever, and William H. Coyl (State
Historical Society of Iowa, Des Moines)*

Federal spoiling attack against the rebel force in the hollow. To clear the way for Vandever's brigade and cover its left flank, Carr shifted Weston's command from the head of Tanyard Ravine and stretched it over the crest of Big Mountain. The resulting thin blue skirmish line at least provided the illusion of Federal strength in that direction.

Vandever's troops discarded their overcoats and packs, dressed their ranks, and loaded their weapons. There was a brief interruption as the battered battalion of the 3rd Illinois Cavalry returned from its encounter with Slack's brigade and passed to the left rear to take a position on Ford Road. The infantrymen glanced uneasily at the wounded riders and riderless horses. Shortly after 1:00 P.M. the two regimental commanders rode forward and shouted what they hoped would be words of encouragement and inspiration. Herron addressed his Iowans in ringing Jacksonian terms: "We have come a long way, boys, to fight them, and by the Eternal, we will fight them right here." Phelps was unusually laconic for a politician turned soldier; the congressman simply said, "Remember men, you are Missourians."[12]

At Vandever's signal the 2nd Brigade advanced. The troops marched around the head of Tanyard Ravine and followed the terrace along the northern side of Big Mountain. Then they wheeled right and descended the steep slope west of Tanyard Ravine that the 3rd Illinois Cavalry had recently visited. As the Federals pressed on, they came under Confederate artillery fire. Vinson Holman of the 9th Iowa said that "cannon balls begin to fly like hail around our heads. We begain to think that we was going right into action in good earnist." The rebel artillery fire was consistently high and caused few casualties among Vandever's troops.[13]

Federal and Confederate skirmishers exchanged a flurry of shots on the rocky hillside and then withdrew to their respective lines of battle. One of the few rebel casualties—possibly the only casualty—of this minor affair was Colonel Slack, the commander of the 2nd Missouri Brigade. Slack was a popular, capable Confederate officer whose one weakness was a tendency to expose himself recklessly. He had been severely wounded at Wilson's Creek and was not yet fully recovered, but he insisted on being at the head of his troops. After the repulse of the 3rd Illinois Cavalry Slack rode forward to see what was happening. He was still well in advance of his own line when Vandever's 2nd Brigade arrived and skirmishing erupted. The fatal bullet struck Slack in the lower abdomen only a few inches from his earlier wound. As the mortally wounded Missouri colonel was carried back to the hospital at the tanyard, command of the 2nd Missouri Brigade passed to Col. Thomas

Rosser. Two miles to the west McCulloch was struck down by Federal skirmishers in much the same manner and at about the same time.[14]

Visibility was extremely limited in Tanyard Ravine, and a Missouri rebel noticed that he could hear the Federals slipping and sliding down the slope several minutes before he could see them. When less than one hundred yards apart the opposing lines became visible to one another and simultaneously opened fire. Vandever's men were outnumbered at least two to one, and at such close range the "whirlwind of fire" from shotguns and smoothbores was murderous. The first rebel volley "was a staggering blow" that knocked down over sixty men in the 9th Iowa and forced the rest to take several steps backward. Vandever ordered everyone to lie down and return fire. Soon the officers and men of the 2nd Brigade were sprawled along the flinty benches or huddled behind trees, engaged with rebels similarly situated. Vandever and Phelps declined to dismount and together had four horses shot from under them; Phelps was also badly bruised by a shell fragment. The steep slope gave the Confederates an additional advantage. "We occupied a masterly position," explained a soldier in Rives's regiment, because "the enemy overshot us and our fire was very destructive." Soon the dry leaves in front of Burbridge's regiment caught fire, adding to the pall of smoke and the terror of the wounded.[15]

Vandever realized that his brigade was up against an "overpowering force" and would have to pull back. After fifteen minutes the Federals scrambled up the hill and disappeared into the haze. Once back on the terrace the troops prepared to receive the expected enemy counterstroke. The Confederates, however, remained inert. Vandever, who seemed to have taken to heart Carr's instructions to keep the rebels on the defensive, again ordered his command to advance.[16]

A Missouri soldier watched the Federals emerge once more into view, "marching and firing by platoons, those in front breaking off to the rear after discharging their pieces and making room for the next platoon." He grudgingly added that the yankees were "certainly finely drilled, and executed the commands admirably." Unfortunately, they were too few to slug it out at close range with the Confederates. Vandever's men halted and sought cover as before but soon carried out a "disorderly retrograde movement" toward the tavern, leaving dozens of dead and wounded comrades.[17]

At some point in the unequal contest Little and Rosser called for assistance. Price responded by shifting three of his smaller units to the western side of Telegraph Road: Greene's 3rd Missouri Brigade, Frost's 7th and 9th

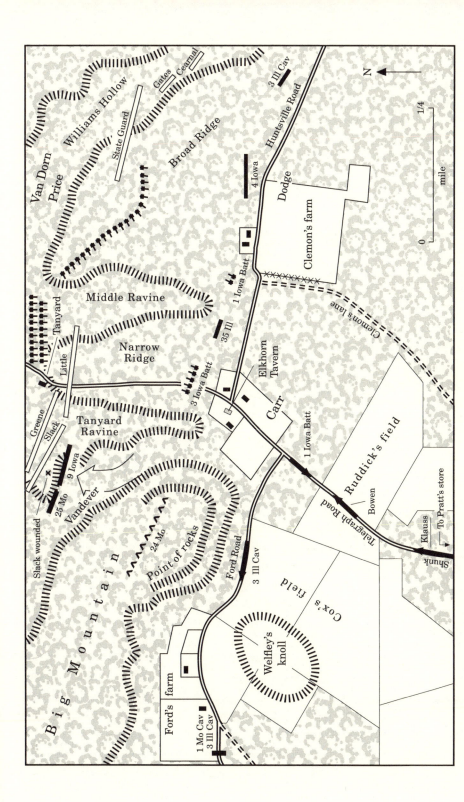

Map 9-1. Elkhorn Tavern: Vandever Attacks Slack

State Guard divisions, and Lindsay's 6th State Guard Division—900 to 1,200 infantrymen and dismounted cavalry. These reinforcements arrived too late to participate in the engagement with Vandever's brigade but increased the strength of the Confederate right wing to between 3,000 and 3,500 soldiers, roughly two-thirds of Price's division.[18]

Vandever's second repulse marked the end of Carr's aggressive spoiling tactics in Cross Timber Hollow. As Carr watched the 2nd Brigade retire in disarray, he decided the time had come to assume a passive defensive posture, as he had intended to do originally. By now he was convinced "that it was no small party merely to annoy the road with whom I was contending, but a very considerable force." Carr rode out Huntsville Road to visit Dodge and see how he was faring. When he learned that the rebels had made no serious attempt to get around the Federal right flank since the first moments of the engagement, he instructed Dodge to close up his 1st Brigade to the left, thereby shortening the Federal right.[19]

Carr returned to the tavern and tidied his left in much the same fashion. He directed Vandever to place his 2nd Brigade across the terrace between Tanyard Ravine and Big Mountain. He placed Weston's battalion of the 24th Missouri and the company of the 4th Iowa under Vandever's command, temporarily incorporating them into the 2nd Brigade. Vandever promptly told Weston to abandon his attenuated skirmish formation and close up to the right in regular line of battle, thereby shortening the Federal left. Carr then ordered Hayden to withdraw his 3rd Iowa Battery from Cross Timber Hollow and take up a new position on the edge of the plateau just north of the tavern. The Iowans left two dead gunners and more than a dozen dead horses as they ascended the hill. At the tavern they were joined by their comrades in the 1st Iowa Battery, who returned to the fight after replenishing their ammunition chests south of Pratt's store.[20]

The new Federal line was shorter and more compact. It was centered on Elkhorn Tavern and consisted, from left to right, of the 24th and 25th Missouri and 9th Iowa west of Telegraph Road; eight guns of the 1st and 3rd Iowa batteries across the road; and the 35th Illinois, two guns of the 1st Iowa Battery, the 4th Iowa, and the 3rd Illinois Cavalry east of the road. The 4th Division was down to around 1,800 infantry, 450 cavalry, and 10 guns. The two batteries had taken a severe pounding, and three of the four infantry regiments had been roughly handled (the 4th Iowa was comparatively unbloodied); but officers and men had performed well and seemed to be confident and in good spirits. Nevertheless, the 4th Division was outnumbered more than two to one in manpower and four to one in artillery by Price's Missourians. Carr sent an aide galloping down Telegraph Road with another plea for reinforcements.[21]

Curtis was reluctant to withdraw his remaining forces from the Little Sugar Creek fortifications until he was absolutely certain of enemy intentions, but he realized Carr was hard pressed and could not be denied a second time. The only unit readily at hand was Bowen's Missouri Cavalry Battalion, a headquarters detachment. Curtis directed Bowen to take two mountain howitzers and one company of cavalry (the latter commanded by Capt. Frederick Benteen of Little Big Horn fame) and go to Carr's support. He also asked Bowen to tell Carr "to stand firm—that more force could be expected soon."[22]

These were not empty words. As Bowen departed for Elkhorn Tavern, Curtis sent a courier racing down Telegraph Road in the opposite direction with an urgent message for Col. William P. Benton. When Davis had led the 3rd Division to Leetown to support Osterhaus, he had left Benton's 8th Indiana and Capt. Martin Klauss's 1st Indiana Battery in the fortifications overlooking the Telegraph Road crossing of Little Sugar Creek. Curtis ordered Benton to send half of his command to Elkhorn Tavern at once. It was not long before Captain Klauss was on his way with three six-pounder rifled guns, followed by Lt. Col. David Shunk and five companies of fresh Hoosier infantry. Benton remained behind with the other half of his command to guard against the fading prospect of an attack from the south on Telegraph Road.[23]

Curtis did not like sending reinforcements to Carr in driblets, but he had great faith in his midwestern soldiers. He told Halleck that "each small accession to the Fourth Division seemed to compensate an overpowering force" of rebels. Carr was far less sanguine about the ability of his men to hold off twice their number. He was disappointed with Bowen's token force and Curtis's brave words, though the sight of Shunk's small column tramping into view raised his spirits a bit. Carr used most of the additional manpower and firepower to shore up Vandever's battered 2nd Brigade. He deployed the battalion of Indiana infantry across the head of Tanyard Ravine between the 9th Iowa and Telegraph Road, and he placed Bowen's two mountain howitzers on the terrace between the 9th Iowa and the 25th Missouri. He added Klauss's three light rifled guns to the two Iowa batteries in the center and sent Benteen's company to reinforce the assorted cavalry units screening his left on Ford Road. The Federal force at Elkhorn Tavern now stood at around two thousand infantry, five hundred cavalry, and fifteen guns.[24]

It was about 2:30 P.M., and the lull in the fighting continued, broken only by sporadic artillery fire and intermittent skirmishing. The outnumbered Federals still clung to the top of the hill and still held the rebels in check in Cross Timber Hollow. The next move was Van Dorn's.

Van Dorn was one of the most aggressive officers in Confederate service, but for several crucial hours on March 7 he was anything but combative. He became cautious and uncertain after meeting unexpected Federal resistance in Cross Timber Hollow, and he became almost completely passive after receiving a message from McCulloch a little after noon. This was the message McCulloch had composed while he was rounding the western end of Big Mountain, about an hour before being drawn into battle on Foster's farm. The Texan informed Van Dorn that his division was advancing "as fast as his men could walk" and that "everything looked favorable" for a rapid reunion of the army at Elkhorn Tavern. Encouraged by this outdated information, Van Dorn assumed that McCulloch's division would soon arrive along Ford Road and would roll up the Federal left flank. He was content, therefore, for Price's division to remain on the defensive and hold the enemy in place for the kill.[25]

Around 2:00 P.M., however, Van Dorn received distressing news regarding the progress of McCulloch's division. Missouri quartermaster Harding reached Cross Timber Hollow after riding around Big Mountain on the Bentonville Detour. Harding found Van Dorn and Price conferring on Broad Ridge and informed them that McCulloch's division was engaged near Leetown and was no longer driving east toward Elkhorn Tavern. Moreover, Harding reported that his initial attempt to reach Price's division by riding directly to Elkhorn Tavern on Ford Road had been blocked by Federal cavalry near the rise between Big and Little mountains. With this new information in hand Van Dorn was left to ponder the wisdom of his hasty decision to divide the Army of the West in the presence of the enemy and, more immediately, to reevaluate his course of action in Cross Timber Hollow.[26]

Then Price was hit. A bullet ripped through his right arm just below the elbow and struck him in the side, causing a severe contusion. Old Pap continued to sit on his horse "as though nothing was the matter" while aides bandaged his arm with handkerchiefs. He calmly informed his shaken staff that "had the bullet come a moment sooner it probably would have killed him," for he had just lifted his right arm to shift the reins of his horse from one hand to another. Meanwhile Van Dorn hovered anxiously nearby, fretting over the bad news from Leetown.[27]

By now Vandever's attack was over, and the Federals were falling back all along the line, initiating what a Missouri officer described as "quite a lull in the storm of battle." In the distance could be heard a swelling roar of musketry as Hébert pressed home his ill-fated assault in Morgan's woods at Leetown.[28]

When Little failed to receive any orders to follow the retreating Federals up the hill, the exasperated Missouri officer took matters into his own hands. He roused the soldiers of his 1st Missouri Brigade and waved them forward. The Missourians soon reached the "scene of wreck and disaster" where the 1st Iowa Battery and the 35th Illinois had stood. "The remains of parts of the Federal battery were scattered around, and the effect of the explosions could be plainly seen," said a rebel. "Dead horses and dead and wounded infantry told of the storm of iron which had beaten them down." Here Little halted his ragged line of battle; the 1st Missouri Brigade was now more than halfway up the hill.[29]

The sudden lurch forward on the right galvanized Van Dorn into action. With McCulloch's division embroiled at Leetown, the Confederate commander realized he would have to fight his way out of Cross Timber Hollow and onto Pea Ridge. The 1st Missouri Brigade had shown the way. After conferring with Price, who was determined to stay on the field despite his wound, Van Dorn ordered the rest of the division to move forward and align with Little's men in preparation for a general attack. Van Dorn's decision to resume an offensive posture was a turning point in the struggle for Elkhorn Tavern, for it followed Carr's decision to assume a passive defensive posture. Also important was an informal change in the Confederate command arrangement apparently agreed to at the same time. The two generals would become, in effect, co-commanders of the Missouri division during the next stage of the engagement: Van Dorn would assume control of the right wing; Price, control of the left wing.

It took another thirty minutes or more for the Missouri forces to receive their orders and reach their new positions. The infantry and dismounted cavalry simply pushed straight up the hill and halted more or less in line with Little's brigade. Moving the artillery forward was far more difficult. Guibor's battery rumbled down Broad Ridge to the tanyard and then toiled up Telegraph Road to the scorched bench lately occupied by the 1st Iowa Battery.

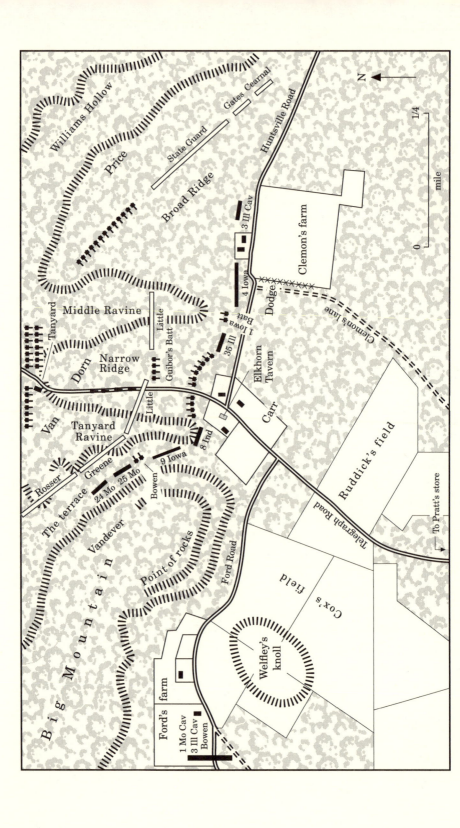

Map 9-2. Elkhorn Tavern: Carr Shortens His Line as Van Dorn Prepares to Attack

Gorham's battery followed suit but could not find a level surface and remained in column on the road behind Guibor's battery. Only these two batteries advanced with the infantry; the other guns remained on Broad Ridge or in reserve at the tanyard for the time being.[30]

Because of limited visibility and extremely difficult terrain, not to mention the large space on Broad Ridge occupied by the batteries, the Confederate infantry line was anything but regular. It snaked in an interrupted fashion from Tanyard Ravine to Williams Hollow, a distance of slightly more than a mile, and overlapped the shorter Federal line at both ends.

While these arrangements were in progress, Van Dorn finally received some good news. Gates reported that the Federal line along Huntsville Road had been shortened and now could be turned more easily. Van Dorn and Price rode up Williams Hollow to see for themselves — perhaps all the way to Huntsville Road. Finally, well after 3:00 P.M. on a late winter day, the two generals were satisfied that the Federal right was indeed vulnerable. Instead of a costly uphill frontal assault all along the line, Van Dorn and Price devised a more complicated but potentially more devastating course of action. The Confederate right wing would attack as originally planned. The Confederate left wing, however, would advance in column up Williams Hollow onto Pea Ridge. There, the Missourians would face west and roll up the exposed Federal right flank. It was a sound plan, but it required much movement of weary men and animals and clumsy artillery over very difficult terrain. At least another hour would be required for the state guard divisions on the left to retire out of sight of the Federals, struggle forward to their new positions, and deploy for an all-out attack.[31]

While Price supervised the agonizingly slow redeployment on the left, Van Dorn returned to Telegraph Road around 4:00 P.M. The Confederate commander struggled to understand the overall shape of the battle from his isolated position in Cross Timber Hollow. He reasoned that McCulloch's powerful division could not have been brought to a halt by anything less than an enormous Federal force. If so, then the number of Federal troops at Elkhorn Tavern must be relatively small — and maybe getting smaller. Van Dorn thought that the abrupt change in Federal tactics in the hollow and the shortening of the Federal line atop Pea Ridge could only be a sign of weakness. He concluded — incorrectly — that Curtis was withdrawing troops from the tavern and sending them to Leetown to deal with McCulloch. Consequently, the forthcoming Confederate attack at the tavern should overwhelm the outnumbered defenders and enable Price's division to gain the high ground at last.

Van Dorn, as always, automatically assumed that the most favorable interpretation was the correct one and that victory was at hand. Unaware that McCulloch had been dead for two hours, he dashed off a message to the Texan, urging him to hold on. "It was evident," Van Dorn later explained, "that if [McCulloch's] division could advance or even maintain its ground, I could at once throw forward Price's left, advance his whole line, and end the battle." This sentence neatly illustrates the Confederate commander's reductionist approach to maneuvering masses of troops and his tendency to think in terms of absolute victory and defeat on the battlefield.[32]

Carr, by contrast, had no illusions about his situation. He concluded that the prolonged lull in the battle meant a major attack was coming. He could not tell where or when, because the dense smoke lingering in the still air made detection of enemy troop movements impossible from his headquarters at the tavern. Not so on the Federal right. After pulling back to Huntsville Road and shortening his line as ordered, Dodge prepared for a fight when long lines of rebels emerged from the haze on Broad Ridge and advanced on his position. Then, inexplicably, the rebels fell back and disappeared. Late in the afternoon, around 4:00 P.M., troopers of the 3rd Illinois Cavalry solved the mystery when they detected a column of Missouri cavalry, infantry, and artillery toiling up Williams Hollow and onto Pea Ridge half a mile east of the Federal right flank. Dodge informed Carr that the rebels had reached the plateau and were deployed across Huntsville Road in great strength. The 4th Division was outflanked.[33]

Carr, in turn, informed Curtis of this ominous development and warned that he could not hold his position much longer without substantial reinforcements. Curtis replied that help was on the way and urged Carr to "persevere" yet a little longer. Carr made what preparations he could to receive the expected enemy attack, instructing Dodge and Vandever to hold their positions as long as possible and then fall back slowly and in good order. "I was constantly expecting re-enforcements," Carr later explained, "which I knew the general was using every effort to get up to me, and if they arrived in time we could hold the ridge.... I therefore determined to hang on to the last extremity."[34]

But Carr would not be alone much longer. Contrary to what Van Dorn believed, by this late hour Curtis had concluded that the enemy force on Telegraph Road was the primary threat. While the rebels in Cross Timber Hollow prepared for their full-scale assault, Curtis was hurrying additional reinforcements to Carr's embattled command from the bluffs above Little Sugar Creek. The struggle for the high ground at Elkhorn Tavern was approaching its climax.

10 High Tide at Elkhorn

The all-out Confederate assault on the thin Federal line at Elkhorn Tavern brought the fighting in Cross Timber Hollow to a terrible climax. Price's Missourians knew they had to drive the stubborn Federals back and gain a foothold atop Pea Ridge. Carr's midwesterners understood they had to hold their position until promised reinforcements arrived from Little Sugar Creek. With daylight slipping away and officers and men on both sides grimly determined to succeed, the resulting struggle at Elkhorn Tavern was the bitterest fighting of the battle.

The rebel attack was painfully slow in getting under way. After Van Dorn left Price in Williams Hollow and returned to Telegraph Road, he told Little to advance "so soon as the heavy firing on our left should give the signal of the attack under General Price." Van Dorn spoke as if he expected the action to commence immediately, but for what must have seemed an interminable length of time, nothing happened. While Price's column on the left slowly pushed up Williams Hollow, hundreds of exhausted soldiers on the right fell asleep on the cold, rocky ground. Others, too keyed up to sleep, noticed that, except for scattered firing along the skirmish lines, the battlefield had become oddly silent. After a while they realized why: the sound of fighting at Leetown had faded.[1]

At 4:30 P.M. artillery fire erupted from the direction of Williams Hollow. This was the signal from Price that Little had been waiting for, and he gave the order to advance. Shouted commands and rolling drumbeats brought the weary rebels to their feet and sent them moving up the slope on both sides of Telegraph Road. The pall of smoke prevented them from knowing the exact location of the Federal line; they would simply plow ahead until they struck something solid.[2]

The Missourians pressed forward in increasing disorder as fatigue, foliage, and the difficult terrain played havoc with military precision. The long line gradually separated into its component parts, each regiment and battalion advancing at its own pace and on its own course. It did not really matter, however; as long as the rebels kept going uphill, they were heading in the right direction with enough strength to compensate for their lack of organization. When only about one hundred yards apart, the opposing forces came into full view through the haze. Vinson Holman of the 9th Iowa was startled at how suddenly the enemy appeared; one moment the steep slope in front of his position was empty, the next it was "covered with Rebels."[3]

Volleys rippled along the edge of the plateau as one Confederate unit after another encountered the Federal line. A Missouri staff officer said the musketry "was extremely heavy and surpassed in severity anything our men had as yet experienced." Another Missourian, a company officer in the very thick of the action, reported that "the firing was terrible" and that "the enemy shot well, for our wounded fell on every side." Asa Payne of Rives's regiment recalled those moments in vivid detail: "The Federal line was in full view and I could hear something going zip, zip all around and could see the dust flying out of the trees and the limbs and twigs seemed to be in a commotion from the concussion of the guns. . . . I remember that I was in the front rank that day, and as soon as we came in view of the Federal lines the boys in the rear rank fired their guns on each side of my head." Payne survived the fire of both friend and foe but heard a ringing in his ears for days afterward.[4]

From the opening volleys the intensity of the battle was terrific. "Such fighting as was done here by the Missourians was hardly ever superseded," declared one rebel. On the Federal side, Alonzo Abernethy of the 9th Iowa stated that the battle "raged with a fury which exceeded our worst apprehensions." Indeed, Jacob Platt, an officer in the 9th Iowa, went so far as to testify, "I charged the battlements of Vicksburg . . . and assisted in driving the Confederates from their almost impregnable position on Missionary Ridge . . . but in all my army experience I did not see any fighting compared with the plain open field conflict that occurred in and around the Elkhorn Tavern on March 7, 1862."[5]

The hill was so steep and Federal resistance so determined, the weary

Confederates could not regain the initiative after halting to fire. Here and there they even lost ground. The "obstinate and bloody" contest became too much for the men of Burbridge's regiment in Tanyard Ravine; they fell back and sought shelter behind a limestone outcropping. While these Missourians huddled in relative safety, "the combat still raged with unabated fury" all around them. Elsewhere on the rugged slope, when they realized that the attack had stalled, Missouri officers called for their men to drop to the ground. As the rebel attack degenerated into a stationary battle of attrition at murderously short range, Vandever, too, ordered his troops to find cover. "Each man sought a tree, a stump or a rock, loaded and fired as rapidly as he could," recalled Nathan Harwood of the 9th Iowa.[6]

With the two opposing forces so close, Van Dorn soon learned that his right extended beyond the Federal left. He ordered Rosser to wheel his 2nd Missouri Brigade to the left atop the terrace and roll up the exposed Federal flank. If the Federals reinforced their left to stave off the 2nd Missouri Brigade, the 1st Missouri Brigade and supporting units would renew their frontal assault against the weakened Federal center and right, seizing the heights and routing the enemy. These were classic textbook tactics. Unfortunately, the textbook did not take into account such factors as fatigue, disorientation, and terrain. By the time the three battalions of the 2nd Missouri Brigade scrambled up the steep slope beyond the Federal left flank and gained the terrace, it was after 5:00 P.M. More time elapsed while Rosser re-formed his winded, disorganized troops and wheeled them around to face the Federal flank.[7]

Vandever responded by refusing the 24th and 25th Missouri until the Federal line west of Telegraph Road formed a shallow V facing both north and northwest. There was as yet little smoke atop the plateau, and the loyal Missourians could see masses of their secessionist counterparts approaching through the open woods on the terrace and the northern slope of Big Mountain. "It seemed to me that the whole world over there was full of rebels," said an unnerved Federal officer. "It was one line after another." The Confederate tide halted while Rosser informed Van Dorn that he was in position and ready to attack.[8]

The commander of the Army of the West was ready for some good news. He had just learned from Major Ross of the 6th Texas Cavalry that McCulloch and McIntosh were dead, that Hébert was missing and presumed dead, and that McCulloch's division was in disarray. Van Dorn sent Ross back to Leetown with the order for Colonel Greer to "hold his position at all hazards." At this critical juncture Van Dorn probably should have left Price in charge in Cross Timber Hollow and accompanied Ross to Leetown to take command of McCulloch's floundering division. Instead, he turned his attention back to personally directing no more than thirty-five hundred Confederate troops against an even smaller number of Federals. "I nevertheless pressed forward with the attack," was how he phrased it. The Van Dorn of old, the romantic warrior happiest in the thick of battle and unconcerned with matters beyond his field of vision, was emerging in the furious struggle for Elkhorn Tavern.[9]

Concentrating once more on events in his immediate front, Van Dorn directed Little and Rosser to proceed with the two-pronged assault. Rosser got his men in motion first. The 2nd Missouri Brigade stepped across the terrace at the double-quick to within eighty yards of the re-fused Federal line, stopping only to unleash a series of volleys. The blasts of bullets generally sailed over the soldiers of the 24th and 25th Missouri, who lay sprawled on the cold ground. A young Federal officer remembered how "it seemed that to hold one's hand two feet higher than the head, as a comrade expressed it, 'with a pint cup you could gather a quart of shot every second.'" The outnumbered Federals brought the rapid Confederate advance to a complete standstill with several volleys of their own. As the conflict raged, Phelps slowly rode back and forth along the line, reminding his men to aim low, urging them to hang on, and promising them that help was on the way. Somehow he and his horse survived the hurricane of fire without a scratch.[10]

Just before the attack commenced on his left, Vandever learned that Weston and Phelps were without artillery support after Bowen's two mountain howitzers ran out of ammunition and withdrew in search of more. On Vandever's orders Captain Hayden of the 3rd Iowa Battery dispatched a six-pounder gun to the threatened flank. Cannon and caisson rumbled around the tavern and halted directly in front of the advancing 2nd Missouri Brigade. An "immense force" of rebels rushed forward and captured the gun before it could be unlimbered, shooting down the horses and scattering the astonished gunners. The triumphant Confederates dragged the light cannon away but failed to turn it on the Federal infantry, probably because they did not know how to operate artillery.[11]

While Rosser's assault against Vandever's left was in progress, Little gave up trying to form the 1st Missouri Brigade and its myriad supporting units into an organized line. He simply ordered everyone to charge up Narrow Ridge and the adjacent ravines. For the first time that day the rebel yell echoed off the rocky walls of Cross Timber Hollow. The Confederates advanced at the double-quick—or at least as quickly as the slope permitted —emitting everything from "the regulation 'yell'" to "a wild cheer." The howling made quite an impression on the anxious men of the 9th Iowa sprawled across the top of the flinty hillside. One of them vividly recalled how the rebels came on "with a yell and a fury that had a tendency to make each hair on one's head to stand on its particular end."[12]

From his position on Telegraph Road Hayden turned his three remaining guns and enfiladed part of the approaching Missouri line on Narrow Ridge at murderously close range. "The battery opened upon us with a sweeping fire, tearing through our lines, crashing among the limbs of the trees and scattering the rocks in the air, now filled with the contents of bursting shells," wrote Ephraim Anderson. The Missourians "recoiled for an instant under the iron hail" of canister, and the impetus of the charge was lost. Then the thin blue line of the 9th Iowa rose at Herron's command and fired a volley that stopped the faltering rebels in their tracks.[13]

For a moment the rebel attack faltered, and the Federals seemed to hold their ground; but the Confederates were too numerous and too determined to be denied. A short time earlier Carr had pulled Shunk's battalion of the 8th Indiana out of line and had sent it to support Dodge's crumbling flank on Clemon's farm. This move gravely weakened Vandever's front. Little's troops steadied and opened a very heavy fire against the 9th Iowa and the 3rd Iowa Battery. "The balls flew like hail around us," recalled an Iowa soldier. The Confederate musketry forced the Federal infantry back down again and even drove the stalwart cannoneers from their weapons.[14]

As Federal small arms and artillery fire decreased, Rives dashed out in front of his regiment and bellowed, "Forward!" His men advanced with another wild yell, walking then running through the dense smoke without halting to fire, rapidly closing on the defenders. Missourians to right and left of Rives's regiment started forward in support, and almost immediately Little's entire command was in motion. Vandever had no reserves available, and he gave the order to withdraw. The men of the 9th Iowa needed no urging. They fired one last uneven volley at the oncoming rebels and then sprinted back toward the tavern, scrambling over the fences in their path.[15]

Confusion reigned supreme as the Confederates reached the edge of the plateau. Each regiment and battalion seemed to select a different objective and veer off in that direction. Burbridge shouted, "On to the battery!" and the officers and men of his regiment ran for their lives toward the three guns

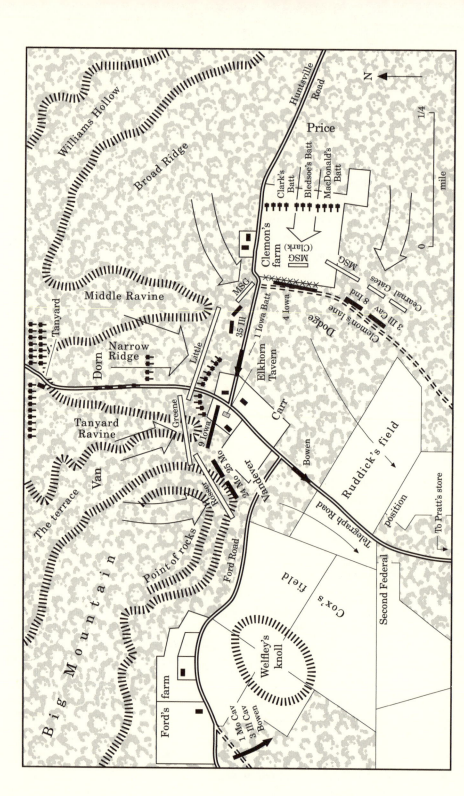

Map 10-1. Elkhorn Tavern: Van Dorn Attacks and Carr Falls Back across Ruddick's Field

of the 3rd Iowa Battery. Other Confederates had the same idea and joined the rush with "a yell of enthusiasm." The gunners had just enough time to unleash a salvo of canister directly into the faces of the approaching rebels. One terrified Missouri infantryman was knocked backward by the "withering, scorching blast" but somehow survived the "torrent of lead and iron" that slaughtered his comrades on every side.[16]

The rebels swarmed around a twelve-pounder howitzer and a six-pounder gun that could not be withdrawn because all of the battery horses had been shot down. In the smoke and confusion Hayden's gunners managed to spike both of these cannons and haul away a six-pounder gun, the last of their operational weapons. The melee permitted the other Federal batteries to limber up and escape at a gallop down Telegraph Road without losing any guns or equipment. Wildly excited Missourians from several units climbed all over their trophies and milled around in total disorder at the junction of Telegraph and Huntsville roads, oblivious to the battle for Elkhorn Tavern that continued to rage a few yards away.[17]

The rest of Little's command closed in on the Federal infantry in an uncoordinated series of short rushes from fence to fence around the tavern. The battle was growing more fluid, and the Federals were in danger of being surrounded and overwhelmed. Carr knew the game was up: "My troops fought with most heroic courage and devotion, officers exposing themselves freely, cheering and encouraging their men, but it was impossible to withstand such overpowering numbers." He told Vandever to save his brigade.[18]

Disengagement was difficult because of the disjointed Federal line and the proximity of the enemy. Fortunately, the spreading billows of smoke helped to obscure men and movements. Herron's Iowans fell back slowly and stubbornly, halting every few paces to fire at the pursuing rebels. The two regiments of loyal Missourians on the terrace got to their feet and retired at the double-quick to avoid being cut off by Little's troops fanning out from Narrow Ridge. The pace picked up, an officer noted, when the rebels "sent a hail-storm of balls after us as a parting salute." The Federals maintained fairly good order despite their perilous position and the chaotic situation. They fell back through the orchard where they had first deployed to the edge of a dense, brushy thicket where the ground began to slope down toward Pratt's store. There Carr and Vandever reestablished a serviceable line behind a rail fence and awaited a renewal of the storm.[19]

It was slow in coming. After the 24th and 25th Missouri had dashed to safety, the men of the 2nd Missouri Brigade arose and marched along the

Elkhorn Tavern, with the head of Tanyard Ravine to its rear and the eastern extremity of Big Mountain in the background (authors' collection)

terrace toward the tavern, firing at dimly seen masses of men moving across their front. These troops belonged to the 1st Missouri Brigade and various state guard divisions, and much frantic shouting and waving of flags ensued. An indignant member of Little's command declared that "it was with great difficulty" that Rosser's Missourians "were prevailed upon to cease firing." Confederate momentum petered out amidst confusion and recriminations as the two ragged lines collided and units intermingled.[20]

Disorganization in the gray ranks grew even worse as soldiers wandered off to loot Weston's campsite, explore the tavern and its outbuildings, and strip the Federal dead and wounded of weapons, clothing, and other valuables. The ravenous Missourians had not eaten since breakfast the day before at Elm Springs, and they rummaged desperately in search of food. When the men of Rives's regiment discovered a sutler's store in an outbuilding, they immediately confiscated the contents in the name of the Confederacy. A rebel recalled how the sutler stood wringing his hands in anguish as the soldier and his famished comrades "filled our haversacks with crackers, oysters, sardines, etc. and I remember some of our boys stuck their bayonets into and carried off a pile of cheese on their shoulders." Thirty minutes of rapidly fading daylight passed before exasperated officers got their men back into ranks and disentangled and aligned the various units.[21]

The Missouri infantrymen had cause to celebrate, for they had gained the high ground on their own. The only Missouri artillery close enough to see and engage the Federal line was Guibor's four-gun battery, which had advanced to the spot formerly occupied by the 1st Iowa Battery. When Van Dorn ordered the right wing forward, Guibor immediately opened fire on the ten Federal guns deployed across Telegraph Road on the edge of the plateau. For the only time that day the Federal cannoneers at Elkhorn Tavern had the advantage, and they attempted to make the most of it. The action had barely begun when a salvo of shells exploded around Guibor's battery, killing dozens of horses and causing three men to bolt downhill at full speed. The Missourians always claimed that one of the men "never stopped until he reached St. Louis."[22]

The situation became even warmer for Guibor's artillerymen when skirmishers from the 35th Illinois inched down the slope and began to snipe at them. The Missourians had to stop firing at the Federal batteries and blast the hillside with canister to keep the skirmishers at a safe distance. Hunt Wilson was sighting down the barrel of his cannon when he saw a Federal infantryman step from behind a tree directly ahead and not sixty yards away. Speaking of himself in the third person, Wilson described how the yankee "took a long deliberate aim at the head of the devoted gunner, whose sensations were horrible at this moment, as he could almost feel the bullet boring a hole between his eyes; a puff of smoke came from the rifle and a sharp metallic ring told that the aim was too low; the ball had struck the face of the muzzle of the gun, leaving a large dent." Wilson staggered back, the lanyard was pulled, and a charge of canister struck down the intrepid skirmisher. Fortunately for Guibor, Little's advancing line compelled the Federal infantry and artillery to fall back before they could do any serious damage to his exposed battery.[23]

As enemy fire died, a riderless black horse came running down Telegraph Road and was caught by one of the cannoneers. The saddlebags contained a fine pair of holstered pistols and, perhaps even more impressive at the moment, a flask of brandy and "a nice lunch of real wheat bread and butter and ham, wrapped in a white napkin." The famished Missourians were awestruck by the dainty delicacies. "How high those fellows lived," wondered Wilson. Fortified by a bite of food and a sip of spirits, Guibor led his battery up Telegraph Road onto Pea Ridge. He forced his way through the

Guibor's battery in action against Carr's beleaguered Federals on the evening of March 7. Certainly the most dramatic visual portrayal of the battle of Pea Ridge, this painting was the work of an amateur, Hunt P. Wilson, a gunner in the battery. (Museum of the Confederacy, Richmond, Va.; photograph by Katherine Wetzel)

crowd of milling infantrymen and unlimbered his cannons atop a slight hump directly in front of Elkhorn Tavern. On high ground at last, the Missouri artillerymen sprayed canister and all manner of shot and shell down Telegraph Road and into the nearby woods where Vandever's men were drawn up in line of battle.[24]

Shortly after Guibor reached the plateau, the disorganized Confederate right wing resumed its assault against Vandever's brigade. The fighting in the thicket resembled what had occurred in Morgan's woods at Leetown earlier in the day. A Missourian said that "there was so much underbrush about that much of the fighting consisted of skirmishing, as small groups of us would try to take portions of the enemy by surprise, and there was a terrible loss of life." Van Dorn, Little, and Rosser had their hands full trying to control their troops in the scrubby forest.[25]

The Federals fought doggedly. They held their position behind the fence for a little while before falling back through the woods to the southern side of Ford Road. They even managed to launch a few counterattacks whenever the Confederates faltered. "It was charge and recharge," recalled a drained Iowa lieutenant. Carr, Vandever, and the regimental commanders were in constant motion, rallying their hard-pressed men and preventing the retreat from becoming a rout. Herron was especially conspicuous. An admiring fellow officer described him as "too brave for his own good." While riding in front of his regiment urging his men to stand fast, Herron fell victim to a canister ball from one of Guibor's guns. The ball ripped through his horse and struck his booted right ankle, breaking several bones. Pinned to the ground by his toppled horse, Herron was taken prisoner by the advancing Confederates. His strenuous efforts to stem the rebel tide earned him the fourth Medal of Honor awarded at Pea Ridge. Command of the 9th Iowa passed to Maj. William H. Coyl, who was slightly wounded but remained on the field.[26]

Despite such heroics Vandever's three infantry regiments lost their hold on Ford Road and were steadily pushed back toward Pratt's store. Phelps, who came through the fight at the tavern miraculously unscathed, was nicked by a rebel bullet in the woods but stayed with his regiment. As casualties mounted and ammunition ran low, the soldiers wavered. "We were pressed terribly," acknowledged an officer in the 25th Missouri, "and had not a battery come to our help, we would have been overpowered." It was not actually one battery but bits and pieces of four different batteries that were waiting in Ruddick's cornfield: the thirteen assorted guns and howitzers that had

Artillery pieces mark the location of Guibor's battery in front of Elkhorn Tavern on the evening of March 7 (authors' collection)

escaped capture at the tavern or that had departed earlier to replenish their ammunition chests and packs. The troops of Vandever's 2nd Brigade emerged from the woods in some disorder and hurriedly crossed to the southern side of the field, where they established a new line behind a fence. The Federal artillery wheeled into place on either flank. The cannons on the right near Telegraph Road opened fire on Guibor's battery in front of the tavern; those on the left began raking the woods with shell and case shot.[27]

With artillery support on both flanks and a clear field of fire in front, Carr made a final effort to halt the Confederate onslaught. Not everyone in blue thought another stand-up fight was a good idea. A soldier in the 9th Iowa, shaken by the harrowing retreat from the tavern, almost gave up hope when the rebels "pored out of the Brush on to us by the Thousands." The Confederates burst from the smoky woods at several points and advanced rapidly across the cornfield. One Missouri rebel admitted that his comrades "had by this time become wildly enthusiastic" and were almost uncontrollable.

Officers could not even get the men to pause and align their ranks. Despite almost unlimited opportunity for maneuver on both sides of Telegraph Road, the disorganized mass of Confederates surged directly toward the Federal position. One of Vandever's infantrymen remembered that, as the rebels approached, he could hear "their cheers and yells rising above the roar of the artillery."[28]

The impetuous Missourians ran into a murderous hail of canister and rifle fire that dropped men by the dozens. Asa Payne was rushing forward when an officer next to him, Lt. Irving Glasscock, was hit. "Strange to say I heard the bullet strike him with a thud. He was so near me that he almost brushed me as he fell. He threw up his hands and said 'O Lord', and fell upon his back and was dead." Though the furrowed cornfield was soon littered with many more dead and wounded, the rebels pressed on, many dressed in the newly issued white uniforms that made them perfect targets in the twilight. "By this time it was almost dark and we got so near the battery that the fire from the guns would pass in jetting streams through our lines," said Payne. In the midst of this hellish scene a young Confederate named William Kennerly stared at "the pale stalks left standing from the previous summer and wonder[ed] why the farmer had not cleared them away." It was, he thought, a striking example of "what foolish things a man will think at times of stress." As the carnage mounted, the rebels wavered and then streamed back to the cover of the woods on the northern side of the field. The men of Vandever's brigade cheered hoarsely at their unexpected triumph. The Federal line had held.[29]

The bloody repulse of the Missourians in Ruddick's field was the high-water mark of the Confederate war effort in the Trans-Mississippi. If Carr's last-ditch defense had failed, the rebels almost certainly would have overrun the Federal headquarters at Pratt's store and seized the trains just beyond. But it was not to be; ebb tide was at hand for Van Dorn and the Army of the West.

Ninety minutes earlier and three-quarters of a mile to the east, Price launched his attack against the Federal right. After a tiring and time-consuming struggle, Old Pap managed to maneuver nearly two thousand men and eleven guns up Williams Hollow and into line atop Pea Ridge. The Missourians faced west across Huntsville Road, their right flank near the edge of the plateau, their left in the woods about five hundred yards to the south. From right to left the line consisted of Rains's 8th State Guard Division, Clark's 3rd State Guard Division, Saunders's 5th State Guard Division, and Gates's, Cearnal's, and Shelby's cavalry units. Bledsoe's, Clark's, and Mac-Donald's batteries waited in column on the road behind Rains's division.[30]

After advancing several hundred yards against nothing more than light harassing fire from troops of the 3rd Illinois Cavalry, the Missourians reached Clemon's farm. There they halted and dressed their ranks along the eastern edge of a square cornfield that lay on the southern side of Huntsville Road. The field was slighty over two hundred yards wide with a marked crown in the center six or eight feet high. Missouri officers rode into the field to see over the crown, squinting into the hazy glare of the late afternoon sun. In the treeline on the opposite side of the field they could make out a dark line of infantry behind a low breastwork of logs and fence rails. Price presumably would have preferred to turn such a strong position, but with daylight fading fast he felt that he had to attempt an immediate frontal assault. He ordered the artillery into the field to shell the woods across the way while the infantry prepared to advance. The batteries rumbled forward and unlimbered just behind the crown in the middle of the field. The eleven guns roared to life and brought the prolonged lull to a crashing conclusion. The guns also signaled Van Dorn that the final attack was commencing.[31]

After learning that a Confederate force threatened his right flank, Dodge had engineered a partial change of front to the east. The 4th Iowa pulled back from Huntsville Road and filed into a narrow lane that ran along the western side of Clemon's field. To fill the gap thus created along Huntsville Road, the 35th Illinois spread out in an attenuated line all the way from Elkhorn Tavern to Clemon's cabin, a distance of four hundred yards. The two six-pounder guns of the 1st Iowa Battery moved to the right angle in the Federal line near the northeastern corner of the field. After harassing Price, the two battalions of the 3rd Illinois Cavalry fell back and occupied the lane on the right of the 4th Iowa. This extended Dodge's line southward into the woods about one hundred yards.[32]

Clemon had spent the winter months uprooting deadened trees and hauling them to the western edge of his cornfield, a tremendous stroke of good fortune for the Federals. The Iowa infantrymen dragged the trunks and branches across the front of their position and then dismantled the fence that bordered the lane and piled the rails on top. The rude but sturdy breastwork was the only field fortification used at Pea Ridge and proved to be a key factor in this phase of the battle.[33]

The Missouri gunners opened fire on the Federal position from a distance of less than two hundred yards. The iron storm erupted as the last company of the 4th Iowa was filing into Clemon's lane. "As we turned to the right the grape were buzzing around our ears at a terrible rate," said Capt. Henry Cummings. "I never knew I could turn a corner so quick—I must have made forty feet in about three jumps." The latecomers joined the other members of the regiment in making themselves as small as possible. Cummings was convinced that "had we not lain down we would not have had ten men to the company. The fire was so terrible." Lt. James A. Williamson, later a brigadier general, felt the same way. He described the "terrible fire" in Clemon's field as the "most terrific cannonading" he experienced during the war. The Iowans made no attempt to shoot back but huddled behind their log breastwork.[34]

Much of the flying metal sailed over the breastwork and caused the forest behind the Iowans to writhe as though ravaged by a terrific windstorm. Trees toppled, branches crashed to the ground, and splinters flew in all directions. Price permitted the bombardment to continue for twenty or thirty minutes and then ordered the infantry forward. The result was a fiasco. Clark's small-ish 3rd State Guard Division occupied the center of the Missouri line. When the cannons fell silent, Clark's command of fewer than five hundred men stepped out alone. They broke ranks briefly to skirt the artillery pieces and then re-formed and pressed on at the double-quick through the dense billows of smoke. At less than one hundred yards they became visible to the waiting Iowa cannoneers, who staggered the approaching line with the last few rounds of canister in their ammunition chests. Worse was to come. "We charged to within twenty steps of their ambush when they turned loose on us," said one Missourian. At the last moment the 4th Iowa rose from behind the breastwork and delivered a volley at point-blank range, which knocked down the front rank of the oncoming Missourians. "We were met by a most terrific and deadly volley of musketry," wrote Clark of the sheet of flame that blazed along the log breastwork, "and for a moment our brave men recoiled before its deadly aim."[35]

Then Clark went down in a heap, his horse killed under him, and the 3rd State Guard Division disintegrated. "The men yielded to their instincts to return the fire without orders," said Lt. Col. Richard H. Musser, who also suddenly found himself afoot in front of the deadly breastwork. "Some of the men took cover and others lay down in the field. The enemy continued to pour in his volleys and we were in a critical situation." After a few minutes the surviving Missourians fled back to the shelter of the crown in the middle of the field.[36]

Clemon's field, looking east from Dodge's position. The pile of brush in the foreground represents the crude breastwork that Dodge's Iowans used in their defense of this field. (authors' collection)

The unsupported charge of the 3rd State Guard Division never had a chance to succeed. The attackers were outnumbered at least three to two by the defenders, who had the additional advantage of fighting from cover. The bungled assault cost the Confederates more than lives. It nullified the demoralizing effect of the cannonade and increased the confidence of the Federal troops.

Price ordered his artillery back into action, and another storm of shot and shell hammered the Federal position. Dodge rode back and forth in Clemon's lane encouraging his men and belittling the danger of artillery fire. The Confederates nearly proved him wrong. An exploding shell tore away his saddle holsters and ripped his pants. ("Never even scratched me," he told his family.) Then a canister ball grazed his left hand, knocking two knuckles out of joint, and a falling branch swept him backward off his horse, cracking two ribs. The Iowa colonel struggled to his feet and remounted. He continued to expose himself recklessly, and by the end of the day he had lost three horses and accumulated six bullet and canister holes in his coat. Others in the Federal ranks were hit by metal or by splintered wood, but most huddled in relative safety behind the breastwork or in the woods to either side.[37]

When the artillery fire ended, the 3rd State Guard Division inexplicably went forward alone a second time. The result was predictable and tragic. As the Missourians reached the line of bodies marking the limit of their first advance, they again "wavered and staggered under the fire of the enemy." Courage could do only so much, and the rebels soon streamed back toward the safety of the lee slope. The sight so affected Price that he trotted forward onto the field. The fleeing troops halted when "their old veteran chief," his arm in a sling, urged them to rally and re-form.[38]

On the other side of the field the reaction was equally emotional. A cheer swept along the Federal line when the attackers broke and fled for the second time. Lieutenant Colonel Galligan and his Iowans stood and waved their hats and weapons. Some even scrambled over the breastwork and dashed into the field to retrieve souvenirs. Dodge was as exultant as any of his men. "I mowed them down in mounds," he crowed. "They charged us time and time again but they could not move us." On this occasion the 4th Iowa had repulsed the 3rd State Guard Division without any assistance from the two guns of the 1st Iowa Battery, which had run out of ammunition and withdrawn.[39]

Price decided to try again with better coordination and more appropriate tactics. Clark's decimated division returned to the middle of the field and joined the three batteries in hammering the breastwork with everything from solid shot to buckshot. This time, however, the Confederates concentrated on the Federal flanks. The 8th State Guard Division advanced through the woods north of Huntsville Road and engaged the right flank of the 35th Illinois. In the woods south of Clemon's field the 5th State Guard Division and the dismounted cavalry units struck the two battalions of the 3rd Illinois Cavalry along Clemon's lane. As the Missourians pushed ahead, their longer line wrapped around the exposed right flank of the Illinois horsemen and slowly forced them back from the lane.[40]

Dodge's euphoria faded as he realized his predicament. He sent an aide back to Carr with a plea for reinforcements to buttress his sagging right flank. Though Vandever's 2nd Brigade was now coming under sustained enemy attack at Elkhorn Tavern, Carr rushed Shunk's battalion of the 8th Indiana to Dodge's relief. The trip from the tavern to Clemon's farm was short but exciting for the Indiana infantrymen. As they moved at the double-quick along Huntsville Road and turned into the lane, they were exposed to a "murderous fire" from the rebels in the cornfield. The Hoosiers fairly sprinted down the lane, bending as low as possible, until they reached the cover of the woods south of the field. Shunk and Dodge somehow missed each other in the narrow lane—the two must have passed within touching distance—but the Indiana colonel found his way to the right place and put his troops into the fight alongside the 3rd Illinois Cavalry.[41]

Price committed all of his available men and guns against Dodge's 1st Brigade, and for the better part of an hour both sides were locked in an "earnest and terrible" battle of attrition. Price described the intense fighting in field and forest as "the fiercest struggle of the day." The Confederate superiority in men and artillery inevitably began to tell, even in the center, where the 4th Iowa was feeling the effect of the prolonged hail of enemy fire. Bullets and canister balls found their way through chinks in the breastwork or struck those who exposed themselves above it, including Galligan, who fell wounded. "Bullets were continually going by us whist-whist-whist," said Captain Cummings. Dodge, who informally resumed command of his old regiment after Galligan went down, was amazed at the way some of his troops behaved after being hit. "Many who were too badly wounded to leave the field stuck to their places, sitting on the ground loading and firing. I have heard of brave acts but such determined pluck I never before dreamt of." The regimental color bearer was twice seriously wounded but continued to clutch the splintered flagstaff until Dodge ordered him carried to the rear. As for the regimental flag, Dodge said it was "riddled—nothing left of it."[42]

Between 5:30 and 6:00 P.M. the Federal position in Clemon's field became untenable. Dodge learned that Carr and Vandever had lost Elkhorn Tavern and were falling back toward Pratt's store under heavy pressure. Evidence of that came shortly afterward when hundreds of Confederate troops from Little's brigade poured down Huntsville Road from the direction of the tavern and struck the 35th Illinois in flank and rear. Lieutenant Colonel Chandler was taken prisoner with about forty of his men as he attempted to fend off this unexpected threat. Company by company the Illinoisans abandoned their position along the edge of the plateau and ran into the woods south of the road. Most ended up alongside Vandever's brigade in Ruddick's field. A similar calamity befell the troops on Dodge's right. The 3rd Illinois Cavalry and the 8th Indiana, fighting stubbornly against twice their number of rebels, finally gave way. A charge by the 5th State Guard Division drove them back from the lane and caused them to lose contact with the 4th Iowa. The Illinois and Indiana troops drifted south toward Vandever's line, drawing some of the Confederates after them.[43]

The men of the 4th Iowa behind the battered breastwork were in imminent danger of being surrounded. The roar of battle and the triumphant yells of the rebels seemed to be all around. Dodge realized it was time to go and ordered his troops to fall into line. The Iowans then faced about and marched into the woods, carrying off most of their wounded comrades. By now the smoke was almost as thick atop Pea Ridge as it had been in Cross Timber Hollow, and the Federals escaped unseen.[44]

Price rode along the thinned line of the 3rd State Guard Division in Clemon's field and "bade them onward to victory." Clark's Missourians went forward a third time toward the strangely silent breastwork. They scrambled over the piles of logs that had caused them so much grief and plowed into soldiers of the 8th State Guard Division advancing through the woods from the north. Only a few nervous shots were fired, but much precious time was lost before order could be restored and the advance renewed.[45]

In the meantime, the yankees got away. Dodge and the 4th Iowa marched through the woods as the Confederate pincers closed behind them. "Had we stood our ground ten minutes longer we would have been cut to pieces," said Captain Cummings. At one point in the shadowy, smoky woods the retiring Federals passed within hailing distance of a body of Confederate troops but were not challenged. The 4th Iowa emerged into Ruddick's cornfield east of Telegraph Road and hurried over the recently abandoned site of the 4th Division's field hospital. They had not quite reached the southern side before a ragged line of pursuing rebels burst from the woods and trotted across the field. The Confederates failed to consider that the fleeing Federals might still have teeth. "I halted and turned on them," Dodge reported, "and with my last ammunition poured so hot a fire into their ranks that they fled in confusion." Dodge shouted in triumph with his men until he realized that the regiment would be defenseless if the rebels tried again. "I never felt such a chilling in my life," he later confided to his father. But there was no further pursuit, and the Iowans reached the fence on the southern side of Ruddick's field without incident. There they joined the men of Vandever's brigade, still excited over their repulse of the Confederate attack fifteen minutes earlier.[46]

The 4th Division—or what was left of it—was now about half a mile south of its original position along the northern edge of Pea Ridge. During the chaotic fighting atop the plateau, the Federals had lost several cannons and had suffered heavy casualties, including two regimental commanders seriously wounded (Smith and Galligan), two slightly wounded (Phelps and Coyl), and two captured (Herron and Chandler), and they were running short of ammunition. Carr was as determined as ever to hold on but doubted whether his troops could withstand another assault. Then he noticed a column of blue-clad infantry and artillery approaching from the south on Telegraph Road. Relief was at hand.

Curtis and Asboth reached Carr's position at the head of an oddly fragmented force: four companies of the 2nd Missouri and five of the 25th Illinois, four six-pounder guns of the 2nd Ohio Battery, and two twelve-pounder howitzers and two six-pounder rifled guns of the 4th Ohio Battery. The little column at one point included the 4th Missouri Cavalry, but the cowardly Meszaros halted his battalion four hundred yards short of Ruddick's field and led it back to camp by a "circuitous route" out of Curtis's sight. The relief force was not very large, but it was effective. As one of Carr's begrimed officers put it, the ammunition "was about exhausted, and so were we." The infusion of five hundred fresh infantrymen carrying forty rounds apiece and eight cannons with full ammunition chests turned the tide of battle. When Asboth formed the reinforcements into line on the western side of Telegraph Road, the chance of a Confederate breakthrough was gone.[47]

Curtis assumed command of the swelling Federal force on Telegraph Road, and for the first time in his military career he personally led men in battle. The general was confident of victory; if anything, he was overconfident. His midwesterners had swept the enemy off the field at Leetown, and he had no doubt that they would do the same at Elkhorn Tavern. "Supposing with my reinforcements I could easily recover our lost ground," Curtis prepared to drive the enemy back into the depths of Cross Timber Hollow.[48]

It was now about 6:30 P.M., and the sun had set. In the woods north of Ruddick's field Confederate officers rode back and forth rounding up strays and stragglers and urging their exhausted soldiers to re-form for one last charge. Units were intermingled, and the men were numb with fatigue. To make matters worse, the Missourians were now at a disadvantage in artillery, for most of the batteries remained behind in Cross Timber Hollow or at Elkhorn Tavern awaiting orders to advance. Van Dorn, excited and distracted, continued to demonstrate little sense of responsibility for McCulloch's division. Though the eastern terminus of Ford Road finally was in his hands, he made no effort to link with the other half of his army somewhere to the west.[49]

Curtis launched his counterattack first. Two dozen Federal cannons hammered the woods north of Ruddick's field and drove the milling rebel infantrymen back in disorder. The barrage also smothered the rebel cannoneers at the tavern and forced some of them to seek shelter. Curtis instructed Dodge to lead the advance and regain the lost ground. When Dodge explained that the 4th Iowa was out of ammunition, the general directed him to make a bayonet attack. Dodge did as ordered. With a wild hysterical shout, the Iowans threw their hats in the air and advanced at the double-quick across the darkening field. "Such a yell as they crossed that field with, you never heard," said the Iowa colonel. "It was unearthly and scared the rebels so bad they never stopped to fire at us or to let us reach them." The entire Federal line followed and pushed into the smoky woods.[50]

Confederate resistance stiffened in the vicinity of Ford Road, and the fighting became fierce and confused. Curtis and Asboth and their staffs were riding directly behind the advancing blue line. Asboth was struck in the right arm by a bullet or a canister ball. He had an aide bind the wound with a handkerchief and, like Price, refused to leave the field despite severe pain. Asboth arranged his cloak to cover his bandaged arm and continued to direct affairs on his side of the road. Curtis rode untouched through the deadly fire, though one of his aides was shot and a bodyguard was decapitated by an artillery round.[51]

When the Federal advance stalled well short of the tavern, Curtis realized nothing more could be accomplished with the means at hand. He had enough force on Telegraph Road to stop the rebels but not enough to drive them from the field. "About this time the shades of night began to gather around us, but the fire on both sides seemed to grow fierce and more deadly," he explained to Halleck. It was time to fall back and regroup before darkness set in. The Federal infantry retired and once again formed a defensive line along the fence on the southern side of Ruddick's field. The Confederates did not counterattack but merely followed as far as the fence on the northern side of the field. Even Van Dorn was satisfied that his men could do no more that night.[52]

Intermittent artillery fire continued for another hour or so, providing a "grand spectacle" in the darkness but accomplishing little. Around 7:30 P.M. the Confederate cannoneers closed with a triumphant salvo, a lavish expenditure of ammunition that they could ill afford. Curtis ordered a defiant response but discovered that his gunners "could not find another cartridge to give them a final round; even the little howitzers responded, 'No cartridges.'" Thus ended the fighting at Elkhorn Tavern on March 7.[53]

Van Dorn's attempt to defeat or destroy the Army of the Southwest with a single stroke had failed. Instead of uniting in the Federal rear and fighting a climactic battle, the two halves of the Army of the West had become bogged down in separate engagements miles apart. McCulloch's division had been defeated at Leetown, and its ranking officers had been killed or captured; Price's division had achieved a limited tactical success at Elkhorn Tavern but only after a long and costly struggle. At the end of the first day the battle was effectively a draw. Victory or defeat on the morrow depended in large part on how well each army prepared during the night for a renewal of the struggle.

11 Soften the Heart

Darkness spread across Pea Ridge and brought an end to the carnage but there was little rest for the weary on the cold, clear night of March 7–8. Moonlight filtering through the lingering haze of battle dimly illuminated a scene of surprising activity. Hundreds of soldiers wandered across the battlefield to succor the wounded or steal from the dead. Thousands more stumbled through thickets and toiled along rutted roads in preparation for the dawn. Still others struggled, sometimes in vain, to replenish empty cartridge boxes and ammunition chests. In the background, sharp in the frigid air, were the terrible sounds of broken men and animals.

Yellow hospital flags hung limply from the simple frame buildings and crude log huts that dotted the battlefield. Many of these frontier structures lacked windows and wooden floors and "were wholly wanting in the usual necessaries found in the more settled regions." Within each cramped and poorly ventilated building surgeons struggled by the light of candles or lanterns to do what they could for the hundreds of wounded. The Army of the Southwest began the campaign without a proper supply of medical stores, and Federal surgeons were desperately short of bandages, dressings, stimulants, and bedding. The handful of Confederate surgeons had even less to work with. "Our preparations were wholly inadequate," declared a Federal doctor. He added that "the enemy had, apparently, made none at all." Nothing could be found in the vicinity to remedy these critical deficiencies.[1]

The stream of wounded overwhelmed the medical facilities of both armies. A nocturnal visitor to Elkhorn Tavern counted sixty men lying on the floor inside and dozens more on the porch and in the yard. Tents were pitched outside the hospital buildings at Leetown and Pratt's store to accommodate the overflow. Wounded soldiers sometimes reached a hospital only to bleed to death before an overworked surgeon had time to tie off an artery or apply a tourniquet. For those with shattered limbs amputation was the only recourse available. A young rebel passing Clemon's cabin was aghast at the sight of a pile of severed limbs outside the door, the "arms in sleeves and legs with boots still on the feet." A mile to the southwest at Pratt's store a slightly wounded Iowa artilleryman described the awful scene at a Federal hospital. "The surgeons were busy cutting and carving like butchers; arms and legs dissevered lay thick around outside, while inside were some of the unfortunate victims of the bloody day. Some were praying, some swearing, some laughing, others crying, some groaning, many dead and dying." After a few minutes the Iowan could stand it no longer and limped off toward his camp. He had learned that "of all sight sickening places it is a field hospital during an engagement."[2]

The exhausted Confederates were woefully slow in retrieving the wounded from the rugged terrain and dense thickets around Elkhorn Tavern. Sgt. Salem Ford of the Missouri State Guard was surrounded by the human debris of the fighting that had surged back and forth in the woods north of Ruddick's field. Many of the casualties were Federals. "I shall never forget that night," said Ford. "They were all around me, and their suffering and calls for water and fire appealed to me and gained my sympathy. Those supplications to God and us for help were enough to soften the heart of even a Missouri soldier." Ford and his men built a roaring fire some distance back in the woods and carried or dragged their helpless enemies to its warmth.[3]

Mary Phelps was an angel of mercy of another sort. The wife of Colonel Phelps had journeyed from Springfield to Little Sugar Creek for what she thought would be a brief visit with her husband. Unable to flee the impending battle because of the rebel presence on Telegraph Road, she appointed herself "medical supervisor, nurse, quartermaster, and commissary" for the battered 4th Division and worked day and night to help the wounded.[4]

The eventual withdrawal of most of the combat forces from Leetown permitted greater freedom of movement for medical personnel in that area. Several Confederate surgeons remained on Foster's farm to tend the wounded. One southern doctor decided not to wait for the wounded to come to him. Washington L. Gammage and a small group of volunteers from the 4th Arkansas and 3rd Louisiana scoured Morgan's woods for casualties. They encountered Federal soldiers engaged in the same humanitarian task and agreed to work together. For hours they carried off those who could be moved and built fires for those who could not. Wounded men of both armies were taken to Leetown, where nearly every building in the village served as a hospital.[5]

Gammage and his little band of Confederates were not in any danger until they attempted to rejoin their comrades on the Bentonville Detour. Wending their way northward they ran into a detachment of Federal infantrymen on picket duty along Ford Road. Gammage casually entered into a conversation with the unsuspecting soldiers. Then three Federal officers rode up. "One of them called out halloa boys, on picket, I suppose!" related Gammage. "I quickly answered yes, sir! and they passed on." Waiting a short time after the officers rode off, the rebels politely took their leave and departed.[6]

Capt. Robert Mathews of the 25th Missouri barely survived the night after being hit in the final Federal counterattack up Telegraph Road. "I thought I was killed," wrote the loyal Missourian. "I was shot somewhere in the heart, I could not tell where, but I was sure it was a death shot, as the blood was flowing from my mouth and I was choking for breath." Mathews turned and staggered back in the company of another wounded officer. The pair got out of the woods but collapsed in Ruddick's field, where prowling Confederates stole their sidearms and rifled their pockets. Not long afterward Federal soldiers crept into the field and rescued them. Mathews's wound was pronounced fatal by a harried surgeon, but he survived with the help of one of his soldiers who held him all night near a fire and kept him from drowning in his own blood. Mathews believed with good reason that if he had remained in the cornfield he would have died, for "many a poor fellow moaned his life away without help or succor under the cold and frosty sky of that bitter night."[7]

For the living as well as the dying the night was indeed bitter. A Missouri rebel named Edward Wall stared at the dark shapes littering Clemon's field and whispered to a comrade, "I hope I never have to hear another gun as long as I live." Another Confederate soldier stationed in the woods along Telegraph Road remembered those terrible hours to the end of his days: "It was a very cold night and it was pitiful to hear the wounded calling all through that night in the woods . . . for some water or something to keep them warm. I hope I will never hear such pleadings and witness such suffering again. Such cruelty and barbarity ought not to be tolerated by civilized nations." Thousands of men in northwestern Arkansas were learning hard lessons about the glory of war.[8]

During the night, most of the demoralized, exhausted survivors of McCulloch's shattered division finally reached Elkhorn Tavern. First to arrive was a woebegone column of two thousand men led by Pike. The troops had not filled their canteens since crossing Little Sugar Creek the night before and were desperate for water. When Pike reached Telegraph Road in Cross Timber Hollow, he turned the column north toward Big Sugar Creek instead of south toward Elkhorn Tavern. Van Dorn learned of Pike's eccentric route and ordered him to countermarch at once. The tired, thirsty, and hungry rebels reached Elkhorn Tavern "long after dark" and crowded around bonfires or huddled together in the woods for warmth, for they were without the coats, blankets, and knapsacks they had discarded before going into battle that morning. They had left their gear on Foster's farm in the confused withdrawal from Leetown.[9]

In the Confederate encampments around Twelve Corner Church another thirty-five hundred of McCulloch's men under Greer's command tried with a similar lack of success to make themselves comfortable. They, too, were tired, thirsty, hungry, and bereft of much personal gear. A handful of desperate souls crept back to Foster's farm and retrieved some items, but few had the energy or courage to venture so near enemy lines. As the temperature dropped below freezing, the hapless soldiers set large bonfires blazing and kept as close to the flames as they dared, often becoming singed on one side but remaining chilled on the other. Those who could not find a place near a fire burrowed into piles of leaves. Every so often nervous pickets awakened everyone by firing at stragglers making their way back toward the fiery beacons.[10]

While his men snatched what fitful rest they could, Greer anxiously pondered his next move. The dispatch from Van Dorn directing him to hold his position had arrived an hour before sunset. After that—nothing. It was as if the Texas colonel had been forgotten. Around 10:00 P.M. Greer conferred with the remaining regimental commanders. Everyone agreed that the troops at Twelve Corner Church should move to join Price as soon as possible. Greer composed a note informing Van Dorn of his intention to march to Elkhorn Tavern unless he received an order to the contrary before 1:00 A.M.[11]

John N. Coleman and A. B. Blocker of the 3rd Texas Cavalry set out eastward along the Bentonville Detour about 11:00 P.M. with Greer's message in hand. The two young cavalrymen nervously made their way over the narrow winding road and through the tangles of felled trees. Once they hid from what they feared was a Federal patrol but was most likely a party of Pike's inconstant warriors heading back to the Indian Territory. Climbing the steep hill out of Cross Timber Hollow, they discovered the human wastage of the struggle for Elkhorn Tavern. The 3rd Texas Cavalry had been held in reserve at Leetown, and this was the two teenagers' first glimpse of a battlefield. Years later Blocker remembered the grim scene: "The dead soldiers of both armies were lying where they had fallen, on both sides of the road, and presented a most ghastly sight when the moonlight would flash out from behind a cloud onto their white, upturned faces."[12]

The two Texans reached Confederate headquarters a little after midnight. Van Dorn and Price were camped in the yard on the northern side of Elkhorn Tavern. The commanding general was lying on the ground, wrapped in a blanket, using a saddle for a pillow. Upon being awakened Van Dorn sat up and silently read Greer's message. He stared into the flickering campfire for a few minutes then abruptly said, "You men return at once to Colonel Greer and tell him to have all his forces in his command on this road by sunup in the morning." Without another word he lay down. Maury began to write the order; but Coleman warned that if they were captured, the enemy would know everything, so Maury permitted him to transmit the order verbally. Coleman need not have worried. The two cavalrymen returned safely to Twelve Corner Church, where they found McCulloch's division assembling for the long, cold march.[13]

An officer in the 4th Arkansas remembered that "we was called into line very Quiet, no nois or loud talking." About 2:30 A.M. the soldiers under Greer's command—every one of them "staggering with fatigue and half-dead with cold and hunger"—set out for Elkhorn Tavern. It was a nightmarish journey. Hundreds of utterly exhausted men stumbled out of the column and collapsed. Those who struggled on reached the tanyard in Cross Timber Hollow only an hour before sunrise. The men fell out by regiments and sprawled on the frozen ground in what one Louisiana soldier called "a sort of stupor." They would have no more than an hour's rest before the battle began anew.[14]

The two halves of the Army of the West were separated for nearly twenty-

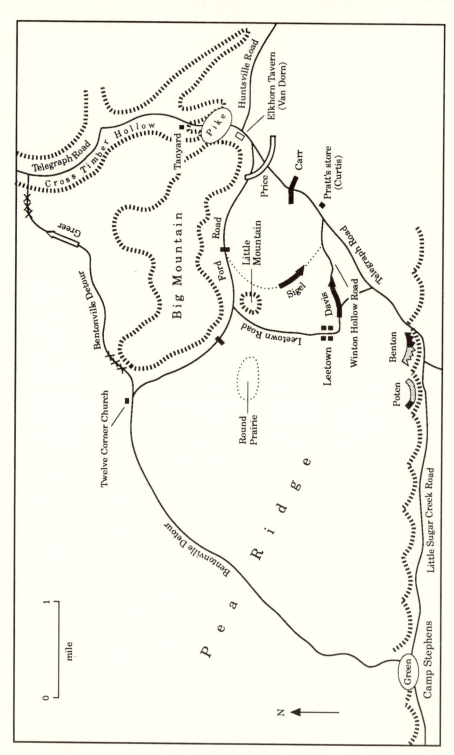

Map 11-1. Pea Ridge: Night of March 7–8

four hours at Pea Ridge. During that time there was remarkably little communication between Van Dorn and the commanders of McCulloch's division. Apparently only four official messages passed around Big Mountain between sunrise and sunset on March 7. Around midmorning McCulloch informed Van Dorn that his division was rounding Big Mountain and turning eastward toward Elkhorn Tavern. In midafternoon Van Dorn urged McCulloch to hold his ground. About the same time, Stone reported the deaths of McCulloch and McIntosh and the deteriorating situation at Leetown. Van Dorn responded to Stone's message with an order for Greer to take command and stand fast. In addition to these official dispatches, Missouri quartermaster Harding told Van Dorn shortly after noon that McCulloch's division was heavily engaged at Leetown. If other messages got through, no record of them has survived.

The loss of McCulloch, McIntosh, and Hébert was a major cause of the breakdown of communications within the Army of the West, but Van Dorn's conduct was an important factor as well. The Confederate commander became so immersed in the fight at Elkhorn Tavern that he effectively abdicated as army commander. On March 7 Van Dorn did not know what was happening on another part of the field; what was worse, he made no serious effort to find out.

Soldiers of Price's division collapsed wherever they happened to be when the fighting stopped at Elkhorn Tavern on March 7. The Confederate line of battle—if such a disjointed, confused mass of intermingled units could be called a line—formed an irregular crescent about one mile in length centered on Telegraph Road. The Missouri rebels were in reasonably good spirits, for they remained ignorant of the debacle at Leetown. "We thought we had gained the day and the victory was ours," recalled a sergeant in Slack's brigade. Though buoyed by their accomplishments, Price's men were in pathetic physical condition. Brigadier General Frost, commanding the 7th and 9th State Guard divisions, observed that the "long fasting and incessant labor" of the past few days "had nearly exhausted the powers of human endurance." The Missouri soldiers had left their coats and blankets in Cross Timber Hollow and suffered severely from the cold. Many huddled together for warmth in the frosty woods, while others drifted toward the blazing fires in the rear areas. Here and there they scavenged for food in the haversacks of fallen yankees.[15]

More fortunate were the several hundred Missourians who consumed the remaining Federal stores and sutler's goods near the tavern. They wolfed down oysters, sardines, cheese, pickles, wine, preserves, and other "delicacies long unknown to the State Guard." The men of Guibor's battery, providentially located only a few steps from this cornucopia of luxuries, were among the blessed that night. They devoured as much as they could and topped off their hasty repast with captured cigars. Afterward, reported gunner Hunt Wilson, "matters assumed a more comfortable aspect." Few—very few—were so lucky.[16]

Another group of Missourians milling around the tavern had an epicurean encounter of a different sort. They ripped open several containers of captured dessicated vegetables ("desecrated vegetables" according to the Federals) and dumped the contents into a large kettle filled with boiling water. The rebels were uncertain about what would happen next and watched the pot expectantly. An officer noted in amusement that "soon the vegetables commenced climbing out over the top of the kettle until at last the pile outside was ten times as large as the amount inside." The famished soldiers, armed with spoons and cups, made short work of the unappetizing mess.[17]

Alas for Van Dorn, no more than a tenth of his troops enjoyed tinned seafood or soggy vegetables that night. His decision to dash forward without an adequate supply train and to subsist on captured enemy rations had been a tremendous gamble. He seemed to have lost; the Army of the West was beginning to starve.

The Confederates also faced a second and more immediate crisis of their own making: during the night Van Dorn neglected to order up the ordnance and supply trains from distant Camp Stephens. The only possible explanation for this stupendous oversight is that Van Dorn did not realize the trains had become separated from the rest of the army and assumed they were close at hand behind Big Mountain or in Cross Timber Hollow. Van Dorn turned in for the night confident that there would be sufficient opportunity to distribute ammunition and emergency rations the next morning. Meanwhile, eleven miles to the southwest at Camp Stephens, Green and his 2nd State Guard Division, joined by a growing number of fugitive Texas, Arkansas, and Indian troops from Leetown, uneasily guarded the trains against the specter of another Federal attack and waited for orders.[18]

The failure to keep the trains close to the rest of the army was the most disastrous error in a campaign awash in errors. The Army of the West was nearly as effectively separated from its trains as the Army of the Southwest was severed from its base at Rolla, the crucial difference being that Curtis had plenty of reserve ammunition on hand but Van Dorn did not.

Oddly enough, the Confederates did receive a modest resupply of artillery ammunition that night courtesy of the Federal army. Four soldiers of the 4th Ohio Battery had taken a caisson to the rear to refill its ammunition chests. Upon returning to the front, they drove straight up Telegraph Road and into Confederate hands. A Missouri officer noted that the Federals were "greatly surprised" to find themselves prisoners of war. The three full ammunition chests were welcomed by the Missouri gunners but hardly compensated for the absence of their own ammunition train.[19]

A sense of gloom hung over the Army of the Southwest that night. The success at Leetown was overshadowed by the setback at Elkhorn Tavern and the knowledge that the Confederates lay across the army's line of supply and retreat. The soldiers of Carr's 4th Division were especially despondent. Captain Cummings of the 4th Iowa noted that many of the regiment's officers "despaired of victory." Even Dodge was affected, though he kept up a bold front. "That night was a gloomy one to those who knew our situation," he acknowledged privately to his family. Byron Carr, visiting his older brother, described the 4th Division's headquarters staff as "about as anxious and downhearted a company as I ever hope to see again." The officers and men of Carr's command spent the long night huddled behind the zigzag fence on the southern side of Ruddick's field.[20]

Physically and emotionally drained by the fury of the battle, most of the Federals did not realize how roughly they had handled the Confederates. "The night was one of deep anxiety, and many of us had gloomy forebodings for the coming day," recalled one soldier. Rumors raced along the lines and from campfire to campfire. The most popular story offered the hope that reinforcements from Missouri and Kansas were approaching the battlefield that very night, but few in the Army of the Southwest placed much stock in these unlikely tales. A soldier in the 37th Illinois disdainfully remarked that "our courage wasn't so shaky yet as to require such stimulants." Despite muttered premonitions of disaster and defeat, there was no talk of surrender. Indeed, many of the shivering troops remained intensely defiant. "We didn't feel whipped," wrote one stalwart infantryman.[21]

One Federal soldier who most assuredly did not feel whipped was Samuel Curtis. As he saw it, the Army of the Southwest had routed the enemy on one battlefield and had fought a dogged delaying action on another. Curtis returned to his headquarters at Pratt's store after helping Asboth and Carr establish a defensive position on the southern side of Ruddick's field. For the next few hours he reviewed the course of the battle, checked troop movements and logistical activities, and made plans for the climactic fight on the morrow. By the time Curtis finally dismissed his staff and turned in for the night, he was "certain of success on the coming day."[22]

Pratt's store was the focal point of Federal activity that night, for it lay directly between the troops and the trains. Ambulances and caissons rattled to and fro along Telegraph Road. Soldiers thronged the roads and lanes, some laden with heavy boxes of small arms ammunition, others draped with canteens and haversacks belonging to their comrades and messmates. Furtive stragglers and milling teamsters added to the stream of traffic. Above the din came the cries of the draft animals, most of whom had not eaten since the previous day. "The braying of the mules—never melodious —became doubly dismal and discordant," said correspondent Knox. "Their usually hoarse tones gradually softened to a low, plaintive moan that was painful to hear."[23]

About midnight the headquarters staff and civilians at Pratt's store enjoyed a bit of comic relief unintentionally provided by Knox's fellow journalist William Fayel. After engaging in a lengthy discussion on the merits of reincarnation, Fayel carelessly placed his bedroll too close to one of the headquarters campfires. Shortly after he dozed off, his beard caught fire. Roused by Fayel's frantic shouts, Knox and others in the vicinity flung off their blankets and valiantly assisted "in staying the conflagration." Singed but undaunted, Fayel adjusted his bedroll and retired a second time.[24]

In contrast to Curtis, Asboth was not at all confident of a Federal victory in the morning. In fact, he was certain the Army of the Southwest was doomed. The Hungarian emigré had performed well in the final clash along Telegraph Road despite receiving a painful arm wound. Mercurial even in the best of times, Asboth was seized by despair as the night wore on. He rode down Telegraph Road, his arm in a sling, and chanced upon the camp of the 3rd Iowa Cavalry near Pratt's store. About sunset the Iowans had been ordered from Leetown to reinforce the 4th Division but had arrived too late to participate in the fighting. When Asboth appeared out of the darkness, Bussey invited him to join in a spartan meal.[25]

Asboth sat beside the fire and poured out his fears to Bussey: their losses were heavy, and captured rebels claimed Van Dorn had forty thousand men firmly astride Telegraph Road. Asboth "did not see what was to prevent the loss of our whole army" and wondered why Curtis did not hold another council of war. Bussey tried unsuccessfully to calm the anxious Hungarian and finally agreed to send his adjutant, Lt. John Noble, to Curtis with Asboth's request for a meeting of the senior commanders. Apparently Asboth felt that Curtis would be more receptive to his idea if it came from a fellow Iowan—another glimpse of the ethnic divisions within the Army of the Southwest.[26]

Noble found Curtis, fully dressed, resting on a blanket spread over a bed of straw in his tent. He dutifully relayed Asboth's dismal assessment of the army's situation and his request for an immediate council of war. Curtis listened patiently—or at least stoically—and then said, "I have ordered Sigel over from Lee Town ... and in the morning I will attack at Elk Horn Tavern and will whip the rebels there, and when I whip them there, I whip them everywhere." In dismissing Noble, Curtis neatly summed up his assessment of the situation and his plan of action.[27]

Asboth was not satisfied. He all but ordered Bussey to go himself to Curtis. "Late as it was," recalled Bussey, Curtis "treated me cordially and asked many questions concerning my observations of the day's battle." Bussey then repeated Asboth's request for a council of war. "Tell General Asboth that no conference or council of war is necessary," said Curtis emphatically. He repeated what he had told Noble, throwing in some additional details. "I have ordered Generals Sigel and Davis to move with their divisions during the night, and form on the left of Carr's division with all their available forces, and be ready to renew the battle at daylight. The enemy will concentrate his whole force at Elk Horn; we will fight him there tomorrow. If we whip him there, he is whipped everywhere." Bussey departed and informed Asboth of his meeting with the commanding general.[28]

Twice rebuffed, Asboth declared with great agitation that Curtis "did not seem to appreciate his great danger" and rode off to his own tent. Still strangely reluctant to face the Federal commander, Asboth wrote a letter recommending that Curtis launch a "decided concentrated movement, with the view of cutting our way through the enemy where you may deem it advisable, and save by this if not the whole at least the larger part of our surrounded army." Curtis did not respond to this missive. He believed that he was in a position not merely to salvage his command but to strike the enemy a smashing blow, and he did not intend to let a nervous subordinate change his mind.[29]

The matter did not quite end there. Shortly after Asboth rode off, Bussey encountered Dodge and told him what had just happened. Dodge rushed to Curtis's tent, apparently under the mistaken impression that the commanding general was falling prey to defeatism (which in Dodge's mind meant that Curtis was listening to foreigners instead of Iowans). Thoroughly irritated by now, Curtis again rose from his bed of straw and explained that there would be no council of war, that his plans for the morrow were made, and that rather than retreat he was going to "fight it out right where they were." Dodge imprudently suggested that, under the circumstances, the entire army should be concentrated against the foe at Elkhorn Tavern. "That is just what I am going to do," snapped Curtis. Satisfied, Dodge returned to his command, and Curtis again tried to rest.[30]

Six hours earlier, as dusk shaded into darkness, Sigel marched from Leetown toward the sound of the guns at Elkhorn Tavern. He rode at the head of a very short column composed of a battalion of the 25th Illinois, two twelve-pounder guns of Welfley's Independent Missouri Battery, and two six-pounder rifled guns of the 4th Ohio Battery. Despite the urgency of the situation, Sigel proceeded cautiously. He was uncertain of the enemy's location, was unfamiliar with the terrain, and unaccountably had neglected to provide his relief column with a cavalry escort. After advancing a short distance beyond Little Mountain, Sigel stopped and waited for Osterhaus to bring up the 12th and 15th Missouri and the 36th and 44th Illinois from Leetown. The reinforced column then resumed its forward movement.[31]

About 7:00 P.M. Sigel called a halt on the edge of Ford's farm. Though darkness had almost completely fallen by now, the Federals had an unobstructed view of the contested ground between Elkhorn Tavern and Pratt's store. Flashes of artillery fire lit up the smoky battlefield like heat lightning on a summer night. Sigel could not appreciate the irony of the situation. For much of the day Van Dorn had waited for McCulloch's division to arrive, but Ford Road had lain empty. The road was filled with troops now, but their uniforms were blue.[32]

No enemy pickets were encountered, and Sigel concluded that the Confederates at Elkhorn Tavern were unaware of his approach. The German general saw no reason to reveal his presence now that fighting had ended for the day. He decided to bivouac where he was and commence operations against the enemy's flank in the morning. After informing Curtis of his intentions, Sigel ordered the scattered detachments of the 1st and 2nd Divisions to join him on Ford's farm, leaving only two companies of the 2nd Missouri and four six-pounder guns of the 2nd Ohio Battery in the Little Sugar Creek fortifications. He prohibited campfires, enjoined everyone to maintain the "strictest silence," and warned the pickets to establish their outposts no more than two or three hundred yards in advance. As the Federals dribbled in over the next few hours, they sought an empty place and settled down to get what rest they could. Officers and men who came directly from Little Sugar Creek had coats and blankets to protect them from the cold; those who came straight from the fight at Leetown generally had neither. Food and water were scarce, and messengers sent off to obtain provisions returned empty-handed.[33]

Around midnight Federal pickets reported hearing faint rumbling noises to the north, seemingly from the far side of Big Mountain. Sigel, bundled inside his enormous overcoat, ventured partway up the sandstone slope. He listened intently for half an hour but heard nothing from the direction of the Bentonville Detour. Sigel pondered the matter. If the youthful ears of the pickets had indeed detected the distant sounds of moving men and vehicles, the rebels defeated at Leetown must be making their way around Big Mountain to join their comrades at Elkhorn Tavern. Sigel was right, but for the wrong reason. It was very unlikely that the Federals heard McCulloch's division on the march along the Bentonville Detour: the hour was wrong and the distance was too great. Sigel's pickets almost certainly heard the sound of Davis's 3rd Division moving from Leetown to Pratt's store on Winton Hollow Road. In the cold, still air the noise made by the Federal column echoed off the rocky southern face of Big Mountain. Therefore Sigel could not hear any sounds coming from the north when he was actually on the side of Big Mountain.[34]

Sigel impulsively decided his men must be properly fed and rested in order to be ready for the coming battle against a united Confederate army. The 1st and 2nd Divisions would march back to the camps near Little Sugar Creek, spend the rest of the night there in relative comfort, and return in the morning. Sigel led his command away from the battlefield and left only detachments of the 4th and 5th Missouri Cavalry to hold the position on Ford's farm. "We silently left our position in the field," recalled a soldier in the 36th Illinois, and spent the next hour "groping our way among the deadened cornstalks, clambering over fences, meandering through woods, falling over logs, ascending steep hills and crossing ravines." The weary, disoriented guides at the head of the Federal column lost their way in the smoky darkness, made at least two wrong turns, and led everyone southeast.[35]

About 2:00 A.M. Sigel found himself at Pratt's store instead of at Little Sugar Creek. Unfazed, he took this opportunity to inform Curtis of his altered plans. Roused yet again from his bed of straw, the commanding general was astonished to learn that Sigel had abandoned his position on Ford Road without seeking permission or, until now, informing anyone of his action. Curtis was even more astonished when he heard Sigel's scheme. With dawn only four hours away and the troops still two miles from their camps, it would be impossible for them to eat, sleep, and return in time to do battle —especially with Sigel in charge. Curtis still was reluctant to give his chief subordinate a direct order, but he forcefully urged him to rest his weary men at Pratt's store and "send for provisions, as the other troops were doing." Taken aback by Curtis's sharp tone, Sigel "readily concurred."[36]

The wandering warriors of the 1st and 2nd Divisions, "dead tired, starved and discouraged," plopped down in the woods surrounding Pratt's store. Some started cooking fires; others scurried off to fill canteens, borrow utensils, and collect rations of flour from the nearby supply trains. Within an hour or so they were dining on flapjacks. The small cooking fires soon became roaring bonfires surrounded by slumbering masses of thinly clad soldiers. "We were thoroughly tired out," recalled one midwesterner, "and had reached a point where sleep, however uncomfortable, was a necessity." Sigel's men were among the few Federals who enjoyed the luxury of campfires that night.[37]

When Asboth learned of the arrival of the 1st and 2nd Divisions at Pratt's store, he hurried over and poured out his fears to Sigel, who was one of his closest friends in the army. Sigel's military career thus far had been highlighted by a series of retreats in Germany, at Carthage and Wilson's Creek in Missouri, and most recently, at Bentonville. By now he was predisposed to think of battle in terms of defeat and escape. Even though Sigel had seen the Federal triumph at Leetown with his own eyes, Asboth had little difficulty persuading him that the overall tactical situation was hopeless. By the time this curious meeting ended, the army's senior division commander had convinced the army's second-in-command that the battle of Pea Ridge was lost and that the Federals could avoid disaster only by making a vigorous fighting withdrawal. Sigel's heart must have quickened as he contemplated the prospect of his second brilliant retreat in three days.

Hours earlier, after Sigel and Osterhaus had marched toward the sound of battle at Elkhorn Tavern, Davis directed the soldiers of his 3rd Division to secure the Leetown battlefield and retrieve the wounded. Not having heard from Curtis in some time, Davis dispatched a company of cavalrymen from the 36th Illinois to check the Winton Hollow Road between Leetown and Pratt's store for rebel ambushes. The troopers found none and reached army headquarters without incident, where they described the final stages of the Federal victory at Leetown to Curtis in detail. Fully satisfied that there no longer was any danger of a renewed Confederate offensive in that quarter, Curtis sent the cavalrymen back to Davis with orders to reinforce Carr and Asboth on Telegraph Road as soon as possible.[38]

Davis formed the "weary, chilled and despondent" soldiers of the 3rd Division on Leetown Road. The dim moonlight filtering through drifting layers of smoke illuminated a landscape turned macabre: dozens of bodies littered the ground where the Peoria Battery had been overrun. An officer in the 59th Illinois wrote that "moonbeams never made a scene more cold or cruel, the air never seemed [more] like drafts from a charnel house, nor our doom more apparent." The column set out about midnight and trudged the two miles to Pratt's store; then they turned up Telegraph Road toward the Federal line of battle at Ruddick's field. Davis and Curtis did not meet. Most likely the Indiana colonel saw no reason to awaken Curtis merely to report his passage.[39]

With Asboth sulking in his tent, Carr was in command when Davis arrived at Ruddick's field. Carr explained the situation to Davis and then led his 4th Division some distance to the east. When the division finally settled down for the night, the position of the two brigades was reversed: Vandever's 2nd Brigade was now on the right, Dodge's 1st Brigade on the left. The 4th Division was nearly fought out, and this shift took it away from the most likely arena of battle in the morning. Davis's 3rd Division deployed squarely across Telegraph Road, Pattison's 1st Brigade on the right and White's 2nd Brigade on the left. While placing his men in line, Pattison came across the battalion of the 8th Indiana and the three guns of the 1st Indiana Battery and directed them to rejoin the brigade. Meanwhile, Weston's 24th Missouri and Bowen's Battalion fell back to Pratt's store for rest and reassignment.[40]

Davis marched his men away from Leetown so quickly that few were able to recover their overcoats and blankets. Now, like so many other soldiers on that frosty battlefield, they suffered greatly from the cold. After the regiments filed into their new positions, one man from each mess was sent to the supply wagons to collect food and water for his comrades. The distribution process was far from perfect—an infantryman in the 18th Indiana complained that he received only "half enough grub"—but at least everyone in the 3rd Division got something to eat without having to march in circles. No fires were permitted along the line of arms, and the soldiers huddled together in shared misery.[41]

The higher ranks in Davis's division did not fare any better than the mass of privates. Surgeon George Gordon of the 18th Indiana wolfed down a few cold biscuits supplemented by a can of sardines. Gordon opened the can in the dark and shared its contents with Colonels Pattison and Washburn. The famished doctor forgot to wash his gory hands before eating. "In the morning," he recalled with a shudder, "I could see by my thumb and two first fingers on my right hand by the absence of blood, how deep my fingers and thumb had been in the Sardines box." None of the three officers had an overcoat, so they "would walk awhile to start the circulation and that would start our teeth to chattering so loud we were afraid it would alarm the rebels, and we did not wish to disturb them in the least." The three then tried huddling together for warmth. "Blessed was the man that got in the middle," recalled Gordon. When that became unbearable, the three officers got up and walked about some more and then lay down again. In this uncomfortable fashion they passed the night.[42]

During the night of March 7–8 Curtis shifted his troops from a widely dispersed array to a compact formation centered on Telegraph Road. The 3rd and 4th Divisions were in Ruddick's field; the 1st and 2nd Divisions were a short distance behind at Pratt's store. The latter two divisions were not on Ford's farm where they were supposed to be, but that error could be remedied quickly at the proper time. Each regiment and battery had been resupplied with ammunition, and every soldier had received something to eat and drink. When the sun rose on March 8, the Federals would be ready to continue the fight.

12 Thunder in the Ozarks

As dawn broke over Pea Ridge on Saturday, March 8, an observer in the Federal camp described the morning sun as a "dull, copper tinted globe, slowly pushing itself up through the murky cloud of cannon smoke that even the long hours of a winter night had not dispelled." The entire battlefield was swathed in wispy layers of white that resembled morning fog. The night had been cold, but the day held promise of warming temperatures.[1]

In the thickets surrounding Elkhorn Tavern the soldiers of the Army of the West rose sluggishly from the frigid earth, stamping their feet and flailing their arms against the bone-chilling cold. With their haversacks and canteens empty, and their cartridge boxes and ammunition chests nearly so, the men must have hoped the day would bring a change in their fortunes. Many had strayed during the night in search of sustenance, warmth, or plunder, but most remained wherever their units had halted at the close of the fighting.

The ragged Confederate line was centered on Telegraph Road and was about one mile in length. Its right flank lay near Ford Road below the rocky promontory of Big Mountain; its left was south of Clemon's field. All of the Missouri soldiers were partially hidden in the scrubby woods that covered so much of Pea Ridge. Nearly all, except the guardsmen on the far left, looked out across an expanse of frost-covered farmland: Ruddick's field to the south and Cox's field to the west. In the rear lay the Arkansas, Texas, Louisiana, and Indian units that had arrived from Leetown with Pike and Greer.

After a reasonably restful night Van Dorn awoke to find that his fever was gone. As he sipped coffee in the tavern yard, he waited to see whether Curtis would surrender or would attempt to find a way out of the trap. If the yankees wanted to continue the fight, the Confederate commander would oblige them, for in his view, the tactical situation favored southern arms. The Army of the West had been victorious in the bitter struggle for Elkhorn Tavern and now lay squarely across the Federal line of communications. Van Dorn did not yet know that the Confederate ordnance and supply trains were hopelessly out of reach at Camp Stephens, nor did he realize that his equally pugnacious counterpart in blue was massing the entire Federal army for a decisive counterstroke.[2]

Following a conference with Price, Little, and other Missouri officers, Van Dorn made few major changes in the disposition of his forces other than to unscramble the jumbled, overlapping formations left from the confused fighting of the previous day. He restored organizational coherence by concentrating the state guard east of Telegraph Road; reinforced his center by bringing forward the 1st Arkansas Mounted Rifles, the 16th and 17th Arkansas, and the 4th Texas Cavalry Battalion from McCulloch's division; and extended his right flank by shifting the 2nd Missouri Brigade until it stretched over the rocky promontory of Big Mountain. To protect the exposed right flank Van Dorn sent the 2nd Cherokee Mounted Rifles to establish a cavalry screen along the top of Big Mountain, a task for which the Indians were reasonably well suited. When he was done, Van Dorn had transformed the curved alignment of the night before into a V-shaped line of battle.[3]

The troops who had only recently come dragging in with Greer lay sprawled in sleep all over Cross Timber Hollow. Van Dorn initially did not want to disturb these men; even he considered them too worn out to be of any use. Within an hour, however, he changed his mind and ordered Greer to bring his command up the hill. The men struggled to their feet and trudged up the steep incline to the plateau. They turned east onto Huntsville Road and halted near Clemon's farm to await further orders. An hour after sunrise most of the two divisions of the Army of the West were finally together atop Pea Ridge at Elkhorn Tavern.[4]

These movements attracted the attention of interested observers on the opposite side of Ruddick's field. The Federals, too, were up early that morning. Sigel sent Osterhaus on a reconnaissance mission toward Ford's farm as soon as there was enough light to see. Osterhaus rode across the country-side and halted atop a cleared, gently rounded ridge four hundred yards west of Telegraph Road. Welfley's Knoll, as this ridge is now known, rises fifty feet above the plateau and runs from northeast to southwest along the western edge of Cox's field. It is the highest point on this section of Pea Ridge after Big and Little mountains and dominates the woods south and west of the tavern where the Confederates were stirring. As he gazed down through the lingering smoke at the surrounding fields and forests, Osterhaus realized that Welfley's Knoll might well be the key to the second day's battle.

Osterhaus trotted back and informed Sigel of the importance of the knoll. He suggested that instead of trudging back to Ford's farm via the round-about route of the previous night, the 1st and 2nd Divisions should march directly up Telegraph Road and form on the left of Davis's 3rd Division. This would save time, would keep the army massed together, and would give the Federals possession of the knoll. Sigel so informed Curtis and received permission to move forward as soon as possible. Seeing the 44th Illinois forming up in Telegraph Road, Sigel told Osterhaus to go ahead and lead that regiment to the proper location; the rest of the 1st and 2nd Divisions would follow shortly.[5]

While Osterhaus rode up Telegraph Road at the head of the 44th Illinois, the crash of artillery unexpectedly rolled across the frozen plateau. Surprised, he turned to Colonel Knobelsdorff and told him to advance at the double-quick. Osterhaus assumed, reasonably enough, that the sudden eruption of artillery fire meant the rebels were preparing to launch an attack against Carr and Davis. In fact, nothing of the sort was happening. A Federal battery, in an almost casual way, had just fired the first shots of the second day's battle.

Davis was curious about Confederate activity directly across Ruddick's field from his 3rd Division. Rebels garbed in what appeared to be "white blankets" were seen moving about in the hazy light of dawn; this was the first glimpse the Hoosiers had of the whitish uniforms worn by Little's Missourians. Davis rode over to Battery A, 2nd Illinois Light Artillery, the much reduced Peoria Battery, whose three remaining cannons were immediately west of Telegraph Road. He directed Captain Davidson to fire into the woods across the way and see how the enemy responded. Davidson's gunners shattered the morning calm by loosing twenty rounds of shell and canister. The sudden barrage created quite a "flutter" among the rebel infantry, who quickly disappeared from view.[6]

After the Peoria Battery ceased firing, an uneasy quiet descended upon the plateau. Some soldiers in the 18th Indiana peered across the smoky field and wondered aloud if the rebels had run away. Little's men had indeed fallen back a short distance into the woods, but as one Indiana soldier remarked, "shure enough they were there." Suddenly a "sheet of flame" erupted from Confederate batteries masked by the trees and brush. Klauss's 1st Indiana Battery, well out in Ruddick's field two hundred yards east of Telegraph Road, was the primary target. Klauss screamed, "Jesus Christ, limber up," and led his men out of the narrow confines of Ruddick's field through a gauntlet of Confederate fire. The three Indiana cannons and caissons raced across the entire front of the 3rd Division from east to west, bounced over Telegraph Road, and sped into the broad fields beyond. Davidson's Illinois cannoneers held out a bit longer even though "shot and shell came thick and fast" from the rebel artillery. After one of his guns was disabled, Davidson also withdrew and joined Klauss on the rising ground two hundred yards northwest of White's 2nd Brigade.[7]

Having disposed of the two Federal batteries with remarkable ease, the Missouri gunners turned their attention to the Federal infantry in their front. The 3rd Division formed a shallow V centered on Telegraph Road: Pattison's 1st Brigade to the east, White's 2nd Brigade to the west. All of the men crouched behind little piles of rails made from disassembled fences, but only those within about one hundred yards of the road enjoyed the additional shelter of trees and brush. The Confederate gunners shifted from canister to shot and shell and hammered at the exposed infantry. "Their first few shots dropped way in our rear," said a soldier in the 37th Illinois, "but nearer and closer they dropped till finally they obtained our range, and a few solid shots hit the piles we lay behind, scattering them and us at a pretty lively rate. Hardly one of us but what had a bruise or bleeding nose or lip, from concussion of rails against us." Tull's Missouri Battery was particularly effective because, from its position east of Telegraph Road, it enfiladed the line of the 2nd Brigade.[8]

Davis withdrew his 3rd Division from the "doubtful shelter" of the rail fences. He re-fused both wings to a second line of fences marking the edges of Cox's and Ruddick's fields. The soldiers were only too happy to go. An officer in the 59th Illinois said that when White waved his sword, "up we jumped and scampered pell-mell southward over the field." Osterhaus, Knobelsdorff, and the 44th Illinois came panting up the road and filed into place on the left of the 2nd Brigade in the midst of the bombardment and then fell back along with everyone else.[9]

Pratt's store on the morning of March 8, as painted by Hunt P. Wilson of Guibor's battery (Museum of the Confederacy, Richmond, Va.; photograph by Katherine Wetzel)

The resulting alignment of the 3rd Division violated any number of military maxims. Davis's troops now formed a narrow, irregular, and potentially vulnerable salient centered on Telegraph Road. Regiments faced in different directions, some at right angles to one another. All of the soldiers, however, were partially concealed and sheltered in the woods. Carr watched the 3rd Division fall back and ordered the 4th Division to do the same; then he re-fused Vandever's 2nd Brigade until his right wing faced almost due east.[10]

The sight of the 3rd and 4th Divisions falling back caused a commotion around Pratt's store and initiated a general exodus of civilians and stragglers to the rear, which was now the rather confined area between Pratt's store and Little Sugar Creek. Medical orderlies placed wounded soldiers atop loaded supply wagons and prepared to carry them to a place of greater safety, if one could be found. It soon became apparent, however, that an evacuation of the hospitals and other facilities at army headquarters would not be necessary.[11]

Van Dorn responded to the Federal retrograde movement by ordering an oddly halfhearted demonstration. The artillery fire ceased, and a line of Missouri and Arkansas troops moved out from the shelter of the woods. The Confederates advanced across Ruddick's field, stepping over the frozen bodies of friend and foe. The six remaining guns of the Peoria and 1st Indiana batteries were in a perfect position to enfilade the Confederate ranks from the west and opened fire. The rebels wavered and then fell back to the shelter of the woods. The Army of the West had executed its last offensive maneuver at Pea Ridge.[12]

The unexpected outburst of artillery fire hastened the 1st and 2nd Divisions on their way and caused Curtis to gallop to the front. Sigel's troops gulped down their last bits of breakfast and marched up Telegraph Road at the double-quick with the little German general himself at their head. Food and rest had dispelled much of the despondency of the previous night; an observer noted that many of the officers and men "were as lively and jovial as if going to a corn husking." They reached Ruddick's field about the time the Confederate infantry retired.[13]

Van Dorn's passivity convinced Curtis that the time had come to seize the initiative. He directed Davis and Carr to return the 3rd and 4th Divisions to the piles of rails marking their original position. He then told Sigel to deploy the 1st and 2nd Divisions on the left of the 3rd Division where the 44th Illinois was located, about three hundred yards southeast of the crest of Welfley's Knoll. Mindful of Sigel's recent behavior, Curtis watched carefully

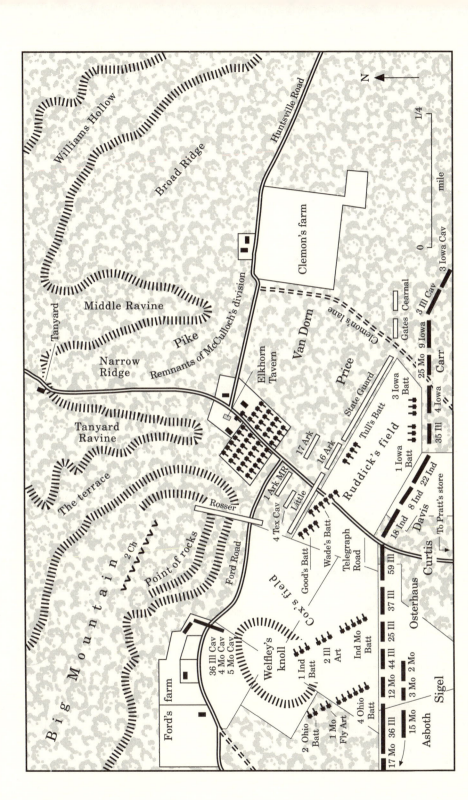

Map 12-1. Elkhorn Tavern: 9:00 A.M., March 8

as the blue column turned off the road to the west and formed a line of battle in the rolling fields. Sigel deployed his two divisions in less than thirty minutes, a record by the sluggish standards of Civil War armies. Curtis was impressed and informed Halleck that the normally deliberate German had moved "with great celerity."[14]

Sigel's remarkable efficiency on March 8 was, ironically, caused by his conviction that the Army of the Southwest was in imminent danger of being compelled to surrender. That morning he had informed his officers that they "would have to pierce through the enemy or be subjugated and submit to captivity." As events soon would demonstrate, Sigel was determined to beat a hasty retreat into Missouri with his two divisions. Whether the rest of the army followed was none of his concern[15]

Sigel initially placed his command on an east-west line behind the same rail fence occupied farther to the east by the 3rd Division. After a certain amount of shifting, the units of the 1st and 2nd Divisions were arrayed from right to left in the following fashion: the 25th and 44th Illinois, five cannons of Welfley's Independent Missouri Battery, the 12th Missouri, six cannons of the 4th Ohio Battery, the 36th Illinois, the 17th Missouri, the two surviving cannons of the 1st Missouri Flying Artillery, and two cannons of the 2nd Ohio Battery. At first the 2nd, 3rd, and 15th Missouri remained in reserve a short distance to the rear; later they moved to a new position on the left of the 17th Missouri, extending the Federal line farther to the left.[16]

Not every soldier in blue was in line of battle that morning. "Idle men stood about in squads away from their companies on a thousand different excuses," wrote a cavalryman of the scene along Telegraph Road. Some stragglers pretended to be sick, while others claimed to have lost their rifles. After the scare caused by the temporary withdrawal of the 3rd and 4th Divisions, the cowardly crowd stayed well to the rear and bombarded everyone returning from the front with anxious questions: "'How is the battle going?' 'Who is retreating?' 'Do the enemy fall back?'" Curtis could hardly have been unaware of the throngs of skulkers so near his headquarters, but he chose to ignore them and to concentrate on the task at hand.[17]

By 8:00 A.M. the four divisions of the Army of the Southwest formed a continuous line of infantry and artillery stretching three-quarters of a mile from Cox's field on the left to a wooded area southeast of Ruddick's field on the right. Cavalry detachments secured and extended the flanks to Ford's farm on the left and to Little Sugar Creek on the right. Curtis was ready to go on the offensive.

A southeasterly breeze sprang up after sunrise and swept away the smoke lingering from the previous day's fighting. The morning sun illuminated a dramatic scene as Sigel's two divisions filed into place on the rising ground west of Telegraph Road. Confederates in the woods north of Ruddick's field and on the rocky slope of Big Mountain had a superb view of the proceedings. A Missouri soldier recalled with awe how "regiment after regiment was deploying constantly into the field." Van Dorn responded with less admiration and more consternation. Realizing that none of his artillery was located opposite the newly arrived Federals, he ordered Good's Texas Battery, parked near the tavern, to advance and break up the enemy formations. The Texans rolled down Telegraph Road and turned west into Ruddick's field. They unlimbered their four twelve-pounder guns and two twelve-pounder howitzers near the sharp angle in the Confederate line. After loading their weapons with shell and case shot, they opened fire on the solid ranks of Federal infantry four to six hundred yards to the southwest. A few minutes later the gunners of Wade's Missouri Battery joined in the barrage.[18]

Van Dorn failed to use his numerical artillery superiority effectively on March 8. No more than three of the fifteen batteries in the Army of the West were in action along the front at any time, and they were ineffective. The rebel gunners consistently overshot the long lines of blue-clad soldiers who lay down as soon as the firing began. As far as can be determined, rebel artillery fire caused only four fatalities among the Federal infantry: one man in the 44th Illinois, another in the 36th Illinois, and two in the 12th Missouri. There were a number of close calls. A lieutenant in the 1st Missouri Flying Artillery managed to dodge a solid shot that passed so close he "could feel the air pressure plainly." Colonels Greusel and Frederick were slightly less fortunate. Both men were knocked out of their saddles by the shock waves from projectiles that passed only inches from their heads, but they were not seriously injured.[19]

At Sigel's command six batteries of varying size wheeled forward to engage the rebel artillery. A total of twenty-one Federal cannons, some of them rifled, now faced the twelve Confederate cannons west of Telegraph Road. In addition to being outgunned, the rebels suffered the great disadvantage of being on lower ground. Welfley's Knoll was directly in front of Sigel's left flank. As the artillery duel got under way, Sigel directed Captain Welfley, for whom the ridge is named, to advance his Independent Missouri Battery to the rounded crest and open fire. Other batteries followed. The knoll was a "splendid position" for artillery, and as Osterhaus had foreseen, its occupation by the Federals was a key factor in the outcome of the battle.[20]

*An artillery piece marking the location of Welfley's battery atop Welfley's Knoll.
Big Mountain is in the distance; its rocky promontory, with an observation
pavilion on its top, is to the right of the center. (authors' collection)*

The Federal gunners were far more effective than their Confederate counterparts, and Sigel deserved much of the credit. The German general took
personal control of the artillery west of Telegraph Road, including the two
fugitive batteries from the 3rd Division. For two hours he moved from battery to battery, frequently sighting the pieces himself and "encouraging the
men and giving his directions as coolly as if on parade." The Federal cannoneers followed his instructions and concentrated their fire on one target at a
time, beginning with the two Confederate batteries in the center. The result
was devastating.[21]

The Federals "opened a perfect storm of round and shrapnell shot and
shell" on Good's exposed position; the trees just behind the Texas battery
were shattered, and the ground all around was "litterally ploughed up with
cannon balls and shell." In less than an hour half of the Texas cannoneers
were down or in flight, and Good told his wife that "it is a perfect miracle
that any of us ever came out." One of the casualties was a fourteen-year-old

Arkansan named William Wilson who had attached himself to the battery when it rumbled past his home in Fayetteville three days earlier. He lost a leg. Lt. James Douglas, a former schoolmaster and fervent secessionist, reluctantly admitted that the yankees fought with "great spirit" and "poured a torrent of shot, shell and canister upon our little band." He estimated that at least one hundred missiles passed within twenty feet of his position. The embattled Texans doggedly fought until their ammunition gave out; then they limbered up and dashed for the rear. In their haste they left their handsome silk flag, a gift of the ladies of Dallas, lying uncased on the shot-torn ground.[22]

Wade's Missouri Battery, in the edge of the woods about two hundred yards east of the Texans, had an equally difficult time. "Such a cyclone of falling timber and bursting shells I don't suppose was ever equaled during our great war," wrote one survivor. With his ammunition depleted and men and horses dropping all around him, Wade followed Good's example and ordered his battery to fall back to the tavern. The Missourians limbered up and stampeded to the rear on Telegraph Road in wild disorder, or what one participant wryly described as "a kind of military tactics not learned at military school."[23]

Van Dorn responded to this disastrous turn of events by belatedly ordering forward Hart's Arkansas Battery and Clark's Missouri Battery, each equipped with four six-pounder guns. The untried Arkansas cannoneers reached the scene first and unlimbered their weapons at Good's former position near the angle in the Confederate line. Whether they actually fired any shots is not known, but within minutes they were so unnerved by the iron storm from the twenty-one Federal cannons that they fled from the field. Upon returning to the tavern Hart lamely explained that "he found the fire so severe he could not stay in it any longer." Furious, Van Dorn placed Hart under arrest for cowardice and sent the battery to the rear in disgrace. Clark, just coming up, received permission to use Hart's unexpended ammunition for his own six-pounders. Van Dorn directed Clark not to venture into Ruddick's field but to plant his battery south of the tavern near the junction of Ford Road and Telegraph Road. Some of the other Missouri batteries around the tavern gave Clark a modicum of support by firing sporadically and ineffectively at the distant Federals.[24]

The men in the 1st Missouri Brigade took a severe pounding during this phase of the artillery duel. Federal projectiles that overshot the Texas, Missouri, and Arkansas batteries smashed directly into Burbridge's and Rives's

Welfley's Knoll, looking west from Telegraph Road across Ruddick's field. The Federal gunners atop the knoll had a commanding advantage over Confederate artillery in the field and Confederate infantry in the woods on the right. (authors' collection)

regiments in the woods north of Ruddick's field. Rebels crouched behind the smallish trees or hugged the ground to avoid the hail of shot and shell and wooden splinters. The action was much worse than anything they had endured the previous day in Cross Timber Hollow. "Such an incessant booming of cannon and bursting of shells I had never heard," recalled a soldier in Rives's regiment. Large branches and sometimes entire trees came crashing down on the unfortunate Missourians. One man remembered that a rifled solid shot struck an oak tree in front of him, bored right through, and "tore off a large slab" as it exited, showering him with bark and splinters and discouraging him from relying on trees for protection against artillery. The Confederate center began to weaken as the barrage of Federal fire gradually drove the white-clad Missouri infantry away from Ruddick's field and back into the woods.[25]

After Hart's battery fled the scene, Sigel directed three of his six batteries to rake the woods on either side of Telegraph Road and three to shift their fire toward the southeastern corner of Big Mountain. The bare, rocky promontory was the most distinctive physical feature on the battlefield. Huge, free-standing columns of sandstone thirty feet high dominated the slope below the crest. Because of the absence of vegetation along this part of the slope the Federals could see the infantrymen of the 2nd Missouri Brigade in line and a battery being hauled toward the crest.[26]

When the Federal gunners opened fire, the imposing promontory became a deathtrap. Incoming artillery rounds smashed into the stone and sent fragments flying in all directions. Infantrymen who sought shelter among the massive formations discovered their error too late. Artillerymen and their horses, standing exposed to the terrible fire, were mowed down. Sigel reported with no exaggeration that "the rocks and stones worked as hard as the shells and shot" to slay the enemy. Within half an hour the Confederate right flank on Big Mountain crumbled, and Van Dorn ordered a withdrawal. Some members of the 2nd Missouri Brigade failed to get the word—or were too frightened to move—and hung on despite the "terrific volley of bombs and balls." The Federal gunners seemed to pursue the fleeing rebels, as errant missiles sailed over the rocky promontory and crashed around Elkhorn Tavern, spreading confusion in the Confederate rear.[27]

The situation in the vicinity of Elkhorn Tavern became even more chaotic when artillery projectiles commenced arriving from the Federal right. After watching the 1st and 2nd Divisions move into position in the broad fields west of Telegraph Road, Curtis rode in the opposite direction. He stopped frequently to speak words of encouragement to the officers and men of the 3rd and 4th Divisions and reached the Federal right flank about the time the artillery duel on the far side of Telegraph Road was at its peak. Curtis ordered the handful of Federal cannons on the right to join the fight. Displaying more enthusiasm than judgment, he personally led the surviving pieces of the 1st and 3rd Iowa batteries forward into the southeastern corner of Ruddick's field and directed them to fire on Elkhorn Tavern, barely visible above the trees on the northern edge of the plateau. As the batteries unlimbered and went into action, Curtis told Carr to wheel Vandever's 2nd Brigade forward and bring it into line with the rest of the 3rd and 4th Divisions. At some point the gunners of Tull's Missouri Battery attempted to repeat their earlier success against Klauss's 1st Indiana Battery by driving off the Iowans. Curtis responded by ordering both Iowa batteries, as well as Davidson's Peoria Battery across the road, to suppress the rebels. Tull's cannons soon fell silent, and the Illinois and Iowa cannoneers resumed firing shells into the Confederate center and rear.[28]

The cannonade lasted a little over two hours. It was the most intense sustained artillery barrage ever to take place on the North American continent up to that time, and it was a stupendous experience for the troops of both armies. Billows of smoke swirled across the plateau and drifted over the crest of Big Mountain. The continuous roar of artillery fire, the shriek of projectiles of every size and shape, and the clatter of shrapnel and flying debris nearly overpowered the senses of the troops. The crashing waves of sound could be heard for more than fifty miles across the Ozark Plateau. A benumbed Federal infantryman tallied over eighteen hundred discharges in the first hour before he lost count—a rate of more than thirty shots per minute, or one shot every two seconds. Even that estimate appears much too conservative, for the 4th Ohio Battery alone fired an astounding 566 rounds during the cannonade.[29]

Every soldier who left an account of the battle struggled to describe what he experienced that morning. "It was a continual thunder, and a fellow might have believed that the day of judgement had come," wrote an Iowan. One Illinois man said that "the constant roar of artillery seemed to shake the ground like an earthquake," while another told his brother that "no recital of the scene can give you any idea of the terrible grandeur of this period of the battle.... It beggars all my powers of description." Henry Cummings of the 4th Iowa was also at a loss for words and simply told his wife, "It was the grandest thing I ever saw or thought of." The Confederates who were on the receiving end of most of the fire were also impressed. A Missouri soldier spoke for many of Van Dorn's hapless warriors when he said that "a more continued and terrific cannonading was certainly never heard."[30]

The cannonade at Pea Ridge on March 8 was more than just sound and fury. It was one of the few times in the Civil War when a preparatory artillery barrage effectively softened up an enemy position and paved the way for an infantry assault. Confederate artillery was dispersed or silenced, and Confederate troops were forced well back into the woods away from the fields to their front.[31]

During the cannonade Sigel systematically advanced and realigned his forces to take advantage of the high ground. A segment of the blue line —both infantry and artillery—pushed forward several hundred yards, while the remainder stayed in place and provided support. Another segment followed, and then another, until the entire line had reached the new position.

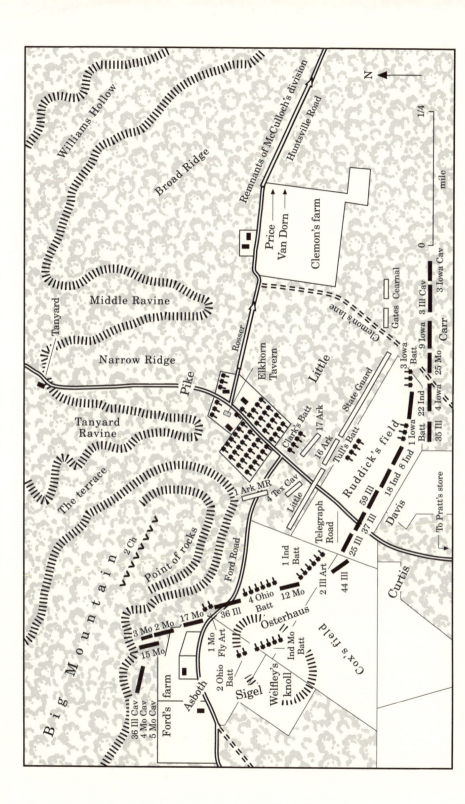

Map 12-2. Elkhorn Tavern: 10:00 AM, March 8

Then the process began anew. When not actually in motion the infantry lay on the ground to avoid sporadic enemy fire, while the artillery pounded the woods at ever-closer ranges. Sigel's incremental maneuvering was reminiscent of siege warfare with its elaborate geometrical system of parallels and approaches. Bit by bit the 1st and 2nd Divisions executed a gigantic right wheel, advancing half a mile and changing front from north to east until the Federal formation roughly corresponded to the battered, V-shaped Confederate line. Around 9:30 A.M. Sigel's left flank reached Ford's farm and linked with the detachments of the 4th and 5th Missouri Cavalry left there the previous night.[32]

By this time Confederate artillery fire had fallen off dramatically, and Confederate infantry had all but disappeared from sight. Sigel sent Osterhaus to inform Curtis of these promising developments. Osterhaus found the commanding general on Telegraph Road observing the effects of the Federal bombardment. After hearing what Osterhaus had to say, Curtis told Davis and Carr to prepare their divisions for an advance and then rode west to see for himself how Sigel was progressing. From time to time he paused to observe the artillerymen at their work. A member of Curtis's escort stated that the commanding general behaved "about as calmly and with as much composure as if overseeing a farm." Shortly after 10:00 A.M. Curtis found Sigel on Ford's farm on the extreme left of the Federal line. The gaggle of horsemen may have attracted the attention of the Missouri gunners near Elkhorn Tavern, for while the two generals were talking, a Confederate shell plunged into the ground almost directly under Curtis's horse. Curtis and Sigel continued to discuss tactical matters and made no move to leave. Their aides watched nervously as a stream of smoke rose from the small crater —the telltale sign of a burning fuse—but the shell failed to explode.[33]

At the close of the conversation Curtis casually told Sigel, "General, I think the infantry might advance now." The two officers saluted, and Curtis returned to the Federal center on Telegraph Road. The long ride to the left flank, like the one to Little Sugar Creek the previous afternoon, seems to have reflected both the Federal commander's innate caution and his uncertainty about Sigel's judgment. Once again reassured that all was well, he set his grand counterstroke in motion. Curtis later said that from this moment on he was convinced that "victory was inevitable."[34]

As commands passed down the chain of command, nearly ten thousand Federal infantrymen got to their feet and dressed their ranks. They stepped forward a few paces, aligned on units to right or left, and awaited the order to attack a roughly equal number of Confederates. The curving blue line, now almost a mile long, ran south from Ford's farm across Cox's field and then turned to the southeast near Telegraph Road and continued along the southern edge of Ruddick's field.

All of the infantry and artillery and most of the cavalry of the Army of the Southwest, except for stragglers and rear guard detachments, was in the open. For what may have been the only time in the Civil War, an entire army was visible in line of battle from flank to flank. It was a scene of martial grandeur right out of a picture book on the Napoleonic Wars, and it generated considerable rubbernecking as many Federals paused to take in the spectacle. "I had heard of such things," Dodge admitted, "but they were far beyond my conception." An awed officer in the 18th Indiana called the splendid array of men at arms "the grandest sight that I had ever beheld." Far over on the left near Ford's farm, Lt. William Burns of the 4th Missouri Cavalry stood in his stirrups for a better view. Many campaigns and battles later he still declared, "I would not have missed that sight for thousands."[35]

Shortly after dawn that morning Price had dispatched a courier to bring up the ordnance and supply trains. Price, like Van Dorn, thought the wagons were parked somewhere close. About the same time a puzzled Green at Camp Stephens sent a messenger in search of Price to explain his situation and ask for instructions. The two riders probably passed each other on the Bentonville Detour somewhere behind Big Mountain; they may even have asked each other for directions, for neither man knew where he was supposed to deliver his message. Upon receiving Price's order to advance, Green dutifully set out on the Bentonville Detour, but the draft animals were weak from lack of forage and progress was slow.[36]

Green's message reached Price at the height of the artillery duel. Old Pap hastened to inform Van Dorn that the reserve ammunition was at Camp Stephens—at least five or six hours away. The Confederate commander was staggered by this news, for it meant that his batteries would run out of ammunition long before Green could arrive. With tears of frustration in his eyes Van Dorn told Price that he had no choice but to retreat and save the army. The tables had been turned: now it was the Confederates, not the Federals, who were in danger of being trapped and compelled to surrender. If the Confederates attempted to retrace their roundabout steps toward Bentonville, the Federals merely had to move west along Ford Road and block the Bentonville Detour at Twelve Corner Church.[37]

In this unexpected crisis Van Dorn demonstrated that his audacity was not tempered by defeat. He decided that the main body of the army would march east on Huntsville Road, cross the White River, and turn south, making good its escape by marching completely around the Army of the Southwest; the trains and other forces at Camp Stephens would head west and then turn south and rendezvous with the main body in the safety of the Boston Mountains. In making this decision Van Dorn remained as indifferent as ever to the matter of logistics and to the enfeebled condition of his men and animals. The land beyond White River was a broken, barren wilderness of rocky trails and hardscrabble farms. Food and forage were scarce when they could be found at all.

Van Dorn brazenly attempted to avoid responsibility for the fiasco of the trains. Several weeks later he told General Albert S. Johnston that during the night of March 7–8 "the officer in charge of the ordnance supplies could not find his wagons, which, with the subsistence train, had been sent to Bentonville." After the war Maury offered a slightly different version of Van Dorn's story, blaming the affair on "the inexcusable incompetency of the ordnance officer who sent our train beyond reach." These deliberately vague statements are false. They were intended to obscure the fact that the trains had become separated from the army without anyone at headquarters noticing and thus to shift blame from Van Dorn and Maury to a wholly imaginary "ordnance officer." It was, in fact, Van Dorn who told Green to save the wagons by taking them through Bentonville to Elm Springs. A little before noon on March 8 Green met his own messenger returning with orders from Van Dorn to turn back and head west as rapidly as possible. Thoroughly perplexed, the Missouri officer nevertheless did as instructed.[38]

Shaken that his dream of capturing St. Louis would not be realized on this campaign, Van Dorn had some difficulty concentrating on the immediate problem of how to disengage and escape. This would not be easy: it was broad daylight, the two armies were only a few hundred yards apart on a wide plateau, and the chosen Confederate escape route led, not rearward into the depths of Cross Timber Hollow, but laterally just behind the vulnerable left flank. Only an assortment of skeletal state guard units stood between the Federals and Huntsville Road. Providentially for Van Dorn, the Federals were massing against the Confederate center and right, not against the left. Moreover, a slight hump near the crest of the densely wooded plateau masked Huntsville Road from the Federals in Ruddick's field.

Price, who had figured so prominently in the fighting on the previous day,

Hunt P. Wilson's painting of the Confederate army just before it began to retreat from the battlefield on March 8. The wounded Price figures much more promi-nently in this depiction, the most richly detailed visual record of the battle, than he did in the fighting that day. (Museum of the Confederacy, Richmond, Va.; photography by Katherine Wetzel)

played a relatively minor role on March 8. After informing Van Dorn of Green's message, his only other notable contribution was his insistence that as many wounded Missourians as possible be brought with the army. Old Pap was suffering from his injured arm, which had become infected and swollen. He soon took to an ambulance and left the field with other disabled members of his division.[39]

Van Dorn acceded to Price's demand. Around 10:00 A.M. he ordered the handful of Confederate ambulances to collect "all the wounded they could bear" and head east on Huntsville Road. Several units of McCulloch's divi-sion and the 2nd Missouri Brigade followed soon after, shuffling along the narrow road in complete ignorance of what was taking place. Van Dorn planned to use his remaining forces to cover the withdrawal or, as he put it, "to deceive the enemy as to my intention, and to hold him in check while executing it." He told Little to stand fast in the center and delay the Federals as long as possible, and he instructed the state guard troops on the left to act in concert with Little's command. After setting the retreat in motion Van Dorn left Elkhorn Tavern and rode along Huntsville Road to Clemon's farm. It was now a question of whether the Confederates could make good their escape before the Federals discovered the retreat and delivered a fatal blow.[40]

13 Victory and Defeat

The final act of the battle of Pea Ridge began about 10:30 A.M. on March 8 when Sigel ordered forward the 1st and 2nd Divisions of the Army of the Southwest. Several batteries advanced to within two hundred yards of the woods west of Telegraph Road and blasted the Confederate position with case shot and canister. Under normal circumstances such a Napoleonic tactic would have been fatal for the cannoneers and their horses, who were well within range of even the motley assortment of weapons carried by the Missourians, but most of the rebel infantrymen had withdrawn or had been forced back into the trees by the weight of the barrage.[1]

Fifteen minutes later Federal skirmishers trotted past the roaring batteries and plunged into the shattered, tangled woods. They met little resistance except along the base of the rocky promontory where some troops of the 1st Arkansas Mounted Rifles fired on skirmishers of the 36th Illinois. Visibility was limited, and one of the Federal soldiers recalled that "the best we could do was to watch for the puffs of smoke and then fire at the spots from whence they came." After a brief and nearly bloodless firefight the rebels faded back into the woods and disappeared.[2]

Just behind the skirmishers the solid blue lines of Federal infantry came stepping briskly across the fields, regimental banners waving in the warming breeze. On Sigel's left the 17th Missouri, followed *en echelon* by the 2nd, 3rd, and 15th Missouri, crossed Ford Road and climbed the slope of Big Mountain. The four Missouri regiments had a surprisingly easy time. Sigel feared Big Mountain would be well defended, but such was not the case. The loyal Missourians exchanged a few shots with dimly seen rebels in the trees—probably Watie's Cherokees—but gained the broad crest without any difficulty. After a pause to catch their breath and to re-form their lines, they descended to the terrace on the northern side of the mountain.

In the center of Sigel's onrushing line the men of the 36th Illinois crossed Cox's field at the double-quick, cheering all the way. They entered the woods north of Ford Road expecting to meet a storm of rebel musketry but found only their own mystified skirmishers. "We scoured the woods in vain to find a live secesh," said one disappointed—or relieved—Illinois soldier.[3]

Upon reaching the base of the rocky promontory Colonel Greusel shifted the 36th Illinois to the left, where the slope was more agreeable to linear formations. After a bit of scrambling the Federals saw the result of artillery fire on the exposed point of Big Mountain. "The scene that presented itself on arriving at the top of the hill was one that can never be forgotten," said Leach Clark. Dozens of dead and wounded soldiers of the 2nd Missouri Brigade, many of them dismembered or horribly mangled by bursting shells and flying metal and rock, lay amidst the sandstone outcroppings and shattered trees. Dead horses, broken muskets, and wrecked artillery vehicles added to the air of devastation. Dazed survivors said that the bombardment had been a "perfect hell." The Illinois soldiers picked their way through the carnage and cautiously descended the steep eastern slope of Big Mountain toward Elkhorn Tavern.[4]

The regiments on Sigel's right struck both sides of the sharp angle in the Confederate line and encountered stiffer resistance. Upon receiving the order to advance, Colonel Coler and the soldiers of the 25th Illinois moved out "with a hurrah." They crossed Ruddick's field at the double-quick and reached the battered treeline on the southern side of the angle without incident. Coler halted his regiment and sent some skirmishers into what he described as "an uncommonly thick growth of oak underbrush." Cautiously prowling ahead the skirmishers found a Confederate line of battle about seventy-five yards from the edge of the woods. The 25th Illinois advanced slowly toward the unseen foe, struggling through a tangle of splintered trees, fallen branches, vines, briers, and logs. During a providential lull in the roar of battle, Coler heard the command "Ready!" ring out directly ahead. He shouted for his men to take cover. The blue ranks dropped to the ground

Sandstone columns on the west face of the rocky promontory on Big Mountain where Federal artillery caused so much carnage. Note the observation pavilion atop the promontory. The 36th Illinois halted here on its climb up the mountain and obliqued to the left to continue its advance. Nine-year-old Jonathan Shea provides a human scale of the promontory's size. (authors' collection)

seconds before a "terrific volley of musketry" tore harmlessly through the vegetation. The Illinoisans opened fire from their prone position, and an intense but static contest erupted with neither side able to see or willing to move very much. The 44th Illinois entered the woods behind the 25th Illinois but could do little except lie down and await developments.[5]

The stalemate was broken by the arrival of the 12th Missouri on the western side of the angle. Hugo Wangelin and his loyal Missourians had started out in concert with Greusel and the 36th Illinois, but the two regiments diverged as the Illinoisans veered northeast toward the rocky promontory. The Missourians threw themselves into the attack with enthusiasm. Osterhaus, their former regimental commander, urged them forward with a shout: "Boys, now strike [so] that the chips fly!" Cheering wildly like everyone else in blue that day, the Missourians rushed eastward across Cox's field. "We advanced like hell and the devil himself on a poor sinner," said an excited young sergeant. The regiment reached the treeline between Ford Road and the angle. There was little underbrush here, and the men moved quickly through the woods, surprised at the lack of enemy resistance. One of the skirmishers found the silk flag belonging to Good's Texas Battery and claimed it for Missouri and the Union.[6]

All of Sigel's regiments except the 25th and 44th Illinois on his far right were driving blindly into the enormous gap left by the 2nd Missouri Brigade, which had left its position shortly before as part of Van Dorn's general withdrawal from the battlefield. The unsupported right flank of the 1st Missouri Brigade, located near the angle, was terribly vulnerable. When Burbridge realized Federal troops were threatening his right and rear, he ordered his men to fall back to Telegraph Road. The Missouri and Texas soldiers disengaged from the 25th Illinois and re-formed behind a fence on the eastern side of the road, where they opened fire on the Federals approaching from the west. Maj. Jacob Kaercher of the 12th Missouri said that the regiment received a "perfect shower of bullets" as it approached Telegraph Road. Wangelin took a spill when his horse was killed under him, and the loyal Missourians wavered for a moment. Then they responded with a "murderous fire" of their own and pushed forward, some crawling, some sprinting from tree to tree. On their right, Coler discerned what was happening and wheeled the 25th Illinois to the right through the thicket, adding the weight of another four hundred rifles to the attack on Burbridge's new position.[7]

While the 1st and 2nd Divisions attacked west of Telegraph Road, the 3rd Division assaulted the Confederate position east of the road. The 25th Illinois had crossed Ruddick's field at a slight angle, so when the regiment reached the treeline, its right flank was across Telegraph Road. Seeing this, Curtis ordered Davis to shift his command. The 37th and 59th Illinois and the 18th, 8th, and 22nd Indiana filed to their right until the entire 3rd Division was east of Telegraph Road. This last-minute adjustment placed half or more of the Hoosier infantry immediately in front of Carr's 4th Division, which formed the Federal right.

Curtis limited the depleted regiments of the 4th Division to a supporting role in the attack. Consequently, he missed a signal opportunity to disrupt the Confederate withdrawal. Had Curtis shifted the 4th Division to the east and sent it forward in concert with the 3rd Division, it would have struck the unsupported Missouri State Guard units charged with holding open Huntsville Road. Carr's troops might not have been able to drive the Missourians

The battlefield of March 8, looking south from the rocky promontory on Big Mountain. Telegraph Road curves south in the center, and Ruddick's field lies on the far left. Curtis's line stretched from the curve in Wire Road to the left and right. (authors' collection)

back to the road, but even an unsuccessful attack in that quarter would have created additional confusion in the Army of the West. Curtis had no idea Van Dorn was retreating on Huntsville Road, but by choosing to attack primarily with his freshest troops—the 1st, 2nd, and 3rd Divisions—on his left and center, he unknowingly selected a course of action that drove the rebels toward their escape route.

Davis gave the word, and the 3rd Division set out across Ruddick's field with measured steps and formal hurrahs for the Union. Then, nearly wild with excitement, the Federals picked up speed until they were practically running, shouting madly all the way. A soldier in the 8th Indiana frantically scribbled his impressions of the dash in his diary. "On the right into line double quick. Lord but how we made things hum. Forward quick time guide right. Marched in on an open space. Halt make ready take aim fire. After first shot load at will.... Our guns a booming. The battery howling. Wounded groaning. Some excited, I might say all. But we was going forward."[8]

"That beautiful charge I shall never forget," wrote an officer in the 37th

Illinois, "with banners streaming, with drums beating, and our long line of blue coats advancing upon the double quick, with their deadly bayonets gleaming in the sunlight, and every man and officer yelling at the top of his lungs. The rebel yell was nowhere in comparison." Sigel also was impressed. Watching the sweeping charge of the 3rd Division from across the battlefield he exclaimed, "Oh, dot was lofely."[9]

Just before reaching the treeline, Davis's five regiments came to a ragged halt, one after another, and loosed a series of volleys into the woods at point-blank range. "The rolling fire of small arms defied description," said one veteran of the charge. Receiving very little fire in return, the Federals resumed their rapid advance. With shouts of triumph the men of the 3rd Division entered the woods and began to pick their way through the torn and tangled vegetation in search of the enemy.[10]

The Confederates east of Telegraph Road were supposed to retire slowly in the face of a determined Federal assault, but some apparently took to their heels with more alacrity than expected. When Davis's 3rd Division entered Ruddick's field, the cannoneers of Tull's Missouri Battery came to life and loosed a four-gun salvo of canister at the oncoming blue line, but their aim was high. They then limbered up and fled to the rear, leaving the infantrymen to fend for themselves. The soldiers of the 3rd Missouri, the 16th Arkansas, and the state guard units, like their comrades west of Telegraph Road, had been forced back into the woods by the artillery barrage and were unable to engage the yankees while they were crossing the field. The rebels were in a difficult situation. In the excitement of the moment Federal artillerymen departed from normal procedure and continued to pound the woods even as troops of the 3rd Division closed in with muskets blazing. "The bark and dirt was flying from off the trees all around and the cannon balls and grape shot and minney balls sang like humming birds and bees in the air," remembered a soldier in the 3rd Missouri.[11]

Despite this prolonged and intense hammering, the beleaguered rebels briefly stood their ground against the Federal onslaught. After the 3rd Division had advanced some distance into the woods, it was met by what one man called "the most terrific discharge of musketry conceivable." The Federals flopped to the ground or crouched behind logs and trees, and for a few minutes the rebels seemed to contest every inch of ground. But Little decided his troops had done enough and ordered a retreat. One after another the long line of Confederate and state guard units east of Telegraph Road fell back through the dense woods toward Clemon's farm, peeling away

The battlefield of March 8, looking southwest from the rocky promontory on Big Mountain. Welfley's Knoll is in the center. The Federal infantry deployed to the left and right roughly along the fence lines, which are partially demarked by snow drifts. (authors' collection)

from right to left in order to cover Huntsville Road until the last possible moment.[12]

The rebels retired hastily but in reasonably good order, though the 1st Arkansas Mounted Rifles, the 17th Arkansas, and three companies of the 2nd Missouri drifted north past Elkhorn Tavern instead of east toward Clemon's farm. Disengaging at such close quarters was dangerous business, and the Confederates did not escape without cost. Benjamin Rives, one of the best regimental commanders in Price's division, was on foot directing the withdrawal of his 3rd Missouri when he was struck in the abdomen. Aides placed him on his horse and brought him to a field hospital, where he died the next day. The Missouri colonel was not the only one of Little's men to fall. "They run like whiteheads," claimed a soldier in the 37th Illinois, "but we stopped some of them in the brush for good."[13]

Van Dorn waited near Clemon's log cabin while a stream of southern soldiers trudged past on Huntsville Road. Officers and men were exhausted but not particularly dispirited, for none realized that they were in full retreat. A lieutenant in the 3rd Missouri recalled that "not one soldier of that regiment knew that we were leaving the field entirely. All thought that we were going to some new position." Even the commander of the 8th State Guard Division, Brigadier General Rains, did not know what was happening until he spoke with Van Dorn on Huntsville Road: "For the first time I realized the fact—the fight was over; the victory within our grasp was lost." Sometime after 11:00 A.M. Van Dorn turned his horse east and rode to the head of the retreating column. He left a substantial portion of his army on the battlefield, still heavily engaged with the Federals.[14]

As the rebels fell back, the woods atop Pea Ridge swelled with an unfamiliar sound: the triumphant shouts of blue-clad infantrymen as they crashed through the timber and brush. "You ought to have heard the whooping when the Secesh commenced to break," wrote a soldier in the 12th Missouri. Like an enormous predator the Army of the Southwest was pressing in for the kill, unaware that the prey was slipping away.[15]

Van Dorn failed to inform the thirteen batteries clustered around Elkhorn Tavern that the Army of the West was retreating—yet another example of the inept staff work that plagued the Confederates at Pea Ridge. Left to their own devices, some of the artillerymen continued to shoot ineffectively at the Federal batteries in the fields; others sprayed canister at Federal infantry in the woods. Nearly all were down to their last few rounds and fired sparingly.

The one exception was Churchill Clark's four-gun battery. Clark's Missourians blazed away with ammunition obtained earlier from the disgraced Arkansas battery. Inevitably, their high rate of fire and advanced location on Ford Road drew a tremendous response from the Federals. Missiles rained down on the battery and broke limbers, disabled guns, exploded ammunition chests, and sprayed men and horses with deadly debris. Just after being ordered by Little to move back from his exposed position, Captain Clark, only nineteen years old and the darling of the Missouri division, was killed by a solid shot that tore off the top of his head. Survivors of the wrecked battery left Clark on the ground and dragged off their crippled weapons. Moments later a stray Confederate infantryman chanced upon what he called "the most horrible spectacle it was my lot to witness during the war." The rebel stared for a moment at the fallen gunners of Clark's battery "lying across each other and mingled with dead horses, all scorched and burned black from the explosion of the ammunition wagon"; then he dashed away to escape the continuing storm of enemy artillery fire.[16]

The battlefield of March 8, looking west from the rocky promontory on Big Mountain. Little Mountain is on the left, Ford Road is in the center, and the west end of Big Mountain is on the right. (authors' collection)

Pike, wandering across the battlefield in search of Van Dorn, was shocked at the chaotic state of affairs at Elkhorn Tavern. "No one was there to give an order," he said. Some of the artillerymen turned to Pike; but he could only suggest that they stand fast, for he did not know that the army was retreating. Pike sent two aides to Clemon's field, where Van Dorn had last been seen, but they returned to say that the Confederate commander was nowhere to be found and the field was full of enemy soldiers. As if to confirm this information, the din of musket and artillery fire was replaced by "immense cheering" from thousands of Federal throats.[17]

As the soldiers of the Army of the Southwest closed in on Elkhorn Tavern from three sides, paralysis in the rebel ranks gave way to a frantic burst of activity. MacDonald's St. Louis Battery fired its last few rounds down Telegraph Road and then limbered up and retreated. At the last moment MacDonald noticed the flag was missing. He galloped back to the orchard south of the tavern, picked up the banner, waved it defiantly toward soldiers of the 12th Missouri only a few yards away, and raced to safety amidst a hail of bullets. The gunners of Bledsoe's Missouri Battery fired off all the metal at hand, including the battery's blacksmithing tools and spare trace chains, before retiring. (After the battle, puzzled Federal soldiers found a trace chain embedded in a tree trunk south of the tavern and cut it out as a souvenir.) One by one the rebel batteries rumbled away from the tavern, fleeing the enemy army and searching for their own.[18]

Without orders or a general officer other than Pike to provide leadership at this critical juncture, the Confederate cannoneers escaped pell-mell, with each of the thirteen batteries very much on its own. Jackson's, Kelly's, Landis's, and MacDonald's Missouri batteries retreated on Huntsville Road. MacDonald had another hairbreadth escape, leading his company on a mad dash to safety past Clemon's cabin just before being cut off by Davis's 3rd Division. Bledsoe's, Clark's, Gorham's, Guibor's, Tull's, and Wade's Missouri batteries, Gaines's and Hart's Arkansas batteries, and Good's Texas Battery fled north down the hill into Cross Timber Hollow. They were the last organized Confederate units to leave the field. The Army of the West was gone.[19]

The two wings of the Army of the Southwest came together at Elkhorn Tavern a little before noon. The 17th, 2nd, 3rd, and 15th Missouri and the 36th Illinois scrambled in and out of Tanyard Ravine and halted along Telegraph Road north of the tavern; they missed intercepting the fleeing Confederate artillery by a matter of minutes. The 12th Missouri and the 25th and 44th Illinois drove up Telegraph Road to the tavern. A few minutes later Sigel, Asboth, and Osterhaus joined the milling mass at the battered hostelry. Behind them came the cavalry and artillery of the 1st and 2nd Divisions.[20]

In the vicinity of the tavern the Federals found burning campfires, discarded weapons, and equipment of every description "scattered in profusion as well as confusion all around," evidence that the rebels had departed in unseemly haste. They also saw the devastation caused by the concentrated fire of their batteries during the final stage of the cannonade. "I had never believed that artillery was capable of such havoc," wrote Henry Voelkner of the 1st Missouri Flying Battery. "The sight was awful." The fields, orchard, corral, yard, and roads contained mangled bodies of men and horses and smashed remnants of vehicles and trees. The "horrid scene" also shocked a Federal cavalryman. "I pray God I may never have occasion to behold such another. Cannon balls and unexploded shells were lying thick over the ground. The trees were cut splintered and torn in every direction. Everything gave ample proof of the horrors of war."[21]

East of Telegraph Road the troops of the 3rd Division drove through the woods on a broad front, veered slightly to the northeast, and reached Hunts-ville Road between the tavern and Clemon's farm. The 4th Division, coming up in support, moved obliquely to the right to get clear of the 3rd Division and struck Huntsville Road on the eastern side of Clemon's farm. Davis and Carr halted their exuberant men and awaited orders.[22]

Curtis rode up Telegraph Road immediately behind his advancing troops, enthralled by the seductive grandeur of battle. "A charge of infantry like that last closing scene has never been made on this continent," he wrote. "It was the most terribly magnificent sight that can be imagined." At the tavern Curtis shook hands with Sigel in the midst of thousands of yelling, weeping, and dancing soldiers. The normally reserved old engineer was as exuberant as everyone else, cheering and waving his hat as he passed each of his regi-ments. "I rode along our line shouting Victory! Victory!" Curtis told his brother, "and such shouts you never heard from mortals as our men gave utterance to."[23]

After three anxious days and nights the Federals "shouted themselves hoarse" in their moment of triumph. Said an officer in the 22nd Indiana, "I could compare the scene to nothing more fitting than a powerful camp meet-ing revival of the days of yore." Rarely was a Civil War battlefield the scene of such an emotional celebration of victory. Many of the cheering midwestern-ers were dazed by what seemed to be an almost incredible turn of events. "It was sometime before I could convince myself we had indeed won, so hard had been the fighting, so hopeless the issue for two days," wrote an officer in the 59th Illinois.[24]

Capt. Silas Miller of the 36th Illinois, whose intrepid skirmishers had slain McCulloch and had led the assault on the rocky promontory, tried to explain to his brothers back home what possessed him and nearly everyone else in the Army of the Southwest at that moment:

> May be you know what joy is, but you do not and never can know the wild delerious extacy which crazes the soldier, or rather an army, when they know they have met and put to route an enemy twice or three times their number, whom they have been fighting with various success for three excited, anxious, *almost eternal days*. What though their comrades moan and shriek with painful wounds! What though hundreds of dead are strown within their very sight! *The victory is ours!* The cost and all else is forgotten. The great joy and wild delight absorbes all else; extacy rules the hour and the man, and gives a life that he never knew before.

For a little while the rebels were forgotten as the sounds of victory echoed off the rocky walls of Cross Timber Hollow and rolled across the wooded plateau of Pea Ridge.[25]

Amidst all the joyous uproar many senior officers made speeches. Osterhaus, caught up in the excitement of the moment, struggled gamely with the English language as he congratulated "der prave poys" of the 36th Illinois. Such unabashed sentiment still had a great effect at this early stage of the war. "Oh, I tell you, it made our boys fairly shake in their shoes," said Jacob Kaercher of the 12th Missouri after a complimentary speech. In regiment after regiment the men responded with "three roaring cheers" for themselves and their leaders.[26]

Unfinished business soon intruded into the celebration. Curtis wondered where the thousands of Confederates had gone. He later confided to his wife that "the rebel army seemed to have sunk into the earth leaving the great plain to our sole and safe occupation." He erroneously assumed that the Confederates were retreating the way they had come and rode down into Cross Timber Hollow to see for himself. Accompanied only by Sigel and two small personal escort companies, the Federal commander boldly but foolishly advanced more than a mile beyond Elkhorn Tavern to the point where Telegraph Road turns sharply northwest. There he saw "straggling teams and men running in great trepidation" away from Pea Ridge. Curtis ordered a battery forward to hasten the rebels on their way. A few minutes later the two twelve-pounder howitzers of the 1st Missouri Flying Battery arrived and went into action at the turn in the road.[27]

Pike was part of the stream of fugitives glimpsed by Curtis and Sigel in Cross Timber Hollow. After rounding the turn he came across the 17th Arkansas standing by the side of the road awaiting instructions. Somehow the Arkansans had been left behind when the rest of McCulloch's division marched east, and they had struck out on the only road they were familiar with. Pike saw an opportunity to establish a defensive line across the hollow using the 17th Arkansas and some of the passing batteries, but he had hardly begun when the Federal howitzers opened fire. "All was immediately in confusion," said Pike, who was clearly unnerved by the unexpected appearance of the enemy's booming cannons so far north of the battlefield. A Missouri soldier described Pike's pathetic attempt to maintain order and his subsequent flight: "An excited officer, carrying a flag, halted, stuck the staff in the ground, called on all to rally and die by it, then spurred away." The makeshift rear guard dissolved amidst the exploding shells. What had been a disorderly retreat degenerated into a rout.[28]

After watching the Missouri artillerymen send several rounds screeching down the hollow, Sigel urged Curtis to order their personal escorts forward to harry the fleeing rebels. Curtis was dubious. His company of Bowen's Battalion and Sigel's company of the 4th Missouri Cavalry contained only about fifty men in all, but he said, "All right, General, if you think best." Curtis realized he had erred in neglecting to bring his mounted forces down the hill. As the escort companies prepared for action, he sent a courier racing back toward Elkhorn Tavern for additional cavalry and artillery.[29]

The escort companies deployed into a short line of battle across Telegraph Road. A few hundred yards ahead, recalled a soldier in Bowen's Battalion, they could see "the retreating rebel army—infantry, cavalry, and artillery, all mingled together in a struggling mass, each individual apparently trying to see who could get out of the way the quickest." So it may have appeared from a distance, but when the Federal horsemen closed in, they discovered that a few of the rebels still had some fight left in them. The three companies of the 2nd Missouri that had become separated from their regiment atop Pea Ridge formed into line and took on the approaching cavalrymen. "They gave us an awful volley which staggered us for a moment," admitted a member of the 4th Missouri Cavalry. Then cannoneers from Guibor's Missouri Battery and Good's Texas Battery wheeled three guns into action farther down the hollow and fired off their last shells—the final Confederate shots of the battle. Faced with this unexpected resistance the fifty Federal cavalrymen chose not to press the pursuit but contented themselves with picking up a few stragglers and awaiting reinforcements.[30]

The horde of Confederates in Cross Timber Hollow took advantage of this development to put some distance between themselves and their pursuers. Good's Texas Battery and Tull's Missouri Battery turned east on a primitive track that offered some hope of reaching Van Dorn and the main body of the Army of the West, while the other batteries continued rolling north toward Keetsville. Hundreds of men from a dozen regiments turned west on the Bentonville Detour. Among them was a disconsolate Pike, who wrote that the road and the woods on either side "were everywhere full of fugitives on foot, singly and in bands of two, three or half a dozen." At Twelve Corner Church Pike again encountered the 17th Arkansas. Colonel Rector, obviously overwrought after the debacle in Cross Timber Hollow, told Pike that all was lost and there was nothing left to do but hide the weapons, disband the regiment, and send the men home. Pike decided the time had come to end his brief and unhappy association with the Army of the West. He left the road and struck out due west toward the Indian Territory on his own. He had no idea what had become of his Cherokees and Texans but assumed they would head in the same direction sooner or later.[31]

Had Pike continued along the Bentonville Detour, he would have come upon the Confederate trains withdrawing down Little Sugar Creek Valley. The creaking wagons were accompanied by a heterogeneous collection of units, including the 1st Choctaw and Chickasaw and 1st Creek, which had arrived only that morning from the Indian Territory, and hundreds of stragglers from Elkhorn Tavern, whose numbers were increasing by the minute. During the late afternoon this motley, dispirited assemblage passed through Bentonville en route to Elm Springs.[32]

As shadows lengthened on March 8 the disintegrating fragments of the Confederate army north and west of the battlefield were in desperate straits. Leaderless and lost, their passage was marked by a trail of abandoned material and exhausted men and animals.

Curtis returned to Elkhorn Tavern after authorizing Sigel to pursue the enemy in Cross Timber Hollow as far as practicable. Sigel's performance on the battlefield that morning had been unimpeachable, and Curtis felt confident to let him deal with the fleeing rebels without supervision. The Federal commander still failed to realize that he and his principal lieutenant were not of one mind. Curtis wanted to capture or destroy as much of the rebel army as possible; Sigel wanted to push the rebel army out of the way and open an escape route to Springfield. As soon as he was on his own, Sigel sent for the 1st and 2nd Divisions to join him in Cross Timber Hollow. While Van Dorn hurried the main body of the defeated Confederate army southeast, Sigel led half of the victorious Federal army on a retreat north.[33]

The officers and men of the 1st and 2nd Divisions believed they were in hot pursuit of the enemy and pressed on doggedly despite fatigue and hunger. Asboth and two brigade commanders even disobeyed instructions from Curtis to remain atop Pea Ridge and went down into Cross Timber Hollow. Cavalry and artillery under Sigel's personal direction broke up one or two feeble Confederate attempts to make a stand—the thing Sigel feared most—and rounded up stragglers by the hundreds. The prisoners, mostly Arkansas and Missouri troops, were an unimpressive lot. One Federal soldier compared them to "scared partridges" and noted that in their panic-stricken flight many had lost not only their weapons but also their hats, coats, and shoes. The landscape north of Elkhorn Tavern spoke eloquently of the desperate and disorganized condition of the enemy. "For miles the road is strewn with rifles, muskets, clothes, blankets and everything calculated to impede their flight," reported a soldier in the 36th Illinois. A Missouri officer concluded that Van Dorn and Price "will have to get out a search warrant to find their army."[34]

Meanwhile, Curtis received the first intimation that his initial assessment of the Confederate retreat was incorrect. Around 1:00 P.M. Carr reported that the 3rd Illinois Cavalry was following a rebel force moving southeast on Huntsville Road. The Federal horsemen found the road littered with debris and the woods on either side filled with "dispersed, ragged, half starved" stragglers. One trooper described the rebel prisoners as being "fatigued until they could not move." Carr sent the rest of Dodge's brigade a short distance out on Huntsville Road in support of the Illinois cavalrymen but eventually called everyone back to help secure the battlefield. No one in the Federal army, including Curtis, realized the importance of this discovery.[35]

About this time Curtis belatedly became aware that a good portion of his army had gone north with Sigel. The Federal commander was puzzled and then annoyed at this odd development. "I heard him remark that it was imprudent to thus separate his forces and scatter them in chasing the enemy," recorded journalist Fayel. Curtis's mood grew darker after 2:00 P.M. when two messages arrived from Sigel in quick succession. In the first message the German general was strangely uninformative. He merely reported that he had reached the eastern terminus of the Bentonville Detour and asked that the divisional trains, including "the wagons carrying the cooking utensils," be sent to that point. Sigel helpfully suggested that the trains could be escorted northward by the few odd detachments of the 1st and 2nd Divisions still remaining on the battlefield.[36]

The second message clearly revealed Sigel's anxious state of mind. "It seems that the enemy's main force retreats towards Keetsville," wrote Sigel. "Let us *follow* him through and get out of this hollow.... Let us do this because Van Dorn may recover and make a stand whilst we now can drive him before us and take a more convenient position at Keetsville." Sigel reminded Curtis to be sure to bring the trains, prisoners, and wounded when he pulled out of Arkansas. This astonishing message infuriated Curtis. "I am going forward, not backward," he announced to his staff, adding that he intended to remain on the battlefield to care for the wounded and to "show the rebels and the rest of mankind that my victory is unquestionable."[37]

Struggling to maintain his composure, Curtis scribbled a message to Sigel. "I regret exceedingly that so much force separated from this position and Colonels Schaefer and Greusel and General Asboth must account to me for neglecting my instructions not to go down the hill." He reminded Sigel that "a cavalry pursuit is all we can make available against an enemy who we know by experience will run all night to avoid embarrassment," and he instructed him to return with his infantry. He refused to release the detachments Sigel had requested but agreed to send provisions to succor the hungry men and animals of the 1st and 2nd Divisions. Curtis mistakenly assumed that Sigel's command would camp near the junction of Telegraph Road and the Bentonville Detour; as yet he was not aware that Sigel had continued to Keetsville without waiting for a reply from his superior.[38]

While Curtis fretted and fumed atop Pea Ridge, his wayward second-in-command pushed into Missouri. Sigel left Colonel Knobelsdorff and his own 44th Illinois, three companies of cavalry, and the two howitzers of the 1st Missouri Flying Battery to secure the junction of Telegraph Road and the Bentonville Detour. Told to "continue the pursuit of the enemy" toward Twelve Corner Church, Knobelsdorff led his small command west on the Bentonville Detour for two or three miles behind Big Mountain. The Federals rounded up dozens of enemy stragglers and forced hundreds more to flee into the woods. Toward sunset Knobelsdorff and his men returned to the junction and camped for the night.[39]

Seven miles north the rest of the 1st and 2nd Divisions ground to a halt around the same time. Men and animals were worn out by the rapid pace. The Federals camped just south of Keetsville and waited for their supply trains to catch up with them. Sigel received Curtis's summons to return, but as events would demonstrate, he was not yet convinced that victory made retreat unnecessary.[40]

The "battle scarred and somewhat battle scared heroes" of the 3rd and 4th Divisions remained atop Pea Ridge. During the afternoon they secured the battlefield, gathered up the wounded, and collected prisoners. One rebel loudly demanded that his captors take him to Colonel Bussey, who warmly shook the rebel's hand and ordered his release. Thus ended the dangerous mission of William Miller of the 3rd Iowa Cavalry, the "deserter" who had warned Curtis of the Confederate advance on March 5 and then returned to Price's division to gather as much information as he could about the enemy.

At the close of the battle Miller hid in the brush until the firing stopped and then surrendered as carefully as possible. Unfortunately, this story does not have a happy ending. Miller was murdered by Confederate guerrillas at his Missouri home on August 14, 1862.[41]

As afternoon slipped into night, thousands of Federal soldiers trudged back to their camps overlooking Little Sugar Creek in search of something to eat and a place to sleep. Most were too weary to wonder where the rebels had gone or what the morrow would bring. They were satisfied that they had survived and triumphed.

While Sigel's forces harried retreating rebels in Cross Timber Hollow, the main body of the Army of the West made good its escape from Pea Ridge. The Confederates left Huntsville Road a few miles east of the battlefield and turned south on a nameless, primitive track that wandered down into the spectacular valley carved by the White River. After fording the icy waters of the White, they finally stumbled to a halt at a tiny settlement called Van Winkle's Mill. Men and animals could go no farther. Indeed, many were not able to go that far; the stream of stragglers was almost as thick as the marching column. Fortunately for the rebels there was no Federal pursuit other than the cautious probe by the 3rd Illinois Cavalry on Huntsville Road.[42]

Gradually the rank and file understood what was happening as the sound of battle died away in the distance. "As we moved on without further orders, it finally dawned on us *we were in retreat*," recalled one soldier. Another noted that "gloom spread over the men in an instant" when they realized the truth. The troops seemed to sag visibly, and the pace of the march, not very fast to begin with, slowed to a shuffle.[43]

By midafternoon dismay and disappointment gave way to anger. A Missouri soldier named Henderson Greene declared that "a madder set of men is hardly ever found than they were when they found they were retreating instead of falling back as they supposed to take a new position." A ripple of outrage spread along the winding column. "It was clear enough that there had been a shameful piece of bungling and mismanagement, and the discontent and clamour became general, and everyone was disgusted," said a soldier in the 3rd Louisiana. Typical was the remark of a Texas cavalryman who fumed, "We got decidedly the best of the fight, and still we retreated." The Missourians were ignorant of the full extent of the disaster at Leetown and were particularly upset by the decision to withdraw. Rumors swept through the ranks that Van Dorn had withdrawn the army over Price's objections. "It was common and current talk that General Price violently opposed the retreat," said John Wilson, a soldier in the state guard, "but was over-ruled and had not sufficient strength to continue the battle with his Missouri army." Even in his old age Wilson was bitter about how he and his comrades put up a valiant fight only to be "robbed in the end."[44]

Enlisted men were not the only ones affected by the disheartening retreat. When a group of disbelieving Missouri soldiers asked Brigadier General Rains of the 8th State Guard Division if it was true that they had lost the battle, the Missouri officer bellowed, "By God, nobody was whipped at Pea Ridge but Van Dorn!" The Confederate commander was well within earshot of this intemperate outburst and promptly placed Rains under arrest. Rains's words were adopted by many soldiers of the Army of the West, who declared to the end of their days that Van Dorn—and only Van Dorn—was whipped on that cold, smoky battlefield in the highlands of northwestern Arkansas.[45]

Upon reaching Van Winkle's Mill late in the afternoon the troops spread over the sparsely settled neighborhood in search of food. A modest supply of corn was found at the mill and distributed among the men and animals. Douglas Cater of the 3rd Texas Cavalry wolfed down a handful of parched corn for his first meal in more than forty-eight hours: "I never enjoyed a supper as well as I did this one." Chickens, hogs, and cattle that had not been spirited away by their owners were pressed into the service of the Confederacy. "Every living biped and quadruped was immediately killed and eaten," said Will Tunnard of the 3rd Louisiana. Some soldiers had not waited. Earlier that afternoon infantrymen shot a hog near the road, hacked the animal apart on the spot, and staggered on, "eating the raw bloody pork without bread or salt."[46]

As darkness fell on March 8, the southeasterly wind moaned through the pines that covered the hills around Van Winkle's Mill. "It seemed awful to listen to it," said a distraught Missouri soldier. "The trees seemed to be wailing our retreat." The rebels endured another night without shelter and huddled around bonfires of rails, boards, and branches. A local resident named Joseph Sanders observed that they "all fell so sound asleep they never posted any centenels and they slept so sound that they burnt their cloths, hats and boots and some got their hair burnt before they awoke." It was his opinion that one hundred Federals could have captured the entire bunch.[47]

So ended the battle of Pea Ridge. But even though the fighting was over, the campaign continued. While the victors coped with the dreadful aftermath of battle, the vanquished struggled to survive in the Arkansas wilderness.

14 The Vulture and the Wolf

Van Dorn awoke early at Van Winkle's Mill on Sunday, March 9, to find that a cold rain was falling. His mood must have matched the dreary weather as he composed a brief message to Johnston in Tennessee. The message contained several evasions and misleading statements. Van Dorn informed his superior that he had fought a battle in northwestern Arkansas but had failed to win. He stated that his "whole army" was located fourteen miles east of Fayetteville after having "gone entirely around the enemy"; then he promptly contradicted himself by stating that his trains were retiring toward the Boston Mountains via Fayetteville. Van Dorn did not mention the inconvenient fact that most of his artillery, several regiments of infantry and cavalry, and great numbers of stragglers and deserters were unaccounted for.[1]

As the morning wore on, Van Dorn busied himself with administrative matters. He sent a company of Missouri cavalry back to Pea Ridge to inter Confederate dead and to offer to exchange prisoners with the Federals. He ordered that all weapons be cleaned and inspected, that the remaining ammunition be distributed evenly among the various units, and that lists of the names of killed and wounded be compiled and submitted to headquarters. Finally, he directed commissary and quartermaster officers to investigate "losses of fences forage poultry etc. and pay for them or give proper receipts for the value of such things taken." Given the desperate circumstances of the army, which was scattered and literally on the verge of starvation, a more futile directive than the last can hardly be imagined.[2]

At some point during the morning Van Dorn decided to shift his base of operations from the Boston Mountains to Van Buren on the Arkansas River. This was a tacit admission that the campaign to liberate Missouri had failed. Van Dorn sent a message to Green instructing him to press on to Van Buren with the trains and to bring the men and material left behind in the Boston Mountains. Then he bid adieu to Price and headed south with a tiny gaggle of aides and guides. Moving at his usual furious pace, the Confederate commander crossed the Boston Mountains and reached Van Buren on March 11. There he began preparations for the arrival of the trains and the army.[3]

Fifteen miles to the southwest, on the far side of White River, Green spent most of March 9 anxiously awaiting orders at Elm Springs. When a small Federal cavalry force appeared at Bentonville in the afternoon and skirmished with his rear guard, Green realized that he was cut off from the main body of the Army of the West. Fearful that the Federals might return in greater strength and destroy the Confederate trains, he decided to head south toward the Boston Mountains.[4]

Green set the wagons in motion on the Elm Springs Road and kept them going for the next thirty hours. He described the retreat to the Boston Mountains as "a very hard, tedious, tiresome march" and noted with some understatement that "it was only through great exertion that the train could be kept moving." Rain fell steadily, and men and animals suffered from fatigue and hunger. Some wagons broke down and were burned, while others were kept moving only by lightening their loads. The path of the trains was marked by carcasses of draft animals and piles of smoldering wood. It was all too much for Pike's warriors. The Cherokees, Choctaws, and Creeks headed west toward the Indian Territory, as Pike assumed they would, and eventually rejoined their rotund commander at Fort Gibson.[5]

William Baxter watched Green's bedraggled column pass through Fayetteville. "The army was a confused mob, not a regiment, not a company in rank, save two regiments of cavalry, which, as a rear guard, passed through near sundown; the rest were a rabble-rout, not four or five abreast, but the whole road about fifty feet wide perfectly filled with men, every one seemingly animated by the same desire to get away.... They were thoroughly dispirited. And thus, for hours, the human tide swept by, a broken, drifting, disorganized mass, not an officer, that I could see, to give an order; and had there been, he could not have reduced that formless mass to discipline or order."

All that day and into the night fragments of the Army of the West flowed and then trickled though the streets of Fayetteville.[6]

Though the townspeople had been roughly treated by these same Confederates in recent weeks, at least a few were so moved by the pitiful condition of the soldiers that they did what they could to help. Little Marion Tebbetts stood by her front gate and passed out corn bread that her mother cooked in the house. Marion thought the hastily prepared bread was rather dense and unappetizing, but "those starved men ate it as a delectable morsel." The Tebbetts yard, so recently occupied by Asboth's blue-clad troopers, was overrun by exhausted rebels. "All night could be heard their groans and curses and prayers," recalled the little girl. The staunchly unionist Tebbettses were not the only samaritans. A hungry Texas cavalryman long remembered the small boy who silently handed him an apple as he walked his horse through the streets of Fayetteville.[7]

On March 10 the column trudged into the Boston Mountains. At Strickler's Station Green received the message from Van Dorn directing him to strip the old campsites along the Illinois River and Cove Creek and to push on to Van Buren. The next morning the rebels made their way down the steep southern slopes of the Boston Mountains into the Arkansas River Valley.[8]

The woebegone soldiers Van Dorn left behind at Van Winkle's Mill on March 9 continued to be at the mercy of the elements. The steady rain caused streams to rise so rapidly that some rebels "were still sound asleep with their heads out of the water and their bodies partially covered." Men and animals who had been in danger of freezing for the past week were now awash in a sea of mud. The troops stoked their sputtering fires and ate a miserable breakfast of soggy parched corn. Then they set out toward the south. The muddy roads and swollen streams made progress slow and fitful. For lack of guides some units wandered miles out of their way; others waded aimlessly back and forth across the twisting White River. Shoes and boots disintegrated and were cast aside. No additional rations were available; one man wrote that all they received was water "which poured down from the heavens in abundance." After less than ten miles the column splashed to a halt on the banks of War Eagle Creek. "I believe we suffered as much that day as any soldier ever did since the war commenced," said a member of the 2nd Missouri Brigade.[9]

The Confederates fell upon the farms along War Eagle Creek in a frenzy of foraging. Officers made no attempt to distribute food or maintain order; it was every man for himself with predictable results. A victimized farmer recalled that his uninvited visitors "killed every fowl of any kind, all the cattle, hogs and sheep, and took all the bacon and corn that they could find for several miles around.... They cooked at our house from 11 o'clock until midnite, until there was nothing left to cook." The farmer left his pillaged homestead in disgust and wandered among the campsites, where he witnessed signs of even more desperate hunger. "I seen lots of men cut out slices of beef and mutton before it was done bleeding and eat it raw. The only bread they had was the corn they had hooked on the road. They threw the ears into the fire and burnt the outside black and eat it."[10]

The handful of subsistence farms provided only a fraction of the food needed to feed thousands of men. "I was so hungry I even picked up turnip peelings out of the mud and ate them, and I saw many others do the same," wrote a sergeant in the 2nd Missouri Brigade. The men of McCulloch's division in the rear of the column were in an even worse plight because the horde of troops ahead of them swept the country clean of everything edible — including turnip peelings. Price, in nominal command, failed to rotate the order of march each day; he put his Missourians on the road first on March 9 and tried to keep them ahead of the Arkansas, Louisiana, and Texas troops for the duration of the retreat.[11]

Price's only significant contribution to the Confederate cause during the retreat was his successful effort to recover the army's missing artillery batteries, which had fled north on Telegraph Road at the close of the battle, hotly pursued by the Federals. On March 10 he sent the 3rd Texas Cavalry and the 1st Missouri Cavalry in search of the batteries. The next morning the horsemen encountered the object of their search a few miles north of Huntsville.[12]

For three days after the battle the wandering artillerymen had lived in constant fear of Federal cavalry. They hauled their cannons and caissons over mountains and ridges "where it was almost impossible to roll a wheelbarrow." After leaving Elkhorn Tavern Good's Texas Battery and Tull's Missouri Battery turned east just south of the Missouri line; the other batteries went all the way to Keetsville before leaving Telegraph Road. The two groups found each other on the eastern side of the White River and slowly made their way southward, hampered by a lack of forage for the animals and a lack of knowledge of the whereabouts of the Army of the West. From Huntsville the cannoneers were escorted back to the main body by the cavalry.[13]

After a particularly dismal night of trying to sleep in a downpour, the Confederates struggled to their feet and plodded away from War Eagle Creek on March 10. "We trudged on in disorder," wrote Maj. Daniel H. Reynolds of the 1st Arkansas Mounted Rifles. "Few men of any of our companies [were] present and even that few were not in order." The trail of the defeated, disorganized army was littered with discarded clothing, weapons, cartridge boxes, knives, coffee pots, and even flags.[14]

The rebels also left a number of wounded compatriots who had been evacuated from the battlefield at Price's insistence. Many of the wounded simply could go no farther over the primitive roads. Capt. Robert C. Carter of the Missouri State Guard was one such unfortunate. By the time the army reached War Eagle Creek, the bullet wound in his thigh had become inflamed and painful. "So I was laid out in a porch by the side of the road," remembered Carter. The next morning he and about ninety other severely wounded soldiers were transferred to a local church and cared for by a surgeon and a few slightly wounded soldiers. Carter was bitter about the way he was treated by his comrades in arms. "I was confined in this loathsome hospital for three months. The army in the retreat took all our clothes and belongings and we were all left in a sorry plight." How many wounded rebels died at War Eagle Creek or along the way is unknown.[15]

After leaving War Eagle Creek the Army of the West marched down into the rugged, winding White River Valley. The landscape was very different from the gently rolling terrain of the Springfield Plateau; a Missouri rebel called it "the worst country I had ever seen." If things were not bad enough, the rain continued to fall in torrents day after day and created a nightmarish world of mud and water. A member of the 3rd Louisiana described the dismal landscape and the army's ordeal in detail:

> There were no roads or bridges; the country was mostly hills covered with scrub oaks, rocks, rivers, and creeks, and very sparsely settled, and so poor, as some of the men expressed it, that turkey buzzards would not fly over it.... Price's army had preceded us; but if they did any good by opening a path, they did us a great deal of harm by clearing the country of everything that could be eaten by man or beast, even to the last acorn, which seemed to be the only thing the country produced. We proceeded to scramble along the best way we could, wading through creeks and rivers and scrambling over rocks and through brushwood. At night we kindled large fires and took off our wet clothes, wrung the water out of them, and dried them the best way we could. Occasionally we passed a small settlement from which the inhabitants had fled, but

everything had been carried away by Price's army. In the gardens we sometimes found the remains of some turnips or onions, which were eagerly dug out of the ground with our [bayonets] and eaten raw.[16]

The Confederates trudged up the narrowing valleys of the middle and western forks of the White River, struggled over the crest of the Boston Mountains, and followed Frog Bayou Road down to the Arkansas River. Organization continued to erode as soldiers constantly strayed in search of an ear of corn or a mouthful of pork. "I never knew what it was to want for something to eat until the last fifteen days," a young Texan confided to his parents after the ordeal was over. More fortunate than most were some Louisiana soldiers who detoured up a side valley and found a few secluded Ozark farms undiscovered by other foragers. The infantrymen gathered up everything edible and dumped it into a large pot. While the cauldron boiled and bubbled, they "danced round it like the witches in 'Macbeth.'" Fortified and refreshed by this repast, the Confederates pushed southward, leaving their unwilling hosts to survive as best they could until the next harvest.[17]

While the rebels were at their weakest, they encountered the Boston Mountains, the southern escarpment of the Ozark Plateau. A soldier in the 2nd Missouri Brigade said that the men had to struggle over "rocks, hills, and bluffs where it seemed to me that no other person had ever been before or ever would be again." On March 14 and 15, while the leading infantrymen plodded through the mountain passes, the heavens opened and produced another deluge. "A heavy and continuous rain has been falling," wrote a stoic Arkansas soldier in his soggy diary. "All night we stood in it and bore it best we could."[18]

The week or more that it took the miserable soldiers of the Army of the West to move from Van Winkle's Mill to Van Buren was among the most trying periods experienced by any Civil War soldiers. A famished trooper of the 3rd Texas Cavalry noted with grim irony that he and his comrades "appeared to be in much greater danger of dying from starvation in the mountains of northern Arkansas than by the enemy's bullets." William Watson of the 3rd Louisiana exaggerated only slightly when he described the desperate situation as a "miniature Moscow retreat." Perhaps the last word on the subject came from another Lone Star trooper who later heard the retreat euphemistically described as a disagreeable experience. "*Disagreeable* hardly supplies the word," snorted Douglas Cater. "It was *bad*."[19]

Near the foot of the Boston Mountains the Confederates found wagon-loads of flour, corn, and bacon waiting for them—the rations Van Dorn had ordered Green to retrieve from Strickler's Station and Cove Creek. One group of Missouri soldiers "baked" their flour in a tin bucket over a smoldering fire during a heavy rainstorm. "I heard many say they thought it was the best bread they had ever eaten and thought so myself," said William Ruyle of his dense, damp meal.[20]

The regiments that had set out from the Boston Mountains two weeks earlier were hardly recognizable when they reached the Arkansas River. The 3rd Louisiana, whose uniforms and military precision had so impressed Van Dorn at the outset of the campaign, was a pitiful sight. "The regiment arrived at Van Buren in straggling squads, tired, hatless, barefooted, hungry, dirty, and ragged," reported Will Tunnard. Only 270 "terribly demoralized" Louisiana soldiers could be accounted for at first, though many others dribbled in over the next few days in pathetic condition. No wonder Tunnard declared that "the retreat was more disastrous than a dozen battles."[21]

Van Dorn assigned each unit a campsite along the lower reaches of Frog Bayou just east of Van Buren. Supplies that had accumulated during the army's absence were dispensed liberally. "Here we found plenty of rations, such as flour, pork, beans, rice, sugar, coffee, beef, and sweet potatoes," said a Missouri soldier. "You should not be surprised if some of us nearly foundered." In addition to food there were piles of tents, bedding, and other items recovered from the camps in the Boston Mountains. As the Confederates recuperated from the rigors of the campaign, they set about constructing proper military encampments.[22]

Work progressed slowly because most of the men were deadly tired and weak. An Arkansas officer apologized for waiting five days to write a letter home: "I have felt so much jaded and worn that I have not felt disposed to write sooner." The entire army was sunk in a lethargy brought on by exhaustion, malnourishment, depression, and a virtual epidemic of colds, pneumonia, and diarrhea. At least the Confederates had few seriously wounded men to care for; most of them were left behind at Pea Ridge or were abandoned at War Eagle Creek.[23]

The morale of the officers and men of the Army of the West at this time was extremely low. "All agree that the late disaster has had a very demoralizing effect upon us," wrote an Arkansas soldier on March 20. But the army gradually came back to life. Major Ross observed that his Texas cavalrymen "were very much disheartened, at first, but are reviving in spirits a little." The effect of rest and full rations had a salutary effect on both men and animals, for as one of Ross's Texans said with masterful understatement, "The last month has been quite a trying one on us all."[24]

The troops took some comfort in the widespread belief that they had bested the Federal army in battle. A typical comment came from a Texas officer who declared that "although we left the field, I think we have taught the Feds a lesson they won't forget soon." Many others were content with the knowledge that they had done their best under desperate circumstances, while still others were happy merely to have survived the campaign.[25]

Stragglers continued to arrive at Frog Bayou until nearly the end of the month, but not all of the missing rebels were so devoted to the cause. Bands of former rebels wandered past the ravaged farmsteads on War Eagle Creek for weeks after the battle. A settler noticed that many of these deserters had thrown away their arms and "none seemed in much of a hurry" to rejoin their former comrades. Without question the rapid advance and the disorganized retreat caused a significant loss of manpower in Confederate ranks, some of it permanent.[26]

Van Dorn's stock, never very high, dropped to new depths and stayed there. A Louisiana soldier wrote that the general was "very unpopular with the whole army." There was absolute unanimity on this score: none of the surviving memoirs, diaries, and letters from the officers and men of the combined Arkansas and Missouri armies contains a kind word about Van Dorn's performance during the Pea Ridge campaign. In less than two weeks the Mississippi general had lost the confidence of his soldiers; he would never regain it.[27]

The rain that fell all day on March 9 washed away the last lingering traces of smoke from the battlefield. Curtis awoke at Pratt's store determined to inflict as much damage as possible on the retreating foe despite the inclement weather. He still believed that Van Dorn had gone the way he had come, so he sent Colonel Bussey and most of the available cavalry in pursuit of the rebel army on the Bentonville Detour.

Bussey's command consisted of his own 3rd Iowa Cavalry, one battalion of the 1st Missouri Cavalry, Bowen's Missouri Cavalry Battalion, and four mountain howitzers. At midmorning the column overtook Colonel Knobelsdorff, who was boldly marching west once again on the Bentonville Detour in search of the enemy. Knobelsdorff and his small force turned back toward Cross Timber Hollow while Bussey pushed on to Bentonville. Early in the afternoon the Federal troopers reached the town and skirmished briefly with

Green's rear guard. The Confederates retreated south across the Osage Prairie, but Bussey declined to pursue because of the weak condition of his mounts. The mud-splattered Federal cavalrymen returned to Pea Ridge that evening with fifty or sixty prisoners. Bussey informed Curtis that the enemy force beyond Bentonville seemed to be composed primarily of trains and stragglers.[28]

While Bussey probed toward Bentonville, Sigel made one last compulsive effort to sweep the rebels off Telegraph Road and open the way to Springfield. Despite instructions to the contrary from Curtis, he sent the 1st and 2nd Divisions north on Telegraph Road toward Keetsville. Sigel put his men in motion without any breakfast (something he had declined to do during the battle) and drove them forward with uncharacteristic urgency. A man in the 36th Illinois declared that "our march towards Keitsville was about the quickest kind of quick time." He added that "but for the name and dishonor of the thing I should have fell out of the ranks and dropped behind." When Sigel discovered that the rebels had left Telegraph Road and turned east toward the White River, he finally called a halt to his "pursuit" and headed back toward the battlefield. The daylong rain soaked his weary men and practically submerged Telegraph Road. Toward evening Sigel directed the 1st and 2nd Divisions to camp north of Elkhorn Tavern in Cross Timber Hollow. He went up the hill to have a strained meeting with Curtis in which he acknowledged that the Confederate force he had followed to Keetsville was not the main body after all.[29]

Around midday, while Bussey and Sigel were busy following bits and pieces of the Confederate army to the west and north, the company of Missouri horsemen sent by Van Dorn approached the battlefield on Huntsville Road. The rebels recklessly clattered up without an obvious flag of truce—the limp white cloth they carried was hard to see in the rain—and threw a fright into the 3rd and 4th Divisions. Shots were fired, the long roll was sounded, and thousands of Federal troops fell into line before calm was restored. Upon being taken to see Curtis at Pratt's store, the rebels requested permission to inter Confederate dead and offered to exchange prisoners as soon as possible. They also volunteered the information that the bulk of the Army of the West had marched from the battlefield on Huntsville Road. An escaped Federal prisoner who reached Pea Ridge later that day said the same thing.[30]

By the evening of March 9 Curtis finally knew for certain that the main body of the rebel army was in full retreat east of the White River. At midnight a courier hurried from Pratt's store with an express communication for Halleck in his saddlebags. The mud-spattered rider reached Springfield the next day and handed the message to Sheridan, who took one look and immediately wired St. Louis. Halleck had been on pins and needles since learning that the rebels were advancing upon the isolated Army of the Southwest. It is not difficult to imagine his relief as he scanned the brief telegram from Curtis, which closed with these words: "Indiana, Illinois, Iowa, Ohio, and Missouri very proudly share the honor of victory which their gallant heroes won over the combined forces of Van Dorn, Price, and McCulloch at Pea Ridge, in the Ozark Mountains of Arkansas."[31]

While newspapers across the North trumpeted the news of the glorious triumph in faraway Arkansas, the soldiers of the Army of the Southwest experienced the grim aftermath of a major battle. The Federals lost 1,384 men at Pea Ridge: 203 killed, 980 wounded (of whom perhaps 150 later died), and 201 missing and presumed captured, roughly 13 percent of the approximately 10,250 troops engaged. Federal losses by division were revealing: 1st Division, 156; 2nd Division, 120; 3rd Division, 344; 4th Division, 682; and unattached headquarters units, 82. What Curtis called the "sad reckoning" of the casualty list clearly reflected that the brunt of the battle was borne by the 4th Division at Elkhorn Tavern on March 7. In one day of combat Carr's men incurred half of all Federal casualties—twice as many as any other division.[32]

Confederate losses are less certain. No formal accounting was made, and Van Dorn's airy statements are highly suspect. Ten days after the battle the Confederate commander estimated his casualties as "not being more than 800 killed and wounded and between 200 and 300 prisoners." After another ten days had passed, he lowered that estimate to "about 600 killed and wounded and 200 prisoners." These round numbers fly in the face of common sense. As the Confederates attacked on March 7 and endured the bombardment on March 8, they almost certainly suffered correspondingly higher casualties than the Federals. The only relatively firm statistics concerning Confederate losses came from the Federals, who forwarded between 450 and 500 unwounded prisoners to St. Louis on March 12. At least 25 additional unwounded prisoners remained in Cassville to help care for casualties flowing in from the battlefield. Thus the Federals captured more than twice as many soldiers of the Army of the West as Van Dorn acknowledged.[33]

Approximately 16,500 Confederates, including emergency men, set out on the campaign from the Boston Mountains and the Indian Territory; fewer than 14,000 reached Pea Ridge, and fewer than 13,000 were engaged. By a conservative estimate, the Army of the West suffered approximately 2,000 casualties during the battle, a loss of at least 15 percent of the troops engaged. Hundreds, perhaps thousands, more were lost to disease and desertion during the arduous advance and retreat. These overall figures are, of course, educated guesses, but they fit well with the handful of surviving regimental and company casualty lists and are far more believable than anything in Van Dorn's official correspondence.

Another measure of an army's success in the Civil War was the number of cannons won or lost, but there was confusion on this score at Pea Ridge. The Federals salvaged the tubes of the three cannons of the 1st Missouri Flying Battery captured and burned on Foster's farm. In addition, Curtis and other officers stated in both official and personal correspondence that the Federals not only recovered the three cannons of the 3rd Iowa Battery lost on March 7 but also captured five abandoned Confederate cannons during the final stages of the engagement on March 8: four on the battlefield near Elkhorn Tavern and a fifth in Cross Timber Hollow. One of the captured guns, described as a "fine 6-pounder brass cannon," was assigned to the 1st Missouri Flying Battery. The fate of the other four is not known. Confederate accounts disagree. Van Dorn stated that his command lost only one cannon, which broke down during the retreat and had to be abandoned, and "brought away" four Federal cannons. On March 17 two of these captured guns were assigned to MacDonald's St. Louis Battery and one to Wade's Missouri Battery. Reconciling the discrepancy between the Federal and the Confederate accounts is impossible.[34]

There is no doubt that the Federals gathered up a considerable amount of weaponry and equipment discarded by the defeated rebels. The 44th Illinois collected 230 firearms, 60 horses, 38 saddles, and piles of haversacks, cartridge boxes, and assorted items during the regiment's two forays along the Bentonville Detour. A soldier said that the battlefield was "strewn with guns and weapons of all kind which our soldiers were busy for days in picking up." Two days after the battle a cache of 200 firearms deposited by the 17th Arkansas was discovered in a hollow near Bentonville and hauled back to camp. Curtis did not exaggerate when he wrote that his men collected "wagon loads" of enemy firearms. The Army of the West could ill afford such losses.[35]

Whatever the precise reckoning of casualties and spoils, large numbers of dead men remained on the battlefield, and the rising temperature made interment a pressing matter. On March 9 Curtis established details to deal with the ghastly task of collecting the corpses and putting them wherever the rocky terrain permitted. "Our men are burying the dead as fast as they can today posibly do it," recorded an Indiana infantryman in his diary. "Just dig a hole and throw them in and cover them up. Always wrap their blankets around them. It looks horrid but they dont know any thing about it poor fellows." The Federals were buried side by side in long trenches, with the name and unit of each victim, if known, marked on a wooden headboard. The grisly business did not always go smoothly. A misguided burial detail dug a trench adjacent to the hospital at Leetown and was filling it up with bodies when Davis happened by. With a furious oath he demanded to know "what — – – —— had ordered a grave dug right in the edge of the village and beside the hospital tents." The chastened burial party removed the dead and interred them nearer the battlefield, out of sight of the wounded.[36]

The Confederate burial party sent by Van Dorn excavated several shallow trenches near Leetown and Elkhorn Tavern and unceremoniously filled them with the remains of their compatriots. "The Rebels in burying their men they dig a large hole and lay them in on top of one another," observed a Federal. "Ones head to anothers feet and sometimes make it so large so as to cross them both ways and then pile the dirt in on them. It almost made us sick to see them at work." No attempt was made at identification. Within a few days the spring rains washed away the loose soil atop the trenches and exposed the decaying bodies of the southern dead. No one bothered to bury Indians or to search diligently for corpses in the dense underbrush. No wonder Curtis soon moved most of his command to Camp Stephens in Little Sugar Creek Valley to get away from "the stench and filth" of the battlefield.[37]

A harsh fate also awaited some of the two thousand or more wounded soldiers. By sunset on March 9 every structure in the vicinity of Pea Ridge was filled with wrecked humanity. Elkhorn Tavern, awash in casualties, was typical. "We found the lower floors occupied with the wounded so thick that it was difficult to step between them," wrote journalist Fayel of the appalling scene.[38]

The Federal army's limited supply of bandages, dressings, stimulants, and bedding proved inadequate. A Federal surgeon angrily declared, "I am fully convinced that no army was (so far as provision for the wounded was concerned) ever sent into the field in such destitute condition as ours, *except the one that it fought and conquered.*" The Western Sanitary Commission, the Trans-Mississippi version of the U.S. Sanitary Commission, rushed forward medical supplies as soon as word of the battle reached St. Louis. Halleck ordered quartermasters and other officers along the tenuous line of communications to speed the parcels to Pea Ridge *"with all reasonable dispatch."* Military surgeons, civilian doctors, and others who volunteered their services also hurried to the scene.[39]

William Fithian of Danville, Illinois, stepfather of John and William Black of the 37th Illinois, was one of the civilian doctors. He reached Pea Ridge on March 21 and was assigned to the hospital at Leetown. A decade of quiet practice in a small town had not prepared Fithian for the carnage caused by a major battle, but he pitched in with such energy and determination that a week passed before he found time to write his wife. "Our men are terribly wounded and in almost every conceivable manner. It is heartrending to attempt to dress their wounds—yet that painful task has to be discharged as a duty." The good doctor was shocked at the meager and monotonous rations available to his patients. He declared that "the wounded are suffering beyond description and some are dieing for want of delicacies." Fithian urged his wife to forward sweet wines and brandies, dried and canned fruit, dried meat, nuts, and spices. He added helpfully that "they should be packed well in dry goods boxes and well hooped; and by all means the Sanitary Committee should be informed of the contents of each box." Fithian warned that under present circumstances it was "entirely useless" to attempt to ship anything to the army unless it was approved by the Western Sanitary Commission as being of medicinal value.[40]

Curtis, appalled by the looming medical catastrophe, ordered to the rear all the Federal wounded who could be moved. The trip over Telegraph Road was cruel punishment for helpless men jammed into jolting ambulances, but it would have been even more cruel to have left them in the Arkansas wilderness. Three days after the battle bloodstained ambulances began unloading crippled men in Keetsville, Cassville, and even Springfield, where improved facilities were available. Houses, churches, and public buildings in those communities were pressed into service as hospitals. A soldier reported that the spartan, crowded conditions within these buildings were "very poor for a sick man but a great deal better than lying on the ground." A representative of the Western Sanitary Commission was not so sure. Arriving in Cassville two weeks after the battle, he found most of the four hundred Federals there "lying in the clothes they fought in, stiff and dirty with blood and soil." He immediately dispensed clean bedclothes and bandages. Some of the rebel wounded remained at Pea Ridge, while others were dispersed across Benton

County. William Slack was one of the latter; he died on March 20 in a farm-house six miles east of the battlefield. Each of these new hospitals, Federal and Confederate, soon had its own small graveyard.[41]

The plight of the wounded cast a pall over the Army of the Southwest. Men not yet hardened to the aftermath of battle were shaken by the sights, sounds, and smells of nineteenth-century military medicine. "It is redicklous how bad the wounded is taken care of," complained an Iowa soldier after a visit to a field hospital. Captain Kinsman of the 4th Iowa concluded a letter home with the bitter observation that "one hard fought battle gives our surgeons more experience in cutting men up than a lifetime of country practice." Another soldier reported that surgeons "are taking off arms, and legs and hands evry day. It is nothing to see them cut a mans arm off or a leg. I hope to God that I wont have to witness the same again. It is to horable to think of."[42]

Nothing was worse than tending comrades slowly dying of agonizing wounds or witnessing the pain of relatives come to collect their loved ones. Vinson Holman of the 9th Iowa recorded the dreadful experience of a friend, shot through the body, who lingered for a week after the battle. "There wasent no Man that suffered any more," wrote Holman after the end had finally come. "I don't believe he would have suffered any more if he had been burnt up." Samuel Herrington of the 8th Indiana told of a young soldier severely wounded in the face and arm. When the soldier's father read about the battle in the newspaper, he started south from Indiana, somehow certain that his son was hurt. "That is the way he found his only boy," concluded Herrington. "Eyes both out and arm gone. WAR. WAR."[43]

The search for dead and wounded led to a gruesome discovery in the lane north of Foster's farm. Eight soldiers of Trimble's detachment of the 3rd Iowa Cavalry had been scalped, and others apparently were murdered as they lay wounded; all had been mutilated to some degree by knives or hatch-ets. When the men of the Confederate burial party departed, they carried a letter from Curtis to Van Dorn complaining about this lapse from "civilized warfare." Van Dorn probably was inclined to believe the worst of Pike's Indi-ans, but he tried to uphold Confederate honor by leveling an unsubstanti-ated charge that German troops had killed Confederate prisoners, a charge Curtis dismissed.[44]

Pike was more forthright than his superior. He had witnessed the killing of one wounded Federal soldier at Leetown and had learned of another atrocity after returning to the Indian Territory. Pike informed Curtis of his "horror" at the two incidents and ordered his Indian troops to refrain from such behavior in the future, but his responsible actions did him little good. He eventually received most of the blame for the deeds of his "savage allies" and was pilloried in newspapers across the north; his prewar reputation as a poet, educator, and intellectual was permanently blighted. The true culprits never were identified.[45]

The scalped and mutilated cavalrymen drew crowds of gawkers, as did any concentration of lifeless bodies. Mangled victims of artillery fire held a peculiar fascination for the young midwesterners. "It was a harrowing sight to see the mutilated and disfigured forms of the dead," recalled Lyman Bennett of the 36th Illinois. "I noticed one that a shell had taken away one-third of the skull and scooped it entirely of brains; another with head entirely blown to atoms; others with limbs entirely gone." A party of Indiana soldiers climbed the rocky promontory to the top of Big Mountain but found the carnage more than they could stomach. "It is terrible up there," wrote a shaken Hoosier. "We could not stay but [a] fiew minutes." The devastated landscape around Elkhorn Tavern also attracted tourists. An Illinois soldier wandering through the shattered woods along Telegraph Road noted that "large sized trees (ten inches through) were cut off and apparently every thing was swept away that stood in the path of the deadly missiles from the batteries." Even after dead and wounded soldiers were interred or removed, the battlefield remained littered with dead horses, spent artillery projectiles, and debris of every description.[46]

The battle was a sobering experience for the victors, including Curtis. A few days after the battle he penned a moving letter to his brother. "The scene is silent and sad. The vulture and the wolf have now the dominion and the dead friends and foes sleep in the same lonely graves. Many a kind friend and bold spirit is there interred. It is a vast grave and a bold rocky mountain on the site where we last struggled and under whose shadow many fell, is a huge gravestone which shall perpetuate the memory of the heroes who fell fighting for Civil and Religious liberty in the Ozark Mountains of Arkansas." Few Federal generals in the field in the spring of 1862 were more active than Curtis or more conscious of the price of military glory and martial reputation.[47]

The Federal commander had precious little time to bask in the glow of victory or to ponder the meaning of man's inhumanity to man before being forced to deal with troubles of every description. Reinforcements turned out to be the least of Curtis's worries. Battlefield losses were largely remedied by the return of Major Conrad's wandering detachment and the arrival of the sizable 13th Illinois from Rolla. After being cut off by the Confederates at Bentonville on March 6, Conrad led his force of about 250 infantrymen and a handful of cavalrymen on a forced march to the vicinity of Keetsville. "It was tramp! tramp! without cessation and whoever could not keep up simply fell behind and were taken prisoner," recalled a loyal Missourian named John Buegel. The next day, while the exhausted infantrymen recuperated, Conrad and his few horsemen probed south along Telegraph Road toward the sound of battle. Near the Bentonville Detour the Federals encountered Confederate cavalrymen, who chased them back to the Missouri line. Cut off once again, Conrad and his troops limped to Cassville. "Our feet were so swollen that we could not stand," said Buegel. On March 9, after marching 125 miles in four days, the footsore Federals finally rejoined their comrades atop Pea Ridge. A week later the 13th Illinois arrived. These infusions of manpower —more fatigued than fresh—brought the army's strength back to about ten thousand men.[48]

While troops dribbled in, Curtis clashed with Sheridan, the army's quartermaster and commissary, who was based in Springfield. The Federal commander had urged Sheridan to use every available means to provide additional cavalry mounts to replace those lost at Little Sugar Creek in February. On March 5 Sheridan fired off an intemperate letter to Curtis in which he declared that "no authority can compel me to Jayhawk or steal" horses from civilians, clearly implying that he felt Curtis was asking him to do just that.[49]

This message reached Curtis in the immediate aftermath of battle when he was tired and troubled. He had Sheridan arrested for insubordination and sent back to St. Louis. In an odd passage that seems to contain more gossip than fact, Curtis informed Halleck that Sheridan "was about fizzled out. He does not seem to have judgement or energy enough. Besides, he has got mixed up with secession lady friends till his sympathies seem almost against us and he frets about the irregularities of our troops which are mainly owing to a want of supplies which he ought to provide." Curtis erred in removing the industrious Sheridan, who had labored heroically to keep the Army of the Southwest in the field, but in so doing he inadvertently struck the Confederacy a mighty blow. Halleck liked the brash Irishman and sent him to Tennessee before a court-martial could take place in St. Louis. Within two years Sheridan was in Virginia as commander of the cavalry corps of the Army of the Potomac. He ended the war in the parlor of Wilbur

McLean's house in Appomattox, a long way from his cramped office in Springfield.[50]

Removing Sheridan proved easier than obtaining adequate supplies. On March 10 Curtis began bombarding officers from Springfield to St. Louis with demands for action. To Halleck: "I *must have* horses or I cannot haul my cannon forward or back. I must also have my Cavalry kept up or I cannot forage." To the commandant at Rolla: "Help forward ammunition, shoes and horses to replenish them in my Command. I have disposed of a considerable quantity of these things in the dispersing of the Arkansas Rebels." To the ordnance officer at Rolla: "I want full new supply of ammunition for my artillery forwarded by express. Shell and fuses were especially scarce at the close of the battle. . . . Shell for the mountain howitzers are needed instanter, as these are constantly useful. I wish you could procure twenty more rigged with strong horses to haul the guns and a light two-horse wagon to carry ammunition." Officers at lesser posts along the long line of communications were instructed to hasten every box and bundle forward without delay.[51]

Curtis wanted 4,650 rounds of solid shot, case shot, shell, and canister and 288,000 rounds of small arms ammunition—a rough measure of the ordnance expended during the campaign, nearly all of it at Pea Ridge. On March 22 he complained to the ordnance officer at Rolla that his men had received only 11 rounds apiece in the two weeks since the battle. He snapped that this pitiful amount was no more than a "drop in the bucket!"[52]

As the days passed, Curtis grew more anxious about his army's condition. He confided to his wife that he had "urged and begged every source of power" for assistance in obtaining supplies but with little success. Halleck, the principal source of power in the Trans-Mississippi, reeled under the barrage of letters and telegrams from northwestern Arkansas. "We are doing everything in our power to supply you," he assured Curtis more than once but pointed out that he was also trying to meet urgent demands from the far larger Federal forces on the Tennessee and Mississippi rivers.[53]

Shoes and clothing continued to be in short supply as well—an Iowa soldier reported that "whole companies are nearly barefooted"—but the most vexing problem proved to be the scarcity of food and forage. "The country is stripped from this point to the Arkansas," wrote Curtis, "and my foraging teams have to make two days' journey north to get anything." The Federal commander reluctantly accepted that his position was untenable; he would have to fall back a short distance into Missouri to allow his command to be resupplied and rebuilt. On March 18 the Army of the Southwest began a gradual withdrawal to the vicinity of Keetsville, north of Cross Timber Hollow, where the terrain was open enough for the army to establish a proper defensive position. Ironically, Sigel led the way north with the 1st and 2nd Divisions, retracing the route he had followed in such haste on March 8. Detachments of varying strength remained on the battlefield to protect the hospitals, to secure the approaches to Cross Timber Hollow, and to maintain a nominal Federal presence in Arkansas.[54]

In the days and weeks after Pea Ridge, unresolved problems of command resurfaced in the Army of the Southwest. The Federal campaign had been hampered from the beginning by the awkward relationship between Curtis and Sigel. The latter's erratic performance at Pea Ridge brought matters to a head. While casting about for some way to resolve a situation that had become intolerable, Curtis received a guarded message from Halleck, written just prior to the battle, that warned him to watch out for Sigel and to keep him under control. Curtis responded immediately in a private letter:

> I may some time hereafter verbally explain to you my trials in regard to detachments and detours which have perilled at various times the very existence of this army. . . . If General Sigel be indeed a good leader of an army, I hope he may have a separate command where he may be satisfied. I cannot understand him and I do not wish to have the honor of commanding him. . . . I have been urged by General Sigel and others to move back, and on the battlefield he urged me to move to Keitsville immediately under the *pretence* of a pursuit (for it would only have been a pretence for any fool knows a frightened retreating army won't run toward his foes) but I have held position in Arkansas and on the battlefield at all hazards knowing that the least backward movement would ruin the moral effect of a complete victory.

These were strong words from a man who had studiously avoided criticizing or antagonizing Sigel since taking command nearly three months earlier.[55]

Halleck replied that he was not surprised at Sigel's conduct at Pea Ridge. He explained that he had recently received information about Sigel's peculiar behavior at Carthage and Wilson's Creek "which destroyed all my confidence in him." Halleck continued: "It was for that reason that I telegraphed you so often not to let Sigel separate from you. I anticipated that he would try to play you a trick by being absent at the critical moment. . . . I am glad that you prevented his projects and saved your army. I cannot describe to you how much uneasiness I felt for you. You saved your army and won a glorious victory by refusing to take his advice."[56]

While Halleck and Curtis exchanged these conspiratorial letters, a controversy erupted over Sigel's role in the battle. Curtis had long been annoyed by the misleading newspaper stories generated during the campaign by Sigel's flacks. The press, he complained to Halleck, was "a medium of false puffing and quack heroes to the disgust of honorable men." Curtis noted that "for a long time after I had this command my brother in Ohio was puzzled to know from the papers whether I had even a subordinate position under General Sigel." Curtis made little or no effort to promote himself in the public eye; he naively expected to have his military accomplishments recognized and reported fairly. Consequently, he was very upset when Sigel garnered the lion's share of the credit for ousting Price from Missouri.[57]

Curtis feared the same thing would happen regarding the victory at Pea Ridge. He insisted on reading (though not actually censoring) Fayel's lengthy account of the battle before it was sent to St. Louis. Fayel's story was fair and accurate, at least by the standards of Civil War journalism. The same could not be said of many other accounts of the battle that glorified Sigel and either ignored or vilified Curtis. These accounts usually emanated from foreign-born officers of the 1st and 2nd Divisions. They uniformly stressed how Sigel cut his way through a horde of surrounding Confederates on March 6, how he eagerly awaited his chance on March 7 while the rest of the army was forced back, and how he led the Federals to victory on March 8. Curtis invariably was dismissed as ineffective. Henry Voelkner described the Federal commander as "an old washerwoman" who "did not know whether the wind blew from the north or the south." Jacob Kaercher echoed Voelkner's sentiments: "Curtis is no account at all. He did not know what to do." Native-born soldiers in the 1st and 2nd Divisions also were affected to some degree by the rampant Sigelmania. An Illinois infantryman declared, "Sigel alone is worth as much as 5000 men to our side.... He ought by rights to be the Commander in place of Curtis." Many such statements were published verbatim in midwestern newspapers or served as the bases of misinformed commentaries on the battle.[58]

The Federal commander became extremely irritated when newspapers singing Sigel's praises began to appear in camp about two weeks after Pea Ridge. Then came letters from Dodge, Vandever, and other Iowans on leave in St. Louis reporting that officers from Sigel's divisions were spreading lies about the course of the battle. The most scurrilous lie of all appeared in a

German language newspaper in Chicago that reported that Curtis wanted to surrender on March 7. According to the story, Sigel persuaded Curtis to give him command of the army, which he led to victory the following day. Curtis sent the offending clipping to Sigel, who issued a carefully qualified denial that any such thing had happened: "I will do all in my power to find out the author of an assertion which is as far as I know, untrue. You did never give the command of the army to me, and I regard it as a calumny, if it is said that you spoke in my presence about surrendering."[59]

In fact, Sigel made no effort to ascertain the person or persons responsible for the surrender story. Embellished versions were disseminated far and wide, and many of the disseminators were located in Sigel's camp. Greusel was a particularly tireless propagandist. "I must say that God and General Sigel were the only saving of our little army," Greusel informed former senator Hamilton Fish of New York after the battle. "General Curtis had made up his mind to capitulate but General Sigel said in my hearing, never, never, I shall sacrifice every one of my Germans, and up went a shout, never, never, let us sell our lives together, mind this came from about 6000 men belonging to General Sigel." This piece of malicious fiction eventually made its way from Fish to Postmaster General Montgomery Blair, who passed it on to Lincoln.[60]

Sigel's role in all this is unclear but does little to enhance his reputation. Even if he did not actively orchestrate or encourage the rumormongering, he did not try to stop it. The fracas poisoned relations between Curtis and Sigel and exacerbated existing ethnic tensions between native-born and foreign-born elements of the Army of the Southwest.

Fortunately, one of the main actors left the stage before the situation got completely out of hand. On March 25, the day after writing the denial to Curtis, Sigel declared himself too unwell to command and requested immediate medical leave. Sigel was afflicted with a chronic throat infection during the winter of 1861–62. Did that illness suddenly flare up again, or did Sigel decide to seek a separate command while his name graced the pages of a hundred newspapers? Asboth expressed surprise that his friend and patron departed "so abruptly" for St. Louis. Lieutenant Noble of the 3d Iowa Cavalry, who traveled partway to St. Louis with Sigel and even shared a room with him one night on the Wilson's Creek battlefield, did not mention the general's illness in his diary. Sigel never returned to the Army of the Southwest. He was promoted to major general, partly for political reasons and partly for his genuine contribution to the Federal victory at Pea Ridge, and

Cyrus Bussey, in 1890, with the Pea Ridge sword presented to him by his loyal 3rd Iowa cavalrymen (State Historical Society of Iowa, Des Moines)

served in Virginia and West Virginia without distinction. His checkered military career ended in 1864 after the debacle at New Market in the Shenandoah Valley.[61]

Curtis was urged by some to counter the campaign of lies and innuendo directed against him by publishing his own version of events, but he declined to do so except in his official report. As warm congratulations poured in from family, friends, and brother officers, he decided the "silly gossip" was unworthy of a reply. "I can survive it," he said.[62]

A number of other unseemly quarrels erupted as officers tried to assign blame or to garner credit for what had transpired at Pea Ridge. The most vindictive campaign was waged by Lieutenant Colonel Trimble of the 3rd Iowa Cavalry. He claimed, among other things, that Bussey had abandoned his command on Foster's farm and had run away. The enlisted men of the 3rd Iowa Cavalry felt differently. When they learned of Trimble's baseless accusations, they purchased a handsome presentation sword for Bussey inscribed with the words "Pea Ridge."[63]

Even genuine heroes were not above such spiteful behavior. Dodge grossly inflated his own role in the battle and belittled the contributions of others, especially foreign-born officers. He charged that the "Dutchman" Osterhaus acted "out of all military usage" and mishandled the Federal cavalry on Foster's farm, and he claimed that Sigel deliberately ignored Curtis's orders to reinforce the 4th Division on March 7. Midwesterners who crossed Dodge did not fare much better. Incensed that Carr's evenhanded report of the struggle for Elkhorn Tavern did not place him at the center of events, Dodge obliquely accused Carr of cowardice and announced that he had "no faith in the division commander." The only Federal soldiers generally safe from Dodge's scathing pen and tongue were his fellow Iowans. Indeed, in a flurry of self-congratulatory letters and telegrams sent to public officials and prominent citizens in his home state immediately after the battle, Dodge made his position clear: "Thank God the bravery of the 4th and 9th Iowa saved our little army."[64]

The risky winter campaign to sweep the rebels out of Missouri had been more successful than Halleck could have hoped. Nevertheless, he did not intend for the Army of the Southwest to resume the offensive into Arkansas but to remain where it was and continue to shield Missouri. The stunning tactical victory at Pea Ridge did not immediately alter the strategic situation. As long as a powerful Confederate army remained in northern Arkansas, it posed a significant threat to Missouri. Consequently, Halleck directed Curtis to maintain his position, at least for the present, and strictly enjoined him not "to advance across Boston Mountains on any consideration." Ever the worrier, Halleck reminded Curtis to be careful of Van Dorn, whom he characterized as "a vigilant and energetic officer ... certain to strike any exposed point." He ignored the possibility that Curtis might already have learned this.[65]

Before long, however, Halleck saw an opportunity to make the isolated Federal army on the Ozark Plateau an integral part of the vast operation unfolding on the Mississippi River. Halleck expected his fleet of gunboats and transports to reach the mouth of the Arkansas River later in the spring and to compel the rebels in Arkansas, including the Army of the West, to fall back into Louisiana. If the plan was successful, the Army of the Southwest could then advance rapidly over the Boston Mountains to the Arkansas River, link with waterborne Federal forces at Little Rock, and join operations against the Confederate heartland.

Halleck's grandiose strategic plan for the conquest of the Mississippi River Valley was sound, if unduly optimistic, but the Confederates in Arkansas refused to cooperate by remaining inert. A few weeks after Pea Ridge Van Dorn and the Army of the West were on the move once again.

15 Marching through Arkansas

While the Army of the West reassembled along the banks of Frog Bayou, Van Dorn stayed close to his headquarters in Van Buren and immersed himself in correspondence and administrative duties. He continued to deny that Pea Ridge was a Federal victory. "I was not defeated, but only foiled in my intentions," he insisted in letters to General Johnston and Secretary of War Benjamin. "I am yet sanguine of success, and will not cease to repeat my blows whenever the opportunity is offered." He declared his determination "to recover as soon as possible and fight again."[1]

The Confederate commander blamed his lack of success at Pea Ridge on a number of factors: a "badly-disciplined army," a "series of accidents entirely unforseen and not under my control," and the poor quality of his subordinates. Elaborating on this last point in remarkably blunt language, Van Dorn told Adjutant General Cooper that he found "the want of military knowledge and discipline among the higher officers to be so great as to countervail their gallantry and the fine courage of their troops.... I cannot convey to you a correct idea of the crudeness of the material with which I have to deal in organizing an army out here. There is an absolute want of any degree of sound military information, and even an ignorance of the value of such information." He asked Cooper to send him several hundred copies of army regulations and manuals on infantry, cavalry, and artillery tactics. Van Dorn's assessment of his officers was unduly harsh, but even if accurate, it leaves him open to censure for initiating the campaign without learning the capabilities and limitations of his subordinates.[2]

Van Dorn took this opportunity to reorganize the remainder of his army. McCulloch's and Price's separate commands were merged into a single, over-sized division commanded by Price, who officially became a Confederate major general on April 8. This unwieldly division was composed of four infantry brigades commanded by Little, Hébert, Green, and A. E. Steene; two cavalry brigades commanded by Greer and Churchill; and an artillery brigade led by Frost.[3]

In view of problems encountered on the way to and from Pea Ridge, the Confederate commander specified that each of the new brigades contain a pioneer force of one hundred able-bodied men, well equipped with tools, who would march at the head of the brigade and would enable it "to pass obstacles in the road with as little delay as possible." He also directed that each brigade contain a provost guard to "prevent straggling and disorder on the march" and to carry out other disciplinary tasks. Van Dorn seemed to have learned that proper planning, organization, and equipment were essential for the success of a major campaign.[4]

Not everyone was pleased with the new arrangement. Former members of McCulloch's division—especially Texans—were incensed about the "amalgamation" of the two forces. They especially resented Van Dorn's undisguised favoritism toward Price and his Missourians. John Good, the Texas battery commander, was outraged at Van Dorn's sketchy official report on Pea Ridge: "I did think myself in that fight until seeing the report but am now 'officially' satisfied it is a mistake. The chivalry of Texas was not upon the battle field of Elkhorn nor was my company. None of us like this. *Texas plays second fiddle to Missouri.*"[5]

Upon learning from the returning Confederate burial party that Curtis was amenable to an exchange of prisoners, Van Dorn sent another party back to the battlefield on March 15 with Lieutenant Colonels Chandler and Herron. Van Dorn proposed that the two Federal officers be exchanged immediately for Colonel Hébert and Major Tunnard. Curtis agreed and released the two Confederates along with eight lesser officers and enlisted men, all the rebels immediately at hand. Representatives of the two commanders then worked out an agreement to exchange the remaining prisoners as soon as possible.[6]

At the end of March the Confederates brought 239 prisoners to Cross

Hollow and turned them over to the Federal army. Counting Chandler and Herron, 241 Federal prisoners (12 officers and 229 enlisted men) were exchanged; roughly one-sixth of these soldiers were captured prior to the battle, the remaining five-sixths in the battle itself, most of them near Elkhorn Tavern. Nearly all of the 450 or 500 unwounded Confederate prisoners were in St. Louis, and several weeks would pass before they could be located. By that time Van Dorn and his army no longer were in Arkansas, so the rebels were sent down the Mississippi River to Fort Pillow and were released. The uncounted hundreds of seriously wounded Confederate soldiers in Federal hands apparently were also exchanged at this time but remained in their makeshift hospitals until they could travel. How many actually returned to Confederate or state guard service is not known.[7]

The exchange of prisoners was marred by a minor squabble over protocol. Colonel Rosser of the 2nd Missouri Brigade refused to return Herron's sword. When Van Dorn learned of this breach of military manners, he directed Price "to impress upon Colonel Rosser the necessity for complying with the usages and courtesy of war," which required that sidearms be returned to exchanged officers. Rosser was ordered to relinquish the sword to the provost marshal of the army, who forwarded it to Herron with Van Dorn's compliments. Such was warfare in the nineteenth century.[8]

Van Dorn was temperamentally unsuited to remain on the defensive. He was anxious to take the field again, and an opportunity to do so came almost immediately. A message from Beauregard had arrived in Van Buren while Van Dorn was away on the campaign. Writing on February 21, Beauregard continued to press for an offensive east of the Mississippi River. He said that the fall of Forts Henry and Donelson had isolated his forces in western Tennessee from those of Johnston in central Tennessee. He suggested that Van Dorn and the Army of the West cross the Mississippi River at New Madrid or Columbus and join him in Tennessee. From there the combined Confederate armies could advance and seize "Cairo, Paducah, the mouths of the Tennessee and Cumberland Rivers, and most probably be able to take also Saint Louis by the river. What say you to this brilliant programme?" Indeed, what could Van Dorn say to such an appealing fantasy? Beauregard was a strategist after his own heart.[9]

A few weeks earlier Van Dorn had rejected a similar overture from Beauregard. Now, after the failure at Pea Ridge, he jumped at the chance to resume the offensive even if it meant leaving the Trans-Mississippi. The first stage of the operation would be essentially identical to Van Dorn's original plan to invade Missouri from northeastern Arkansas. This time, instead of marching directly upon St. Louis, he would lift the Federal siege of New Madrid and then cross the Mississippi River and cooperate with Beauregard as suggested. On March 16 Van Dorn advised the Louisiana general that his command would leave Van Buren within a week and would reach Jacksonport in northeastern Arkansas by April 7. Though Johnston was the ranking Confederate officer in the West, neither Beauregard nor Van Dorn asked his permission to initiate this movement; this omission was one of many indications that Beauregard had assumed effective leadership from Johnston in the aftermath of the debacle at Forts Henry and Donelson. Van Dorn followed Beauregard's lead, offhandedly informing Johnston on March 17 of his intention to "assist the army on the Mississippi." Van Dorn's communications with his two immediate superiors illustrated his tendency to play fast and loose with large round numbers; he informed Beauregard that he would bring twenty thousand men, but the next day he told Johnston that he would bring only fifteen thousand.[10]

To cover the projected eastward movement of the Army of the West, Van Dorn sent Colonel Churchill and four regiments of cavalry on a raid against the Federal supply depot at Springfield on March 22. After six days of constant struggle over difficult Ozark terrain the Confederates reached the White River near Forsyth, just north of the Missouri line, only to find that spring rains and melting snow made the river impassable. The weary rebels and their worn-out horses turned eastward toward Jacksonport. This abortive raid was the last offensive action carried out by the Army of the West in the Trans-Mississippi.[11]

The promise of a bold stroke on a massive scale galvanized Van Dorn. He hastened the refitting of his army and ordered that recruits and supplies all across Arkansas be sent to Jacksonport. Then, on the eve of his departure from Van Buren, he learned of the Federal capture of New Madrid. For the second time in a month aggressive Federal operations in Missouri had nullified Van Dorn's planned course of action. "What do you now advise?" he asked Beauregard. "Answer me at once, please." Van Dorn was so overwrought that he literally could not stay in one place and wait for Beauregard's reply. He boarded a steamboat on March 22 and headed for Jacksonport, instructing Price to follow with the army as soon as possible.[12]

While Van Dorn churned down the Arkansas River, Beauregard met with Johnston in Tennessee. He urged Johnston to wrest the initiative from Halleck by concentrating the scattered Confederate forces in the West for a mighty blow against Grant's army at Pittsburg Landing on the Tennessee River. This was essentially an expanded version of the idea Beauregard had been advocating since his arrival in the West. Johnston fell under the spell of the dominating Creole general and ordered all of his forces to proceed to Corinth, Mississippi, a few miles south of Pittsburg Landing.[13]

The Army of the West was a vital part of the new plan. Van Dorn's troops were hundreds of miles from Corinth and would not enjoy the luxury of traveling by railroad until they reached the eastern bank of the Mississippi River. Nevertheless, Beauregard and Johnston could not pass up the opportunity to add twenty thousand (or fifteen thousand) veterans to the ranks of what would become the Army of Tennessee. On March 23 Johnston directed Van Dorn to "move your command to Memphis by the route in your judgement the best and most expeditious." Beauregard followed with a message that same day in which he urged Van Dorn to use eastern Arkansas's navigable waterways: "Could you not come to Memphis via river?" asked the Creole. "I will send you all the boats you may require."[14]

By the time Van Dorn received these messages on March 25, he was in Jacksonport. He promptly instructed Price and Churchill, the latter wandering across the Ozark Plateau with his cavalry brigade, to change the direction of their march to Des Arc, a port about fifty miles south of Jacksonport on the White River. Van Dorn informed Johnston that the order to move to Memphis "will be executed as promptly as possible"; he then took a steamboat to meet with Beauregard and to plan how best to move his troops, animals, equipment, and stores from Des Arc to Memphis.[15]

As the busy days passed, Van Dorn slipped from under the cold shadow of Pea Ridge and forgot the lessons he had only recently learned about proper preparations and realistic objectives. He wrote to his wife that the combined armies east of the Mississippi should be able to recover Tennessee, liberate Kentucky, and invade Ohio: "Then huzza for the Confederacy." The Mississippi cavalier was himself again. From the comfort of hotel rooms and steamboat cabins Van Dorn repeatedly urged his subordinates to quicken the pace of the march, but his nagging exhortations had little effect. The movement of the Army of the West from Van Buren to Des Arc was exceedingly difficult; the spring rains that had made the retreat from Pea Ridge so miserable returned to drench the troops, soak the roads, and swell the creeks in their path. North of Little Rock the Confederate column descended into the vast alluvial bottomland of the Mississippi River Valley. The soggy landscape seemed submerged. "I never saw worse roads than we have had for this last two days," wrote a Texan. "The roads are over a flat spongy country and in many places the bottom seems to have fallen out." Little's brigade reached Des Arc on April 6 and departed for Memphis the next day aboard a small flotilla of steamboats, but the rest of the army was far behind. Hébert's brigade, last to leave Van Buren, did not reach the White River until April 15 and did not get away until April 24 or 25.[16]

The delay really made no difference. Fearful that Grant's army at Pittsburg Landing would be reinforced, Johnston decided he could not wait any longer for Van Dorn's distant command. While Little's Missourians filed onto the boats at Des Arc on April 6, Johnston led his soldiers into battle near Shiloh Church along the banks of the Tennessee River. When the shooting stopped the next day, Johnston was dead, and the shattered remnants of his army were falling back to Corinth. By the time Van Dorn's soldiers finally trickled into northern Mississippi a week later, their numbers barely compensated for the staggering losses incurred at Shiloh. The great Confederate gamble in the West had failed.

The concentration at Corinth had a devastating impact on the defense of the Trans-Mississippi Confederacy. In his haste and enthusiasm Van Dorn did not merely move the Army of the West to the eastern side of the Mississippi; he abandoned Arkansas and Missouri to the enemy. He directed that all arms, ammunition, food, and other supplies in Arkansas be sent to Memphis after the army; that all machinery and stores at the Little Rock arsenal be shipped to Vicksburg; and that all unserviceable horses and wagons left behind at Des Arc be moved south to newly established depots on the Ouachita and Red rivers near the Louisiana line. In brief, Van Dorn stripped his district of its military manpower and equipment. His actions guaranteed that the Trans-Mississippi Confederacy never again would be able to support a force comparable in size and power to the Army of the West.[17]

While the controversy with Sigel simmered in the newspapers, Curtis continued to concentrate on refitting his ragged command. Slowly the Army of the Southwest recovered its fighting trim. The spring weather and the absence of any serious threat made these few weeks in late March and early April an idyllic interlude for the survivors of so much hard marching and fighting. Nearly every day Curtis enjoyed solitary strolls through the flowering woods and meadows, "looking at the spring buds and leaves with the same interest I used to watch my seeds in the garden." The warming temperatures made Curtis hopeful that he would be permitted to resume active campaigning. As the days passed without any word from Halleck, he began to fidget over the inactivity of his army.[18]

March 27 was unforgettable for the Federal commander. That morning two dozen officers of the 1st and 2nd Divisions arrived at headquarters to congratulate Curtis on his nomination for promotion to major general. Asboth made a formal complimentary speech, and Curtis replied in kind, attributing his success to the valor and endurance of his troops. The general was pleased by the little ceremony. He remarked that he wished an artist or photographer had been present to record the scene. But in the afternoon his pleasure turned to grief when he learned that his daughter Sadie, twenty years old, had died of typhoid fever in St. Louis. She had contracted the disease while visiting the army's sprawling camps at Rolla in January.[19]

Curtis was crushed by the news. That night, privately mourning in his tent, he wrote, "The whole world seems sad and melancholy. . . . Honor and fame are indeed empty shadows." He grew even more despondent when he realized that he would be unable to attend his daughter's funeral and comfort his stricken wife. "I could not leave my post," he confided to his brother. "The German Generals could not carry on a campaign like this." The Federal commander was so distracted by the loss of his youngest child that he withdrew for long periods into the seclusion of his tent, abandoned writing in his daily journal for a month, and for several days was barely able to tend to his duties: "The care that my command involves seems to overshadow my grief, but the two are more than I can well carry along. . . . I try to keep up, but I fear I am not fit for the place. I wish . . . some experienced educated General was here to whom I could turn over the Command." Fortunately for the cause of the Union, Sadie Curtis died at a time when the Army of the Southwest was not in need of dynamic leadership.[20]

During the last week of March rumors reached the Federal camp that Van Dorn was on the move. By the end of the month Curtis was almost certain that the Confederate army was marching down the Arkansas River Valley, destination unknown. The grief-stricken Federal commander pondered this news. The rebels had failed to force their way back into Missouri from northwestern Arkansas; now it appeared they were sidling to the east in order to threaten the state from northeastern Arkansas. Curtis's primary responsibility remained the safety of Missouri. There was no other Federal force in the Trans-Mississippi capable of meeting Van Dorn's command, so Curtis concluded that he must shift his own army eastward to cover Missouri's long and vulnerable southern flank. Yet he hesitated to take such a drastic step without consulting Halleck. As luck would have it, the telegraph line between Keetsville and St. Louis failed at this crucial juncture, and Curtis was reduced to dashing off an urgent letter.[21]

Four days passed. By April 4 Curtis was growing impatient. "I have about concluded to move eastward," he told his division commanders that morning, "get your troops ready to march at a moment's warning." Curtis planned to cross the White River and move eastward across northern Arkansas, keeping his own army between the enemy and Missouri. When the White River proved too deep to ford (as Churchill and his Confederate cavalrymen had discovered), Curtis selected an alternate route that passed north of the swollen stream and wandered across the southern periphery of Missouri.[22]

On April 5, as the Army of the Southwest broke camp, a message arrived from Halleck over the restored telegraph line. Halleck confirmed that Van Dorn was in Jacksonport, apparently in advance of his army, and concurred in Curtis's decision to move eastward. Moreover, he announced that Brigadier General Frederick Steele's division-sized force, presently stationed in southeastern Missouri, would advance and join Curtis's column somewhere along the Arkansas-Missouri line. And so the Army of the Southwest once more set out on the march. The final stage of the campaign was under way.[23]

Curtis had no illusions about crossing the central portion of the Ozark Plateau. "I have a long, rough road before me, and the matters of supplies may retard me," he wrote Halleck. But the difficulties were even greater than he had expected. The meandering highland roads of southern Missouri were mere tracks through the wilderness, winding along rocky ridges and plummeting into narrow valleys flooded by the spring rains. Creek crossings were major amphibious operations that often required building causeways and impromptu pontoon bridges composed of wagon boxes. Sometimes men, animals, and wagons were swept away and lost in the roaring floods. Progress was reduced to a snail's pace, and supplying the army became a nightmare. The endless forests offered little in the way of food or forage, and rations were reduced to dangerously low levels. The army spread out across a broad front forty miles wide and devoured everything in its path. "I leave nothing for man or brute in the country passed over by my army," reported Curtis without exaggeration. Despite these difficulties the Federals inched eastward from Cassville to Forsyth, Vera Cruz, and West Plains.[24]

While the Army of the Southwest struggled against the elements and the limits of overland transportation on the frontier, Halleck learned that Van Dorn, Price, and the Army of the West had crossed the Mississippi River and had joined Beauregard at Corinth. Much relieved, he informed Secretary of War Edwin M. Stanton that "Missouri may be regarded as safe, or at least not seriously threatened." With the state secure from invasion for the first time since the beginning of the war, Halleck was free to concentrate on operations on and east of the Mississippi River. He left St. Louis and took personal command of the battered but victorious Federal force at Pittsburg Landing.[25]

Halleck now regarded operations in the Trans-Mississippi as peripheral. He decided that the thousands of Federal troops trudging through the wilds of Arkansas and Missouri might be better employed elsewhere. Halleck directed Curtis and Steele to push their respective columns into northeastern Arkansas and meet near Jacksonport. From there the reinforced Army of the Southwest was to continue moving eastward and threaten Memphis in conjunction with a Federal flotilla driving down the Mississippi River. At Memphis Halleck hoped to repeat the combined army-navy operations that had proved successful at Forts Henry and Donelson, New Madrid, and Island No. 10.[26]

The van of the Army of the Southwest reached West Plains in south-central Missouri on April 27. Curtis, back on rolling terrain for the first time in more than three weeks, unleashed another flurry of requests for teams, wagons, rations, and supplies of every sort for his long-suffering men and animals. "The cry is for shoes (horse mule and men) and pants," he wrote. The harried quartermaster in St. Louis promised to help but cautioned Curtis that there was a scarcity of everything because "the army in Tennessee is all-absorbing."[27]

Despite the unpromising supply situation Curtis turned his army south toward Jacksonport in accordance with Halleck's instructions. That simple change of direction acted as a tonic: the worn and weary Federals surged forward as if once again pursuing Price down Telegraph Road. Dour, taciturn Carr, of all people, boasted to his commander that "my Division made twenty-two miles today handsomely; if they had some shoes I could beat the world in marching." Caught up in the excitement, Curtis shook off the depression that had dogged him for weeks and showed a flash of his old aggressiveness. When the head of the long blue column reentered Arkansas on April 29, Curtis took personal command of the cavalry and dashed forward toward Batesville, a bustling little port on the White River. On May 2 the hard-riding Federals stormed into the town and scattered a large band of rebel irregulars.[28]

Two days later advance elements of Steele's column rode into Jacksonport,

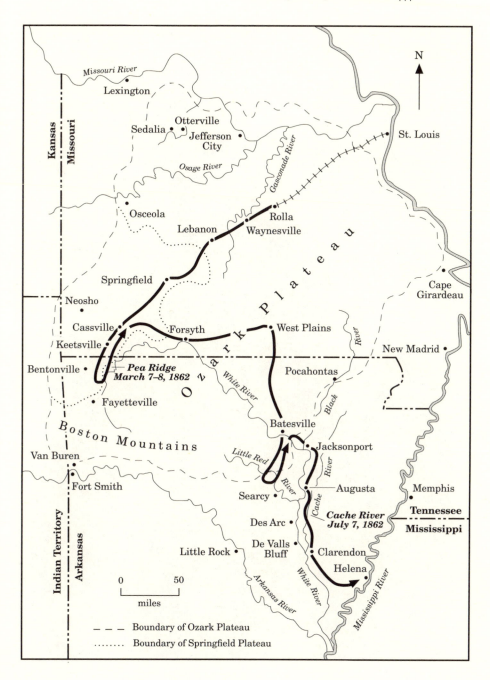

Map 15-1. March of the Army of the Southwest, February–July 1862

Frederick Steele
(Massachusetts Commandery, U.S. Army Military History Institute)

a dozen miles down the White River from Batesville, and made contact with the Army of the Southwest. During the next week, long lines of infantry, cavalry, and artillery and miles of trains rumbled into the two towns and spread over the surrounding countryside in search of food, forage, and suitable campsites. Curtis planned to stay in Batesville only for a few days before pushing on toward Memphis. Scouts soon reported, however, that the low-lying alluvial plain between Jacksonport and the Mississippi River was "an endless lake of water." When Halleck learned that eastern Arkansas was impassable, he concluded that the navy would have to capture Memphis on its own. He instructed Curtis to send half of his infantry regiments to Cape Girardeau in southeastern Missouri, where the troops could be transported to Pittsburg Landing by steamboat.[29]

Displeased at losing half of his veteran infantry "while I am so far in advance of other armies," Curtis nonetheless did as ordered. He detached eight regiments from his own command (the 25th, 35th, 36th, 44th, and 59th Illinois, the 2nd and 15th Missouri, and the 22nd Indiana) and two from Steele's command (the 21st and 38th Illinois) and formed them into two divisions under Asboth and Davis. Even at this point in the campaign Curtis was careful to maintain a rough balance between the ethnic components of his army, including division commanders. On May 10 the chosen officers and men set out for Cape Girardeau and the war east of the Mississippi River.[30]

Over the next few days Curtis reorganized the shrunken Army of the Southwest into three divisions based largely on ethnic and geographical factors. Each of the new divisions consisted of three or four regiments of infantry, three or four regiments of cavalry, and three or four batteries of artillery. The 1st Division, commanded by Steele, was composed primarily of Indiana troops. Carr's 2nd Division included mostly soldiers from Iowa and Illinois. Osterhaus's 3rd Division was almost entirely made up of Missouri troops, most of them Germans. Sigel's departure, the reassignment of Asboth and Davis, and several months of experience in the field finally enabled Curtis to arrange a more rational organization of his army.[31]

With Memphis out of reach, Halleck reversed himself and directed Curtis to march on Little Rock, one hundred miles south in the heart of Confederate Arkansas. Once in possession of the city, Curtis was to declare himself military governor of the state and rule by martial law. Curtis was agreeable to the change in orders—it combined his preference for the offensive with his experience as a military administrator in Mexico—but he was uncertain whether his tenuous overland supply line could be stretched all the way to

Little Rock. Halleck assured him that in the coming weeks every effort would be made to establish a waterborne supply line via the Mississippi and White rivers.[32]

Governor Henry M. Rector of Arkansas panicked when Federal forces entered northeastern Arkansas and occupied Batesville and Jacksonport. He called out the militia and issued a proclamation furiously denouncing Confederate authorities for abandoning the Trans-Mississippi. Then he boxed up the state archives and hastened from Little Rock. Rector was not alone in his dissatisfaction and alarm. Brig. Gen. John S. Roane, the only Confederate general officer in Arkansas, succinctly informed Beauregard of the situation: "No troops—no arms—no powder—no material of war —people everywhere eager to rise, complaints bitter." Roane announced that he was halting all Texas troops passing through Little Rock bound for Corinth and urged that a high-ranking officer be sent at once to take command.[33]

The uproar in Arkansas prompted Jefferson Davis to write to Van Dorn, mildly chiding his old friend for failing to see the political ramifications of his hasty departure from the Trans-Mississippi. Van Dorn explained that prior to leaving Arkansas he had "taken particular pains" to inform Rector of "the military necessity of the Army of the West joining General Beauregard at Corinth." He also pointed out that he had already directed Roane to raise partisan bands (cautioning Roane to "be very careful that none but men of respectable character" command such bands) to attack Federal supply trains and foraging parties.[34]

While Davis and Van Dorn exchanged letters, Beauregard moved to stabilize the situation west of the Mississippi. At the end of May he acceded to Roane's request and appointed Maj. Gen. Thomas C. Hindman, a fervent Arkansas secessionist and a veteran of Shiloh, to command the Trans-Mississippi District in Van Dorn's absence. When Hindman arrived in Little Rock, he was shocked. "I found here almost nothing," he complained to Adjutant General Cooper. "Nearly everything of value was taken away by General Van Dorn." Hindman had to assemble an army and establish a logistical base from scratch in the least populous and least developed part of the Confederacy. Undaunted by the herculean task before him, Hindman went to work with a furious, driving energy. He offended practically everyone with his abrasive, single-minded manner, but he got things done. Within a few weeks he had scraped together four thousand cavalry, mostly Texans;

fifteen hundred infantry, mostly Arkansans; and a battery of light guns and had placed a handful of heavy guns along the Arkansas and White rivers.[35]

Hindman needed time to organize and drill his embryonic army at Little Rock. Casting about for some way to slow the approaching Federals, he called for an increase in the scope and intensity of irregular warfare. He announced that "for the more effectual annoyance of the enemy" all males of military age should organize themselves into guerrilla bands and "cut off Federal pickets, scouts, foraging parties, and trains, and to kill pilots and others on gunboats and transports, attacking them day and night, and using the greatest vigor in their movements." Hindman was less concerned than Van Dorn about the social consequences of unleashing hordes of armed civilians. He cared only about stopping the yankees.[36]

The Army of the Southwest, the cause of so much anxiety in Little Rock, Corinth, and Richmond, steadily extended its component parts south from Batesville. The town lay near the eastern edge of the Ozark Plateau and was an excellent point of departure for offensive operations to the south and east. On May 7 troops of Osterhaus's 3rd Division crossed the White River on a "miserable" rope ferry. Four days and forty miles later, they reached the Little Red River just north of Searcy. Little Rock lay only about sixty miles away across a stretch of low ridges and level bottomlands. The Little Red was unfordable, however, and the Federals, without benefit of engineering expertise, set about building a bridge. Meanwhile, the White River claimed eleven men of the 3rd Illinois Cavalry when the rickety ferry capsized. The fatal accident graphically demonstrated the vulnerability of the Federal position. Steele's 1st Division at Jacksonport was separated from Carr's 2nd Division at Batesville by the Black River. Both were separated from Osterhaus's 3rd Division by the White River and, soon, the Little Red River as well. Curtis realized that "it will not do to have our forces separated by so many rivers." He halted any farther advance until Steele's pontoon bridge arrived.[37]

The Federal commander was concerned that Osterhaus's isolated command could not be supported by the rest of the army if it ran into trouble. Batesville was abuzz with rumors that Texas regiments en route to Corinth were being halted in Little Rock and were being organized into a makeshift defensive force. Curtis informed Halleck that Governor Rector had issued a "flaming proclamation calling out the militia" and that "some troops are collecting at Little Rock." After contemplating the vulnerability of his extended supply line and the difficulty of guarding wide-ranging foraging

"Pioneers from Carr's Division, May 21, 1862," by Robert O. Sweeny. This sketch vividly illustrates the logistical difficulties the Federals faced in the alluvial bottomlands where their effort to capture Little Rock foundered. (State Historical Society of Missouri)

parties, Curtis concluded that Rector's call for militia "is likely to give me trouble in Arkansas." The capture of Little Rock now appeared to be a more formidable undertaking than the Federals had first imagined.[38]

Osterhaus confirmed that the Confederates were coming alive and causing serious complications for the overextended Federals. He reported that parties of rebels "harass my pickets and forage parties almost on every trip they make outside of our lines." He warned that his small cavalry force was "not sufficient to keep these stealing, murdering bands in the proper distance." Consequently, Osterhaus's command was very low on forage and could not stay long in its present position.[39]

Not only were the Confederates becoming more active, they were raising the level of violence. The troops opposing Osterhaus were a mix of undisciplined Texas cavalrymen and local irregulars who fought from ambush and took few prisoners. Those unfortunate Federals who did fall into their hands were often beaten and mutilated before being murdered. Osterhaus angrily declared that "the enemy on the other side of the river are certainly a set of outlaws and do by no means deserve the name of soldiers." Curtis emphatically agreed. He told Osterhaus that "such villains" were "not to be taken as prisoners."[40]

The intensity of the skirmishing increased dramatically on May 19 when a Federal foraging party ventured south of the Little Red River and was attacked by Texas cavalrymen near Searcy. After a fierce firefight several hundred Texans surrounded two companies of the 17th Missouri. The Federals tried to surrender, but the Confederates shouted "D—n you, we want no prisoners" and murdered a number of Missouri infantrymen, including several lying wounded on the ground. Federal losses amounted to 15 killed, 32 wounded, and 2 missing. Confederate casualties are uncertain, but the Federals claimed the departing cavalrymen left 18 dead. The barbarous behavior of the rebels in this encounter infuriated Curtis, and he reiterated his order to Osterhaus: "Instruct your scouting parties to take no more prisoners of armed banditts."[41]

On May 20 Carr's 2nd Division joined Osterhaus's command on the Little Red River. Confident that he now had enough strength to brush aside the rebels in his front and capture Little Rock, Curtis ordered a general forward movement for the next day. But before the advance could get under way, a letter arrived from Capt. Frederick S. Winslow, the army's new quartermaster, and his assistant, Captain Carr. The two officers informed Curtis in no uncertain terms that the Army of the Southwest—finally—had reached the end of its tether. The supply line, stretching three hundred miles across the Ozark Plateau from Rolla to Batesville, had broken down. In addition to the difficulties caused by spring rains, guerilla raids, and a shortage of draft animals, the army's wagons and harnesses were "in a condition of great insufficiency ... having now been in constant service for five months without time for necessary repairs or refits." Winslow and Carr declared that the army could not be maintained much longer where it was and most certainly could not be supported if it moved any farther south. Curtis canceled the planned offensive and returned to Batesville.[42]

After carefully reviewing the logistical situation with Winslow and Carr, Curtis concurred that a continuation of the advance on Little Rock was *"absolutely impossible."* Nothing more could be done until a waterborne supply line was established via the Mississippi and White rivers. The Federal commander refused to give up the initiative altogether, however, and decided to strike a limited blow against the rebels in his front. He instructed Carr and Osterhaus to launch a coordinated series of cavalry raids and foraging expeditions across the Little Red River on May 27. The sudden burst of activity caught the Confederates off guard and forced them back ten or fifteen miles. A fair amount of food and forage was collected, some of it from rebel camps.[43]

News of the successful operation raised the Federal commander's spirits. "I am crowded a little but I am troubling Rebeldom in Arkansas considerably," he wrote. Nevertheless, on June 4 the troops along the Little Red began pulling back to Batesville. Curtis informed Halleck of his deteriorating logistical situation and noted that he might even have to retire into Missouri unless a more effective means of supplying his army could be put into effect. Halleck had not been paying much attention to events in the Trans-Mississippi during his methodical approach to Corinth, which fell to Federal forces on May 30, but now he became alarmed over the possibility of losing much of what had been gained in Arkansas. "Rely on it I will reinforce you as soon as possible," he promised Curtis. Halleck was as good as his word. "It is of pressing importance that you immediately send some gunboats down the Mississippi and up White River to Jacksonport," he wrote to Commodore Charles H. Davis, commander of the Federal flotilla that had recently captured Memphis. "It is the earnest wish of the War Department that this be done without delay." Davis was agreeable, and by mid-June a heavily escorted convoy of transports loaded with 100,000 bushels of grain, 2,500 bales of hay, and several regiments of infantry was churning down the Mississippi. In a fine example of interservice cooperation the expedition was jointly commanded by Col. Graham Fitch of the army and Lt. James Shirk of the navy.[44]

After turning into the narrow, looping White River in eastern Arkansas, the convoy fought its way upstream for 170 miles. On June 17 the Federal vessels engaged Confederate batteries at St. Charles and suffered a serious loss when rebel fire struck the steam drum of the ironclad *Mound City*. Scalding steam killed half the gunboat's crew and injured most of the rest. After the infantry got ashore and overran the batteries, the expedition pressed on to Clarendon before being stopped by low water. When Curtis learned of this development, he decided to move downriver, saying that since the transports could not come to him, "I must go to them." And so, in a surprisingly casual manner, Curtis made the momentous decision to sever his supply line with Rolla, put his command in motion, and live off the southern countryside until he could make contact with the navy. In the last week of June the Federals tramped out of Batesville and proceeded down the eastern bank of the White River: the March to the Mississippi was under way.[45]

For the next two weeks the Army of the Southwest operated in eastern Arkansas independent of a base of supplies, the first time in the Civil War a Federal army attempted such a daring maneuver. It would not be repeated until eleven months later, when Grant chose a similar course of action during the Vicksburg campaign. Curtis was less inclined than ever to promote himself after the controversies with Sigel, and he never made much of his break with military convention, at least not in public. Nevertheless, Curtis realized that he had accomplished something quite remarkable. In a private letter he proudly informed his older brother Henry that "I have marched further over worse roads than any other General and subsisted my force in the country. Nobody else has done this."[46]

The Federals had struggled over the windswept Ozark Plateau in the dead of winter; now they trudged across the endless alluvial plain of the Mississippi River Valley at the height of a southern summer. Men and animals suffered from heat, dust, insects, and a lack of potable water but found adequate supplies of food in the rich bottomlands. Curtis did not envisage his march across eastern Arkansas as a form of strategic economic warfare, but it had that effect. The troops foraged, pillaged, and destroyed on an unprecedented scale. "Desolation, horrid to contemplate, marks every section of the country through which the army has passed," wrote an Illinois soldier, "and an air of sickening desolation is everywhere visible." An Arkansan believed that "no country ever was, or ever can be, worse devastated and laid waste than that which has been occupied, and marched over, by the Federal army. Every thing which could be eaten by hungry horses or men has been devoured, and not content with foraging upon the country, almost every thing which could not be eaten was destroyed." Property damage in one county was estimated at $1.5 million.[47]

The presence of the Army of the Southwest sounded the death knell of slavery in Arkansas's premier agricultural region. Curtis emancipated slaves on a mass scale, ignoring the fact that in mid-1862 he lacked the authority to do any such thing. In towns along the way soldiers commandeered printing presses and produced stacks of emancipation forms. News of what the Federals were doing spread like wildfire, and by the end of the campaign, more than three thousand refugee slaves, "freedom papers" in hand, trailed the dusty blue column en route to an uncertain future. Thousands more headed north toward Missouri. Few of the midwesterners in the army had seen a black person before the campaign, but they quickly adjusted to having men, women, and children of African descent "wandering around the camp as thick as blackberries."[48]

When Hindman learned that the Federals had abandoned their drive on Little Rock and were marching down the White River, he issued a remarkable proclamation. It began with a situation update as seen from Confederate headquarters in Little Rock. "The Yankee General, Curtis, is attempting to escape," announced Hindman. "His position has become untenable. He is appalled at the dangers that surround him." Hindman challenged Arkansans to deal with the fleeing Federals as the Minutemen of old had dealt with the Redcoats: "Attack him day and night, kill his scouts and pickets, kill his pilots and his troops on transports, cut off his wagon trains, lay in ambush and surprise his detachments, shoot his mounted officers, destroy every pound of meat and flour, every ear of corn and stack of fodder, oats and wheat that can fall into his hands; fell trees, as thickly as rafts, in all the roads before him, burn every bridge and block up the fords. Hang upon his front, flanks and rear, and make the ring of your rifles and shot-guns the accompaniment of every foot of his retreat." This call for a general uprising and a scorched earth policy did not have the desired effect. Some fervent secessionists did poison wells, fell trees, burn bridges, and snipe at the Federals, but most Arkansans were interested primarily in protecting their lives and property. Hindman later admitted to Cooper that "my instructions for devastating the country were not executed."[49]

Hindman's assurance that the Confederate army would do its part also proved chimerical: the only organized attempt to halt the Federals was a costly fiasco. On July 7 the Army of the Southwest began crossing the Cache River, a sluggish stream surrounded by swampy ground. Brig. Gen. Albert Rust, commanding a handful of poorly armed Texas cavalry regiments, foolishly attacked the Federal column while it was straddling the river. He ordered the 12th and 16th Texas Cavalry to strike the vanguard of Curtis's army on the eastern side of the stream. The vanguard was a detached force of about four hundred men from the 11th Wisconsin and the 33rd Illinois under the command of Col. Charles E. Hovey, until recently president of the Illinois Normal School. The undisciplined Confederates charged, "yelling like savages and swearing like demons," but several volleys from the Federal infantry "threw them into confusion, tumbling horse and rider indiscriminately over each other." Hovey's command was reinforced by a battalion of the 1st

Indiana Cavalry and two three-inch rifled cannons. When the Federals coun-terattacked, the Texans broke and ran.[50]

Curtis remained well to the rear and forwarded reinforcements as he had done at Little Sugar Creek. He was pleased that Steele's inexperienced sol-diers had done well and informed Halleck that the battle of Cache River was "a complete rout of the rebel army of Arkansas. They ran in all directions." The Federals lost 6 killed and 57 wounded, but the Confederates suffered much heavier casualties: probably 136 dead and at least as many wounded, along with 66 horses killed. One shaken Texan informed his mother that "we got the worst of it considerably." Cache River was the last time the Confed-erates attempted to engage the Army of the Southwest.[51]

After the battle the Federals pushed on to Clarendon, where they believed the convoy was waiting. The head of the column reached the little riverport on July 9 only to discover that the gunboats and transports had gone back down the river the day before. Fitch and Shirk had become discouraged just a bit too quickly by their inability to make contact with the Army of the Southwest. Curtis fired cannons and sent messengers galloping after the boats, but to no avail. The attempt to establish a waterborne supply line up the White River had failed by the slimmest of margins, and Curtis privately acknowledged that "the disappointment is most overwhelming." Clarendon was located in a swampy lowland incapable of supporting a large number of men and animals. Curtis decided he had no choice but to abandon the line of the White River and proceed to Helena on the Mississippi, about forty-five miles east. He had considered marching to Helena as early as June 25 but had decided against it because relocating there meant giving up any imme-diate chance of resuming operations against Little Rock. Curtis now con-cluded that reestablishing a secure supply line and refitting his run-down command was more important than gaining more territory. Little Rock could wait.[52]

On July 12 the van of the Army of the Southwest reached Helena after a nightmarish march in stifling heat and dust, "with only filthy, slimy water from the swamps to drink." The troops climbed atop the levee and flagged down passing Federal transports, which soon stopped and disgorged rations, clothing, shoes, and all manner of supplies. Curtis salved his disappointment at failing to capture Little Rock by moving into Hindman's elegant mansion in Helena and flying a large United States flag from the roof. The rest of the army, trailed by thousands of refugee slaves, straggled in over the next few days. Since leaving Pea Ridge the Federals had marched five hundred miles in slightly more than three months. Now they could rest; the campaign was over.[53]

After a string of dramatic victories at Fort Donelson, Pea Ridge, Island No. 10, Shiloh, New Orleans, and Corinth, Federal offensive operations in the Mississippi Valley and the Trans-Mississippi sputtered to a halt. Somewhat undone by their own success, the Federals needed time to consolidate their gains and prepare future operations. Their relative inactivity during the second half of 1862 allowed the Confederates to regain the strategic initiative for a brief time.

When the bulk of Confederate forces west of the Appalachians embarked on an invasion of Kentucky, Van Dorn and the Army of the West remained behind in Mississippi and made a vain attempt to recover western Tennessee. The resulting battle at Corinth on October 3–4, 1862, was one of the bloodiest Confederate defeats of the war. At Corinth Van Dorn demonstrated that his impetuous nature had not been tempered by his experience in Arkansas.[54]

Van Dorn was criticized heavily after Corinth, and he asked for a court of inquiry to clear his name. The court, headed by Sterling Price, pondered charges strongly reminiscent of the Pea Ridge campaign. Van Dorn was accused of beginning the operation with inadequate supplies and forcing his army to take whatever was needed from the enemy, of failing to familiarize himself with the Federal position before attacking, and of marching his men in a "hastily and disorderly manner" that caused much needless suffering, especially on the retreat. Van Dorn denied committing any errors and appealed to the court's regard for a soldier's honor by declaring that "my reputation is all that belongs to me." He was exonerated.[55]

Corinth was the final campaign for the ill-starred Army of the West. Van Dorn's command was broken up, and the troops were incorporated into other armies. Some went into the trenches at Vicksburg and Port Hudson; others ended up at Stone's River and Chickamauga. Van Dorn was assigned to a cavalry force. He scored his only victory of the Civil War when he destroyed a Union supply base at Holly Springs, Mississippi, in December 1862 and effectively halted Grant's first thrust toward Vicksburg. Van Dorn finally seemed to have found a role that fit his temperament and abilities. Unfortunately, he had precious little time left. On May 7, 1863, he was murdered by a jealous husband at Spring Hill, Tennessee. Thus ended an ambiguous chapter in the annals of Confederate military history.[56]

Price became disgusted with Jefferson Davis's reluctance to support the liberation of Missouri. He returned to Arkansas after the defeat at Corinth and devoted his flagging energy to the redemption of his home state. His final quixotic act was a desperate, doomed offensive directed against St. Louis in the fall of 1864. After losing a good part of his ragtag army at Pilot Knob, Price turned away from St. Louis and wandered aimlessly across Missouri. In a series of engagements around Kansas City in October 1864, his army was wrecked by a hastily gathered collection of Federal forces and Kansas militia led by none other than Samuel Curtis.[57]

The Army of the Southwest did not participate in the effort to counter the brief Confederate resurgence in the late summer and fall of 1862. Curtis and his men spent those months in Helena in military limbo. The midwesterners endured smothering heat and humidity and suffered from a murderous array of subtropical diseases. The situation did not improve when Helena became a mecca for hordes of northern traders eager to obtain cotton from the locals for resale to northern textile factories. The traders engaged in bribery, larceny, and theft in their frenzied efforts to obtain cotton. These illegal activities involved some army officers and contributed to an erosion of morale among the rank and file. As medical and moral conditions deteriorated, Curtis struggled to protect his soldiers, to curb the avaricious practices of the traders, to sustain the thousands of freedmen in Helena, and to maintain some semblance of discipline in an army without a mission. But when Curtis replaced Halleck as commander of the Department of the Missouri on September 19, 1862, leadership of the Army of the Southwest passed to Frederick Steele. A conservative Democrat, Steele reversed Curtis's enlightened measures toward freedmen and permitted cotton traders to conduct their unsavory business without interference from army headquarters.[58]

The Army of the Southwest gradually dissolved as regiment after regiment was incorporated into the Army of the Tennessee and took part in the siege of Vicksburg. Hard campaigning and fighting followed at Chattanooga, Kennesaw Mountain, and the March to the Sea. Atop Missionary Ridge on November 25–26, 1863, veterans of the old 1st and 3rd Divisions, who had been detached at Batesville, had a battlefield reunion with their comrades of the old 2nd and 4th Divisions when their respective new units camped near one another.[59]

Curtis missed all of this. Despite his accomplishments in the field, the aging general spent most of the rest of the war at a desk. When Curtis's radical Republican views made working smoothly with the more conservative governor of Missouri impossible, Lincoln removed him from the Department of the Missouri and named him commander of the Department of Kansas. During his tenure in Kansas he led troops in battle for the last time, destroying Price's army and ending forever any Confederate threat to Missouri. He was transferred to the Department of the Northwest in January 1865 and spent the next year dealing with frontier problems. After leaving the army Curtis joined the great adventure of building a transcontinental railroad, a project he had vigorously supported for over a decade. On December 26, 1866, he returned from an inspection tour of Union Pacific activities on the Great Plains and walked across the frozen Missouri River from Nebraska to Iowa. The day was extremely cold and windy, and Curtis had a difficult passage. Moments after reaching the soil of his adopted state, the old soldier slumped to the ground and died.[60]

Confederate veterans of Pea Ridge always recalled with deep regret what might have been, while Union veterans remembered with pride what had been accomplished against imposing odds. After enduring ice storms and stultifying heat, marching over seven hundred miles across mountains and swamps, fighting and winning one of the largest battles west of the Mississippi, and pioneering a novel form of mobile warfare, the officers and men of the Army of the Southwest had reason to feel proud. No other Federal operation at this stage of the Civil War lasted as long, covered as much territory, and achieved its objectives as effectively. Surely no one in that little army could have predicted at the outset of the campaign that their efforts, initially defensive in nature, would wreak such havoc on the course of the rebellion in the Trans-Mississippi. By the time Curtis led his dusty blue column into Helena in the summer of 1862, Missouri was safe for the Union, half of Arkansas was lost to the Confederacy, and the strategic balance in the Mississippi Valley was altered permanently.[61]

Conclusion
A Military Analysis of Pea Ridge

The Pea Ridge campaign was one of the earliest sustained operations of the Civil War. It provides a window through which we can glimpse the evolution of warfare in America in the mid-nineteenth century. While the campaign was traditional in many respects, the use of repeating rifles, dessicated vegetables, and telegraphic communication reflected the impact of industrialization. Moreover, the ready reliance on fieldworks at Little Sugar Creek and the social and economic impact of operations along the White River anticipated the trench warfare and strategic raids that dominated the war in 1864–65. The campaign also illuminated some of the problems involved in maneuvering and fighting across the undeveloped, wooded, and often rugged landscape of the western Confederacy.

STRATEGY

The campaign was an integral part of Halleck's overall strategy for Union success in the West. He rightly believed that establishing Federal control of St. Louis and as much of Missouri as possible was essential before beginning large-scale offensive operations in Tennessee and the Mississippi Valley. Halleck, so often maligned by contemporaries and historians as an ineffectual nag, deserves much of the credit for the success of the Pea Ridge campaign. He conceived the risky winter operation, placed Curtis and Sheridan in key positions, granted permission to march on his own authority, and provided crucial moral and logistical support during the initial months of campaigning. The result was one of the first Federal incursions into the Confederacy and the most successful Federal operation ever carried out in the Trans-Mississippi.

Ironically, the Federal victory at Pea Ridge was so complete that it has obscured the magnitude of the Confederate threat to Missouri in 1862. Van Dorn commanded the most powerful rebel force ever assembled in the Trans-Mississippi. It made little difference whether he led the Army of the West northward with a firm grasp of the strategic situation in his head or with only a burning desire for glory in his heart. Had Van Dorn not been turned back at Pea Ridge, he might well have reached the Missouri River and might even have threatened St. Louis. At the very least, a sizable Confederate force rampaging around central Missouri would have caused tremendous havoc and would have forced Halleck to divert thousands of troops and tons of supplies from the river offensives.[1]

Pea Ridge reshaped the strategic balance of forces in the West. Van Dorn was so jolted by his defeat that he readily agreed to Beauregard's suggestion that he transfer his command to the eastern side of the Mississippi. He had been appointed to command the Trans-Mississippi two months earlier in order to win a major strategic advantage. When he crossed the river, all Confederate hopes of controlling that region ended. Curtis's victory at Pea Ridge was the turning point of Federal efforts to dominate the Trans-Mississippi. The departure of the Army of the West from the Trans-Mississippi eliminated the primary reason for the presence of the Army of the Southwest atop the Ozark Plateau. Federal operations in the Trans-Mississippi after Pea Ridge ceased to have much effect on the overall strategic situation in the West, but they continued to have a tremendous impact on military, political, social, and economic affairs in the immediate theater of operations. In the course of their movements across northern and eastern Arkansas, the Federals ravaged the countryside, engaged in wholesale emancipations of dubious legality, and came within a whisker of capturing Little Rock.

After Curtis turned away from Little Rock, the nature of Federal operations in Arkansas changed. What had been a more or less orthodox invasion became the first strategic raid of the Civil War. The economic impact on eastern Arkansas of the March to the Mississippi was comparable to the effect of later raids on portions of Mississippi, Alabama, Georgia, and the Carolinas. By the time his army reached the Mississippi River at Helena,

Curtis found that he no longer was in the forefront of the strategic picture. The Federal advance down the Mississippi, made possible in part by his accomplishments, had preceded him.

LOGISTICS

During the first few weeks of the campaign the Army of the Southwest drove over two hundred miles across a sparsely settled and often hostile frontier region from the railhead at Rolla, which itself was a hundred miles from the primary Federal depot at St. Louis. Lacking railroads or water-borne transportation, the Federals relied on wagon trains struggling over primitive roads in winter weather for ammunition, equipment, clothing, and much of their food. As the trains did not always arrive at regular intervals, the Federals survived their odyssey into the wilderness by foraging vigor-ously and, when all else failed, by stoically enduring reduced rations and other shortfalls for weeks at a time. "I doubt if there was any campaign in the whole war where there was greater physical suffering and more manly endurance displayed than in this campaign," declared one veteran. The strik-ing overland mobility of the lightly equipped Army of the Southwest was in stark contrast to the relative immobility of other Federal forces at this point in the war, such as the Army of the Potomac, which enjoyed enormously greater logistical support yet lumbered only short distances overland and accomplished little.[2]

After Pea Ridge the Army of the Southwest continued to test the limits of overland logistics by marching another five hundred miles across Missouri and Arkansas. Curtis eventually cut loose from faraway Rolla and drove down the White River Valley in an unsuccessful attempt to establish a waterborne supply line. This maneuver, the March to the Mississippi, demonstrated for the first time in the Civil War that a large mobile force, independent of a base of supplies, could operate effectively for a sustained period in a rich agricul-tural area. Aside from having to endure a surfeit of dust and mosquitoes, Curtis and his men survived quite well while marching through Arkansas. Unfortunately, no one in the Union high command seems to have noticed.

GENERALSHIP

Curtis was the central figure in the campaign. He understood his strategic mission and achieved all of his original objectives. His administrative ability helped to keep the Army of the Southwest operating in the field for six months, much of that time under exceptionally trying circumstances. It is no exaggeration to say that in 1862 Curtis was among the most successful Union generals; only Grant accomplished more in the field.

Hardly had the campaign concluded, however, before Curtis began to fade into the shadows. Only in Iowa was his memory, and the memory of his accomplishments in the Trans-Mississippi, kept alive with statues and monuments. Dodge outlived his old commander by fifty years and closely followed the course of Civil War historiography. He was puzzled by the treatment accorded Curtis. "I have never thought that General Curtis has received the credit he was entitled to" for the Pea Ridge campaign, wrote Dodge. "This campaign demonstrated early in the war what could be accomplished by a small Army 300 miles away from any rail or water communication, in a rugged, mountainous, sparsely settled country, marching in winter, and virtually subsisting upon the country." Dodge was not alone in his opinion. Sheridan did not allow the postbattle dispute over insubordination to affect his admiration for Curtis. In his memoirs Sheridan did what he could to restore the Iowa general to his rightful place in history: "I was always convinced that Curtis was deserving of the highest commendation, not only for the skill displayed on the field, but for a zeal and daring in campaign which was not often exhibited at that early period of the war." Such efforts had little effect. Today, if Curtis is remembered at all, it is as a minor figure who participated in marginal activities somewhere in the West. He deserves better.[3]

Despite his lack of experience in battle, Curtis performed creditably and usually made the correct decision, sometimes against the advice of his subordinates. Curtis decided that the Army of the Southwest would stand and fight rather than fall back into Missouri. He initiated the counterattacks that kept the two halves of the Confederate army separated, and he supervised the extraordinary change of front carried out by the Federal army in the middle of the fight. He held much of his force in reserve until he could determine the true nature of the rebel threat, an act that required considerable moral courage given the desperate state of affairs at Elkhorn Tavern. Curtis recognized that Leetown was the most important sector of the battlefield on March 7 because it offered rebel forces the easiest approach to Pratt's store, the rear of the Little Sugar Creek fortifications, and the rear of Carr's embattled command at Elkhorn Tavern. The heroic perseverance of the 4th Division gave Curtis time to secure the Leetown front and concentrate, without a moment to spare, on holding a position astride Telegraph Road far enough north to safeguard his operational base at Pratt's store. Later that day Curtis understood the altered tactical situation following the Confederate collapse at Leetown and refused to allow nervous officers like Asboth to derail his plans for victory. Finally, he used interior lines to concentrate his army during the night of March 7–8 and directed the deployment of his army the following morning.

During the battle Curtis generally left tactical matters to his subordinates. Carr, Osterhaus, and Davis had complete freedom of action on March 7 to fight their separate engagements as they saw fit. Even during his brief appearance in Cross Timber Hollow that day Curtis did not interfere with Carr's direction of the fight. Nevertheless, Curtis kept overall control of matters in his own hands. The Federal commander was well served by his small staff of relatives and other Iowans. Curtis kept himself abreast of the progress of the battle, interpreted events with increasing accuracy as the hours passed, and maintained communication with his principal subordinates despite the scattered deployment of his forces on March 7.

For the most part Curtis was blessed with very competent division and brigade commanders. Osterhaus and Davis, deftly assisted by Greusel, won the fight at Leetown in large part by combining aggressiveness with careful handling of available troops. Carr, ably supported by Vandever and Dodge, accomplished his difficult mission at Elkhorn Tavern by exhibiting aggressiveness, stubbornness, and tactical flexibility under great pressure. Only Sigel and Asboth failed their commander, at least in spirit, by falling prey to defeatism during the battle. Despite this, Sigel turned in a stellar performance on the morning of March 8, although he intended to run from the enemy rather than pursue him. Sigel was erratic throughout the campaign, but on the whole he made a genuine contribution to victory at Pea Ridge that somewhat offset his tragicomic performance at Wilson's Creek.

Confederate generalship at Pea Ridge was dismal. Van Dorn was an irresponsible general who was continually in overdrive. He bore the primary responsibility for the debacle. Though his objective was strategically sound, his lack of logistical preparation was almost criminal, and his obsession with speed and surprise wore down his troops and led to the division of his army in the presence of the enemy. Once the campaign was under way, Van Dorn failed as an army commander in almost every respect. He neglected to assemble an efficient staff and was never able to exercise effective control of his own army. Worse, the hastily assembled staff, composed of Maury and a handful of volunteers from McCulloch's and Price's divisions, committed numerous errors that Van Dorn failed to notice or correct. Losing track of the ordnance trains was a mistake with enormous consequences. In the midst of battle Van Dorn shed his responsibilities as army commander and immersed himself in tactical matters at Elkhorn Tavern better left to his division and brigade commanders. Instead of taking steps to keep himself informed of the progress of McCulloch's division at Leetown, he relied on whatever messengers various officers of that division chanced to send his way.

Van Dorn's decision to envelop the Federal army was self-defeating: it did not allow the Federals an escape route and resulted in the Confederates being cut off from their own trains. Van Dorn could have conducted a shorter flanking movement around the Federal right by advancing along the Bentonville Detour and turning south at Twelve Corner Church, the route ultimately taken by McCulloch's division. On the flat terrain near Leetown Van Dorn could have concentrated and brought to bear his superior numbers and firepower. With a line of retreat open along Telegraph Road, Curtis might have decided to abandon the useless Little Sugar Creek fortifications and to fall back into Missouri through the narrow confines of Cross Timber Hollow. Keetsville, seventeen miles north, was the first relatively open space where Curtis could have deployed his entire army for battle. Along the way, McIntosh's large mounted brigade could have hounded the cavalry-poor Federals without mercy. But the rebel general was reaching for the complete destruction or capture of the yankee army and was uninterested in a partial victory. The flaw in Van Dorn's plan was that it allowed him no options; it was a make or break endeavor.

Throughout his military career Van Dorn failed to consider the effect of what Clausewitz called "friction," the application of Murphy's Law to military operations: "Countless minor incidents—the kind you can never really forsee—combine to lower the general level of performance, so that one always falls far short of the intended goal. Iron will-power can overcome this friction; it pulverizes every obstacle, but of course it wears down the machine as well." Clausewitz might have been writing about the Pea Ridge campaign.[4]

Unlike Curtis, Van Dorn was not well served by his subordinates. McCulloch handled the opening stages of the Leetown engagement correctly, but it was absurd for a division commander to act like a scout while his staff did nothing. McIntosh, like Van Dorn, was a cavalryman out of his element and could not have replaced McCulloch even had he lived. Hébert performed well in a limited role until captured, but Pike was hopelessly ineffectual, and Greer took command too late to demonstrate any ability he may have possessed. Price was something of an enigma at Pea Ridge. He was more effective as an inspirational leader than as a division commander at Elkhorn Tavern on March 7, and his injury forced him to play a greatly reduced role the next day. Slack had promise but was mortally wounded before the battle had barely begun. The one exception to the litany of Confederate ineptitude and misfortune was Henry Little. During the course of the battle he gradually assumed more and more responsibility until he became the de facto commander of Price's division during the last hours that the Army of the West was on the field. His death at Iuka later that year was a blow to the Confederate cause in the West, where good officers were in dreadfully short supply.

It became a tenet of Lost Cause mythology to blame fate for the outcome of the fighting at Leetown and, subsequently, the overall battle. "If Gens. McCulloch and McIntosh had not been killed," a Louisiana captain wrote, "we would have gained a complete victory, for we had the enemy's right repulsed, their battery taken, and all in full train for a complete rout if our reserve had been ordered up at this juncture." If those reserves had been deployed properly and at the right time, they might have won the fight at Leetown, but the officers on Foster's farm were good soldiers. Although eager to join the battle, they dutifully waited for orders that never came. It was the opportunity of a lifetime for a bold officer to lead his regiment forward and pitch in to support Hébert's assault, but no one was willing to take that step. Confederate commanders at the army, division, and brigade levels either failed to seize opportunities or made too many mistakes. Sul Ross sized it up when he wrote, "We have had a Battle, and been whipped, or rather, we whipped ourselves."[5]

TACTICS

Pea Ridge was an oddly fragmented engagement that lasted two days and extended across several miles of varied terrain, or three days and dozens of miles of even more varied terrain if Sigel's retreat from Bentonville is considered part of the battle. Not surprisingly, there were diverse tactical situations. "It was a battle of all kinds of surprises and accidents," remarked Sigel, "of good fighting and good manoeuvering." Correspondent Fayel, disoriented by the woods and hills, remembered that "a scene of inextricable confusion prevailed generally. The battle was simply a melee, a sort of French and Indian war fight in the woods, with a great deal of bravery displayed on both sides, but less skill or design controlling the movements. It was a mere collision of force with force, fire and fall back until the ammunition gave out. I saw no manoeuvering of battalions, no strategic combinations and skillful tactics that we read of in the pages of Jomini, Marmont and Napier, or see on dress parade."[6]

The normally astute Fayel was off the mark. On a minor tactical level, that of regiments and companies, Pea Ridge was indeed a furious and often blind fight in the woods. But on a higher level, that of divisions and brigades, officers exercised reasonably firm direction of tactical evolutions that determined victory or defeat.

The battlefield at Pea Ridge encompassed a mix of topographical features. At Leetown there were level fields and prairies enclosed by thickets of scrubby timber and dense brush. The most intense fighting there occurred in thick woods crisscrossed by ravines. Vegetation reduced visibility, disrupted formations, and caused opposing infantry to engage at very close range, usually less than seventy-five yards. Surprise characterized the confrontation of opposing forces, resulting in brief but frenetic exchanges of gunfire. Half of the units that saw action at Leetown engaged in little more than brief firefights along the fringes of open areas. Major Wangelin of the 12th Missouri remarked that the coolness and firmness of his men enabled them to retain formation and "drive the enemy off with great loss, without being subject themselves to a very protracted fire." The side that could maintain cohesion longer than the other not only won the contest but also lost fewer men.[7]

The Elkhorn Tavern sector was also characterized by a variety of terrain and vegetation. Cross Timber Hollow was very rugged, but the woods were less cluttered with underbrush than at Leetown, making infantry and artillery fire more effective. Only when the Confederates smashed their way onto the relatively level terrain atop the plateau did they encounter fields and tangled, brushy thickets. There the troops on both sides experienced many of the same problems encountered by their colleagues at Leetown. Only on March 8 did successful assaults take place across open areas.

Lateral control of infantry movements, always a problem in the Civil War, was intensified by the terrain and vegetation at Pea Ridge and by the inexperience of regimental and brigade officers. White lost control of his brigade of Illinois regiments in Morgan's woods and was forced to disengage in order to save his command from disintegrating. Within the 37th and 59th Illinois, coordination broke down between companies as well. Davis directed the movement of Pattison's brigade of Indiana regiments with skill and fortuitous timing, but Pattison could not control the movements of his two regiments in the woods. His command emerged more or less victorious largely because of the even greater confusion in Confederate ranks.

At Elkhorn Tavern, after the Missourians broke Carr's line and pushed it back late on March 7, lateral coordination of the multitude of small units in Price's command evaporated. A more efficiently organized division might have maintained cohesion and exploited the advantage it had gained at a terrible cost in lives. Conceivably, Price could have pushed Carr all the way back to Pratt's store and changed the course of the battle. The worst example of Price's failure to maintain lateral control occurred during the poorly managed attacks against Dodge's Iowans that littered Clemon's field with dead and dying rebels.

When fighting occurred in open ground on the first day at Pea Ridge, it naturally was costly. The Confederate attack on the Peoria Battery in Oberson's field cost many casualties among both attackers and defenders. After the battle an Illinois soldier found fourteen dead rebels "in a space not larger than would be occupied by two guns of a battery." The Missouri troops who surged across Clemon's and Ruddick's fields suffered appalling losses. Firepower, not shock, dominated the battlefield at Pea Ridge.[8]

In no other area was there such a sharp contrast between Leetown and Elkhorn Tavern than in the significance of artillery. At Leetown only one Confederate and parts of four Federal batteries were in action, and two of the Federal batteries were rendered inoperative in the course of the fight. The thick vegetation hindered the fire of the yankee guns as much as the breakdown of command hobbled the rebel artillery. The Federal guns clearly played a role in driving the Confederates out of the belt of timber but did not play a significant part in the fighting east of Leetown Road.

In contrast, the artillery shone brilliantly on both days at Elkhorn Tavern. On March 7 cannoneers in blue and gray engaged in a spectacular artillery duel in Cross Timber Hollow. The Confederates gradually gained the upper hand and severely hammered the outnumbered Federal batteries. Later that day, rebel gunners advanced in support of the infantry and did good work, especially in Clemon's field. By the close of the day, however, the tide had turned. The array of Federal cannons in Ruddick's field helped to repulse the final Confederate assault. Federal artillery was utterly dominant on March 8 as Sigel demonstrated his true talents as a field artillerist. Blue-coated cannoneers acting under his immediate supervision concentrated their fire on isolated rebel batteries and drove them from the field, one after the other. Then the Federal guns steadily advanced upon the defenseless rebel infantry, pushing them back from their exposed positions and paving the way for a successful infantry assault.

At Leetown cavalry was employed in almost all possible ways. Horsemen were used initially by Curtis as part of the all-arms reconnaissance force that Osterhaus led to Foster's farm. McCulloch responded with a classic cavalry assault across open ground—tried and true shock tactics—which scattered the Federal force. Most of the Confederate horsemen were then dismounted and served as a reserve for the infantry, while the Federal troopers were re-formed and served as flank guards and scouts for their own infantry. Osterhaus failed to use his horsemen in another classic role, to harass his enemy's flanks by sending Bussey through the gap in the belt of trees onto Foster's farm. The Federals concluded cavalry operations at Leetown with a small but graphic demonstration of the changing role of cavalry on the mid-nineteenth-century battlefield. The ill-advised attack by Meszaros's troopers illustrated that shock tactics against infantry were woefully outdated. Cavalry was not effectively used at Elkhorn except when shock tactics were abandoned and the horsemen were used as flank guards.

Other noteworthy tactical features of Pea Ridge included the unique employment of emergency men by the Confederates. It was a fiasco that contradicted all modern guidelines for mobilizing manpower. It was impossible to tell how many completely green soldiers stood in rebel ranks at Pea Ridge, men who were indifferently armed and had only a few days' worth of drill. Companies of emergency men in the Arkansas regiments fired into other Confederate troops by mistake and were among the first to disintegrate under the impact of Federal counterattacks. The Civil War was no place for minutemen.

The fieldworks erected by Dodge's Iowans along the western edge of Clemon's field consisted of material that happened to be at hand. This was typical of field fortifications during the first half of the war, when soldiers rarely dug a trench but sometimes erected barriers of logs, planks, rocks, or whatever else fortune placed at their disposal. As the war progressed and the armies engaged in continuous campaigning within striking distance of one another, soldiers began to dig into the ground whenever there was even a modest prospect of battle. The result was the elaborate field fortifications that characterized the operations of 1864–65 on both sides of the Appalachians.

THE WESTERN WAR

Pea Ridge was fought during the springtime of northern hopes. The first major Federal victory of the war had occurred at Fort Donelson only three weeks earlier. A month after Pea Ridge came the terrible Federal victory at Shiloh, followed in quick succession by the capture of Nashville, Island No. 10, Corinth, Memphis, and New Orleans, which gave the Federals control of central and western Tennessee and most of the Mississippi Valley. In faraway New Mexico Federal troops defeated a Confederate column in Glorieta Pass. In the east the *Monitor* drove off the *Virginia* in Hampton Roads, and McClellan finally put his powerful but ponderous army in motion toward Richmond in what would become known as the Peninsula Campaign. It seemed as if the great rebellion might collapse before the year was out.

That was not to be, but the impact of this uninterrupted string of Federal successes, nearly all of them in the vast expanse between the Appalachian Mountains and the Great Plains, was tremendous. Yet better-publicized events in the East all too often eclipsed more significant events in the West, a state of affairs that still hampers our understanding of the Civil War. Sherman, among others, was disturbed by this perversion of history. "Somehow, few men realized the full value of the victories of Pea Ridge, Donelson, and Shiloh," wrote the famed general a quarter-century after the guns fell silent. "Though not conclusive, they gave the keynote to all subsequent events of the war. They encouraged us and discouraged our too sanguine opponents, thereby leading to all our Western successes which were conclusive of the final result. The more you study the Civil War, the more you will discover that the Northwestern States 'saved the Union.'"[9]

Appendix 1 The Legacy of Pea Ridge

Pea Ridge lived on as a potent force in the lives of the participants and in the collective consciousness of the nation. Because it was an early battle, it spawned many new military leaders. Three Federal generals fought at Pea Ridge (Curtis, Sigel, and Asboth), and twelve officers of lower rank later became generals; half of these men rose in rank as a direct result of their performance at Pea Ridge. Of the four Federal division commanders, three went on to become part of that large corps of highly competent and reliable mid-level generals who made victory in the West possible. Only Asboth failed to capitalize on his experience at Pea Ridge. His unreliable behavior led superiors to shunt him into progressively less important commands.[1]

Four Confederate generals were at Pea Ridge (Van Dorn, McCulloch, McIntosh, and Pike), and two of them died there. Twenty-four other Confederate and state guard officers, including Price, eventually rose to the rank of general, but few achieved distinction. Hébert, for example, went on to perform competently at Corinth and Vicksburg and then faded from the scene. Greer spent the rest of his military career as an administrator in the Trans-Mississippi. Not every prominent southern officer prospered after Pea Ridge.[2]

For every survivor whose career was advanced by the battle there were dozens whose lives were crushed. Herman Tuerck, a lieutenant in the 12th Missouri, was blinded by "an inimical shot" on March 8 as his regiment rolled forward to victory. Congress granted him a pension of $300 per year in 1863, and Tuerck returned to his native Germany. The pension was not large enough to retain an educated servant to care for him. More than eight years after Pea Ridge, Tuerck wrote to various American political figures, including President Grant, in search of help. He could find no one to take up his cause. "Yes! It is indeed hard and bitter, that I who have sacrificed so much for the U.S. get so little from them in return, and am forced to take this humiliating step!!! I think they might have given me so much, so as to keep off sorrows and cares yet plaguing my dark, miserable life!!"[3]

Because Pea Ridge was the first battle for so many of its participants, it became a benchmark for future experience. Just before the Federal assault on the Dead Angle at Kennesaw Mountain, Georgia, on June 27, 1864, a man in the 22nd Indiana surveyed the menacing Confederate earthworks and said to a friend, "Aye! God, Jim, that hill's going to be worse'n Pea Ridge. We'll ketch hell over'n them woods." The benchmark was not always used seriously. Jefferson C. Davis, who rose to become one of Sherman's most trusted corps commanders, told a story about a soldier who went home to marry without telling his army friends about it. "Why, when I got married I let anybody and everybody know it that wanted to," said Davis. "I thought it was a *big thing*. Pea Ridge was considerable, but nothing by the side of getting a wife."[4]

The worst Pea Ridge legacy in the minds of Civil War contemporaries—and the most exotic in the minds of present-day students—was the controversial role of the Cherokees. Pea Ridge was the only major Civil War battle involving Indians, and the atrocities that occurred at Leetown horrified the North. Rumors circulated freely that the natives had been "dosed with whiskey in advance" and had gone "utterly wild and shot and scalped both sides indiscriminately." The Federal soldiers who experienced this sort of warfare became bitter and wary. Two months after the battle Capt. Eugene Payne of the 37th Illinois informed his wife, "These Indians are blood thirsty and savage. We know when we fight them that we have to fight on a different principle than we would white men. We must be constantly on our guard as if we were fighting wildcats." Feelings were particularly intense among members of the 3rd Iowa Cavalry. "There was two of them infernal indians taken prisoner," wrote Capt. Oliver Hazard Perry Scott, "and we have seen one that was killed. I wish it had been the last of that race. There was quite a number of our men scalped by them, two of our company. . . . There will be no quarter shown them after this, that is certain."[5]

A few days after the battle Curtis expressed his hope to Van Dorn that "this important struggle may not degenerate to savage warfare." Henry Z. Curtis, the general's son and a member of his staff, reasoned that using Indians in battle was simply asking for trouble. "The employment of Indians involves a probability of savage ferocity. . . . Bloody conflicts seem to inspire their ancient barbarities; nor can we expect civilized warfare from savage tribes. If any presumption has been raised in their favor on the score of civilisation, it has certainly been demolished by use of the tomahawk, war-club, and scalping knife at Pea Ridge."[6]

In Washington the Joint Congressional Committee on the Conduct of the War investigated the atrocities at Pea Ridge. In submitting his evidence Curtis issued an uncharacteristically bitter condemnation of Indians; perhaps the former congressman could not resist the temptation to engage in the hyperbolic oratory common to nineteenth-century politics. He declared that the "savages" engaged in warfare "with all the barbarity their merciless and cowardly natures are capable of." Pike did not learn of the scalpings, mutilations, and murders until after his return to the Indian Territory, whereupon he immediately issued orders forbidding a recurrence of this practice, court-martialed a soldier for shooting a wounded Federal, and informed Curtis of all the steps he had taken. Curtis was hardly mollified and chided Pike for using Indians in battle. Pike was unable to disassociate himself from the atrocities and resigned his commission in July 1862. He continued to be crucified in the northern press and was even indicted in Federal court after the war for encouraging atrocities. The nation could not forget and neither could the Cherokees. For decades after Pea Ridge, partisans of each of the two Cherokee regiments blamed the other for the incident.[7]

The image of the barbaric Indian elicited the ultimate horror associated with the untamed frontier, lending to Pea Ridge a strong exotic element. Only after the western Indians had been subdued and the passage of decades had softened the bitterness of the war could people look upon the role of the Cherokees at Pea

Ridge as an amusing interlude. Years afterward John Noble of the 3rd Iowa Cavalry dreamed up a condescending description of the Indians as they milled around the captured cannons on Foster's farm: "Here and there a 'ward of the nation' might be seen with the harness of an artillery horse on, the trace chains clanging at his heels and a collar over his neck, exclaiming as such have been known to do on other occasions, 'Me big In'gen, big as horse.'"[8]

Pea Ridge was an enormous event in the lives of its participants. From that experience emanated a wealth of folk memories expressed in song and story. Immediately after the battle all sorts of wild anecdotes circulated by word of mouth and through the newspapers. Some of them apparently were based on fact, but most were pure fiction. Among the more believable: a soldier in the 12th Missouri was saved when a bullet was stopped by a twist of tobacco the man had stolen the night before and stuffed into his coat pocket; a member of the 18th Indiana was hit by a bullet that shattered the glass of a daguerreotype of his sweetheart but did him no harm; a man in the 36th Illinois survived because a book of bawdy songs stopped a bullet. Among the less credible: a soldier in the 59th Illinois went mad over the scalping of his brother and lost his own life in a frenzied attempt to kill as many rebels as possible; an officer of the 9th Iowa, after killing a Texan in hand-to-hand combat, had to pry his opponent's hands loose from his hair in order to free himself; a cavalry mount lost a leg to an artillery shell but ran three-fourths of a mile on three legs before dropping. In the excitement following the first victory, no story was too wild to share around the campfire or to include in letters home.[9]

Yet there was value in these stories, for they represented the collective oral memory of Pea Ridge and gave meaning to the battle. Songs played the same role. Folklorist Vance Randolph, who lovingly collected oral artifacts of Ozark culture, heard "The Pea Ridge Battle" sung as late as 1928. Dan Martin, the protagonist, participated in the battle and retreated with the Confederate army on March 8.

> An' with that dread confusion
> We was forced to leave the ground.
> The rollin' storms of iron balls
> Was cuttin' thousands down.
>
> To see our friends a-fallin'
> It did us so provoke,
> The sun was dim, the sky was hid
> With clouds of rollin' smoke.

McCulloch is a doomed hero and Price is an inspiring leader, but Van Dorn is only a subject of abuse.

> It was at the Pea Ridge fight
> That Van Dorn lost his hat,
> An' for about a half a mile
> He laid the bushes flat.

> Jumped over stumps an' scattered tents,
> All this he did not dread.
> The most that lay upon his mind
> It was a lump of lead.

The verses were altered and rearranged over the years, but the tone and texture varied little.[10]

Pea Ridge also found its way into popular literature. In 1871 Edward Zane Carroll Judson, better known as Ned Buntline, published a melodrama entitled *Buffalo Bill, the King of Border Men*. The tale features kidnappings, hairbreadth escapes, and fierce fights between the good guys (Buffalo Bill and his partner, Wild Bill Hickock) and the bad guys (an evil lot of border ruffians led by Dave Tutt). The climax comes during the closing moments of the battle of Pea Ridge. Buffalo Bill's company of scouts (which includes Wild Bill) charges a rebel battery in order to save Carr's division. McCulloch is killed in the attack, and Wild Bill is in turn killed by the female lover of Dave Tutt. Not to be upstaged, Van Dorn also gets himself killed. Buffalo Bill's heroic charge saves the Federal army and wins the battle even though every man in the company is killed or wounded. Buntline claimed the story was "founded entirely on fact."[11]

Similarly fantastic stories circulated regarding Hickock's alleged role at Pea Ridge, but these were folktales rather than products of Buntline's overheated imagination. Hickock, usually described as a Federal scout or teamster, is said to have climbed atop Big Mountain and picked off thirty-five rebels, including McCulloch. After Pea Ridge Hickock supposedly served on Curtis's staff and occasionally doubled as a spy. There is no factual basis for any of this. Hickock had no connection with Pea Ridge or the Army of the Southwest.[12]

The only reasonably accurate literary treatment of Pea Ridge in the nineteenth century came from the pen of Thomas Knox. In 1894 the former war correspondent published *The Lost Army*, a lengthy novel based on his wartime experiences in Missouri and Arkansas. The heart of the novel, which is aimed at a youthful audience, is a fictionalized account of the entire Pea Ridge campaign from Rolla to Helena as seen through the eyes of two Iowa teenagers, Jack and Harry. Knox gets the two boys into a number of thrilling fictional adventures along the way, such as scouting and outwitting rebel guerillas, but for the most part he hews closely to the actual events of the campaign. For example, Jack is captured with Herron at Elkhorn Tavern and accompanies him to Van Buren to tend his injured leg. Jack and Harry are wise beyond their years—they have an encyclopedic knowledge of world military history—but otherwise they are stylized literary youths of Knox's day, sort of early versions of the Hardy boys. Knox draws heavily on his own wartime dispatches, reciting them almost verbatim in some places, and conveys a convincing sense of what actually happened at Pea Ridge.[13]

Nearly ninety years passed before another solid fictional treatment of Pea Ridge appeared. In 1980 Douglas C. Jones published *Elkhorn Tavern*, the story of the Hasford family, whose farm is located on the battlefield. The novel deals primarily with family survival. The father is fighting in Virginia, and the mother and children contend with soldiers, guerillas, bandits, and the turmoil of the war, embodied in the terrible struggle for the tavern just a short distance from their farmstead. Jones, a native of the Boston Mountains and a retired army officer, describes the landscape and the lost Ozark way of life in loving detail and relates the fighting in vivid, authentic terms.[14]

Most visual images, like most literary treatments, fail to depict the battle in an accurate or meaningful way. No photographer or battlefield artist accompanied either army. Thus, the weekly newspapers in the North illustrated their accounts of Pea Ridge with generic battlefield scenes. *Harper's Weekly* portrayed the conflict in a grand panorama of sweeping battle lines. The hilly terrain looked much like some areas of the Ozark Plateau, but no attempt was made to fit the historical incidents of the battle to the tableau. With no firsthand visual documentation available, publishers relied on poetic license, not journalistic veracity, to convey the image. The same was true of postwar lithographs. An 1889 Kurz and Allison print shows Confederate cavalry, including a large contingent of Plains-type Indians, charging Federal guns. Like all such prints it is highly stylized and wildly inaccurate. No Indians took part in the mounted charge on Foster's farm. A print of Sigel at Pea Ridge, issued immediately after the battle, also is stylized myth. It depicts the German general giving orders while striking a vigorous pose on his horse with the battle raging in the background. It is an example of the Civil War heroic style at its best.[15]

A talented amateur artist did join Curtis's army immediately after the battle. Robert O. Sweeny was a pharmacist who traveled with his brother-in-law, a Federal commissary officer, to northwestern Arkansas. Sweeny produced three sketches relating to Pea Ridge. Two of the sketches are of little historic or artistic value, but the third, a drawing of Elkhorn Tavern, is particularly interesting. It depicts the building in detail with a cannonball hole in one side and a shattered tree in the yard.[16]

The only filmed representation of Pea Ridge is further evidence that visual images of the battle tend to be generic. In 1989 the Oklahoma Educational Television Authority produced a five-hour miniseries titled *Oklahoma Passage*. It presents the story of the fictional Benton family of mixed Cherokee-white blood from the Trail of Tears to the present. Joseph Benton joins Stand Watie's Cherokee regiment and fights at Pea Ridge. The battle scenes were filmed with reenactors in the summer of 1988 at the Honey Springs battleground in Oklahoma. No attempt was made to recreate the course, character, or texture of the historical event. The scalpings are mentioned in passing and only reinforce Joseph's growing realization of man's evil and inhumanity. The larger implications of the atrocities for the Cherokee people, in particular the tension between their ethnic heritage and their acculturation into white society, are ignored.[17]

Probably the best-known image of Pea Ridge was created by Hunt Wilson, a veteran of Guibor's Missouri Battery. Several years after the war he painted a

"Elkhorn Tavern, Battle Ground of Pea Ridge, Ark.," by Robert O. Sweeny (State Historical Society of Missouri)

triptych that is the most authoritative visual documentation of the battle. The center piece depicts the final Federal attack from the Confederate perspective. It is all-embracing, covering Elkhorn Tavern on the right, the Ford homestead and the advancing Federals in the center, and the Confederate left wing preparing to retreat. The wounded Price is in the foreground urging his men to fall back, but Van Dorn is nowhere to be seen. The painting grandly depicts the swirl and scope of the fighting on March 8, which was unusually visible for all to see. The left panel of the triptych shows the congested area around Pratt's store on March 8. It is the only representation of the store and of Curtis's headquarters tent, and it conveys the sense of expectancy the Federals felt on the morning of the second day. The right panel is Wilson's most evocative, depicting his battery in action in Telegraph Road directly in front of the tavern late on March 7. In vivid colors and dramatic detail Wilson gives a true image of war. Bleeding bodies lie on the ground, the tavern stands naked and exposed, and troops hug the ground for dear life in the background while the gunners toil feverishly over their guns. No one else captured the visual drama of Pea Ridge so well.[18]

The only person with a vision comparable to Wilson's was an anonymous illustrator who portrayed the 37th Illinois in action in Morgan's woods on March 7.

The 37th Illinois battling Hébert's brigade in Morgan's woods, March 7, 1862. An unknown artist painted this "from a Photo Sketch made after the Battle." (George W. Herr, Episodes of the Civil War: Nine Campaigns in Nine States *[San Francisco, 1890], frontis.)*

Working from a photograph of the battlefield taken after the war, the artist accurately portrayed the regimental line of battle with the colors prominently displayed in the foreground. The picture successfully conveys the character of the Leetown battle; the viewer is immediately impressed by the dense woods and drifting smoke. It is not known if the artist was a veteran of Pea Ridge, but the work is a true historical document.[19]

Artists who lacked precise information about the encounter sometimes produced impressive but unenlightening portrayals of Pea Ridge. Andrew Jackson Houston, son of the Texas revolutionary leader, painted Good's Texas Battery in action on March 8. His watercolor was done in the 1880s and exemplifies the nonspecific art often used to represent the battle. It is a good depiction of a battery in action, well executed artistically, but there are no recognizable physical features or troop dispositions that mark it as a Pea Ridge image.[20]

Unlike other early battles, such as Shiloh, Pea Ridge inspired no songs from the popular music industry. The only music associated with the contest was a short piece by "Ch. Bach" entitled the "Pea Ridge March." It is only four pages of piano music without lyrics—a throwaway product of a thriving sheet music industry that capitalized on public interest in the war.[21]

Herman Melville, whose *Moby Dick* had not yet earned him a reputation as one of America's greatest writers, included a poem titled "Inscription for the

Graves at Pea Ridge, Arkansas," in his *Battle-Pieces*, a collection of poems inspired by the war. *Battle-Pieces* contains many works of deep interest for the cultural history of the Civil War, but "Pea Ridge" is not one of them. It is superficial and detached.

> Let none misgive we died amiss
> When here we strove in furious fight:
> Furious it was; nathless was this
> Better than tranquil plight,
> And tame surrender of the Cause.[22]

Later generations found the battle a fertile source of poetic inspiration, although only a small portion of that inspiration resulted in good verse. By far the best was "Return to Pea Ridge," written by Edsel Ford.

> Spirits remembered are not spirits dead...
> Now in this peaceful place I pause to name
> Each man who fell unknown, each man who bled
> His way to glory. Theirs was not the shame.
> But, driven by some inner source of pride,
> Each must have known while dying in this lea
> His sacrifice would somehow fit the wide
> And widening pattern of a destiny.
>
> How cold that other March time must have been!
> How bleak those wooded fields in the attack!
> I stand now where a thousand nameless men
> Laid down their lives in war, and looking back,
> I know I must remember—I must give
> A name to every one, that he may live.[23]

The most impressive legacy of Pea Ridge for many people was the impact of the fighting on the land. The battlefield itself was the most enduring reminder of the conflict. The fields and forests of Leetown and Elkhorn Tavern were littered with debris after the battle. Dozens of Bowie knives were found at Foster's farm, dropped by Texans who naively thought they could use them in battle. Lyman Bennett of the 36th Illinois industriously picked up bullets and canister balls from the field and sent them home as souvenirs. Most awe-inspiring were the thousands of scars on trees and bushes. Surgeon William Fithian took time from his bloody duties in the Leetown hospitals to examine the ground where his stepsons in the 37th Illinois had fought. He found that for two hundred yards in front of the regiment's position not a tree or bush was spared the mark of bullets. The vegetation healed slowly. In October 1862, Federal troops commanded by Francis Herron camped near the tavern and explored the shattered forest. "The woods present a scene as if a tornado had passed through it and spent its vengeance in snapping limbs and twisting huge trees from the main trunk," wrote Benjamin McIntyre of the 19th Iowa. "I noticed many cannon balls still remaining in the trees—some had passed entirely through."[24]

The passage of years gradually softened the ravaged landscape. When Noble Prentis and John Black visited the battlefield in 1888, they found many things changed. Elkhorn Tavern, burned by bushwhackers late in 1862, had been rebuilt in 1885. Clemon's log house was gone, as was the tanyard in Cross Timber Hollow, though the two Union veterans managed to find the vats used in the tanning process. Some sections of Telegraph Road were no longer in use because a railroad had been built through the area, offering better transportation than the rocky road.[25]

There still was enough metal lying around to indicate that some serious fighting had once taken place there. In fact, while the two men walked along Telegraph Road, a local boy tried to talk them into buying relics. Joseph Cox, the current proprietor of the tavern, claimed that five tons of shot, shell, and bullets had been carried away by souvenir hunters. Cox had turned the tavern into a visitor center of sorts. One of the ground-floor rooms was a museum, complete with a blueprint map of the battlefield hanging on the wall. Positions of both armies were marked on the map. Down the hill from the tavern Prentis and Black found a board nailed to a tree, rudely marking the spot where William Slack had been mortally wounded.[26]

Overall, the trees most haunted Prentis. The effects of the battle were clearly visible in "the broken tops of the old oaks, wounded so that a quarter-century has not healed them. It is doubtful if a human being ever entirely recovered from a square blow from an ounce or half-ounce ball, and trees do not seem to outgrow their battle scars. Saying nothing of the effects of artillery fire, the mark of a musket-ball is permanent. The trees on the field of Pea Ridge have been carefully searched for bullets as relics, and in some cases it has been found that the ball after striking the tree has bounded back, but there is the blue-black mark in the wood at the point where the missile ceased to penetrate." Even as late as the 1920s the trees of Pea Ridge still held their wounds, and in the 1950s, just before the creation of Pea Ridge National Military Park, farmers and relic hunters continued to turn up debris of the battle.[27]

The land and vegetation took longer to heal than did the emotions of men. Putting the heartache and bitterness behind them, northerners and southerners assumed the duty of properly caring for the dead and commemorating the battle. The Federal government established a small national cemetery in Fayetteville in 1867 and interred bodies of those killed in the many battles and skirmishes in northwestern Arkansas. Of the identified dead in the cemetery, 110 fell at Pea Ridge. Sympathetic women of the area organized the Southern Memorial Association of Fayetteville in 1872 and established a Confederate cemetery on a hilltop east of town. Over a period of several years they gathered rebel dead from the area, including Slack. Of the 622 soldiers buried there, only 121 are identified. How many died at Pea Ridge is not known.[28]

To commemorate the battle several reunions were held, and two small monuments were erected on the field. On September 1, 1887, Confederate veterans unveiled a suitably stark monument to their dead. The obelisk was described at the time as a "plain, unpretentious shaft of marble that does credit to the donors," the citizens of Benton County. The monument is located about one hundred yards south of the tavern. It bears the names of McCulloch, McIntosh, and Slack and is inscribed with a curiously morbid poem.

> O give me the land with a grave in each spot,
> And names in the graves that shall not be forgot.
> Yes, give me the land of the wreck and the tomb;
> There's a grandeur in graves, there's a glory in doom.[29]

Two years later, on September 3–9, 1889, a reunion of both yankee and rebel veterans was held on the battlefield to erect another monument dedicated to "A United Soldiery." The assembled veterans adopted a resolution acknowledging the defeat of the Confederacy and the restoration of the Union, although one southern speaker made some remarks that were interpreted by a few northerners as indicating a willingness to start the war anew. This minor controversy was settled peacefully. The plain marble shaft, located only a few steps from the 1887 Confederate memorial, was as nonpolitical as possible. One of the three stanzas of verse inscribed on the monument epitomized the spirit of the gathering:

> Spirit of eternal light,
> Keep silent vigil o'er the brave;
> The untarnished Blue,
> The unsullied Gray,
> In peace and love unite.[30]

Unlike a number of other Civil War battlefields that are awash in postwar monuments of every size and style imaginable, Pea Ridge boasts only these two weathered obelisks set in the rocky ground by Telegraph Road.

Aging Pea Ridge veterans continued to return to the battlefield on their own. Jacob Platt, formerly a lieutenant in the 9th Iowa, went back in 1904. "It has been said by a famous orator that 'the past rises before us,' and I am fully convinced that the statement is true," wrote Platt. He found the field little changed, save for the dozens of empty graves that had not been refilled after the bodies had been removed to the cemeteries in Fayetteville. The ragged grooves in the ground brought the battle back to Platt more powerfully than anything else: "Those terrible scenes and incidents are written on the pages of my memory as though graven with the pen of fire."[31]

Asa Payne, who had served in Little's brigade, visited Pea Ridge in 1911. "I was, yet I was not, the beardless boy that marched away, but an old, gray bearded man," recalled Payne. He, too, found the field remarkably familiar despite the passage of half a century, and the experience unleashed a flood of memories and melancholy thoughts.

I stayed all night in the old tavern but all was quiet, the booming of cannon and the wails of the wounded were hushed forever. While seated on its porch beyond the eastern hills the full moon rose like a copper disk and shed its light just as fifty years before over the bloody field. I was lulled to sleep by the tinkling of cow bells in the near by mountain and was awakened only by the hoot of owls which seemed to me were hooting their last long hoot in memory of the past. Next morning I tried to find the place [in Ruddick's field] where Lieutenant Glasscock breathed his last but there was nothing to indicate that he once was. He lives only in the memory of his fast disappearing comrades or perhaps in Randolph County some old sister or brother or perhaps niece or nephew may think or have heard of him.[32]

Memories of the past did not die with the passing of the Pea Ridge veterans, for succeeding generations mounted efforts to preserve the battlefield. Attempts to establish a national military park on the site began in 1914 and were repeated in 1924, 1928, 1936, and 1939. All failed because the federal government judged other battlefields to be more significant than Pea Ridge. In the 1950s, with Civil War centennial fever beginning to sweep the nation, another effort was made. This time it succeeded, and President Dwight D. Eisenhower signed the bill establishing Pea Ridge National Military Park on July 20, 1956.[33]

The state of Arkansas purchased the land in 1957 and deeded it to the federal government in 1960. Following three years of planning and construction the park was dedicated on May 31, 1963, culminating the decades-long effort to commemorate the battle and preserve the field. These efforts were nobly seconded by the Pea Ridge Memorial Association, a local Benton County group dedicated to identifying sites associated with the Pea Ridge campaign. Between 1961 and 1963 the association placed historical markers at Camp Stephens, Cross Hollow, and other important locations outside the park boundaries.[34]

The 4,210 acres of Pea Ridge National Military Park encompass all the ground on which significant action occurred and include a detached section that preserves a portion of the Little Sugar Creek fortifications. The restored vegetation, roads, and fences are reasonably accurate, though there is far too much open space around the visitor center. Only the area around Foster's farm is entirely unsatisfactory: the alternating patches of forest, fields, and prairie which existed in 1862 have been replaced by a huge expanse of open grassland. The park is inadequately supplied with interpretive markers and artillery pieces, but the tour road, hiking trail, and bridle path provide access to most of the areas where important events took place. Elkhorn Tavern is a reconstruction of the 1885 structure, similar but not quite identical to the building that stood on the same foundations in 1862. The elk horns or antlers that adorn its roof today are not the ones that survived the battle. They were taken north by Carr and returned in 1885. When last seen, the antlers were resting in a private museum in the area.[35]

Today, Pea Ridge is one of the more heavily visited national parks in the south-central United States. A sizable herd of deer roam the pastoral fields and browse in the thickets. On wintry days, when the empty battlefield is a stark palette of grays and browns, visitors can easily lose themselves on what veterans called sacred ground. Next to contributing in its own way to the saving of the Union, this is the most precious legacy of Pea Ridge.

Appendix 2 Order of Battle

1st and 2nd Divisions
Brig. Gen. Franz Sigel

1st Division
Col. Peter J. Osterhaus

1st Brigade—Col. Peter J. Osterhaus

25th Illinois—Col. William N. Coler
Losses: 24 (3 k, 18 w, 3 m)

44th Illinois—Col. Charles Knobelsdorff
Losses: 3 (1 k, 2 w)

17th Missouri—Maj. August H. Poten
(Co. A absent on Conrad's expedition)
Losses: 10 (0 k, 2 w, 8 m)

2nd Brigade—Col. Nicholas Greusel

36th Illinois—Col. Nicholas Greusel
(Co. F absent on Conrad's expedition; regiment included two cavalry
   companies)
Losses: 75 (4 k, 37 w, 34 m)

12th Missouri—Maj. Hugo Wangelin
(Co. E absent on Conrad's expedition)
Losses: 34 (3 k, 29 w, 2 m)

Artillery

4th Independent Battery, Ohio Light Artillery—Capt. Louis Hoffman
Four 6-pounder rifled guns and two 12-pounder howitzers
Losses: 5 (1 w, 4 m)

Welfley's Independent Battery, Missouri Light Artillery—Capt. Martin Welfley
Four 12-pounder howitzers and two 12-pounder guns (one howitzer absent on
   Conrad's expedition)
Losses: 5 (5 w)

2nd Division
Brig. Gen. Alexander S. Asboth (w)

1st Brigade—Col. Frederick Schaefer

2nd Missouri—Lt. Col. Bernard Laiboldt
Losses: 54 (8 k, 34 w, 12 m)

15th Missouri—Col. Francis J. Joliat
(Co. B absent on Conrad's expedition)
Losses: 11 (11 m)

Artillery

1st Missouri Flying Battery—Capt. Gustavus M. Elbert
Four 6-pounder rifled guns and two 12-pounder howitzers
Losses: 19 (3 k, 8 w, 8 m)

2nd Independent Battery, Ohio Light Artillery—Lt. William B. Chapman
Four 6-pounder guns and two 12-pounder howitzers
Losses: 3 (1 k, 2 w)

Not brigaded

3rd Missouri—Maj. Joseph Conrad
(Cos. B, C, and E present at Pea Ridge; Co. F absent on Conrad's expedition;
   remainder absent on duty in Missouri)
Losses: 0

4th Missouri Cavalry (Frémont Hussars)—Maj. Emeric Meszaros
(Cos. A, C, D, E, F, and I present at Pea Ridge; remainder absent on duty in
   Missouri)
Losses: 16 (5 k, 8 w, 3 m)

5th Missouri Cavalry (Benton Hussars)—Col. Joseph Nemett
Losses: 17 (3 k, 11 w, 3 m)

3rd Division
Col. Jefferson C. Davis

1st Brigade—Col. Thomas Pattison

8th Indiana—Col. William P. Benton
Losses: 32 (5 k, 27 w)

18th Indiana—Lt. Col. Henry D. Washburn
Losses: 26 (3 k, 23 w)

22nd Indiana—Lt. Col. John A. Hendricks (k), Maj. David W. Daily, Jr.

(Co. B absent on duty in Missouri)
Losses: 42 (9 k, 33 w)

1st Battery Indiana Light Artillery—Capt. Martin Klauss
Four 6-pounder rifled guns and two 6-pounder guns
Losses: 11 (5 w, 6 m)

2nd Brigade—Col. Julius White

37th Illinois—Lt. Col. Myron S. Barnes
Losses: 144 (20 k, 121 w, 3 m)

59th Illinois (formerly 9th Missouri)—Lt. Col. Calvin H. Frederick
Losses: 66 (9 k, 57 w)

Battery A, 2nd Illinois Light Artillery (Peoria Battery)—Capt. Peter Davidson
Two 6-pounder rifled guns, two 6-pounder guns, and two 12-pounder howitzers
Losses: 17 (17 w)

Not brigaded

1st Missouri Cavalry—Col. Calvin A. Ellis
(Cos. B, F, G, H, I, K, L, and M present at Pea Ridge; remainder absent on duty
   in Kansas)
Losses: 6 (2 k, 2 w, 2 m)

4th Division
Col. Eugene A. Carr (w)

1st Brigade—Col. Grenville M. Dodge (w)

4th Iowa—Lt. Col. John Galligan (w)
Losses: 160 (18 k, 139 w, 3 m)

35th Illinois—Col. Gustavus A. Smith (w), Lt. Col. William P. Chandler (c)
Losses: 113 (14 k, 47 w, 52 m)

1st Independent Battery, Iowa Light Artillery—Capt. Junius A. Jones (w), Lt.
   Virgil A. David
Four 6-pounder guns and two 12-pounder howitzers
Losses: 17 (3 k, 14 w)

3rd Illinois Cavalry—Maj. John McConnell
Losses: 58 (9 k, 36 w, 13 m)

2nd Brigade—Col. William Vandever

9th Iowa—Lt. Col. Francis J. Herron (w, c), Maj. William H. Coyl (w)
Losses: 218 (38 k, 176 w, 4 m)

25th Missouri (Phelps's Independent Missouri Regiment)—Col. John S. Phelps (w)
Losses: 94 (12 k, 71 w, 11 m)

3rd Independent Battery, Iowa Light Artillery (Dubuque Battery)—Capt. Mortimer M. Hayden
Four 6-pounder guns and two 12-pounder howitzers
Losses: 22 (2 k, 17 w, 3 m)

Headquarters Units

24th Missouri—Maj. Eli W. Weston
(Cos. A, B, F, H, and I present at Pea Ridge; remainder absent on duty in Missouri)
Losses: 26 (3 k, 16 w, 7 m)

3rd Iowa Cavalry—Col. Cyrus Bussey
(Cos. A, B, C, D, and M present at Pea Ridge; remainder absent on duty in Missouri)
Losses: 50 (24 k, 17 w, 9 m)

Bowen's Missouri Cavalry Battalion—Maj. William D. Bowen
Four companies of cavalry and four 12-pounder mountain howitzers
Losses: 6 (1 k, 3 w, 2 m)

ARMY OF THE WEST
Maj. Gen. Earl Van Dorn

McCulloch's Division
Brig. Gen. Benjamin McCulloch (k)
Brig. Gen. James M. McIntosh (k)
Col. Elkanah Greer

Hébert's Infantry Brigade—Col. Louis Hébert (c), Col. Evander McNair

3rd Louisiana—Maj. Will F. Tunnard (c), Capt. W. L. Gunnells
Losses: 67 (10 k, 15 w, 42 m)

4th Arkansas—Col. Evander McNair, Lt. Col. Samuel Ogden
Losses: 54 (16 k, 38 w) according to McNair, but 55 (5 k, 36 w, 14 m) according to regimental surgeon Gammage, and 79 (22 k, 23 w, 34 m) according to *Arkansas True Democrat*, April 3, 1862.

14th Arkansas—Col. William C. Mitchell (c)
Losses: unknown

15th Arkansas—Col. Dandridge McRae
Losses: unknown

16th Arkansas—Col. John F. Hill
Losses: unknown

17th Arkansas—Col. Frank A. Rector
Losses: unknown

1st Arkansas Mounted Rifles (dismounted)—Col. Thomas J. Churchill
Losses: 5 (5 k)

2nd Arkansas Mounted Rifles (dismounted)—Col. Benjamin T. Embry
Losses: 27 (4 k, 15 w, 8 m)

4th Texas Cavalry Battalion (dismounted)—Maj. John W. Whitfield
(Battalion consisted of three companies of Texas troops and one of Arkansas
   troops)
Losses: unknown

McIntosh's Cavalry Brigade—Brig. Gen. James M. McIntosh (k)

3rd Texas Cavalry—Col. Elkanah Greer, Lt. Col. Walter P. Lane
Losses: 14 (2 k, 12 w)

6th Texas Cavalry—Col. B. Warren Stone
Losses: 19 (3 k, 3 w, 13 m)

9th Texas Cavalry—Col. William B. Sims (w), Lt. Col. William Quayle
Losses: unknown

11th Texas Cavalry—Col. William C. Young
Losses: unknown

1st Arkansas Cavalry Battalion—Maj. William H. Brooks
Losses: 41 (11 k, 30 w)

1st Texas Cavalry Battalion—Maj. R. Phillip Crump
Losses: unknown

Artillery

Hart's Arkansas Battery—Capt. William Hart
Four 6-pounder guns
Losses: unknown

Provence's Arkansas Battery—Capt. David Provence
Two 6-pounder guns and two 12-pounder howitzers
Losses: unknown

Gaines's Arkansas Battery—Capt. James J. Gaines
Two 12-pounder rifled guns and two 12-pounder howitzers
Losses: unknown

Good's Texas Battery—Capt. John J. Good
Four 12-pounder guns and two 12-pounder howitzers
Losses: 17 (1 k, 14 w, 2 m)

Pike's Indian Brigade—Brig. Gen. Albert J. Pike

1st Cherokee Mounted Rifles—Col. John Drew
Losses: unknown

2nd Cherokee Mounted Rifles—Col. Stand Watie
Losses: unknown

1st Choctaw and Chickasaw—Col. Douglas H. Cooper
Losses: unknown (not engaged)

1st Creek Mounted Rifles—Col. Daniel N. McIntosh
Losses: unknown (not engaged)

Welch's Texas Cavalry Squadron—Capt. Otis G. Welch
Losses: unknown

Unassigned

19th Arkansas—Lt. Col. P. R. Smith
Losses: unknown

20th Arkansas—Col. George W. King
Losses: unknown

Price's Division
Maj. Gen. Sterling Price (w)

Confederate Units

1st Missouri Brigade—Col. Henry Little

2nd Missouri—Col. John Q. Burbridge
Losses: unknown

3rd Missouri—Col. Benjamin A. Rives (k), Lt. Col. James A. Pritchard
Losses: 104 (26 k, 45 w, 33 m)

Wade's Missouri Battery—Capt. William Wade
Two 6-pounder guns and four 12-pounder howitzers
Losses: unknown

Clark's Missouri Battery—Capt. S. Churchill Clark (k), Lt. James L. Farris
Four 6-pounder guns
Losses: unknown

1st Missouri Cavalry—Col. Elijah Gates
Losses: unknown

2nd Missouri Brigade—Col. William Y. Slack (k), Col. Thomas H. Rosser

Hughes's Missouri Infantry Battalion—Col. John T. Hughes
Losses: 8 (1 k, 3 w, 4 m)

Bevier's Missouri Infantry Battalion—Maj. Robert S. Bevier
Losses: 15 (3 k, 8 w, 4 m)

Rosser's Missouri Infantry Battalion—Col. Thomas H. Rosser
Losses: unknown

Landis's Missouri Battery—Capt. John C. Landis
Two 12-pounder howitzers and two 24-pounder howitzers
Losses: unknown

Jackson's Missouri Battery—Capt. William Lucas
Four 6-pounder guns
Losses: unknown

Riggins's Missouri Cavalry Battalion—Col. George W. Riggins
Losses: unknown

3rd Missouri Brigade—Col. Colton Greene

(Brigade consisted of several partially organized battalions and companies of
infantry and cavalry in the process of transferring to Confederate service:
parts of Col. Thomas R. Freeman's and Lt. Col. John A. Schnable's Missouri
State Guard regiments and Capt. L. C. Campbell's cavalry company)
Losses: 65 (6 k, 59 w)

Headquarters Units

Cearnal's Missouri Cavalry Battalion—Lt. Col. James T. Cearnal (w), Maj. D.
Todd Samuels
Losses: 20 (2 k, 6 w, 12 m)

Missouri State Guard

2nd Division—Brig. Gen. Martin E. Green

(Division consisted of various unidentified infantry and cavalry units)
Losses: unknown

Kneisley's Battery—Capt. James W. Kneisley
Five 12- and 6-pounder guns
Losses: unknown

3rd Division—Col. John B. Clark, Jr.

1st Infantry—Maj. John F. Rucker
Losses: 11 (1 k, 5 w, 5 m)

2nd Infantry—Col. Congreve Jackson
Losses: 47 (5 k, 17 w, 15 m)

3rd Infantry—Maj. Robert R. Hutchinson
Losses: 27 (1 k, 20 w, 6 m)

4th and 5th Infantry—Col. J. A. Poindexter
Losses: 47 (3 k, 37 w, 7 m)

6th Infantry—Lt. Col. Quinton Peacher
Losses: 33 (2 k, 23 w, 8 m)

Tull's Battery—Capt. Francis M. Tull
Two 6-pounder rifled guns and two 6-pounder guns
Losses: unknown

5th Division—Col. James P. Saunders

(Division consisted of various unidentified infantry and cavalry units)
Losses: 41 (9 k, 32 w)

Kelly's Battery—Capt. Joseph Kelly
Five 12- and 6-pounder guns
Losses: unknown

6th Division—Maj. D. Herndon Lindsay

(Division consisted of various unidentified infantry and cavalry units)
Losses: 47 (13 w, 34 m)

Gorham's Battery—Capt. James C. Gorham
Four 6-pounder guns
Losses: unknown

7th and 9th Divisions—Brig. Gen. Daniel M. Frost

(Divisions consisted of various unidentified infantry and cavalry units from
   Frost's and Brig. Gen. James H. McBride's divisions)
Losses: unknown

Guibor's Battery—Capt. Henry Guibor
Two 6-pounder guns and two 12-pounder howitzers
Losses: unknown

MacDonald's St. Louis Batttery—Capt. Emmett MacDonald
One 6-pounder gun and two 12-pounder howitzers
Losses: unknown

8th Division—Brig. Gen. James S. Rains

1st Infantry—Col. William H. Erwin
Losses: unknown

2nd Infantry—Lt. Col. John P. Bowman
Losses: unknown

3rd Infantry—Lt. Col. A. J. Pearcy
Losses: unknown

4th Infantry—Lt. Col. John M. Stemmons
Losses: unknown

Shelby's Cavalry Company—Capt. Joseph O. Shelby
Losses: unknown

Bledsoe's Battery—Lt. Charles W. Higgins
Three 12-pounder Napoleons and one 12-pounder gun ("Sacramento")
Losses: unknown

Note: Casualty figures for Confederate units are incomplete or otherwise inaccurate.

Notes

ABBREVIATIONS

AHC   Arkansas History Commission, Little Rock, Ark.
BPL   Belleville Public Library, Belleville, Ill.
BU   Baylor University, Waco, Tex.
CHS   Chicago Historical Society, Chicago, Ill.
DPL   Denver Public Library, Denver, Colo.
DU   Duke University, Durham, N.C.
HL   Huntington Library, San Marino, Calif.
IHS   Indiana Historical Society, Indianapolis, Ind.
ISHL   Illinois State Historical Library, Springfield, Ill.
ISL   Indiana State Library, Indianapolis, Ind.
KSHS   Kansas State Historical Society, Topeka, Kans.
LC   Library of Congress, Washington, D.C.
LFC   Lake Forest College, Lake Forest, Ill.
MH   Minnesota Historical Society, Minneapolis, Minn.
MHS   Missouri Historical Society, St. Louis, Mo.
NARA   National Archives and Records Administration, Washington, D.C.
NYHS   New-York Historical Society, New York, N.Y.
OR   U.S. War Department. *The War of the Rebellion: A Compilation of the Official Records of the Union and Confederate Armies.* 70 vols. in 128. Washington, D.C., 1880–1901. All citations of *OR* refer to series 1, unless indicated otherwise.
PRNMP   Pea Ridge National Military Park, Pea Ridge, Ark.
SHSIDM   State Historical Society of Iowa, Des Moines, Iowa
SHSIIC   State Historical Society of Iowa, Iowa City, Iowa
SHSW   State Historical Society of Wisconsin, Madison, Wis.
SU   Stanford University, Palo Alto, Calif.
TSL   Texas State Library, Austin, Tex.
TSLA   Tennessee State Library and Archives, Nashville, Tenn.
TU   Tulane University, New Orleans, La.
UAF   University of Arkansas at Fayetteville, Fayetteville, Ark.
UIC   University of Illinois, Champaign-Urbana, Ill.
UM   University of Michigan, Ann Arbor, Mich.
UMC   University of Missouri—Columbia, Columbia, Mo.
UMR   University of Missouri—Rolla, Rolla, Mo.
UNC   University of North Carolina at Chapel Hill, Chapel Hill, N.C.
USAMHI   U.S. Army Military History Institute, Carlisle Barracks, Pa.
UT   University of Texas at Austin, Austin, Tex.

PREFACE

1. Dodge, *Address*, 40; Crabtree, "Recollections," 211.

CHAPTER ONE

1. The first five paragraphs are based on Snead, "First Year of the War in Missouri," 1:269–71; Phillips, *Damned Yankee*, 129–256; Castel, *Sterling Price*, 3–65, and "Battle of Pea Ridge"; and Bearss, *Wilson's Creek*.

2. Thomas to Cameron, Oct. 21, Lincoln to Hunter, Oct. 24, Hunter to Thomas, Nov. 11, 1861, *OR* 3:540–49, 553–54, 569. Frémont intended to drive across southwestern Missouri and northwestern Arkansas and then follow the Arkansas River to the Mississippi, thus outflanking fortified rebel strong points on the Mississippi at Columbus, Island No. 10, and Fort Pillow. On paper it seemed a good way to neutralize Price and open the Mississippi River at the same time, but Frémont failed to consider the difficulty of moving an army across the Ozark Plateau. Schofield, *Forty-Six Years*, 48–49.

3. Castel, *Sterling Price*, 60–64; Kirkpatrick, "Admission of Missouri," 369–79; Jackson to Davis, Nov. 5, 1861, *OR* 53:754–55; Ephraim M. Anderson, *Memoirs*, 111.

4. General Orders No. 1, Nov. 19, 1861, *OR* 8:369; Thorndike, *Sherman Letters*, 138.

5. McClellan to Halleck and Buell to Halleck, Jan. 3, Lincoln to Halleck, Jan. 1, and Halleck to Lincoln and to Buell, Jan. 6, 1862, *OR* 7:527–29, 926, 532–33, 926.

6. Special Orders No. 92, Dec. 25, 1862, ibid., 8:462.

7. Gallaher, "Curtis," 331–41; Curtis to his brother, Dec. 16, 1861, Curtis Papers, HL.

8. Gallaher, "Curtis," 338–39; Curtis, "Army of the South-West," 3:218n; Guyer, "Journal and Letters," 215.

9. Curtis, "Army of the South-West," 4:641; St. Louis *Daily Missouri Democrat*, Jan. 1, 1862; General Orders No. 1, Dec. 28, 1861, *OR* 8:473.

10. Hess, "Sigel's Resignation"; Curtis to Halleck, Dec. 29, 1861, *OR* 8:471–72.

11. Colton, "Frontier War Problems," 308–9; Mar. 28, 1862, Noble Diary, SHSIIC.

12. Halleck to McClellan, Dec. 10 and 19, 1861, *OR* 8:818–19, 448–49.

13. Castel, *Sterling Price*, 60–64; Halleck to Curtis, Dec. 27, 1861, and Jan. 1, 1862, Curtis to Carr, Dec. 28, and to Halleck, Dec. 29 and 27, 1861, Jan. 2 and 5, 1862, Special Orders No. 1, Dec. 28, 1861, Carr to Curtis, Jan. 3, and Halleck to McClellan, Jan. 9, 1862, *OR* 8:468–69, 471–75, 480–81, 483–84, 489, 7:540.

14. Halleck to McClellan, Jan. 9, and Halleck to Curtis, Jan. 12, 1862, *OR* 7:540, 8:496.

15. Curtis to Halleck and Halleck to Curtis, Jan. 13, Curtis to Carr and to Halleck, Jan. 14, Halleck to McClellan, Jan. 14 and 20, and Halleck to Curtis, Jan. 18, 1862, ibid., 8:498–501, 503–4, 506, 508–10; Curtis, "Army of the South-West," 4:675.

16. Sheridan, *Personal Memoirs*, 1:126–31; Special Orders No. 2, Dec. 29, 1862, General Orders, NARA; Curtis, "Army of the South-West," 4:673–74.

17. Curtis to Halleck, Jan. 22, 1862, *OR* 8:513–14; Curtis, "Army of the South-West," 4:644–45; Special Orders No. 75, Feb. 7, 1862, *OR* 8:549; Herr, *Episodes*, 364–65; Curtis to his mother, Feb. 9, 1862, Curtis Papers, USAMHI.

18. Conkling and Conkling, *Butterfield Overland Mail*, 1:123–230; Ormsby, *Butterfield Overland Mail*, 9–20; Lemke and Worley, *Butterfield Overland Mail*.

19. Prentis, *Kansas Miscellanies*, 13.

20. Curtis, "Army of the South-West," 4:676–77.

21. Curtis to Asboth, Feb. 1, 1862, Letters Sent, NARA; Asboth to Curtis, Feb. 1, and Sigel to Curtis, 2 Feb. 1862, Letters Received, NARA; Curtis to Halleck and to Sigel, Feb. 1, Curtis to Halleck, Feb. 2, and Asboth to Curtis, Feb. 6, 1862, *OR* 8:540–42, 545–46; Jan. 15–17 and 22–24, 1862, Kircher diary, Engelmann-Kircher Collection, ISHL; St. Louis *Missouri Republican*, Feb. 5, 1862; Marcoot, *Five Years*, 11–12.

22. Halleck to McClellan, Jan. 20, Pope to Halleck, Jan. 21, Halleck to Curtis, Jan. 22, 23, and Feb. 6, and Curtis to Halleck, Jan. 24, 31, and Feb. 1, and to Sigel, Jan. 25, 1862, *OR* 8:509, 512, 514, 516, 523–26, 538–40, 544; A. W. Sanford letter, Indianapolis *Daily Journal*, Mar. 11, 1862; Feb. 2, 1862, Gordon diary, Gordon Papers, USAMHI.

23. Sunderland, *Five Days to Glory*, 24–25; E. A. letter, Chicago *Tribune*, Feb. 13, 1862; Jan. 30, 1862, Holman Diary, SHSIIC; Marcoot, *Five Years*, 11.

24. Special Orders No. 80, Feb. 9, 1862, *OR* 8:550; Curtis, "Army of the South-West," 4:680–81.

25. Curtis to Halleck, Feb. 12, 1862, *OR* 8:553–54.

26. St. Louis *Daily Missouri Democrat*, Dec. 6 and 24, 1861, Jan. 13, 15, 25, 27, 28, and 30, 1862; Phelps to Gamble, Aug. 8, 1861, Gamble Papers, MHS; Flint, "War on the Border," 413; Mathews, "Souvenir," UMC. As many as five thousand unionists fled southwestern Missouri when Hunter evacuated Springfield. To aid these loyal refugees Halleck confiscated and sold the property of known rebels in St. Louis. By March 1862 he had raised over $16,000. W. Wayne Smith, "Experiment in Counterinsurgency," 363–67.

27. Fayel, "From Rolla to Springfield."

28. Curtis to his brother, Jan. 30, 1862, Curtis Papers, HL.

29. Shalhope, *Sterling Price*, 1–196; Ephraim M. Anderson, *Memoirs*, 47.

30. Rose, *McCulloch*, 28–122; Gunn, "Ben McCulloch: A Big Captain," 19, and "Life of Ben McCulloch," 78–112; Tunnard, *Southern Record*, 158–59.

31. Jackson to Davis, Oct. 12 and Dec. 30, Jackson to Price, Dec. 30, Davis to Jackson, Dec. 3, 1861, and Jan. 8, 1862, Clark to Price, Dec. 13, and McCulloch to Benjamin, Oct. 14, Nov. 19, and Dec. 4 and 22, 1861, *OR* 3:718, 743–49, 8:686, 701–2, 725–26, 733–34, 53:761–63; Price to Cooper, Jan. 28, 1862, Price Correspondence, TU; Lemke, "Paths of Glory," 344–45.

32. Davis to Harris, Dec. 3, 1861, *OR* 8:701.

33. Morrison, *Memoirs of Henry Heth*, xxi–xxii, xxviii–xxxii, lvii, 159–60.

34. McCulloch to Benjamin, Nov. 8, Benjamin to Bragg, Dec. 27, 1861, and Bragg to Benjamin, Jan. 6 and Feb. 18, 1862, *OR* 3:733–34, 6:788–89, 797–98, 826–27; McWhiney, *Braxton Bragg*, 197–98.

35. Beauregard to Van Dorn, Jan. 10, 1862, Van Dorn Papers, LC; Hartje, *Van Dorn*,

x, 6–15, 21–43; Emily Van Dorn Miller, *Soldier's Honor*, 18, 23, 48, 52–53.

36. Taylor, *Destruction and Reconstruction*, 36; Havins, *Beyond the Cimarron*, 53–55, 59.

37. Benjamin to Polk, Jan. 16, Special Orders No. 8, Jan. 10, and General Orders No. 1, Jan. 29, 1862, *OR* 7:833, 8:734, 745.

38. Van Dorn to Price, Feb. 7, 1862, ibid., 8:748–52; Emily Miller, *Soldier's Honor*, 62–63.

39. Tunnard, *Southern Record*, 28–29; Report of McCulloch's Division, Jan. 1, and Effective Total of McCulloch's Division, Mar. 2, 1862, *OR* 8:728, 763.

40. Ephraim M. Anderson, *Memoirs*, 133–40; General Orders Nos. 7, 9, and 26, Jan. 5, 7, and 23, and Price to Jackson, Feb. 25, 1862, *OR* 8:733, 739–41, 756; Ruyle Memoir, UMR; McDaniel Memoir, USAMHI.

41. Duncan, *Reluctant General*, 14–182; Dale, "Cherokees in the Confederacy"; Morton, "Confederate Government Relations," 199, 299, 303; Franks, "Implementation of the Confederate Treaties," 33; Britton, "Union and Confederate Indians," 1:335–36; Abel, *American Indian as Participant*, 23–25; Gaines, *Confederate Cherokees*, 6–33; Pike to Benjamin, Nov. 27 and Dec. 25, 1861, and May 4, 1862, *OR* 8:697–98, 719–22, 13:819.

42. Price to Hébert, Jan. 21 and 26, and to McIntosh, Jan. 26 and 31, 1862, Price Correspondence, TU; McIntosh to Price, Jan. 24, 1862, *OR* 8:741–42.

43. Price to Hébert, Jan. 31, to McIntosh, Jan. 31, and to Van Dorn, Feb. 8 and 9, 1862, Price Correspondence, TU.

44. Lemke, "Paths of Glory," 345; McCulloch to Brown, Feb. 15, 1862, Brown Papers, UT.

45. Price to Hébert, Feb. 9, 1862, Price Correspondence, TU.

CHAPTER TWO

1. Curtis, "Army of the South-West," 4:723; Special Orders No. 81, Feb. 9, 1862, *OR* 8:550–51.

2. Price to Jackson, Feb. 25, 1862, *OR* 8:757; Price to Hébert, Feb. 13, 1862, Price Correspondence, TU.

3. Carr to Curtis, Mar. 10, 1862, *OR* 8:257; Ellis to Davis, Feb. 25, 1862, Davis Papers, ISL (the only extant copy of Ellis's official report of his activities during the pursuit is this penciled draft in the Davis Papers); letter from unidentified 1st Missouri Cavalry soldier, St. Louis *Daily Missouri Democrat*, Mar. 11, 1862; Curtis to his wife, Feb. 18, 1862, Curtis Papers, USAMHI; Charles Black to his mother, Feb. 19, 1862, Black Family Papers, ISHL.

4. Bevier, *First and Second Missouri*, 87; Bull Memoirs, MHS; Ephraim M. Anderson, *Memoirs*, 140–44; Jines, "Civil War Diary," 15; Price to Van Dorn, Feb. 13, 1862, Price Correspondence, TU.

5. Mathews, "Souvenir," UMC; Cummings to his wife, Feb. 19, 1862, Cummings Papers, SHSIDM; Randolph V. Marshall, *Twenty-Second Indiana*, 13; Lathrop, *Fifty-*

Ninth Illinois, 63–65.

6. Curtis, "Army of the South-West," 4:725; A. W. Sanford letter, Indianapolis *Daily Journal*, Mar. 11, 1862; Curtis to Halleck, Feb. 13, 1862, Letters Sent, NARA; Feb. 13, 1862, Holman Diary, SHSIIC.

7. Curtis, "Army of the South-West," 4:726; Feb. 13, 1862, Ames diary, Ames Papers, USAMHI; Quaife, *Absalom Grimes*, 36–37.

8. Curtis, "Army of the South-West," 4:726–27; Asboth to Curtis, Carr to Curtis, and Asboth to Sigel, Feb. 13, 1862, Letters Received, NARA; St. Louis *Daily Missouri Democrat*, Feb. 22, 1862; William Fayel letter, Rolla (Mo.) *Express*, Feb. 24, 1862; Mathews, "Souvenir," UMC.

9. Stuart, *Iowa Colonels*, 111; Herr, *Episodes*, 365.

10. Curtis, "Army of the South-West," 4:727–28; New York *Tribune*, Mar. 10, 1862. *Tribune* correspondent Junius H. Browne, a Sigel partisan, remained in St. Louis during the campaign. His dispatches are based on a mix of rumors and reliable information and must be used with caution.

11. During the winter months Halleck received unsettling information about Sigel's role in the Union defeat at Wilson's Creek. He learned that it was Sigel who had convinced Lyon to divide his small army in the presence of the enemy, a move that led directly to disaster. On February 15 Halleck sent Curtis a cryptic message cautioning him not to let Sigel talk him into dividing his own army. Several days passed before the warning caught up with the Army of the Southwest, by which time Curtis was beginning to develop his own doubts about Sigel's judgment and reliability. Hess, "Sigel's Resignation," 556.

12. Herr, *Episodes*, 365; Ephraim M. Anderson, *Memoirs*, 144.

13. Ephraim M. Anderson, *Memoirs*, 144; Bennett and Haigh, *Thirty-Sixth Illinois*, 115; Burns, *4th Missouri Cavalry*, 23; Sigel, "Pea Ridge Campaign," 1:316–17; Curtis to Halleck, Feb. 16, 1862, *OR* 8:558; Hesse, "Battle of Pea Ridge," MHS.

14. Curtis, "Army of the South-West," 4:728; Lathrop, *Fifty-Ninth Illinois*, 73; Feb. 14, 1862, Holman Diary, SHSIIC; Black to his mother, Feb. 19, 1862, Black Family Papers, ISHL. Much of Telegraph Road south of Springfield is still in use today whether graded, graveled, or paved. The two sections which best retain their original appearance are in Wilson's Creek National Battlefield and in Cross Timber Hollow just south of Washburn, as Keetsville is now known. U.S. Geological Survey topographic maps are an invaluable resource for locating Telegraph Road and other nineteenth-century roads atop the Ozark Plateau.

15. Ephraim M. Anderson, *Memoirs*, 144–46; Smith Memoirs, UMC.

16. Ellis to Davis, Feb. 25, 1862, Davis Papers, ISL; Bowen to Curtis, Mar. 10, 1862, *OR* 8:269. Each mountain howitzer weighed 231 pounds and could be pulled by a single horse along a road or disassembled and hauled over mountainous terrain by three mules.

17. Harding, "Reminiscences"; Rose, *Ross' Texas Brigade*, 55.

18. Fayel, "From Rolla to Springfield"; letter from unidentified 1st Missouri Cavalry soldier, St. Louis *Daily Missouri Democrat*, Mar. 11, 1862; Curtis to Sigel, Feb. 14 and 15, 1862, *OR* 8:59–60.

19. Feb. 15, 1862, Holman Diary, SHSIIC.

20. Feb. 16, 1862, Kircher diary, Engelmann-Kircher Collection, ISHL; Asboth to Curtis, Feb. 16, 1862, Letters Received, NARA; Curtis, "Army of the South-West," 4:728; New York *Tribune*, Mar. 10, 1862.

21. Ephraim M. Anderson, *Memoirs*, 146–51; Smith Memoirs, UMC; Wilson Memoir, UMC; Ruyle Memoir, UMR; Bevier, *First and Second Missouri*, 89–90.

22. McDaniel Memoir, USAMHI.

23. Bennett and Haigh, *Thirty-Sixth Illinois*, 116; Herr, *Episodes*, 53; W. R. Irwin letter, Muncie (Ind.) *Delaware County Free Press*, Mar. 6, 1862; J. L. K. letter, St. Louis *Missouri Republican*, Feb. 23, 1862; Curtis to Halleck, Feb. 16, 1862, *OR* 8:558.

24. Mathews, "Souvenir," UMC; Elmore to his parents, Sept. 29, 1862, Elmore Papers, CHS; Harwood, *Pea Ridge Campaign*, 114.

25. Feb. 16 and 17, 1862, Holman Diary, SHSIIC; Fayel, "Curtis' Advance"; Lathrop, *Fifty-Ninth Illinois*, 78–79.

26. Special Correspondent letter, Chicago *Tribune*, Feb. 25, 1862; Herr, *Episodes*, 53; Elmore to his father, Sept. 30, 1862, Elmore Papers, CHS; letter from unidentified 44th Illinois soldier, Mar. 18, 1862, Jump Papers, IHS; David R. Sparks to his wife, Feb. 28, 1862, Herrick-Reasoner Papers, ISHL; Cooper and Worley, "Letters," 463.

27. Smith Memoirs, UMC.

28. Ephraim M. Anderson, *Memoirs*, 150; Ellis to Davis, Feb. 25, 1862, Davis Papers, ISL. On some modern maps this northernmost section of Cross Timber Hollow is labeled Washburn Hollow.

29. Ephraim M. Anderson, *Memoirs*, 148–51; Feb. 16, 1862, Mothershead Diary, TSLA; Ellis to Davis, Feb. 25, 1862, Davis Papers, ISL.

30. Ephraim M. Anderson, *Memoirs*, 151; Bevier, *First and Second Missouri*, 90; Feb. 16, 1862, Mothershead Diary, TSLA; Jines, "Civil War Diary," 16; Curtis to Halleck, Feb. 16, 1862, Letters Sent, NARA; Ellis to Davis, Feb. 25, 1862, Davis Papers, ISL. A historical marker located on Telegraph Road just south of the state line refers to this engagement as the battle of Pott's Hill.

31. "Autobiography," Hébert Papers, UNC; McIntosh to Hébert and to Price, Feb. 14, 1862, Curtis Papers, SHSIDM; Price to Hébert, Feb. 15, 1862, Price Correspondence, TU; Lemke, "Paths of Glory," 346; McCulloch to Brown, Feb. 15, 1862, Brown Papers, UT; Special Orders No. 12, Feb. 15, 1862, Special Orders, Van Dorn's Command, NARA.

32. Landry to McCulloch, Feb. 16, 1862, *OR* 8:752; Watson, *Confederate Army*, 271–73; letter from unidentified 3rd Louisiana soldier, New Orleans *Commercial Bulletin*, Mar. 14, 1862; Tunnard, *Southern Record*, 123.

33. Harding, "Reminiscences"; J. H. S. letter, Little Rock *Arkansas True Democrat*, Feb. 20, 1862; Tunnard, *Southern Record*, 123; Smith Memoirs, UMC; Ephraim M. Anderson, *Memoirs*, 152.

34. Feb. 17, 1862, Kircher diary, Engelmann-Kircher Collection, ISHL; John C. Black to his mother, Feb. 19, 1862, Black Family Papers, ISHL; A. W. Sanford letter, Indianapolis *Daily Journal*, Mar. 11, 1862; Curtis to Halleck, Feb. 16, 1862, Letters Sent, NARA; Special Order No. 90, Feb. 18, 1862, General Orders, NARA. Telegraph

Road enters Arkansas in eastern Benton County, passes through Pea Ridge National Military Park, intersects U.S. 62, crosses Little Sugar Creek Valley, and continues south through modern-day Brightwater and Avoca. Nearly all of the original road still exists between the state line and Avoca, a distance of about seven miles. A one-mile dirt section inside the park is closed to vehicular traffic.

35. Ellis to Davis, Feb. 25, 1862, Davis Papers, ISL.

36. Ibid.; Carr to Curtis, Mar. 10, 1862, *OR* 8:257; Lathrop, *Fifty-Ninth Illinois*, 76.

37. Map of Little Sugar Creek Valley, General Asboth's Report, Union Battle Reports, NARA.

38. Watson, *Confederate Army*, 273.

39. Ibid.; Ephraim M. Anderson, *Memoirs*, 152–53; Feb. 17, 1862, Mothershead Diary, TSLA. Dunagin's farm was located on Telegraph Road between modern-day Brightwater and Avoca, half a mile south of the historical marker referring to the battle.

40. Ellis to Davis, Feb. 25, 1862, Davis Papers, ISL; Wright to Carr, Feb. 17, 1862, Curtis Papers, SHSIDM; Feb. 17, 1862, Mothershead Diary, TSLA.

41. Tunnard, *Southern Record*, 123–24; Jines, "Civil War Diary," 16; Ellis to Davis, Feb. 25, 1862, Davis Papers, ISL.

42. Wright to Carr, Feb. 17, 1862, Curtis Papers, SHSIDM.

43. Ellis to Davis, Feb. 25, 1862, Davis Papers, ISL; Harwood, *Pea Ridge Campaign*, 115; Bowen to Curtis, Mar. 10, 1862, *OR* 8:270; Garver to his sister, Feb. 24, 1862, Garver Papers, UNC.

44. Cummings to his wife, Feb. 18, 1862, Cummings Papers, SHSIDM.

45. Watson, *Confederate Army*, 274.

46. Wright to Carr, Feb. 17, 1862, Curtis Papers, SHSIDM; Ellis to Davis, Feb. 25, 1862, Davis Papers, ISL; Curtis, "Army of the South-West," 4:730; Fayel, "Curtis' Advance From Springfield"; Feb. 18, 1862, Ames diary, Ames Papers, USAMHI; Feb. 19, 1862, Herrington Diary, USAMHI; Mar. 1, 1862, William P. Black diary, Black Family Papers, ISHL.

47. Feb. 18, 1862, Cummins Diary, ISHL; Mar. 4, 1862, Bennett diary, Bennett Papers, UMR; Garver to his sister, Feb. 24, 1862, Garver Papers, UNC; Swain Marshall to his parents, Mar. 6, 1862, Marshall Collection, IHS. Trott's store was located on the eastern side of Telegraph Road in Little Sugar Creek Valley immediately south of the stream.

48. Dodge to [?] Harriman, Feb. 23, 1862, Dodge Papers, SHSIDM; Clarke, *Warfare along the Mississippi*, 19–20.

49. Rufus K. Garland letter, Washington (Ark.) *Telegraph*, Mar. 5, 1862; Harding, "Reminiscences"; Feb. 17, 1862, Mothershead Diary, TSLA; Tunnard, *Southern Record*, 123; Smith Memoirs, UMC.

50. Curtis to Halleck, Feb. 18, 1862, *OR* 8:559; Carr to his father, Feb. 23, 1862, Carr Papers, USAMHI; Curtis to his brother, Feb. 25, 1862, Curtis Papers, HL.

CHAPTER THREE

1. Curtis to his brother, Feb. 25, 1862, Curtis Papers, HL; Carr to his father, Feb. 23, 1862, Carr Papers, USAMHI; Curtis to Halleck, Feb. 20, 1862, *OR* 8:561. Telegraph Road passes through Cross Hollow about four miles southeast of modern-day Rogers and just east of modern-day Lowell. No trace remains of the hundreds of buildings that once filled the hollow.

2. Hess, "Asboth," 181–84; Curtis to Halleck, Feb. 21, Asboth to Curtis, Feb. 18, and to Sigel, Feb. 19, 1862, *OR* 8:62–64; Curtis to his brother, Feb. 25, 1862, Curtis Papers, HL; Bennett and Haigh, *Thirty-Sixth Illinois*, 125; J. Dickson Black, *History of Benton County*, 96–97. A Confederate payroll officer on his way to Van Buren encountered the Federal cavalryman at the edge of town and shot him twice, the second time in the head at close range. The second bullet left a ragged gash which led the search party to conclude that the victim had been felled by an axe. The terrified residents of Bentonville made the error of attempting to hide the body in an outhouse. Fayel, "After Pea Ridge."

3. Curtis to his brother, Feb. 25, 1862, Curtis Papers, HL.

4. Rose, *McCulloch*, 198; Jines, "Civil War Diary," 16; Tunnard, *Southern Record*, 124.

5. Harding, "Reminiscences"; Price to Van Dorn, Feb. 19, 1862, Price Correspondence, TU.

6. Ephraim M. Anderson, *Memoirs*, 154–55; Tunnard, *Southern Record*, 124–25; Stone to Van Dorn, Apr. 14, 1862, *OR* 8:302; Jines, "Civil War Diary," 16.

7. Tunnard, *Southern Record*, 125; Watson, *Confederate Army*, 278–79; Smith Memoirs, UMC; Ephraim M. Anderson, *Memoirs*, 156–57.

8. George Taylor to Rebecca, Mar. 3, 1862, Stirman-Davidson Papers, UAF; Gammage, *Camp, Bivouac, and Battle Field*, 23; Baxter, *Pea Ridge*, 46–50.

9. Baxter, *Pea Ridge*, 53–56; David Pierson to William H. Pierson, Feb. 22, 1862, Pierson Family Papers, TU; Banes, "Tebbetts Family History," 11. The Female Institute was located at the corner of Dickson and College streets.

10. Conkling, *Butterfield Overland Mail*, 1:209; Maury, "Recollections of Elkhorn," 184–85. State Highway 265 follows the route of Telegraph Road from Fayetteville south to Strickler's Station.

11. Price to McCulloch, Feb. 23, to Van Dorn, Feb. 19, and to Pike, Feb. 20, 1862, Price Correspondence, TU; Ross to his wife, Mar. 1, 1862, Ross Family Papers, BU.

12. Tunnard, *Southern Record*, 127–28; Feb. 22, 1862, Hoskin Diary, UMC; Feb. 26–28, 1862, Mothershead Diary, TSLA; Harding, "Reminiscences"; Ephraim M. Anderson, *Memoirs*, 161; Smith Memoirs, UMC.

13. General Orders Nos. 48, 50, 53, and 54, Feb. 23, 25, 28, 1862, General and Division Orders, NARA.

14. Carr to Curtis, Mar. 10, 1862, *OR* 8:258; Asboth to Curtis, Feb. 21, 1862, Letters Received, NARA. At Mudtown three officers and forty-three privates of the 4th and 5th Missouri Cavalry became ill after consuming provisions left behind by the Confederates. All eventually recovered except Capt. Louis Dülfer of the 5th Missouri

Cavalry who died the next day. An officer in the 4th Missouri Cavalry wrote that Dülfer had broken into a deserted pharmacy and had mistaken poison for liquor. Dülfer was buried "by starlight in a beautiful spot, in 'Cross Hollow,' but in a wild and lonely grave, Gen. Asboth acting as the chaplain." When Halleck learned of this incident, he ordered that soldiers and civilians guilty of such crimes should be treated as criminals, not as prisoners of war, and hanged. There is no evidence that the rebels attempted to poison their pursuers. Hesse, "Battle of Pea Ridge," MHS; New York *Tribune*, Feb. 25, 1862; Compiled Service Records, NARA; General Orders No. 49, Feb. 27, 1862, *OR* 8:570–71; Burns, *4th Missouri Cavalry*, 24–25.

15. Curtis to his brother, Feb. 25, 1862, Curtis Papers, HL; Mar. 1, 1862, Holman Diary, SHSIIC; Mar. 5, 1862, Bennett diary, Bennett Papers, UMR; Lathrop, *Fifty-Ninth Illinois*, 80–81; Cummings to his wife, Feb. 24, 1862, Cummings Papers, SHSIDM; Knox, *Camp-Fire*, 129–30; Curtis to his mother, Mar. 2, 1862, Curtis Papers, USAMHI.

16. Sigel to Curtis, Feb. 22, 1862, Letters Received, NARA; Herr, *Episodes*, 369; Mar. [?], 1862, Gordon diary, Gordon Papers, USAMHI; Bek, "Civil War Diary," 319.

17. Lathrop, *Fifty-Ninth Illinois*, 88; Sam Black, *Soldier's Recollections*, 4; Harwood, *Pea Ridge Campaign*, 13; Curtis to his wife, Feb. 23, 1862, Curtis Papers, USAMHI; Frederick to Curtis and Barnes to Curtis, Feb. 26, and Ellis to Davis, Mar. 2, 1862, Letters Received, NARA; Carr to James W. Singleton, Feb. 27, 1862, Reavis Papers, CHS; Marrett to his wife, Mar. 1, 1862, Marrett Papers, DU; General Orders No. 6, Feb. 23, 1862, Order Book, UIC.

18. Curtis to Halleck, Feb. 22, and Halleck to Curtis, Feb. 26, 1862, *OR* 8:562, 568; Bussey, "Pea Ridge Campaign," 4–5.

19. Curtis to Halleck, Feb. 26 and Mar. 4, 1862, *OR* 8:567–68, 589; Curtis to his brother, Mar. 13, 1862, Curtis Papers, HL.

20. Curtis to Halleck, Mar. 4, 1862, *OR* 8:589.

21. Sigel, "Pea Ridge Campaign," 1:317; Curtis to Halleck, Apr. 1, 1862, *OR* 8:196.

22. Halleck to Curtis, Feb. 22 and 26, and Halleck to McClellan and McClellan to Halleck, Feb. 21, 1862, *OR* 8:563, 568, 7:645–46; Curtis, "Army of the South-West," 4:732.

23. Curtis to Asboth, Feb. 22, 1862, *OR* 8:562–63; Asboth to Curtis, Feb. 23, 1862, Letters Received, NARA; Feb. 23, 1862, Dysart Diary, PRNMP; Banes, "Tebbetts Family History," 13; Hess, "Asboth," 181–91. The Tebbetts house still stands at 118 E. Dickson in Fayetteville. It is known as Headquarters House and is maintained by the Washington County Historical Society.

24. Asboth to Curtis, Feb. 23, 1862, *OR* 8:69–71; Curtis to Asboth, Feb. 24, 1862, Letters Sent, NARA; Feb. 23, 1862, Reynolds diary, Reynolds Papers, UAF. A few days after Asboth's departure Tebbetts was arrested by the rebels for collaborating with the Federals and was jailed in Fort Smith. He was released after the battle. Baxter, *Pea Ridge*, 76–77.

25. Curtis to Halleck, Apr. 1, and Richardson to Harding, Feb. 26, 1862, *OR* 8:196, 71; Feb. 25, 1862, Bennett diary, Bennett Papers, UMR; Sheridan, *Personal Memoirs*, 1:127–31; Feb. 21, 1862, Boyer Diary, MH.

26. Ross to his wife, Mar. 1, 1862, Ross Family Papers, BU; Billingsley, "'Such Is War,'" 248; Wright to Curtis, Feb. 27, 1862, *OR* 8:74–76.

27. Van Dorn to Bragg, Mar. 27, to McCarver, Feb. 22, and to Johnston, Feb. 24, 1862, *OR* 8:283, 753–55.

28. Maury, "Recollections of Elkhorn," 181–83; Emily Van Dorn Miller, *Soldier's Honor*, 73–74; Hartje, *Van Dorn*, 115–16.

29. McCulloch to Van Dorn, Mar. 1, 1862, *OR* 8:763; Van Dorn to McCulloch, Mar. 1, and Price to Van Dorn, Mar. 2, 1862, Price Correspondence, TU.

30. Maury, "Recollections of Elkhorn," 183–85; Douglas, *Douglas's Texas Battery*, 182. In 1858 a traveler described Telegraph Road between Lee's Creek and Strickler's Station as follows: "I might say the road was steep, rugged, jagged, rough and mountainous and then wish for more impressive words." Lemke and Worley, *Butterfield Overland Mail*, 7. This section of the old road is now a county road connecting State Highways 265 and 220.

31. Maury, "Recollections of Elkhorn," 185–86. Confederate Maj. Gen. Thomas C. Hindman also used Morrow's house as his headquarters during the Prairie Grove campaign in December 1862. The house has been moved to Prairie Grove Battlefield State Park west of Fayetteville. The log buildings at Strickler's Station were burned during the war, but Strickler's house was later rebuilt on the original stone foundation and still stands today in the hamlet of Strickler on Highway 265.

32. Van Dorn to Bragg, Mar. 27, 1862, *OR* 8:283; Emily Van Dorn Miller, *Soldier's Honor*, 63.

33. Effective Total of McCulloch's Division, Mar. 2, 1862, *OR* 8:763; Harding, "Reminiscences." Alwyn Barr concludes that there were only fifty-nine guns in the Army of the West. Barr, "Confederate Artillery," 243–44.

34. Smith Memoirs, UMC; Tunnard, *Southern Record*, 129; General Orders No. 57, Mar. 3, 1862, General and Division Orders, NARA; Kerr, *Ross' Texas Cavalry Brigade*, 13; George Taylor to Rebecca Stirman, Mar. 3, 1862, Stirman-Davidson Papers, UAF.

35. Tunnard, *Southern Record*, 129; Ephraim M. Anderson, *Memoirs*, 162.

36. Van Dorn to Pike, Mar. 3, and Pike to [?], May 4, to Davis, July 31, and to Van Dorn, Mar. 14, 1862, *OR* 8:763–65.

37. McCulloch proclamation, Little Rock *Arkansas True Democrat*, Feb. 20, 1862; Watson, *Confederate Army*, 280; Special Orders No. 16, Mar. 3, 1862, Special Orders, Van Dorn's Command, NARA.

38. C. M. Ohlson and P. R. Smith letters, Washington (Ark.) *Telegraph*, Mar. 19 and Apr. 2, 1862.

39. Curtis to Sigel, Mar. 3, 1862, *OR* 8:583–84; Sigel to Curtis, Mar. 4, 1862, Letters Received, NARA; Curtis to Sigel, Mar. 4, 1862, Letters Sent, NARA.

40. Curtis to Sigel, Mar. 4, 1862, Letters Sent, NARA; Baxter, *Pea Ridge*, 88.

41. Cummings to his wife, Mar. 2–5, 1862, Cummings Papers, SHSIDM; Sigel to Curtis, Mar. 3 and 4, and Asboth to Sigel, Mar. 1, 1862, Letters Received, NARA.

42. Sigel to Curtis, Mar. 15, and Conrad to Sigel, Mar. 13, 1862, *OR* 8:208–9, 278–79; Burns, *4th Missouri Cavalry*, 27–28.

43. Vandever to Carr, Mar. 13, and Carr to Curtis, Feb. 28, 1862, *OR* 8:266, 575.

CHAPTER FOUR

1. General Orders Nos. 59 and 62, Mar. 3, 1862, Price's Command, and General Orders Nos. 24 and 25, Mar. 3, 1862, General and Division Orders; Special Orders No. [?], Mar. 3, 1862, Special Orders, Van Dorn's Command, NARA; Sparks, *War Between the States*, 172.

2. Maury, "Recollections of Elkhorn," 185–86.

3. Harding, "Reminiscences"; Worley, *At Home in Confederate Arkansas*, 58.

4. Jines, "Civil War Diary," 16; Cater, *"As It Was,"* 124; Worley, *War Memoirs*, 11–12; Mar. 5, 1862, Reynolds diary, Reynolds Papers, UAF; Tunnard, *Southern Record*, 130; Rose, *McCulloch*, 201; Ephraim M. Anderson, *Memoirs*, 164.

5. Ruyle Memoir, UMR; Watson, *Confederate Army*, 283–84.

6. Van Dorn to Bragg, Mar. 27, Greer to Van Dorn, Mar. [?], and Stone to Van Dorn, Apr. 14, 1862, *OR* 8:283, 297, 303; Lemke, "Paths of Glory," 348; Ross to D. R. Tinsley, Mar. 13, 1862, Ross Family Papers, BU.

7. Greer to Van Dorn, Mar. [?], 1862, *OR* 8:297.

8. Harding, "Reminiscences"; Logan, "Memories," 7; Hollinsworth, "Battle of Elkhorn," 133; Payne, "Battle of Pea Ridge," PRNMP. Elm Springs Road from Fayetteville to Bentonville is now State Highway 112.

9. Van Dorn to Bragg, Mar. 27, 1862, *OR* 8:283; Musser, "Battle of Pea Ridge"; Kerr, *Ross' Texas Cavalry Brigade*, 14.

10. Ephraim M. Anderson, *Memoirs*, 164; Lemke, *Journals*; Maury, "Recollections of Elkhorn," 186; Greer to Van Dorn, Mar. [?], 1862, *OR* 8:297. North of Elm Springs, State Highway 112 is straighter and shorter than the old road and no longer passes Osage Spring. Several new bridges span the twisting stream that caused Van Dorn so much grief.

11. Greer to Van Dorn, Mar. [?], 1862, *OR* 8:297.

12. Price to Van Dorn, Mar. 22, 1862, ibid., 305. Bentonville is still visible from several miles away on State Highway 112 despite numerous trees planted as windbreaks.

13. Curtis to Halleck, Apr. 1, 1862, ibid., 197.

14. Curtis to Sigel, Mar. 5, 1862, ibid., 592.

15. Ibid.; Bussey, "Pea Ridge Campaign," 7–9; Ingersoll, *Iowa and the Rebellion*, 401.

16. Fayel, "Curtis' Advance"; Mar. 6, 1862, Noble Diary, SHSIIC; Sam Black, *Soldier's Recollections*, 4; Harwood, *Pea Ridge Campaign*, 14; Cummings to his wife, Mar. 14, 1862, Cummings Papers, SHSIDM; Dodge, *Fiftieth Anniversary*, 12; J. Weiss letter, Greenville (Ill.) *Advocate*, Mar. 27, 1862. In his report Curtis stated that the 4th Division began moving out of Cross Hollow at 6:00 P.M., but that seems far too early.

17. Vandever to Carr, Mar. 13, 1862, *OR* 8:266; Mar. 4–5, 1862, Holman Diary, SHSIIC; Mar. 5, 1862, Boyle Journal, SHSIDM.

18. Mathews, "Souvenir," UMC; Abernethy, "Incidents," 403–4; Mar. 6, 1862, Holman Diary, SHSIIC.

19. Herr, *Episodes*, 66, 369; Mar. 5, 1862, Gordon diary, Gordon Papers, USAMHI;

E. F. Kemball letter, Richmond (Ind.) *Palladium*, Apr. 6, 1862; Curtis to Halleck, Apr. 1, 1862, *OR* 8:197; Clarke, *Warfare along the Mississippi*, 23–24; A. W. Sanford letter, Indianapolis *Daily Journal*, Mar. 19, 1862; "Tattle Tale" letter, Aurora (Ill.) *Beacon*, Mar. 27, 1862.

20. Mar. 6, 1862, Herrington Diary, USAMHI; Curtis to Halleck, Apr. 1, Davis to Curtis, Mar. 16, and Pattison to Davis, Mar. 10, 1862, *OR* 8:197–98, 245–46, 249. An Arkansas rebel examined the position several months later and declared that "if the Confederate army had come in as they (Feds) designed; it would have been one of the most disasterous battles of modern times." Shibley to his parents, Sept. 12, 1862, Shibley Letters, UAF. The earthworks occupied by Pattison's brigade west of Telegraph Road are preserved in a detached portion of Pea Ridge National Military Park.

21. Sigel to Curtis, Mar. 15, 1862, *OR* 8:208–9; Sigel, "Pea Ridge Campaign," 1:319–20; Burns, *4th Missouri Cavalry*, 27–28.

22. Sigel to Curtis, Mar. 15, 1862, *OR* 8:208–9; Mar. 6, 1862, Bennett diary, Bennett Papers, UMR; Burns, *4th Missouri Cavalry*, 27–28; Bennett and Haigh, *Thirty-Sixth Illinois*, 129–30; Clark, "Battle of Pea Ridge," 362; John A. Porter letter, Monmouth (Ill.) *Atlas*, Apr. 11, 1862; Hesse, "Battle of Pea Ridge," MHS.

23. Sigel to Curtis, Mar. 15, 1862, *OR* 8:209–10; Sigel, "Pea Ridge Campaign," 1:320. The old road from Osage Mill to Bentonville no longer exists.

24. Sigel to Curtis, Mar. 15, 1862, *OR* 8:210; Voelkner to his parents, Mar. 18, 1862, Voelkner Papers, UMC. Sigel returned to Bentonville in 1887 and stayed at the Eagle House, then known as the Eagle Hotel. Local legend has it that every morning he sat at the same table and ate the same breakfast as he had done a quarter of a century earlier. J. Dickson Black, *History of Benton County*, 248–50. The old hotel no longer exists, but a historical marker stands on the site one block west of the square on State Highway 72.

25. Bennett and Haigh, *Thirty-Sixth Illinois*, 130. Sigel informed Curtis rather cryptically that the departure of the 2nd Missouri was due to "a misunderstanding of my order" which had been "satisfactorily explained by Colonel Schaefer." Sigel to Curtis, Mar. 15, 1862, *OR* 8:210.

26. Greer to Van Dorn, Mar. [?], 1862, *OR* 8:297.

27. Warner, *Generals in Gray*, 202–3; Greer to Van Dorn, Mar. [?], 1862, *OR* 8:297.

28. Greer to Van Dorn, Mar. [?], 1862, *OR* 8:297; Lale, "Boy Bugler," 157.

29. Barron, *Lone Star Defenders*, 64–65; Sparks, *War Between the States*, 172. The old road which McIntosh followed from Bentonville north to Little Sugar Creek is now U.S. 71B. Little Sugar Creek Road is now a county road. In reconstructing the wartime landscape and road network around Pea Ridge, the authors have relied heavily upon a detailed set of maps compiled by Lyman G. Bennett of the 36th Illinois. "Route of the Army of the Southwest from March 1st to July 10th, 1862," Bennett Papers, UMR.

30. Price to Van Dorn, Mar. 22, 1862, *OR* 8:305; Calkin, "Elkhorn to Vicksburg," 13.

31. Sigel to Curtis, Mar. 15, 1862, and Nemett to Sigel, [Mar. ?, 1862], *OR* 8:210, 244.

32. Ross to D. R. Tinsley, Mar. 13, 1862, Ross Family Papers, BU; Billingsley, "'Such Is War,'" 249; Jacob Kaercher letter, Belleville (Ill.) *Advocate*, Mar. 13, 1896.

33. Jenks to Greusel, Mar. 14, 1862, *OR* 8:230; "Tattle Tale" letter, Aurora (Ill.) *Beacon*, Mar. 27, 1862. The Bentonville Road from the town square to the knoll is now State Highway 72. Because of the clutter of commercial structures, the knoll no longer offers a commanding view of the prairie.

34. Nemett to Sigel, [Mar. ?], and Wangelin to [Greusel], [Mar. ?, 1862], *OR* 8:230, 244, 228; Wangelin to Sigel, Mar. 14, 1862, 12th Missouri Regimental Papers, and Wangelin to Sigel, Mar. 18, 1862, Union Battle Reports, NARA; "Tattle Tale" letter, Aurora (Ill.) *Beacon*, Mar. 27, 1862; Mar. 6, 1862, Kircher diary, Engelmann-Kircher Collection, ISHL.

35. French Brownlee and John M. Turnbull letters, Monmouth (Ill.) *Atlas*, May 16 and Mar. 28, 1862; Little to Price, Mar. 18, 1862, *OR* 8:307. In his report and his history of the campaign Sigel erroneously stated that it was the 2nd Missouri that was ambushed in the woods. Sigel to Curtis, Mar. 15, 1862, *OR* 8:210; Sigel, "Pea Ridge Campaign," 1:320n. Only fragments of the Bentonville Road exist today between the knoll and Little Sugar Creek because of the construction of U.S. 71. State Highway 72 turns sharply north at the knoll, rather than northeast as did the old road, and generally follows a route slightly west of the old road.

36. John M. Turnbull letter, Monmouth (Ill.) *Atlas*, Mar. 28, 1862.

37. Calkin, "Elkhorn to Vicksburg," 13; Jenks to Greusel, Mar. 14, and Little to Price, Mar. 18, 1862, *OR* 8:230, 307; "Tattle Tale" letter, Aurora (Ill.) *Beacon*, Mar. 27, 1862; Sigel to Curtis, Mar. 20, 1862, in Curtis, "Army of the South-West," 5:821; Jacob Kaercher letter, Belleville (Ill.) *Advocate*, Mar. 13, 1896.

38. Voelkner to his parents, Mar. 18, 1862, Voelkner Papers, UMC. The mouth of the gorge is seven hundred yards east of the point where State Highway 72 crosses Little Sugar Creek Valley. The old road still exists inside the gorge. The gorge actually leads into Brush Creek Hollow, which in turn leads almost immediately into Little Sugar Creek Valley, but the authors have simplified matters for the sake of narrative coherence.

39. Mar. 6, 1862, Kircher diary, Engelmann-Kircher Collection, ISHL; Bennett and Haigh, *Thirty-Sixth Illinois*, 137; F. O. W. letter, Aurora (Ill.) *Beacon*, Mar. 27, 1862; Voelkner to his parents, Mar. 18, 1862, Voelkner Papers, UMC; Jenks to Greusel, Mar. 14, 1862, Smith to Greusel, [Mar. ?], and Wangelin to [Greusel], [Mar. ?, 1862], *OR* 8:230, 231, 228.

40. The Y-shaped junction was located about three hundred yards east of the point where State Highway 72 crosses Little Sugar Creek Valley.

41. Greer to Van Dorn, Mar. [?], 1862, *OR* 8:297–98.

42. Ibid.; Sparks, *War Between the States*, 172–73; Hollinsworth, "Battle of Elkhorn," 134–35; Lale, "Boy Bugler," 157–58.

43. Hollinsworth, "Battle of Elkhorn," 134–35; Lane, *Adventures*, 90–91; Sparks, *War Between the States*, 172–73; Lale, "Boy Bugler," 157–58; Barron, *Lone Star Defenders*, 65–66; Jacob Kaercher letter, Belleville (Ill.) *Advocate*, Mar. 13, 1896; Greer to Van Dorn, Mar. [?], 1862, *OR* 8:298. The initial engagement occurred about one mile east of the point where State Highway 72 crosses Little Sugar Creek Valley. The skirmishing which followed extended another half-mile up the valley.

44. Lale, "Boy Bugler," 157–58; Greer to Van Dorn, Mar. [?], 1862, *OR* 8:298.

45. Curtis to Halleck, Apr. 1, Osterhaus to Curtis, Mar. 14, and Asboth to Sigel, Mar. 16, 1862, *OR* 8:198, 216, 241; Bennett and Haigh, *Thirty-Sixth Illinois*, 132–33; Mar. 6, 1862, Bennett diary, Bennett Papers, UMR.

46. Curtis to Halleck, Apr. 1, Osterhaus to Curtis, Mar. 14, and Asboth to Sigel, Mar. 16, 1862, *OR* 8:198, 216, 241; Hesse, "Battle of Pea Ridge," MHS; Mar. 6, 1862, Dysart Diary, PRNMP.

47. Sigel to Curtis, Mar. 15, Osterhaus to Curtis, Mar. 14, Hoffman to Greusel, Mar. 14, and Greer to Van Dorn, Mar. [?], 1862, *OR* 8:210, 216, 237, 298; Bennett and Haigh, *Thirty-Sixth Illinois*, 133–35; Mar. 6, 1862, Bennett diary, Bennett Papers, UMR; Lathrop, *Fifty-Ninth Illinois*, 90.

48. Sigel to Curtis, Mar. 15, Smith to Greusel, [Mar. ?], and Conrad to Sigel, Mar. 13, 1862, *OR* 8:208–9, 231, 278–79; Burns, *4th Missouri Cavalry*, 28–29; Bennett and Haigh, *Thirty-Sixth Illinois*, 138–39.

49. Van Dorn to Bragg, Mar. 27, 1862, *OR* 8:283.

50. Tunnard, *Southern Record*, 130; Douglas, *Douglas's Texas Battery*, 183; Ruyle Memoir, UMR.

51. Ross to D. R. Tinsley, Mar. 13, 1862, Ross Family Papers, BU. Camp Stephens was an imprecise geographical term. The 1861 encampment extended for about two miles along Little Sugar Creek Valley between State Highways 72 and 94. The authors generally use the term to refer to that portion of the valley near the junction of Little Sugar Creek Road and the Bentonville Detour.

52. Tunnard, *Southern Record*, 136–37; Ruyle Memoir, UMR; Pike to Van Dorn, Mar. 14, 1862, *OR* 8:287.

53. Van Dorn to Bragg, Mar. 27, 1862, *OR* 8:283; Maury, "Recollections of Elkhorn," 187; Lemke, "Wartime Diary," 6–7; Funk, "Twelve Corner Church"; "Route of the Army of the Southwest from March 1st to July 10th, 1862," Bennett Papers, UMR. The southern terminus of the Bentonville Detour at Camp Stephens is located 250 yards west of the point where State Highway 94 crosses Little Sugar Creek. This portion of the detour extends northward up a moderate incline for 1.5 miles and disappears after it intersects State Highway 72 atop Pea Ridge. The middle portion of the detour, which lay south and east of the modern-day town of Pea Ridge, no longer exists. The northern portion of the detour reappears a short distance west of Twelve Corner Church and zigzags in a northeasterly direction for 3.5 miles. It intersects Telegraph Road in Cross Timber Hollow 0.8 miles south of the Missouri state line. The original Twelve Corner Church has been replaced by a modern structure.

54. Hollinsworth, "Battle of Elkhorn," 139; Van Dorn to Bragg, Mar. 27, 1862, *OR* 8:283; Wilson Memoir, UMC; Memphis *Daily Appeal*, Mar. 29, 1862.

55. Ross to D. R. Tinsley, Mar. 13, 1862, Ross Family Papers, BU (authors' italics).

56. Sigel to Curtis, Mar. 15, 1862, *OR* 8:211; Voelkner to his parents, Mar. 18, 1862, Voelkner Papers, UMC; Mar. 6, 1862, Dysart Diary, PRNMP.

57. Dodge to A. P. Wood, [n.d.] 1866, Dodge Papers, SHSIDM; Dodge, *Battle of Atlanta*, 19–20; "Correspondent" letter, Council Bluffs (Iowa) *Weekly Nonpareil*, Apr. 12, 1862. By the time Dodge published a history of the battle in 1911, he had

decided that Iowa's two greatest military heroes should have conversed more formally. He improved Curtis's words to read: "You take a portion of your command and go there and blockade the road." Dodge, *Fiftieth Anniversary*, 56.

58. Dodge to A. P. Wood, [n.d.] 1866, Dodge Papers, SHSIDM; Dodge, *Battle of Atlanta*, 19–20; "Correspondent" letter, Council Bluffs (Iowa) *Weekly Nonpareil*, Apr. 12, 1862; Dodge, *Fiftieth Anniversary*, 56. The first blockade was located where the Bentonville Detour crosses a ravine about one mile east of Twelve Corner Church; the second was located in the ravine where the detour descends into Cross Timber Hollow.

59. Sigel to Curtis, Mar. 15, and Asboth to Sigel, Mar. 16, 1862, *OR* 8:211, 240; Sigel, "Pea Ridge Campaign," 1:321; letter from unidentified 44th Illinois soldier, Mar. 18, 1862, Jump Papers, IHS. Twenty-five years later Sigel claimed it was he, not Curtis or Dodge, who suspected Van Dorn would use the Bentonville Detour to move around the Federal right flank. He also claimed that his scouts discovered the Confederate movement and that he rode out to the Bentonville Detour to see the enemy column for himself. These statements are uncorroborated by anything he said or wrote in 1862. Sigel, "Pea Ridge Campaign," 1:321.

60. Ross to D. R. Tinsley, Mar. 13, 1862, Ross Family Papers, BU.

61. Pike to Van Dorn, Mar. 14, 1862, *OR* 8:287; Gammage, *Camp, Bivouac, and Battle Field*, 24; Tunnard, *Southern Record*, 137.

62. Tunnard, *Southern Record*, 130–31; Lemke, "Paths of Glory," 348.

63. Van Dorn to Bragg, Mar. 27, and Little to Price, Mar. 18, 1862, *OR* 8:283, 307.

64. Frost to Price, Mar. 19, 1862, ibid., 8:323; Ross to D. R. Tinsley, Mar. 13, 1862, Ross Family Papers, BU; Mar. 6, 1862, Reynolds diary, Reynolds Papers, UAF.

65. Van Dorn to Bragg, Mar. 27, and Little to Price, Mar. 18, 1862, *OR* 8:283–84, 307.

66. Van Dorn to Bragg, Mar. 27, 1862, ibid., 8:283–84; Lemke, "Paths of Glory," 348; "Autobiography," Hébert Papers, UNC. Long after the war, when all of the ranking Confederate leaders at Pea Ridge were dead, Maury attempted to absolve Van Dorn and to blame McCulloch for the division of forces and the subsequent defeat, but this clearly is incorrect. Maury, "Recollections of Elkhorn," 187. Big Mountain is often incorrectly referred to as Pea Ridge in National Park Service publications and other accounts of the battle.

67. Lemke, "Paths of Glory," 348; Watson, *Confederate Army*, 290. The western terminus of Ford Road intersected the Bentonville Detour a short distance east of Twelve Corner Church. There is an intersection at that point today, but the modern road which leads due south from the intersection is not Ford Road. The modern road delineates part of the boundary of Pea Ridge National Military Park. Only a few faint traces remain of the mile-long curving section of Ford Road which ran off in a southeasterly direction from the intersection and rounded the western end of Big Mountain. The Park Service has placed no markers in the northwestern quadrant of the park, nor has it made any effort to identify, preserve, or restore the lost section of Ford Road.

CHAPTER FIVE

1. Weston to Curtis, Mar. 10, 1862, *OR* 8:270–71.

2. Barris to Weston and Lewis to Weston, Mar. 9, and Weston to Curtis, Mar. 10, 1862, ibid., 275, 277, 271.

3. Lewis to Weston, Mar. 9, and Curtis to Halleck, Apr. 1, 1862, ibid., 277, 199.

4. Dodge to A. P. Wood, [n.d.], 1866, Dodge Papers, SHSIDM.

5. Curtis to Halleck, Apr. 1, and Osterhaus to Curtis, Mar. 14, 1862, *OR* 8:199, 217.

6. Hess, "Osterhaus"; Osterhaus to Curtis, Mar. 14, 1862, *OR* 8:217.

7. Curtis to Halleck, Apr. 1, 1862, *OR* 8:199.

8. Curtis to Halleck, Apr. 1, and Carr to Curtis, Mar. 10, 1862, ibid., 199, 258; Dodge to A. P. Wood, [n.d.], 1866, Dodge Papers, SHSIDM.

9. Snelling, "Leetown," 19–20. Nothing remains of Leetown. The site of the hamlet is marked by a field.

10. Mar. 7, 1862, Rogers Journal, SHSIDM; Bussey to Curtis, Mar. 14, 1862, *OR* 8:232. Traces of the southern part of Leetown Road are visible in the brush north of the open area marking the site of Leetown. This section of the road is located about fifty yards west of the point where the tour road turns to the north. The old road and the tour road converge a few hundred yards to the north along the eastern edge of Oberson's field. No trace remains of Foster's lane.

11. Osterhaus to Curtis and Bussey to Curtis, Mar. 14, 1862, *OR* 8:217, 232–33. Because Oberson's field was composed of at least four different parcels of land, it was subdivided by fences. The Park Service has not reconstructed these fences. A trace of the north-south fence that separated Oberson's and Mayfield's property still exists and may be located along the southern edge of Oberson's field about three hundred yards west of the tour stop.

12. Ibid. The Park Service has not reconstructed or identified the location of buildings, fields, fences, and lanes on Foster's farm and has cleared an enormous area. In terms of historical accuracy and interpretation, this vast grassy expanse is hopelessly incorrect and misleading. It is by far the least satisfying part of the battlefield today. To compound the error, the Park Service has mislocated a prairie restoration project on the *eastern* side of Leetown Road, more than half a mile east of the original Round Prairie, in an area which in 1862 was a densely wooded thicket.

13. Ibid. Bussey's report makes confusing reading because the colonel was turned around and thought that east was north. A map of the engagement at Foster's farm accompanied Bussey's report and helps to clarify the situation. The map is in Colonel Bussey's Report, Union Battle Reports, NARA.

14. Osterhaus to Curtis and Bussey to Curtis, Mar. 14, 1862, and Nemett to Sigel, [Mar. ?, 1862], *OR* 8:217, 233, 245.

15. Osterhaus to Curtis and Bussey to Curtis, Mar. 14, 1862, ibid., 217, 233; Mar. 7, 1862, Boyle Journal, SHSIDM; Mar. 7, 1862, Reynolds diary, Reynolds Papers, UAF.

16. Osterhaus to Curtis, Mar. 14, 1862, *OR* 8:217.

17. Harding, "Reminiscences."

18. Sparks, *War Between the States*, 174; Barron, *Lone Star Defenders*, 67; Wat-

son, *Confederate Army*, 293.

19. Ross to D. R. Tinsley, Mar. 13, 1862, Ross Family Papers, BU; Coleman to his parents, Mar. 18, 1862, Coleman-Hayter Letters, UMC; Billingsley, "'Such Is War,'" 250–51; Tunnard, *Southern Record*, 137, 140; Watson, *Confederate Army*, 293–94.

20. Sparks, *War Between the States*, 174; Fitzhugh, *Cannon Smoke*, 162–63.

21. Greer to Van Dorn, Mar. [?], 1862, *OR* 8:298.

22. Fitzhugh, *Cannon Smoke*, 162–63; Lane, *Adventures*, 90; Barron, *Lone Star Defenders*, 68; Greer to Van Dorn, Mar. [?], 1862, *OR* 8:298; Coleman to his parents, Mar. 18, 1862, Coleman-Hayter Letters, UMC.

23. Barron, *Lone Star Defenders*, 68; Billingsley, "'Such Is War,'" 251; "Eleventh Texas Cavalry," TSL. The Confederate charge occurred on a slight downhill gradient, which allowed the rebels to build up considerable momentum.

24. Osterhaus to Curtis, Mar. 14, 1862, *OR* 8:217; Billingsley, "'Such Is War,'" 251; St. Louis *Daily Missouri Democrat*, Mar. 18, 1862; Crump Papers, UAF.

25. Mar. 7, 1862, Rogers Journal, SHSIDM; Mar. 7, 1862, Dysart Diary, PRNMP.

26. Osterhaus to Curtis, Mar. 14, 1862, *OR* 8:217–18.

27. Voelkner to his parents, Mar. 18, 1862, Voelkner Papers, UMC.

28. Bussey to Curtis and Pike to Van Dorn, Mar. 14, 1862, *OR* 8:233, 287.

29. Ibid.; S. A. Griffith letter; St. Louis *Daily Missouri Democrat*, Mar. 22, 11, and 18, 1862; *United States Biographical Dictionary*, 695; Mar. 7, 1862, Boyle Journal, SHSIDM.

30. *Medal of Honor*, 193.

31. Ross to D. R. Tinsley, Mar. 13, 1862, Ross Family Papers, BU (original italics); Mar. 7, 1862, Dysart Diary, PRNMP; Greusel to Osterhaus, Mar. 12, and Hoffman to [Greusel], Mar. 14, 1862, *OR* 8:226, 237. The gap in the belt of trees lies about three hundred yards west of State Highway 72.

32. Harding, "Reminiscences"; Pike to Van Dorn, Mar. 14, 1862, *OR* 8:288. There is no reliable evidence that the Indians committed atrocities in the vicinity of the cannons, though Thomas F. Anderson, a white man serving in the 2nd Cherokee Mounted Rifles, claimed to have seen an Indian scalp a Federal artilleryman who was pretending to be dead. When the Indian cut off a piece of scalp about the size of a silver dollar, the soldier jumped to his feet and ran away. Instead of shooting, the Confederates yelled, "Go it, Yank, we have a lock of your hair!" This jocular account is suspect for a number of reasons. Thomas F. Anderson, "Indian Territory," 86.

33. Kerr, *Ross' Texas Cavalry Brigade*, 15; Crump Papers, UAF.

34. Bussey to Curtis and Pike to Van Dorn, Mar. 14, 1862, *OR* 8:235, 288; Lale, *Civil War Letters*, 49; Kerr, *Ross' Texas Cavalry Brigade*, 14–15; Mar. 7, 1862, Rogers Journal, SHSIDM; unidentified letter, Richmond (Va.) *Whig*, Apr. 9, 1862. Bussey believed that "the loss of my command is greater in proportion to my force than perhaps any other engaged." Bussey to Curtis, Mar. 14, 1862, *OR* 8:235.

35. Barron, *Lone Star Defenders*, 67; Tunnard, *Southern Record*, 132–33; Hollinsworth, "Battle of Elkhorn," 135; S. A. Griffith letter.

36. Sam Scherer and "Tattle Tale" letters, Aurora (Ill.) *Beacon*, Mar. 27, 1862; St. Louis *Daily Missouri Democrat*, Mar. 18, 1862.

37. Sam Scherer and "Tattle Tale" letters, Aurora (Ill.) *Beacon*, Mar. 27, 1862; Castle, *Grandfather*, 28.

38. Bennett and Haigh, *Thirty-Sixth Illinois*, 146; Clark, "Dreams That Came to Pass," 331; Mar. 7, 1862, Bennett diary, Bennett Papers, UMR; Osterhaus to Curtis, Mar. 14, and Greusel to Osterhaus, Mar. 12, 1862, *OR* 8:217, 226.

39. Osterhaus to Curtis, Mar. 14, and Greusel to Osterhaus, Mar. 12, 1862, *OR* 8:217, 226.

40. Osterhaus to Curtis, Mar. 14, 1862, ibid., 218.

41. Bussey to Curtis, Mar. 14, Nemett to Sigel, [Mar. ?], and Sigel to Curtis, Mar. 15, 1862, ibid., 234, 245, 211; Mar. 7 and Apr. 20, 1862, Boyle Journal, SHSIDM; Dec. [?], 1862, Dysart Diary, PRNMP; Mar. 7, 1862, Rogers Journal, SHSIDM. After the battle the Iowans circulated a petition calling for Perry's resignation.

42. Greusel to Osterhaus and Hoffman to [Greusel], Mar. 14, 1862, *OR* 8:226, 237.

43. Welfley to Sigel, Mar. 11, 1862, ibid., 236.

44. Osterhaus to Curtis, Mar. 14, 1862, and Wangelin to [Greusel], [Mar. ?, 1862], ibid., 217, 228.

45. Greusel to Osterhaus, Mar. 12, 1862, ibid., 226.

46. Ibid.

47. Greusel to Osterhaus, Mar. 12, and Greer to Van Dorn, Mar. [?], 1862, ibid., 226, 298–99; Tunnard, *Southern Record*, 137–40.

48. Tunnard, *Southern Record*, 137, 140; Rose, *McCulloch*, 203–4.

49. Lane, *Adventures*, 91–92; Greer to Van Dorn, Mar. [?], and Stone to [Van Dorn], Mar. 12, 1862, *OR* 8:298–99, 301; Lale, "Boy Bugler," 158–59; Douglas, *Douglas's Texas Battery*, 184; Ross to D. R. Tinsley, Mar. 13, 1862, Ross Family Papers, BU.

50. Yeary, *Reminiscences*, 775.

51. Stirman, "Career of M'Culloch," 173; Rose, *McCulloch*, 203–4.

52. Rose, *McCulloch*, 204; Joseph M. Bailey, "Confederate Soldier," TSL, and "Death of General McCulloch," 175.

53. See note 52 above.

54. Rose, *McCulloch*, 204; John H. Brown letter, Houston *Weekly Telegraph*, Aug. 11, 1862. McCulloch received a sword from Howell Cobb during his visit to Richmond but never wore it.

55. Bennett and Haigh, *Thirty-Sixth Illinois*, 148; Rose, *McCulloch*, 204.

56. Rose, *McCulloch*, 204–5; John H. Brown letter, Houston *Weekly Telegraph*, Aug. 11, 1862. The exact site of McCulloch's death cannot be determined today. A cairn of rocks erected near the spot after the battle has disappeared. McCulloch was struck down in the belt of trees about one hundred yards west of State Highway 72. The interpretive marker placed by the Park Service in Oberson's field gives the incorrect impression that the general was killed much nearer to Leetown Road. St. Louis *Daily Missouri Democrat*, Mar. 20, 1862; Seamster, "Reunions of Blue and Gray," 43.

57. Clark, "Dreams That Came to Pass," 331; "Aurora" [probably Nicholas Greusel] letter, Chicago *Tribune*, Apr. 23, 1862; Bennett and Haigh, *Thirty-Sixth Illinois*, 148. Because Pelican took McCulloch's watch, he was (and still is) widely credited

with firing the fatal shot. It is not known which Federal skirmisher killed McCulloch; Pelican was merely the first to reach the body. Pelican gave or sold the watch to Greusel. None of the Federals got the general's Colt revolver, engraved with the words, "Ben. McCulloch, Presented by the Inventor." Fayel, "Second Day at Pea Ridge"; John H. Brown letter, Houston *Weekly Telegraph*, Aug. 11, 1862.

58. Joseph M. Bailey, "Confederate Soldier," TSL, and "Death of General McCulloch," 175.

59. See note 58 above. The published and unpublished versions of Bailey's story are essentially identical.

60. Rose, *McCulloch*, 205; Joseph M. Bailey, "Confederate Soldier," TSL, and "Death of General McCulloch," 175. McCulloch is buried in the Texas State Cemetery in Austin. Nearby is the grave of Albert S. Johnston, who was struck down a month later at Shiloh.

CHAPTER SIX

1. Ross to D. R. Tinsley, Mar. 13, 1862, Ross Family Papers, BU.

2. Clark, "Dreams That Came to Pass," 331.

3. Ibid.

4. Ibid.; Bennett and Haigh, *Thirty-Sixth Illinois*, 148.

5. Greusel to Osterhaus, Mar. 12, 1862, *OR* 8:226; Clark, "Dreams That Came to Pass," 331, and "Battle of Pea Ridge," 363; Bennett and Haigh, *Thirty-Sixth Illinois*, 149; letter from unidentified 37th Illinois soldier, Chicago *Tribune*, Mar. 24, 1862.

6. Pompey O. Breeden to his wife, Mar. 21, 1862, Moose Papers, UAF; Rose, *McCulloch*, 205; John H. Brown letter, Houston *Weekly Telegraph*, Aug. 11, 1862. McIntosh was killed near the southern edge of the belt of trees about two hundred yards east of State Highway 72, or three hundred yards east of the point where McCulloch died. A cairn of stones marking the approximate site has disappeared. The large interpretive marker placed by the Park Service in Oberson's field does not mention McIntosh. Seamster, "Reunions of Blue and Gray," 43.

7. Rose, *McCulloch*, 205; John H. Brown letter, Houston *Weekly Telegraph*, Aug. 11, 1862. McIntosh is buried in Fort Smith National Cemetery, an unusual resting place for a Confederate general.

8. Greusel to Osterhaus, Mar. 12, 1862, *OR* 8:226. Greusel reported that twenty skirmishers were wounded; one of Miller's men reported that twenty-four were wounded, one mortally. Clark, "Dreams That Came to Pass," 332.

9. James F. Harris letter, New Orleans *Commercial Bulletin*, Apr. 16, 1862; Tunnard, *Southern Record*, 137–38.

10. McNair to Van Dorn, Apr. 29, 1862, *OR* 8:295; Worley, *War Memoirs*, 9.

11. "Autobiography," Hébert Papers, UNC.

12. McNair to Van Dorn, Apr. 29, 1862, *OR* 8:295; Watson, *Confederate Army*, 294. Morgan's woods is much the same today as in 1862: forested, brushy, and dissected by ravines. The heaviest fighting at Leetown took place in this thicket, but the Park

Service has not placed any markers in the area. The park hiking trail passes through Morgan's woods between the two ravines.

13. McNair to Van Dorn, Apr. 29, 1862, *OR* 8:295.

14. Ibid.; Tunnard, *Southern Record*, 135, 140; Rufus K. Garland letter, Washington (Ark.) *Telegraph*, Apr. 2, 1862.

15. Curtis to Halleck, Apr. 1, 1862, *OR* 8:199.

16. Ibid.

17. Ibid. Dodge, for example, said that a "great mistake was made in the morning" when Curtis sent only the 4th Division to Elkhorn Tavern. Dodge to C. Baldwin, Mar. 15, 1862, Dodge Family Papers, DPL.

18. Curtis to Halleck, Apr. 1, 1862, *OR* 8:199

19. White to Davis, Mar. 11, and Pattison to Davis, Mar. 10, 1862, ibid., 253, 249; D. M. Callaghan letter, Waukegan (Ill.) *Weekly Gazette*, Apr. 12, 1862.

20. Eugene B. Payne letter, Waukegan (Ill.) *Weekly Gazette*, Mar. 29, 1862.

21. Crabtree, "Recollections," 219.

22. Davis to Curtis, Mar. 16, 1862, *OR* 8:246; Clarke, *Warfare along the Mississippi*, 25; Mar. 7, 1862, Boyer Diary, MH; D. W. Henderson letter, Litchfield (Ill.) *Journal*, Mar. 26, 1862; Payne Journal, UM. The two cannons which the Park Service has placed in the southeast corner of Oberson's field misrepresent the size, location, and direction of fire of the Peoria Battery. The six guns of the Peoria Battery were located much closer to the fence along the southern edge of the field and faced northeast toward Morgan's woods. The Park Service has not placed any cannons to mark the sites of the 4th Ohio Battery and Welfley's Independent Missouri Battery in Oberson's field.

23. White to Davis, Mar. 11, 1862, *OR* 8:253; Anderson, "Battle of Pea Ridge," USAMHI; Eugene B. Payne letter, Waukegan (Ill.) *Weekly Gazette*, Mar. 29, 1862.

24. Ketzle Memoir, Mullins Collection, Wayne, N.J.; George R. Bell letter, Chicago *Evening Journal*, Apr. 5, 1862; Blodgett, "Army of the Southwest," 305–6; John W. Noble, "Battle of Pea Ridge," 231.

25. M. L. Anderson letter, Monmouth (Ill.) *Atlas*, Apr. 11, 1862.

26. Herr, *Episodes*, 37, 370–71; Lathrop, *Fifty-Ninth Illinois*, 93.

27. Watson, *Confederate Army*, 294; Tunnard, *Southern Record*, 135; Logan, "Memories," 7; Yeary, *Reminiscences*, 355.

28. George R. Bell letter, Chicago *Evening Journal*, Apr. 5, 1862; John M. Turnbull letter, Monmouth (Ill.) *Atlas*, Mar. 28, 1862; James P. Douglas letter, Tyler (Texas) *Reporter*, [Mar. ?, 1862]; Douglas, *Douglas's Texas Battery*, 184.

29. Herschel Felton to E. Schafer, Mar. 12, 1862, Mullins Collection, Wayne, N.J.; Ash to his fiancée, Mar. 11, 1862, Ash Papers, USAMHI; John W. Noble, "Battle of Pea Ridge," 231; Herr, *Episodes*, 371; Curtis to his mother, Mar. 30, 1862, Curtis Papers, USAMHI; Fielding to his mother, Mar. 21, 1862, Fielding Papers, ISHL.

30. E. A. letter, Chicago *Tribune*, Mar. 24, 1862; Herr, *Episodes*, 371; Ash to his fiancée, Mar. 14, 1862, Ash Papers, USAMHI; Eugene B. Payne letters, Waukegan (Ill.) *Weekly Gazette*, Mar. 29 and Apr. 5, 1862; Curtis to his mother, Mar. 28, 1862, Curtis Papers, USAMHI.

31. M. L. Anderson letter, Monmouth (Ill.) *Atlas*, Apr. 11, 1862; Ash to his fiancée, Mar. 11, 1862, Ash Papers, USAMHI.

32. Letter from unidentified 37th Illinois soldier, Chicago *Tribune*, Mar. 24, 1862; David Hick letter, Rock Island (Ill.) *Weekly Argus*, Mar. [?], 1862; letter from unidentified 37th Illinois soldier, Jan. 4, 1863, Black Family Papers, ISHL; Lathrop, *Fifty-Ninth Illinois*, 94.

33. Payne to his wife, Mar. 12, 1862, Payne Papers, LFC; Curtis to his mother, Mar. 23, 1862, Curtis Papers, USAMHI. Curtis's cap and bullet-riddled coat are on display in the Visitor Center at Pea Ridge National Military Park.

34. Davis to Curtis, Mar. 16, 1862, *OR* 8:246, 248.

35. Randolph V. Marshall, *Twenty-Second Indiana*, 15–16; Indianapolis *Daily Journal*, Apr. 17, 1862; Daily to Davis, Mar. 9, 1862, Order Book, 22nd Indiana Regimental Papers, NARA (Daily's report is not in the *OR*). The deadly projectile later was displayed in the Indiana State Library.

36. Davis to Curtis, Mar. 16, and Pattison to Davis, Mar. 10, 1862, *OR* 8:246, 249–50; Washburn to Pattison, Mar. 8, 1862, in Moore, *Rebellion Record*, 4:248 (Washburn's report is not in NARA or the *OR* and survives only in Moore's compilation); Clarke, *Warfare along the Mississippi*, 26–27; Payne Journal, UM. A faint trace of the lane remains, but it is not marked by the Park Service.

37. Watson, *Confederate Army*, 294–95; Lathrop, *Fifty-Ninth Illinois*, 93; Herr, *Episodes*, 37.

38. Ash to his wife, Mar. 11, 1862, Ash Papers, USAMHI; DeWolf, *Swap*, 11; Clarke, *Warfare along the Mississippi*, 25–26.

39. Payne to his wife, Mar. 12, 1862, Payne Papers, LFC; Clarke, *Warfare along the Mississippi*, 25–26.

40. St. Louis *Daily Missouri Democrat*, Mar. 22, 1862; DeWolf, *Swap*, 11.

41. DeWolf, *Swap*, 11–12; letter from unidentified 37th Illinois soldier, Chicago *Tribune*, Mar. 24, 1862; St. Louis *Daily Missouri Democrat*, Mar. 22, 1862.

42. Davis to Curtis, Mar. 16, 1862, *OR* 8:246; Herr, *Episodes*, 371.

43. Pattison to Davis, Mar. 10, 1862, *OR* 8:250; Washburn to Pattison, Mar. 8, 1862, in Moore, *Rebellion Record*, 4:248. After the war, rumors spread about White's poor performance at Leetown, prompting some former officers of the 37th Illinois to write a testimonial letter defending their old colonel. White Testimonial Letter, UAF.

44. Clarke, *Warfare along the Mississippi*, 25–27.

45. Watson, *Confederate Army*, 295; Tunnard, *Southern Record*, 133, 138; James F. Harris letter, New Orleans *Commercial Bulletin*, Apr. 16, 1862.

46. Worley, *War Memoirs*, 9–10; McNair to Van Dorn, Apr. 29, 1862, *OR* 8:295–96; Black to his mother, Mar. 9, 1862, Black Family Papers, ISHL; John C. Black, "Our Boys," 451–52; *Medal of Honor*, 32. Black was the brother of Maj. John C. Black, wounded earlier in the thicket. His Company K lost more men in the struggle for the Peoria Battery than at any other stage of the battle. The 37th Illinois suffered 133 casualties at Leetown, twice as many as the 59th Illinois. White to Davis, Mar. 11, 1862, *OR* 8:254.

47. Jacob C. Hansel letter, Peoria *Daily Transcript*, Mar. 31, 1862.

CHAPTER SEVEN

1. Watson, *Confederate Army*, 295. It is uncertain how—or if—the Confederates disabled the two cannons. Watson claimed the weapons were spiked; an Arkansas captain stated, "We cut the Gun carriages down as we could not move ordnance." Both were writing long after the event. Federal records do not mention any damage to the cannons. Worley, *War Memoirs*, 9.

2. Watson, *Confederate Army*, 295; Tunnard, *Southern Record*, 134, 140.

3. Tunnard, *Southern Record*, 134–35; "Autobiography," Hébert Papers, UNC.

4. Watson, *Confederate Army*, 296–300.

5. "Autobiography," Hébert Papers, UNC.

6. Sigel to Curtis, Mar. 15, 1862, *OR* 8:211; Gen. Orders No. 26, June 23, 1862, General Orders, NARA; Burns, *4th Missouri Cavalry*, 29–30.

7. Gen. Orders No. 26, June 23, 1862, General Orders, NARA; Burns, *4th Missouri Cavalry*, 29–30.

8. Burns, *4th Missouri Cavalry*, 30–32. Burns later heard Meszaros give the newspaper correspondent Thomas Knox "a glowing account of the successful charge he had made."

9. Ibid.; Watson, *Confederate Army*, 298. Watson declared that his comrades opened a "steady continued fusillade" against the cavalry, but it seems unlikely that the disorganized rebels were capable of that.

10. Burns, *4th Missouri Cavalry*, 30–31.

11. Ibid.

12. Pattison to Davis, Mar. 10, 1862, *OR* 8:250; Washburn to Pattison, Mar. 8, 1862, in Moore, *Rebellion Record*, 4:248; Mar. 7, 1862, Johnson Diary, LC; Judson Tyler to his cousin, Apr. 4, 1862, Harding Collection, IHS.

13. Washburn to Pattison, Mar. 8, 1862, in Moore, *Rebellion Record*, 4:248.

14. "Autobiography," Hébert Papers, UNC; Tunnard, *Southern Record*, 141.

15. Randolph V. Marshall, *Twenty-Second Indiana*, 17–18.

16. Ibid.

17. Ibid.; interview with Colonel Hendricks's brother, Cincinnati *Daily Gazette*, Mar. 20, 1862.

18. Randolph V. Marshall, *Twenty-Second Indiana*, 17–18; Mar. 7, 1862, Johnson Diary, LC; Pattison to Davis, Mar. 10, 1862, *OR* 8:250; Tunnard, *Southern Record*, 141.

19. Washburn to Pattison, Mar. 8, 1862, in Moore, *Rebellion Record*, 4:248; Tunnard, *Southern Record*, 141; Greer to Van Dorn, Mar. [?], 1862, *OR* 8:299.

20. "Autobiography," Hébert Papers, UNC.

21. Washburn to Pattison, Mar. 8, 1862, in Moore, *Rebellion Record*, 4:248.

22. Bennett and Haigh, *Thirty-Sixth Illinois*, 150–51; Osterhaus to Curtis, Mar. 14, 1862, *OR* 8:218.

23. Mar. 7, 1862, Kircher diary, and Kircher to his mother, Nov. 28, 1862, Engelmann-Kircher Collection, ISHL; Wangelin to [Greusel], [Mar. ?], and Osterhaus to Curtis, Mar. 14, 1862, *OR* 8:228, 218.

24. Osterhaus to Curtis and Hoffman to [Sigel], Mar. 14, 1862, *OR* 8:218, 237–38.

25. Osterhaus to Curtis, Mar. 14, 1862, ibid., 218; Bennett and Haigh, *Thirty-Sixth Illinois*, 150–51.

26. McNair to Van Dorn, Apr. 29, 1862, *OR* 8:295; Rufus K. Garland letter, Washington (Ark.) *Telegraph*, Apr. 2, 1862; James F. Harris letter, New Orleans *Commercial Bulletin*, Apr. 16, 1862; Silas Miller letter, Aurora (Ill.) *Beacon*, Mar. 27, 1862.

27. Pattison to Davis, Mar. 10, Osterhaus to Curtis, Mar. 14, and Davis to Curtis, Mar. 16, 1862, *OR* 8:250, 218–19, 247.

28. Ross to D. R. Tinsley, Mar. 13, 1862, Ross Family Papers, BU; Joe M. Scott, *Four Years' Service*, 10.

29. Joe M. Scott, *Four Years' Service*, 11; Mar. 7, 1862, Graves Diary, UT.

30. Pike to Van Dorn, Mar. 14, 1862, *OR* 8:288; Tunnard, *Southern Record*, 133; Mar. 7, 1862, Graves Diary, UT. Pike believed "it was not reasonable to expect much of a small body of Indians" in a pitched battle and suggested that his horsemen could have been better used as a mobile force to harry the Federal flanks and rear. Pike to [?], May 4, 1862, *OR* 13:820.

31. Pike to Van Dorn, Mar. 14, 1862, *OR* 8:288–89.

32. Hollinsworth, "Battle of Elkhorn," 139; Pike to Van Dorn, Mar. 14, and Stone to Van Dorn, Apr. 14, 1862, *OR* 8:289, 303.

33. Pike to Van Dorn, Mar. 14, and Stone to Van Dorn, Apr. 14, 1862, *OR* 8:288, 303–4.

34. Cater, *"As It Was,"* 130; Greer to Van Dorn, Mar. [?], 1862, *OR* 8:299.

35. See note 34 above.

36. Greer to Van Dorn, Mar. [?] and 19, 1862, *OR* 8:299, 293.

37. Ibid.

38. Ross to D. R. Tinsley, Mar. 13, 1862, Ross Family Papers, BU; Greer to Van Dorn, Mar. 19, 1862, *OR* 8:293–94; Rose, *Ross' Texas Brigade*, 59.

39. Curtis to Halleck, Apr. 1, 1862, *OR* 8:200.

40. Ibid.

41. Curtis to Halleck, Mar. 10, Sigel to Curtis, Mar. 15, and Asboth to Sigel and to Curtis, Mar. 16, 1862, ibid., 200, 212, 241, 242.

42. Sigel to Curtis, Mar. 15, 1862, ibid., 212.

43. Sigel to Curtis, Mar. 15, Knobelsdorff to Osterhaus, Mar. 11, Smith to Greusel, [Mar. ?], and Curtis to Halleck, Apr. 1, 1862, ibid., 212, 224, 231, 200.

44. Coler to Osterhaus, Mar. 9, 1862, ibid., 221.

45. Green to Price, Mar. 21, and Price to Van Dorn, Mar. 22, 1862, ibid., 316–17, 304; Rufus K. Garland and P. R. Smith letters, Washington (Ark.) *Telegraph*, Apr. 2, 1862. The first Federals to arrive at Leetown—Bussey's cavalrymen—caught a glimpse of the buff-topped Confederate wagons to the west on the Bentonville Detour shortly after the trains turned back to Camp Stephens. Bussey to Curtis, Mar. 14, 1862, *OR* 8:232.

46. Green to Price, Mar. 21, and Poten to Sigel, Mar. 18, 1862, *OR* 8:317, 280; Rufus K. Garland and P. R. Smith letters, Washington (Ark.) *Telegraph*, Apr. 2, 1862; unidentified Confederate soldier's letter, Memphis *Daily Appeal*, Mar. 29, 1862; Lemke, *Journals*.

47. Stone to Van Dorn, Apr. 14, and Green to Price, Mar. 21, 1862, *OR* 8:304, 317; Ross to D. R. Tinsley, Mar. 13, 1862, Ross Family Papers, BU; P. R. Smith letter, Washington (Ark.) *Telegraph*, Apr. 2, 1862.

48. Smith to Greusel, [Mar. ?, 1862], *OR* 8:231–32; "Autobiography," Hébert Papers, UNC.

49. Sigel to Curtis, Mar. 15, and Hoffman to [Sigel], Mar. 14, 1862, *OR* 8:212, 238.

50. Knobelsdorff to Osterhaus, Mar. 11, 1862, ibid., 224–25; letter from unidentified 44th Illinois soldier, Mar. 18, 1862, Jump Papers, IHS; Tunnard, *Southern Record*, 134–35; certificate of Tunnard's personal effects signed by Eli Weston, Mar. 21, 1862, Gale Papers, CHS. While a prisoner Tunnard learned that McCulloch's watch, pilfered by Peter Pelican, was in Greusel's possession. Tunnard was a great admirer of McCulloch and offered Greusel $500—presumably Confederate money—for the timepiece, but Greusel declined the offer. Chicago *Tribune*, Apr. 23, 1862.

51. Sigel to Curtis, Mar. 15, and Davis to Curtis, Mar. 16, 1862, *OR* 8:212, 247; Clarke, *Warfare along the Mississippi*, 29; Knobe Memoir, ISL.

CHAPTER EIGHT

1. Carr to Curtis and Weston to Curtis, Mar. 10, 1862, *OR* 8:258–59, 271; King, *War Eagle*, 3–55.

2. The tavern was burned by secessionists in December 1862 and was reconstructed with some modifications on the original foundations in 1885. The handsome present-day structure is an accurate Park Service reconstruction of the postwar tavern and therefore does not precisely represent how the tavern appeared at the time of the battle. The Park Service has not reconstructed the barn, blacksmith shop, and other outbuildings or otherwise restored the area around the tavern. There are two depictions of the original tavern: Hunt P. Wilson's well-known postwar painting of Pea Ridge, now in the Museum of the Confederacy in Richmond, and Robert Sweeny's recently published postbattle sketch. Wilson was a Confederate artilleryman; Sweeny, a civilian artist accompanying the Army of the Southwest. Bond, "History of Elkhorn Tavern"; Goodrich, "Robert Ormsby Sweeny," 165.

3. The section of Telegraph Road between the tanyard and the tavern is closed to vehicular traffic. The upper half of the old road was in use through the 1950s and has a modern, "improved" appearance. The lower half, abandoned decades ago when a new roadbed was cut into the western side of the ridge, is now part of the park hiking trail. The Park Service has cleared and marked the site of the tanyard.

4. Weston to Curtis, Mar. 10, and Fyan to Weston, Mar. 9, 1862, *OR* 8:271, 274–75.

5. Weston to Curtis, Mar. 10, 1862, ibid., 271.

6. Ibid.

7. Carr to Curtis, Mar. 10, 1862, *OR* 8:259.

8. Carr to Curtis, Weston to Curtis, and Dodge to Carr, Mar. 10, 1862, ibid., 259, 271, 263; Dodge, "Colonel Kinsman," 245.

9. Carr to Curtis, Mar. 10, 1862, *OR* 8:259.

10. Carr to Curtis, Mar. 10, and Jones to Dodge, Mar. 9, 1862, ibid., 259, 265.

11. Carr to Curtis, Mar. 10, 1862, ibid., 259.

12. Van Dorn to Bragg, Mar. 27, 1862, ibid., 284.

13. Cearnal to Price, Mar. 21, 1862, ibid., 329; Smith Memoirs, UMC; Ephraim M. Anderson, *Memoirs*, 167–68; Hunt P. Wilson, "Battle of Elkhorn." The foragers belonged to Weston's command and had set out before Weston learned of the Confederate presence beyond Big Mountain. Three wagons loaded with forage, with teams and drivers, were lost. Precisely where the foragers were captured is unclear. Weston to Curtis, Mar. 10, and Fyan to Weston and Lewis to Weston, Mar. 9, 1862, *OR* 8:272, 275, 277–78.

14. Van Dorn to Bragg, Mar. 27, 1862, *OR* 8:284.

15. Little to Price, Mar. 18, 1862, ibid., 307; Ephraim M. Anderson, *Memoirs*, 169–70.

16. Rosser to Price, Mar. 21, 1862, and Hughes to Price, [Mar. ?, 1862], *OR* 8:312, 314.

17. Greene to Price, Mar. 20, Frost to Price, Mar. 19, Rains to Price, Mar. 20, Clark to Price, Mar. 11, Saunders to Price, Mar. 17, and Lindsay to Price, Mar. 19, 1862, *OR* 8:325, 323, 327, 319, 321, 322.

18. Little to Price, Mar. 18, 1862, ibid., 307.

19. Price to Van Dorn, Mar. 22, 1862, ibid., 305; Hunt P. Wilson, "Battle of Elkhorn."

20. Hunt P. Wilson, "Battle of Elkhorn."

21. Little to Price, Mar. 18, 1862, *OR* 8:307.

22. Sam Black, *Soldier's Recollections*, 6; Jones to Dodge, Mar. 9, 1862, *OR* 8:265.

23. Jones to Dodge, Mar. 9, and Carr to Curtis, Mar. 10, 1862, *OR* 8:259, 265; Sam Black, *Soldier's Recollections*, 6.

24. Hunt P. Wilson, "Battle of Elkhorn"; Harding, "Reminiscences"; Carr to Curtis, Mar. 10, and Jones to Dodge, Mar. 9, 1862, *OR* 8:259, 265–66; Carr to his father, Mar. 15, 1862, Carr Papers, USAMHI.

25. Rains to Price, Mar. 20, 1862, *OR* 8:327.

26. Sam Black, *Soldier's Recollections*, 6–7, 10.

27. Jones to Dodge, Mar. 9, 1862, *OR* 8:265–66.

28. Ephraim M. Anderson, *Memoirs*, 170; Jines, "Civil War Diary," 17; Payne, "Battle of Pea Ridge," PRNMP.

29. Johnson to his wife, Mar. 27, 1862, Johnson Letters, UMC; New York *Herald*, Mar. 19, 1862.

30. Hunt P. Wilson, "Battle of Elkhorn"; Little to Price, Mar. 18, 1862, *OR* 8:307.

31. See note 30 above.

32. Map with notes on Pea Ridge, vol. 144, Dodge Papers, SHSIDM.

33. Price to Van Dorn, Mar. 22, 1862, *OR* 8:305.

34. Little to Price, Mar. 18, 1862, ibid., 308.

35. Dodge to Carr, Mar. 10, 1862, ibid., 263; Cummings to his wife, Mar. 14, 1862, Cummings Papers, SHSIDM; William H. Kinsman letter of Mar. 10, 1862, Council Bluffs (Iowa) *Weekly Nonpareil*, Mar. 29, 1862; Dodge, *Fiftieth Anniversary*, 13.

36. Carr to Curtis and Dodge to Carr, Mar. 10, 1862, *OR* 8:259, 263; Warner, *Generals*

in Blue, 458. Smith survived and returned to active duty after a long convalescence.

37. Sam Black, *Soldier's Recollections*, 6–7; Dodge, *Fiftieth Anniversary*, 13; Mar. 7, 1862, Mothershead Diary, TSLA.

38. Fayel, "Curtis' Withdrawal"; Curtis to his wife, Mar. 10, 1862, Curtis Papers, SHSIDM; Curtis to his brother, Mar. 13, 1862, Curtis Papers, HL.

39. Curtis, "Army of the South-West," 6:154; Fayel, "Curtis' Withdrawal"; Kirkland, *Pictorial Book*, 328. The Chicago *Tribune* said Pea Ridge was a "singularly homely name" but did not criticize the choice. The origin of the preferred Confederate name, Elkhorn Tavern, is obvious. Van Dorn used the words "Elkhorn, Ark." in a telegram dated Mar. 9. A few days later printer Richard Hubbell composed the headline "Battle of Elkhorn" for an issue of the Missouri State Guard's *Army Argus*. Editorial in the Chicago *Tribune*, Mar. 19, 1862; Van Dorn to Johnston, Mar. 9, 1862, *OR* 8:281; Hubbell Reminiscences, MHS.

40. Crabtree, "Recollections," 218; Curtis to Halleck, Apr. 1, 1862, *OR* 8:199.

41. Crabtree, "Recollections," 218; Curtis to Halleck, Apr. 1, and Carr to Curtis, Mar. 10, 1862, *OR* 8:199, 259.

42. Carr to his father, Mar. 15, 1862, Carr Papers, USAMHI; Fayel, "Curtis' Withdrawal."

43. See note 42 above.

CHAPTER NINE

1. Hayden to Vandever, Mar. 9, and Carr to Curtis, Mar. 10, 1862, *OR* 8:268, 259.

2. Sigel to Curtis, Mar. 15, 1862, ibid., 211.

3. Carr to Curtis, Mar. 10, 1862, ibid., 259; *Medal of Honor*, 51.

4. Truman, "Battle of Elk Horn," 169; Hayden to Vandever, Mar. 9, 1862, *OR* 8:268; Mar. 7, 1862, Mothershead Diary, TSLA; Fayel, "Curtis' Withdrawal"; Mathews, "Souvenir," UMC.

5. Hunt P. Wilson, "Battle of Elkhorn"; Fayel, "Curtis' Withdrawal"; New York *Herald*, Mar. 19, 1862.

6. Hunt P. Wilson, "Battle of Elkhorn"; Fayel, "Curtis' Withdrawal."

7. Hunt P. Wilson, "Battle of Elkhorn"; Bond, "History of Elkhorn Tavern," 3–15; New York *Herald*, Mar. 19, 1862.

8. Carr to Curtis, Mar. 10, 1862, *OR* 8:261.

9. Hunt P. Wilson, "Battle of Elkhorn."

10. Rosser to Price, Mar. 21, 1862, and Hughes to Price, [Mar. ?, 1862], *OR* 8:312–13, 314.

11. Vandever to Carr, Mar. 13, 1862, *OR* 8:266–67; Mathews, "Souvenir," UMC; Mar. 7, 1862, Holman Diary, SHSIIC.

12. Mathews, "Souvenir," UMC; Abernethy, "Incidents," 405.

13. Mar. 7, 1862, Holman Diary, SHSIIC.

14. Dr. Keith to Mrs. Slack, Dec. 26, 1862, Slack Papers, UMC; Harding, "Reminiscences"; Rosser to Price, Mar. 21, 1862, *OR* 8:312. Rosser wrote that Slack's fatal

injury "was a severe loss to the Missouri troops, as he was a man of much more than ordinary ability, cool and clear-headed, and a more gallant soldier never lived. His men were devotedly attached to him and to them he was a model of soldierly bearing."

15. Vandever to Carr, Mar. 13, and Carr to Curtis, Mar. 10, 1862, *OR* 8:267; Ephraim M. Anderson, *Memoirs*, 170; Harwood, *Pea Ridge Campaign*, 16; Mathews, "Souvenir," UMC; Smith Memoirs, UMC; Payne, "Battle of Pea Ridge," PRNMP.

16. Vandever to Carr, Mar. 13, 1862, *OR* 8:267.

17. Ibid.; Ephraim M. Anderson, *Memoirs*, 170.

18. Greene to Price, Mar. 20, and Frost to Price and Lindsay to Price, Mar. 19, 1862, *OR* 8:325, 323, 322;

19. Carr to Curtis, Mar. 10, and Hayden to Vandever, Mar. 9, 1862, ibid., 259–60, 268.

20. Carr to Curtis, Mar. 10, 1862, ibid., 260.

21. Ibid.

22. Curtis to Halleck, Mar. 10, 1862, *OR* 8:200; Carroll, *Benteen-Goldin Letters*, 237. As Bowen's battalion departed, Fayel observed that the "insignificant little howitzers, in contrast with twelve-pounders, looked like small puppies compared with large mastiffs as they bounded along over the rough road." Fayel, "Curtis' Withdrawal."

23. Shunk to Carr, Mar. 13, 1862, *OR* 8:252; A. W. Sanford letter, Indianapolis *Daily Journal*, Mar. 19, 1862; J. P. W. letter, Richmond (Ind.) *Palladium*, Apr. 26, 1862; Mar. 7, 1862, Herrington Diary, USAMHI.

24. Curtis to Halleck, Carr to Curtis, and Bowen to Curtis, Mar. 10, 1862, *OR* 8:200, 260, 270.

25. Harding, "Reminiscences."

26. Ibid. The Federal force that Harding encountered on Ford Road probably was a company of the 1st Missouri Cavalry, part of Weston's command, which reported "breaking up" a small party of rebels attempting to outflank Carr's position. Lewis to Weston, Mar. 9, and Weston to Curtis, Mar. 10, 1862, *OR* 8:278, 272.

27. Harding, "Reminiscences"; Van Dorn to Bragg, Mar. 27, 1862, *OR* 8:285.

28. Harding, "Reminiscences."

29. Little to Price, Mar. 18, 1862, *OR* 8:308.

30. Ibid.; Hunt P. Wilson, "Battle of Elkhorn."

31. Harding, "Reminiscences"; Van Dorn to Bragg, Mar. 27, and Saunders to Price, Mar. 17, 1862, *OR* 8:284, 321.

32. Van Dorn to Bragg, Mar. 27, 1862, *OR* 8:284.

33. Dodge to Carr and Carr to Curtis, Mar. 10, 1862, ibid., 263, 260.

34. Curtis to Halleck and Carr to Curtis, Mar. 10, 1862, ibid., 200, 260–61; Fayel, "Curtis' Withdrawal."

CHAPTER TEN

1. Little to Price, Mar. 18, 1862, *OR* 8:308.

2. Ibid.; Harding, "Reminiscences."

3. Mar. 7, 1862, Holman Diary, SHSIIC.

4. Harding, "Reminiscences"; Mar. 7, 1862, Mothershead Diary, TSLA; Payne, "Battle of Pea Ridge," PRNMP. The Federals tended to aim high because they were firing downhill. The result was an unusually large number of Confederates with head wounds. "They was most all shot in the head," reported an Iowa soldier. Mar. 9, 1862, Holman Diary, SHSIIC.

5. Jines, "Civil War Diary," 17; Abernethy, "Incidents," 405; Platt Memoir, PRNMP.

6. Ephraim M. Anderson, *Memoirs*, 171; Harwood, *Pea Ridge Campaign*, 17; Mar. 7, 1862, Mothershead Diary, TSLA; Carroll, *Benteen-Goldin Letters*, 237.

7. Rosser to Price, Mar. 21, 1862, *OR* 8:313.

8. Mathews, "Souvenir," UMC.

9. Ross to D. R. Tinsley, Mar. 13, 1862, Ross Family Papers, BU; Van Dorn to Bragg, Mar. 27, 1862, *OR* 8:284; Maury, "Recollections of Elkhorn," 193.

10. Bowen to Curtis, Mar. 10, 1862, *OR* 8:270; Mathews, "Souvenir," UMC.

11. Hayden to Vandever, Mar. 9, Carr to Curtis, Mar. 10, Rosser to Price, Mar. 21, 1862, and Hughes to Price, [Mar. ?, 1862], *OR* 8:269, 260, 313, 314.

12. Harding, "Reminiscences"; Hunt P. Wilson, "Battle of Elkhorn"; Harwood, *Pea Ridge Campaign*, 16.

13. Ephraim M. Anderson, *Memoirs*, 171.

14. Carr to Curtis, Mar. 10, 1862, *OR* 8:261; Mar. 7, 1862, Holman Diary, SHSIIC.

15. Smith Memoirs, UMC; Mar. 7, 1862, Mothershead Diary, TSLA. In 1862 the area around the junction of Telegraph and Huntsville roads was a maze of different types of fences enclosing the tavern, various outbuildings, a corral, an orchard, a garden, a yard, etc. The Park Service has failed to reconstruct any of these fences accurately.

16. Ephraim M. Anderson, *Memoirs*, 171; Mar. 7, 1862, Mothershead Diary, TSLA.

17. Carr to Curtis, Mar. 10, and Hayden to Vandever, Mar. 9, 1862, *OR* 8:261, 269.

18. Carr to Curtis, Mar. 10, 1862, ibid., 261.

19. Ibid.; William H. Kinsman letter, Council Bluffs (Iowa) *Weekly Nonpareil*, Mar. 29, 1862. The clearing presently occupied by the two monuments just south of the tavern roughly corresponds to the orchard crossed by the Federals. The Park Service has not placed interpretive markers in this area or restored the fence on the southern side of the orchard.

20. Smith Memoirs, UMC.

21. Payne, "Battle of Pea Ridge," PRNMP; Ephraim M. Anderson, *Memoirs*, 172; Frost to Price, Mar. 19, 1862, *OR* 8:324.

22. Hunt P. Wilson, "Battle of Elkhorn."

23. Ibid.

24. Ibid.; Bull Memoirs, MHS.

25. Kennerly, *Persimmon Hill*, 242.

26. Platt Memoir, PRNMP; Carr to Curtis, Mar. 10, 1862, *OR* 8:261; William H. Kinsman letter, Council Bluffs (Iowa) *Weekly Nonpareil*, Apr. 12, 1862; St. Louis *Missouri Republican*, Mar. 31, 1862; *Medal of Honor*, 115.

27. Mathews, "Souvenir," UMC.

28. Mar. 7, 1862, Holman Diary, SHSIIC; Mar. 7, 1862, Mothershead Diary, TSLA;

Mathews, "Souvenir," UMC.

29. Payne, "Battle of Pea Ridge," PRNMP; Kennerly, *Persimmon Hill*, 243.

30. Rains to Price, Mar. 20, 1862, *OR* 8:327–28.

31. Price to Van Dorn, Mar. 22, 1862, and Rains to Price, Mar. 20, 1862, ibid., 305, 327; Musser, "Battle of Pea Ridge." The foundations of Clemon's cabin are visible, and the field on the southern side of Huntsville Road has been restored; but there are no interpretive markers or artillery pieces on this section of the battlefield.

32. Dodge to Carr, Mar. 10, 1862, *OR* 8:263; Dodge, *Battle of Atlanta*, 21. The section of Clemon's lane occupied by Dodge's brigade is part of the battlefield hiking trail. Not only has the Park Service failed to place interpretive markers in this area, but it uses Dodge's position as an unsightly dumping ground for sand, gravel, and other maintenance materials.

33. See note 32 above.

34. Map with notes on Pea Ridge, vol. 144, Dodge Papers, and Cummings to his wife, Mar. 14, 1862, Cummings Papers, SHSIDM; Dodge, *Fiftieth Anniversary*, 14.

35. Clark to Price, Mar. 11, 1862, *OR* 8:319; Westlake Memoir, UMC.

36. Musser, "Battle of Pea Ridge"; Clark to Price, Mar. 11, 1862, *OR* 8:319–20.

37. Dodge to Calvin Baldwin and to his brother, Mar. 15, 1862, Dodge Family Papers, DPL; Dodge, *Battle of Atlanta*, 36.

38. Rains to Price, Mar. 20, and Dodge to Carr, Mar. 10, 1862, *OR* 8:327.

39. "Gasconade" letter, St. Louis *Missouri Republican*, Mar. 31, 1862; Dodge to his brother, Mar. 15, 1862, Dodge Family Papers, DPL.

40. Dodge, *Battle of Atlanta*, 32; Dodge to Carr, Mar. 10, 1862, *OR* 8:263.

41. Dodge to Carr and Carr to Curtis, Mar. 10, and Shunk to Carr, Mar. 13, 1862, *OR* 8:263, 261, 252; Dodge, *Battle of Atlanta*, 31–32; A. W. Sanford letter, Indianapolis *Daily Journal*, Mar. 19, 1862.

42. Price to Van Dorn, Mar. 22, and Clark to Price, Mar. 11, 1862, *OR* 8:305, 319; Cummings to his wife, Mar. 14, 1862, Cummings Papers, SHSIDM; Dodge to his sister, Apr. 2, 1862, Dodge Family Papers, DPL.

43. Dodge to Carr, Mar. 10, 1862, *OR* 8:263–64; Smith Memoirs, UMC; Mar. 7, 1862, Mothershead Diary, TSLA; Dodge, *Battle of Atlanta*, 21–22.

44. Dodge to Carr and Carr to Curtis, Mar. 10, 1862, *OR* 8:264, 261. Fifty years after the battle, Dodge incorrectly stated that he formed the 4th Iowa in column and retreated southward along the lane. This was impossible (the lane was blocked by the 5th State Guard Division) and contradicts what he wrote in his official report and in several contemporary letters. Dodge, *Battle of Atlanta*, 22.

45. Clark to Price, Mar. 11, and Rains to Price, Mar. 20, 1862, *OR* 8:319, 327.

46. Dodge to Carr, Mar. 10, 1862, ibid., 264; Cummings to his wife, Mar. 14, 1862, Cummings Papers, SHSIDM; Dodge, *Battle of Atlanta*, 22, 35–36.

47. General Orders No. 26, June 23, 1862, General Orders, NARA; Burns, *4th Missouri Cavalry*, 32; Asboth to Sigel, Mar. 16, 1862, *OR* 8:242; Mathews, "Souvenir," UMC. The troopers of the 4th Missouri Cavalry complained to Asboth and Sigel about Meszaros's cowardly behavior at Leetown and Elkhorn Tavern. Meszaros was arrested and court-martialed but received only a reprimand for disobedience of orders. Curtis

was furious at this "very mild" punishment for "the most serious of military offences." When the Army of the Southwest reached Helena in July, Meszaros resigned and headed north on the first available steamboat. His men felt "unalloyed satisfaction" at his departure. General Orders No. 26, June 23, 1862, General Orders, NARA; Burns, *4th Missouri Cavalry*, 36, 39, 44, 47.

48. Curtis to Halleck, Apr. 1, 1862, *OR* 8:200; Dodge to A. P. Wood, [n.d.], 1866, Dodge Papers, SHSIDM.

49. Maury, "Recollections of Elkhorn," 188; Hunt P. Wilson, "Battle of Elkhorn."

50. Payne, "Battle of Pea Ridge," PRNMP; Curtis to Halleck, Apr. 1, and Dodge to Carr, Mar. 10, 1862, *OR* 8:200, 264; Dodge, *Battle of Atlanta*, 22, 36.

51. Hunt P. Wilson, "Battle of Elkhorn"; Curtis to Halleck, Apr. 1, and Asboth to Sigel, Mar. 16, 1862, *OR* 8:200–201, 241; Hesse, "Battle of Pea Ridge," MHS; Mathews, "Souvenir," UMC; Curtis to his brother, Mar. 13, 1862, Curtis Papers, HL.

52. Curtis to Halleck, Apr. 1, 1862, *OR* 8:201. Maury believed that if the Confederates had continued to press the Federals, they might have won the battle that night. He declared that "the cessation of our attack then was a fatal error." Maury, "Recollections of Elkhorn," 189.

53. Letter from unidentified 36th Illinois soldier, Chicago *Tribune*, Mar. 24, 1862; Curtis to Halleck, Apr. 1, 1862, *OR* 8:201.

CHAPTER ELEVEN

1. McGugin, "Extracts from a Report," 1(1):340–41; Forman, *Western Sanitary Commission*, 28–32; "Omega" letter, Chicago *Tribune*, Apr. 11, 1862.

2. Hunt P. Wilson, "Battle of Elkhorn"; Kennerly, *Persimmon Hill*, 242; Sam Black, *Soldier's Recollections*, 8.

3. Johnson to his wife, Mar. 27, 1862, Johnson Letters, UMC; Ford Reminiscences, MHS.

4. Mathews, "Souvenir," UMC.

5. Gammage, *Camp, Bivouac, and Battle Field*, 27–28.

6. Ibid.

7. Mathews, "Souvenir," UMC.

8. Stewart, "Battle of Pea Ridge," 189; Smith Memoirs, UMC.

9. Pike to Van Dorn, Mar. 14, 1862, *OR* 8:290; Fitzhugh, *Cannon Smoke*, 164; Mar. 7, 1862, Reynolds diary, Reynolds Papers, UAF.

10. Watson, *Confederate Army*, 304; Tunnard, *Southern Record*, 135.

11. Greer to Van Dorn, Mar. 19, 1862, *OR* 8:294; Rose, *Ross's Texas Brigade*, 59–60; Sparks, *War Between the States*, 176–77.

12. Lale, "Boy Bugler," 159–61.

13. Harding, "Reminiscences"; Lale, "Boy Bugler," 161; Sparks, *War Between the States*, 177. Presumably Van Dorn's ambulance was engaged in transporting the wounded.

14. Greer to Van Dorn, Mar. 19, and Lane to Greer, Mar. 18, 1862, *OR* 8:294, 300;

Worley, *War Memoirs*, 10–11; Watson, *Confederate Army*, 304–5; Barron, *Lone Star Defenders*, 71–72.

15. Ruyle Memoir, UMR; Frost to Price, Mar. 19, 1862, *OR* 8:324.

16. Ephraim M. Anderson, *Memoirs*, 172; Smith Memoirs, UMC; Harding, "Reminiscences"; Hunt P. Wilson, "Battle of Elkhorn."

17. Harding, "Reminiscences."

18. Green to Price, Mar. 19, Pike to Van Dorn, Mar. 14, and Stone to Van Dorn, Mar. 12, 1862, *OR* 8:290, 317, 303–4.

19. Hoffman to [Sigel], Mar. 14, and Little to Price, Mar. 18, 1862, ibid., 238, 309; Harding, "Reminiscences."

20. Cummings to his wife, Mar. 14, 1862, Cummings Papers, SHSIDM; Dodge to his sister, [Apr. 2, 1862], Dodge Family Papers, DPL; Carr to his father, Mar. 18, 1862, Carr Papers, USAMHI.

21. Crabtree, "Recollections," 221; Voelkner to his parents, Mar. 18, 1862, Voelkner Papers, UMC; St. Louis *Daily Missouri Democrat*, Mar. 18, 1862; Ketzle Memoir, Mullins Collection, Wayne, N.J.; Burns, *4th Missouri Cavalry*, 32.

22. Curtis to Halleck, Apr. 1, 1862, *OR* 8:201.

23. Fayel, "Curtis' Withdrawal"; Knox, *Camp-Fire*, 141; New York *Herald*, Mar. 19, 1862.

24. Knox, *Camp-Fire*, 141.

25. Bussey, "Pea Ridge Campaign," 16; Hess, "Asboth," 181–91. Asboth's conduct on the night of Mar. 7 was consistent with his erratic behavior at other times in his Civil War career.

26. See note 25 above.

27. John W. Noble, "Battle of Pea Ridge," 238. Noble stated that Asboth accompanied him to Curtis's tent; Bussey declared that Asboth remained behind at the 3rd Iowa Cavalry's camp. Bussey's account is more convincing.

28. Bussey, "Pea Ridge Campaign," 16–17.

29. Ibid., 17; Asboth to Curtis, Mar. 8, 1862, *OR* 8:239.

30. Dodge to A. P. Wood, [n.d.] 1866, Dodge Papers, SHSIDM.

31. Sigel to Curtis, Mar. 15, 1862, *OR* 8:212–13; Sigel, "Pea Ridge Campaign," 325.

32. See note 31 above.

33. Sigel to Curtis, Mar. 15, Osterhaus to Curtis, Mar. 14, and Greusel to Osterhaus, Mar. 12, 1862, *OR* 8:212–13, 219, 226; Mar. 7, 1862, Kircher diary, Engelmann-Kircher Collection, ISHL.

34. Sigel, "Pea Ridge Campaign," 325–26.

35. Ibid., 326; Sigel to Curtis, Mar. 15, 1862, *OR* 8:213; Bennett and Haigh, *Thirty-Sixth Illinois*, 161.

36. Sigel, "Pea Ridge Campaign," 326; Sigel to Curtis, Mar. 15, and Curtis to Halleck, Apr. 1, 1862, *OR* 8:213, 201.

37. Voelkner to his parents, Mar. 18, 1862, Voelkner Papers, UMC; Mar. 7, 1862, Kircher diary, Engelmann-Kircher Collection, ISHL; Bennett and Haigh, *Thirty-Sixth Illinois*, 161–62.

38. Davis to Curtis, Mar. 16, 1862, *OR* 8:247.

39. Clarke, *Warfare along the Mississippi*, 30.

40. Davis to Curtis, Mar. 16, and Pattison to Davis, Mar. 10, 1862, *OR* 8:247, 250; Moore, *Rebellion Record*, 4:249.

41. Knobe Memoir, ISL.

42. Mar. 10, 1862, Gordon diary, Gordon Papers, USAMHI.

CHAPTER TWELVE

1. New York *Herald*, Mar. 19, 1862; Kennerly, *Persimmon Hill*, 242.

2. Van Dorn made contradictory statements regarding his intentions on March 8. Shortly after Pea Ridge he stated that when he saw the Federals "in a new and strong position, offering battle[,] ... I made my dispositions at once to accept the gage." A few days later, however, he claimed that "the strong position of the enemy" left him "no alternative but to retire from the contest" and that he fought "for the purpose only of getting off the field without the danger of a panic." The initial statement sounds most like classic Van Dorn: belligerent and confident. Van Dorn to Johnston, Mar. 9, to Bragg, Mar. 27, and to Benjamin, Mar. 18, 1862, *OR* 8:284, 281–82.

3. Jines, "Civil War Diary," 17; Mar. 8, 1862, Reynolds diary, Reynolds Papers, UAF; Rosser to Price, Mar. 21, Pike to Van Dorn, Mar. 14, and Little to Price, Mar. 18, 1862, *OR* 8:313, 290, 309.

4. Greer to Van Dorn, Mar. 19, 1862, *OR* 8:294; Tunnard, *Southern Record*, 139.

5. Osterhaus to Sigel, Mar. 14, and Sigel to Curtis, Mar. 15, 1862, *OR* 8:219, 214; Sigel, "Pea Ridge Campaign," 1:328.

6. Mar. 10, 1862, Gordon diary, Gordon Papers, USAMHI; Ketzle Memoir, Mullins Collection, Wayne, N.J.; St. Louis *Missouri Republican*, Mar. 23, 1862; Davis to Curtis, Mar. 16, and White to Davis, Mar. 11, 1862, *OR* 8:247, 254–55.

7. Knobe Memoir, ISL; Mar. 10, 1862, Gordon diary, Gordon Papers, USAMHI; Truman, "Battle of Elk Horn," 170; Jacob C. Hansel letter, Peoria (Ill.) *Daily Transcript*, Mar. 31, 1862; Little to Price, Mar. 18, Davis to Curtis, Mar. 16, and Pattison to Davis, Mar. 10, 1862, *OR* 8:309, 247–48, 250.

8. Ketzle Memoir, Mullins Collection, Wayne, N.J. The Park Service has placed several cannons in Ruddick's field to represent Tull's battery, but they are too close to Telegraph Road.

9. Herr, *Episodes*, 74–75; Clarke, *Warfare along the Mississippi*, 31; Davis to Curtis, Mar. 16, Pattison to Davis, Mar. 10, White to Davis and Knobelsdorff to Osterhaus, Mar. 11, 1862, *OR* 8:247–48, 250–51, 254–55, 225.

10. Vandever to Carr, Mar. 13, 1862, *OR* 8:267.

11. Mar. 8, 1862, Dysart Diary, PRNMP.

12. Knobe Memoir, ISL; St. Louis *Missouri Republican*, Mar. 23, 1862.

13. Osterhaus to Sigel, Mar. 14, and Sigel to Curtis, Mar. 15, 1862, *OR* 8:219, 214; Mar. 8, 1862, Dysart Diary, PRNMP.

14. Curtis to Halleck, Apr. 1, 1862, *OR* 8:202.

15. Voelkner to his parents, Mar. 18, 1862, Voelkner Papers, UMC.

16. Sigel to Curtis, Mar. 15, Osterhaus to Sigel, Mar. 14, and Asboth to Sigel, Mar. 16, 1862, *OR* 8:214, 219–20, 242–43.

17. Mar. 8, 1862, Dysart Diary, PRNMP.

18. Mar. 8, 1862, Mothershead Diary, TSLA; Douglas, *Douglas's Texas Battery*, 185.

19. Cooper and Worley, "Letters," 464; Bennett and Haigh, *Thirty-Sixth Illinois*, 166; Mar. 8, 1862, Kircher diary, Engelmann-Kircher Collection, ISHL; Voelkner to his parents, Mar. 18, 1862, Voelkner Papers, UMC; Lathrop, *Fifty-Ninth Illinois*, 96; Herr, *Episodes*, 371; Burns, *4th Missouri Cavalry*, 33.

20. Burns, *4th Missouri Cavalry*, 33. Adjutant Noble of the 3rd Iowa Cavalry, a staunch member of the Iowa clique and no friend of Sigel, nevertheless asserted that the German general had a "quick eye and clear apprehension for advantageous positions for artillery." John W. Noble, "Battle of Pea Ridge," 239. The Park Service has placed five unidentified cannons, presumably representing Welfley's Independent Missouri Battery, atop the knoll.

21. Bennett and Haigh, *Thirty-Sixth Illinois*, 165; Ingersoll, *Iowa and the Rebellion*, 154.

22. Fitzhugh, *Cannon Smoke*, 164, 171, 172, 185–86; James P. Douglas letter, Tyler (Tex.) *Reporter*, [Mar. or Apr. 1862]; Douglas, *Douglas's Texas Battery*, 186.

23. Truman, "Battle of Elk Horn," 170.

24. Fitzhugh, *Cannon Smoke*, 164, 173; Maury, "Recollections of Elkhorn," 191–92; Harding, "Reminiscences"; Little to Price, Mar. 18, 1862, *OR* 8:310; Hunt P. Wilson, "Battle of Elkhorn." After the battle Hart's Arkansas Battery was disbanded for "shameful conduct in the presence of the enemy," and its cannons were reassigned to MacDonald's St. Louis Battery. Eight enlisted men of the battery were exonerated from the general censure. General Orders No. 15, July 17, 1862, *OR* 8:330.

25. Smith Memoirs, UMC; Payne, "Battle of Pea Ridge," PRNMP.

26. Sigel to Curtis, Mar. 15, 1862, *OR* 8:214; Mar. 8, 1862, Bennett diary, Bennett Papers, UMR. A small observation pavilion located atop the rocky promontory offers a superb view of the March 8 battleground from the Confederate perspective. The massive stone formations below the pavilion are now partially obscured by trees. Reforestation began soon after the battle, due to the depopulation of the area. When Sigel returned to Pea Ridge in 1887, he noticed that "the rocky summits of Big Mountain" no longer were "discernible from the fields below." Sigel, "Pea Ridge Campaign," 1:329n.

27. Sigel to Curtis, Mar. 15, Asboth to Sigel, Mar. 16, Rosser to Price, Mar. 21, 1862, and Hughes to Price, [Mar. ?, 1862], *OR* 8:214, 243, 313, 315; Hunt P. Wilson, "Battle of Elkhorn"; Tunnard, *Southern Record*, 136; Burns, *4th Missouri Cavalry*, 34.

28. Curtis to Halleck, Apr. 1, Carr to Curtis and Dodge to Carr, Mar. 10, and Hayden to Vandever, Mar. 9, 1862, *OR* 8:202, 262, 264, 269; Crabtree, "Recollections," 222.

29. Squires Map, PRNMP; Hoffman to Sigel, Mar. 14, 1862, *OR* 8:238; Fitzhugh, *Cannon Smoke*, 174.

30. "Union" letter, Davenport (Iowa) *Daily Democrat and News*, Apr. 2, 1862; Clark, "Battle of Pea Ridge," 365; H. N. Frisbie letter, Chicago *Evening Journal*, Apr. 5, 1862; Cummings to his wife, Mar. 14, 1862, Cummings Papers, SHSIDM; Jines,

"Civil War Diary," 17; James P. Douglas letter, Tyler (Tex.) *Reporter*, [Mar. or Apr. 1862].

31. McWhiney and Jamieson, *Attack and Die*, 60, 67, 116–25.

32. Sigel to Curtis, Mar. 15, 1862, *OR* 8:214–15; Sigel, "Pea Ridge Campaign," 1:329. A recent characterization of Sigel's tactics as an "Indian rush" of skirmishers is ridiculously inaccurate. Paddy Griffith, *Battle Tactics*, 156.

33. Curtis to Halleck, Apr. 1, and Osterhaus to Curtis, Mar. 14, 1862, *OR* 8:202, 220; Mar. 8, 1862, Dysart Diary, PRNMP; Crabtree, "Recollections," 222.

34. Crabtree, "Recollections," 223; Curtis to Halleck, Apr. 1, 1862, *OR* 8:202.

35. Dodge to his sister, [Apr. 2, 1862], Dodge Family Papers, DPL; Mar. 10, 1862, Gordon diary, Gordon Papers, USAMHI; Burns, *4th Missouri Cavalry*, 33.

36. Green to Price, Mar. 19, 1862, *OR* 8:290.

37. Hartje, *Van Dorn*, 159.

38. Van Dorn to Bragg, Mar. 27, and Green to Price, Mar. 19, 1862, *OR* 8:284, 290; Maury, "Recollections of Elkhorn," 188, 190; Harding, "Reminiscences"; Mar. 8, 1862, Hoskin Diary, UMC.

39. Bevier, *First and Second Missouri*, 107; Smith Memoirs, UMC.

40. Van Dorn to Bragg, Mar. 27, Greer to Van Dorn, Mar. 19, Little to Price, Mar. 18, and Rosser to Price, Mar. 21, 1862, *OR* 8:284, 294, 310, 313; Maury, "Recollections of Elkhorn," 189.

CHAPTER THIRTEEN

1. Sigel to Curtis, Mar. 15, 1862, *OR* 8:214–15.

2. Mar. 8, 1862, Reynolds diary, Reynolds Papers, UAF; Clark, "Battle of Pea Ridge," 365; Silas Miller and Merritt L. Joslyn letters, Aurora (Ill.) *Beacon*, Mar. 27 and Apr. 10, 1862.

3. Benson, *Soldier's Diary*, 13.

4. Mar. 8, 1862, Bennett diary, Bennett Papers, UMR; Bennett and Haigh, *Thirty-Sixth Illinois*, 167–68; Clark, "Battle of Pea Ridge," 365; Silas Miller letter, Aurora (Ill.) *Beacon*, Mar. 27, 1862; Harwood, *Pea Ridge Campaign*, 20. The downhill portion of the park tour road, just below the observation pavilion, cuts across the slope where the 36th Illinois ascended Big Mountain. A hiking trail from Ford Road to the pavilion approximates the regiment's line of advance; the trail continues down the eastern face of Big Mountain to Elkhorn Tavern. The pavilion is located roughly in the center of the area devastated by the Federal cannonade.

5. Coler to Osterhaus, Mar. 9, 1862, *OR* 8:222–23; Henry Voelkner to his parents, Mar. 18, 1862, Voelkner Papers, UMC; Ephraim M. Anderson, *Memoirs*, 177–78.

6. Wangelin to [Greusel], [Mar. ?, 1862], *OR* 8:229; Bek, "Civil War Diary," 321; Mar. 8, 1862, Kircher diary, Engelmann-Kircher Collection, ISHL.

7. Wangelin to [Greusel], [Mar. ?], and Little to Price, Mar. 18, 1862, *OR* 8:229, 310; Jacob Kaercher letter, Belleville (Ill.) *Advocate*, Mar. 13, 1896; Silas Miller and Merritt L. Joslyn letters, Aurora (Ill.) *Beacon*, Mar. 27 and Apr. 10, 1862; Ephraim M. Ander-

son, *Memoirs*, 178.

8. Pattison to Davis, Mar. 10, 1862, *OR* 8:251; Mar. 8, 1862, Herrington Diary, USAMHI. The authors have added punctuation and capitalization to Herrington's graphic but ungrammatical account.

9. Eugene B. Payne, *37th Illinois*, 11. That morning Curtis finally permitted the five companies of the 8th Indiana and the three cannons of the 1st Indiana Battery to abandon the Little Sugar Creek fortifications. The Hoosiers hurried up Telegraph Road but arrived too late to participate in the final charge. Pattison to Davis, Mar. 10, 1862, *OR* 8:251.

10. George R. Bell letter, Chicago *Evening Journal*, Apr. 5, 1862; Eugene B. Payne letter, Waukegan (Ill.) *Weekly Gazette*, Mar. 29, 1862.

11. Little to Price, Mar. 18, and Frost to Price, Mar. 19, 1862, *OR* 8:310, 324; Payne, "Battle of Pea Ridge," PRNMP; Mar. 8, 1862, Mothershead Diary, TSLA.

12. George R. Bell letter, Chicago *Evening Journal*, Apr. 5, 1862; Frost to Price, Mar. 19, 1862, *OR* 8:324.

13. Little to Price, Mar. 18, 1862, *OR* 8:310–11; Smith Memoirs, UMC; White, "Sketch of Colonel Rives," MHS; Maury, "Recollections of Elkhorn," 189; Ash to his fiancée, Mar. 11, 1862, Ash Papers, USAMHI. The 37th Illinois may have captured a flag from the 16th Arkansas or one of Little's Missouri regiments, though there is no mention of this in any official correspondence. Mullins, *Fremont Rifles*, 75, 427n.

14. Mar. 8, 1862, Mothershead Diary, TSLA; Musser, "Battle of Pea Ridge"; Greer to Van Dorn, Mar. 19, Lane to Greer, Mar. 18, and Rains to Price, Mar. 20, 1862, *OR* 8:294, 300, 328; Barron, *Lone Star Defenders*, 71–72; Lale, "Boy Bugler," 162.

15. Frost to Price, Mar. 19, and Greene to Price, Mar. 20, 1862, *OR* 8:324, 326; Mar. 8, 1862, Herrington Diary, USAMHI; Henry N. Frisbie letter, Chicago *Evening Journal*, Apr. 5, 1862; Jacob Kaercher letter, Belleville (Ill.) *Advocate*, Mar. 13, 1896.

16. Hunt P. Wilson, "Battle of Elkhorn"; Payne, "Battle of Pea Ridge," PRNMP; Harding, "Reminiscences."

17. Hunt P. Wilson, "Battle of Elkhorn"; Pike to Van Dorn, Mar. 14, 1862, *OR* 8:290–91; Pike letter, Little Rock *Arkansas State Gazette*, June 28, 1862.

18. Hunt P. Wilson, "Battle of Elkhorn"; Little to Price, Mar. 18, 1862, *OR* 8:310–11; Douglas, *Douglas's Texas Battery*, 186; Fayel, "Second Day at Pea Ridge."

19. Pike to Van Dorn, Mar. 14, 1862, *OR* 8:290–91; Pike letter, Little Rock *Arkansas State Gazette*, June 28, 1862; Fitzhugh, *Cannon Smoke*, 162, 166; Hunt P. Wilson, "Battle of Elkhorn."

20. Greusel to Osterhaus, Mar. 12, 1862, *OR* 8:227.

21. Mar. 8, 1862, Bennett diary, Bennett Papers, UMR; Voelkner to his parents, Mar. 18, 1862, Voelkner Papers, UMC; Mar. 8, 1862, Rogers Journal, SHSIDM.

22. Davis to Curtis, Mar. 16, Pattison to Davis, Mar. 10, and White to Davis, Mar. 11, 1862, *OR* 8:248, 251, 255; Dodge to A. P. Wood, [n.d.] 1866, Dodge Papers, SHSIDM.

23. Curtis to his brother, Mar. 13, 1862, Curtis Papers, HL; Curtis to his wife, Mar. 10, 1862, Curtis Papers, SHSIDM.

24. Bennett and Haigh, *Thirty-Sixth Illinois*, 168; Clarke, *Warfare along the Mississippi*, 32; Marshall, *Twenty-Second Indiana*, 20.

25. Silas Miller letter, Aurora (Ill.) *Beacon*, Mar. 27, 1862.

26. Jacob Kaercher letter, Belleville (Ill.) *Advocate*, Mar. 13, 1896; Bennett and Haigh, *Thirty-Sixth Illinois*, 168.

27. Curtis to his wife, Mar. 10, 1862, Curtis Papers, SHSIDM; Curtis to his brother, Mar. 13, 1862, Curtis Papers, HL; Curtis to Halleck, Apr. 1, 1862, *OR* 8:202.

28. Pike to Van Dorn, Mar. 14, 1862, *OR* 8:291; Pike letter, Little Rock *Arkansas State Gazette*, June 28, 1862; Hunt P. Wilson, "Battle of Elkhorn." The men of the 17th Arkansas fled so precipitously that they left their regimental flag by the side of the road in Cross Timber Hollow. Burbridge's Missourians retrieved the banner and carried it back to Van Buren. When the Arkansans attempted to recover their flag, the Missourians "were loath to give it up," arguing that "men who would throw away their colors did not deserve any." Van Dorn had to issue two emphatic orders before the flag was handed over. Harding, "Reminiscences."

29. Crabtree, "Recollections," 223–24; Curtis to Halleck, Apr. 1, and Sigel to Curtis, Mar. 15, 1862, *OR* 8:202, 215.

30. Crabtree, "Recollections," 223–24; Bowen to Curtis, Mar. 10, and Little to Price, Mar. 18, 1862, *OR* 8:270, 311; Burns, *4th Missouri Cavalry*, 34; Hunt P. Wilson, "Battle of Elkhorn"; Douglas, *Douglas's Texas Battery*, 186.

31. Douglas, *Douglas's Texas Battery*, 186; James P. Douglas letter, Tyler (Tex.) *Reporter*, [Mar. or Apr. 1862]; Pike letter, Little Rock *Arkansas State Gazette*, June 28, 1862; Pike to Van Dorn, Mar. 14, 1862, *OR* 8:292.

32. Pike to Van Dorn, Mar. 14, Stone to Van Dorn, Apr. 14, and Green to Price, Mar. 21, 1862, *OR* 8:292, 304, 317–18; Harding, "Reminiscences."

33. Curtis to Halleck, Apr. 1, and Sigel to Curtis, Mar. 15, 1862, *OR* 8:202, 215.

34. Voelkner to his parents, Mar. 18, 1862, Voelkner Papers, UMC; John M. Turnbull letter, Monmouth (Ill.) *Atlas*, Mar. 28, 1862; Mar. 8, 1862, Bennett diary, Bennett Papers, UMR; Mar. 8, 1862, Kircher diary, Engelmann-Kircher Collection, ISHL; "Gasconade" letter, St. Louis *Missouri Republican*, Mar. 23, 1862. One plausible estimate places the number of Confederates captured in Cross Timber Hollow at between three hundred and four hundred. Bennett and Haigh, *Thirty-Sixth Illinois*, 170.

35. Dodge to A. P. Wood, [n.d.], 1866, Dodge Papers, SHSIDM; Dodge to C. Baldwin, Mar. 15, 1862, Dodge Family Papers, DPL; "Gasconade" letter, St. Louis *Missouri Republican*, Mar. 23, 1862; Sparks Memoir, Herrick-Reasoner-Milnor-Sparks Family Papers, ISHL; Mar. 8, 1862, Boyle Journal, SHSIDM. Dodge later claimed that he discovered the rebels were retreating on Huntsville Road and pursued them for miles with his brigade. This sort of exaggeration is typical of much of Dodge's voluminous postwar writings about his Civil War career.

36. Fayel, "Second Day at Pea Ridge"; Sigel to Curtis, Mar. 8, 1862, Curtis Papers, SHSIDM; Curtis to Sigel, Mar. 8, and Sigel to Curtis, Mar. 15, 1862, *OR* 8:598, 215.

37. Sigel to Curtis, Mar. [8], and Curtis to his wife, Mar. 10, 1862, Curtis Papers, SHSIDM; Bussey, "Pea Ridge Campaign," 21–22; Dodge to A. P. Wood, [n.d.], 1866, Dodge Papers, SHSIDM.

38. Curtis to Sigel, Mar. 8, and Osterhaus to Curtis, Mar. 14, 1862, *OR* 8:598, 220. On March 9 Curtis ordered the three offending officers to report to him for a lecture on

obedience of orders. Special Orders No. 108, Mar. 9, 1862, ibid., 601.

39. Knobelsdorff to Osterhaus, Mar. 11, and Pike to Van Dorn, Mar. 14, 1862, ibid., 255, 292.

40. Osterhaus to Curtis, Mar. 14, and Asboth to Sigel, Mar. 16, 1862, ibid., 220, 242; Osterhaus, "What I Saw of the War," 5, BPL.

41. Sam Black, *Soldier's Recollection*, 10; Bussey, "Pea Ridge Campaign," 23.

42. Van Dorn to Bragg, Mar. 27, and Lane to Greer, Mar. 18, 1862, *OR* 8:284, 300.

43. Wilson Memoir, UMC; Calkin, "Elkhorn to Vicksburg," 14; Payne, "Battle of Pea Ridge," PRNMP; Mar. 8, 1862, Mothershead Diary, TSLA; Smith Memoirs, UMC.

44. Jines, "Civil War Diary," 18; Watson, *Confederate Army*, 311; Hollinsworth, "Battle of Elkhorn," 138; Wilson Memoir, UMC; Mar. 8, 1862, Mothershead Diary, TSLA; Carter, "Short Sketch," UMC; Ford Reminiscences, MHS.

45. Stewart, "Battle of Pea Ridge," 190; David Pierson to [William Pierson], [Mar. ?, 1862], Pierson Family Papers, TU; Truman, "Battle of Elk Horn," 170. After being released from arrest, Rains demanded a court-martial and was temporarily relieved from duty. He was reinstated on April 8. Van Dorn to Price, Mar. 18, 1862, Letters and Telegrams Sent, NARA; Price to Rains, Mar. 19, 1862, Price Collection, CHS.

46. Cater, "*As It Was,*" 134; Mar. 8, 1862, Reynolds diary, Reynolds Papers, UAF; Tunnard, *Southern Record*, 145; Ruyle Memoir, UMR; Barron, *Lone Star Defenders*, 73.

47. Smith Memoirs, UMC; Donat, "Diary of Joseph Sanders," 7.

CHAPTER FOURTEEN

1. Van Dorn to Johnston, Mar. 9, 1862, *OR* 8:281. The transcription in the *OR* erroneously states that the Confederate army was fourteen miles *west* of Fayetteville.

2. Special Orders No. [?], [Mar. 9, 1862], General and Division Orders, NARA.

3. Van Dorn to Stone, Mar. 12, 1862, *OR* 8:777–78; Kerr, *Ross' Texas Cavalry Brigade*, 15.

4. Green to Price, Mar. 21, 1862, *OR* 8:317–18. While at Elm Springs on March 9, Green received two messages directing him to return to the battlefield with the ammunition trains. It is not known who sent these messages. Ibid.; P. R. Smith letter, Washington (Ark.) *Telegraph*, Apr. 2, 1862.

5. Green to Price, Mar. 21, 1862, *OR* 8:318; Lemke, *Journals*; Pike to Van Dorn, Mar. 15, 1862, Mesker Collection, MHS.

6. Baxter, *Pea Ridge*, 98–101; Banes, "Tebbetts Family History," 19.

7. Banes, "Tebbetts Family History," 19; Mar. 9, 1862, Graves Diary, UT.

8. Mar. 12, 1862, Graves Diary, UT.

9. Ford Reminiscences, MHS; Ruyle Memoir, UMR.

10. Donat, "Diary of Joseph Sanders," 7; Ruyle Memoir, UMR.

11. Ruyle Memoir, UMR; Lale, "Boy Bugler," 162; Dacus, *Reminiscences*, 3.

12. Lane to Greer, Mar. 18, 1862, *OR* 8:300–301; Barron, *Lone Star Defenders*, 74–75.

13. Fitzhugh, *Cannon Smoke*, 162, 165; James P. Douglas letter, Tyler (Tex.) *Reporter*, [Mar. or Apr. 1862]; Douglas, *Douglas's Texas Battery*, 183.

14. Mar. 9, 1862, Reynolds diary, Reynolds Papers, UAF; Donat, "Diary of Joseph Sanders," 7.

15. Carter, "Short Sketch," UMC.

16. Smith Memoirs, UMC; Watson, *Confederate Army*, 319–21. Much of the route of the Confederate retreat between Pea Ridge and State Highway 16, due east of Fayetteville, is now submerged beneath Beaver Lake.

17. Coleman to his parents, Mar. 18, 1862, Coleman-Hayter Letters, UMC; Watson, *Confederate Army*, 320. U.S. 71 generally follows the route of the retreat from just south of the Fayetteville airport, where the highway first crosses the western fork of the White River, to modern-day Winslow.

18. Ruyle Memoir, UMR; Lemke, *Journals*; Mar. 14, 1862, Graves Diary, UT; Mar. 13, 1862, Reynolds diary, Reynolds Papers, UAF. The most difficult part of the retreat was south of modern-day Winslow. Here the old road veers west from U.S. 71 and follows Frog Bayou down to the Arkansas River.

19. Barron, *Lone Star Defenders*, 73–74; Watson, *Confederate Army*, 320; Lemke, *Journals*; Cater, "*As It Was*," 137. The only comparable episode in the Civil War was the retreat of the Confederate Army of New Mexico across the desert after the battle of Glorieta Pass in 1862.

20. Smith Memoirs, UMC; Ruyle Memoir, UMR; Jines, "Civil War Diary," 18; Wilson Memoir, UMC. The rendezvous with the relief train took place near modern-day Mountainburg.

21. Tunnard, *Southern Record*, 139, 146–47; Watson, *Confederate Army*, 338; Ephraim M. Anderson, *Memoirs*, 178.

22. Ruyle Memoir, UMR; Watson, *Confederate Army*, 340–41; Douglas, *Douglas's Texas Battery*, 189.

23. Rufus K. Garland letter, Washington (Ark.) *Telegraph*, Apr. 2, 1862; Kerr, *Ross' Texas Cavalry Brigade*, 15; Lale, *Civil War Letters*, 50.

24. Lemke, *Journals*; Ross to D. R. Tinsley, Mar. 13, 1862, Ross Family Papers, BU.

25. James P. Douglas letter, Tyler (Tex.) *Reporter*, [Mar. or Apr. 1862]; Wilson Memoir, UMC.

26. Mar. 18 and 19, 1862, Mothershead Diary, TSLA; Ross to D. R. Tinsley and to Elizabeth Ross, Mar. 13, 1862, Ross Family Papers, BU; Donat, "Diary of Joseph Sanders," 7.

27. Pierson to [William Pierson], [Mar. ?, 1862], Pierson Family Papers, TU; Billingsley, "'Such Is War,'" 251; Douglas, *Douglas's Texas Battery*, 186; W. H. Crawford to Terrissa, Mar. 9, 1862, Shahan Family Papers, TSLA; Loughborough to his wife, Mar. 18, 1862, Loughborough Letters, AHC.

28. Curtis to Halleck, Mar. 9, Bussey to Curtis, Mar. 14, Bowen to Curtis, Mar. 12, and Knobelsdorff to Osterhaus, Mar. 11, 1862, *OR* 8:192, 235, 270; Bussey, "Pea Ridge Campaign," 22; Mar. 9, 1862, Noble Diary, SHSIIC; Mar. 9, 1862, Boyle Journal, SHSIDM.

29. Sigel to Curtis, Mar. 9, 1862, Curtis Papers, SHSIDM; Mar. 9, 1862, Bennett diary,

Bennett Papers, UMR; Sigel to Curtis, Mar. 15, and Osterhaus to Curtis, Mar. 14, 1862, *OR* 8:215, 220–21.

30. Curtis to Halleck, Mar. 10, 1862, Curtis Papers, SHSIDM; Van Dorn to Curtis, Mar. 9, 1862, *OR* 8:193–94; Mar. 9, 1862, Herrington Diary, USAMHI; Fayel, "Second Day at Pea Ridge"; Mar. 9, 1862, Holman Diary, SHSIIC.

31. Curtis to Halleck, Mar. 10, 1862, *OR* 8:191–93.

32. Curtis or a member of his staff made several minor arithmetical errors in compiling the casualty list. Corrected figures are used in the text. Curtis to Halleck, Apr. 1, 1862, ibid., 203–6. A federal surgeon counted 968 instead of 972 Federal wounded. McGugin, "Extracts from a Report," 341. A week after the battle the Federal death toll had risen to at least 212. Dodge to C. Baldwin, Mar. 15, 1862, Dodge Family Papers, DPL.

33. Van Dorn to Benjamin, Mar. 18, and to Bragg, Mar. 27, and Curtis to Halleck, Mar. 11, 1862, *OR* 8:282, 285, 194; Mar. 12, 1862, Noble Diary, SHSIIC; Mar. 19, 1862, Dysart Diary, PRNMP; Mar. 18, 1862, Holman Diary, SHSIIC; Samuel Edwards letter, Richmond (Ind.) *Palladium*, Apr. 6, 1862; M. G. Galloway letter, Little Rock *Arkansas True Democrat*, June 12 and Mar. 27, 1862; Mar. 12 and 13, 1862, Rogers Journal, SHSIDM. William Watson of the 3rd Louisiana was convinced Van Dorn falsified his losses to conceal the magnitude of the Confederate defeat at Pea Ridge. Watson, *Confederate Army*, 344.

34. Curtis to his brother, Mar. 13, 1862, Curtis Papers, HL; Curtis to Halleck, Mar. 13, Osterhaus to Curtis, Mar. 14, Greusel to Osterhaus, Mar. 12, Van Dorn to Benjamin, Mar. 18, and to Bragg, Mar. 27, Rosser to Price, Mar. 21, 1862, and Hughes to Price, [Mar. ?, 1862], *OR* 8:195, 220, 227, 237, 282, 285, 313, 315; Special Orders No. 27, Mar. 18, 1862, Special Orders, Van Dorn's Command, NARA.

35. Knobelsdorff to Osterhaus, Mar. 11, and Curtis to Halleck, Mar. 15, 1862, *OR* 8:225, 618; Knobelsdorff to Curtis, Mar. 11, 1862, Letters Received, NARA; letter from unidentified 44th Illinois soldier, Mar. 18, 1862, Jump Papers, IHS; Mar. 11, 1862, Bennett diary, Bennett Papers, UMR; Curtis to his brother, Mar. 13, 1862, Curtis Papers, HL.

36. General Orders No. 107, Mar. 9, 1862, General Orders, NARA; Mar. 9, 1862, Herrington Diary, USAMHI; Fayel, "Second Day at Pea Ridge"; Britton, *Memoirs of the Rebellion*, 169.

37. Apr. 4, 1862, Herrington Diary, USAMHI; Marsh to his father, Mar. 21, 1862, Marsh Papers, ISHL; "Correspondent" letter, Chicago *Tribune*, Mar. 29, 1862; Britton, *Memoirs of the Rebellion*, 169; Curtis to his wife, Mar. 10, 1862, Curtis Papers, SHSIDM; Curtis to his wife, Mar. 13, 1862, Letters Sent, NARA. There is a slight irregular terrain feature in the cleared area south of Elkhorn Tavern where the two monuments are located. This may be a trace of one of the Confederate burial trenches.

38. Voelkner to his parents, Mar. 18, 1862, Voelkner Papers, UMC; Mar. 9, 1862, Boyle Journal, SHSIDM; Fayel, "Second Day at Pea Ridge".

39. Forman, *Western Sanitary Commission*, 28–34. Curtis later expressed his thanks to the Western Sanitary Commission for the timely shipment of medical

supplies, saying that "in the destitute condition of our hospitals it seemed like a providential interposition in our behalf." Ibid., 34; Curtis to Halleck, Mar. 24, 1862, *OR* 8:640.

40. William Fithian to his wife, Mar. 29 and 30, 1862, Black Family Papers, ISHL.

41. Mar. 16 and 17, 1862, Holman Diary, SHSIIC; Mar. 12 and 14, 1862, Dysart Diary, PRNMP; Lathrop, *Fifty-Ninth Illinois*, 105; "Omega" letter, Chicago *Tribune*, Apr. 11, 1862; Forman, *Western Sanitary Commission*, 28–32; John M. Turnbull letter, Monmouth (Ill.) *Atlas*, Mar. 28, 1862; Bridges, "Confederate Hero," 233–37. Slack was buried on Roller Ridge near modern-day Gateway; after the war he was reinterred in the Confederate cemetery in Fayetteville. Seamster, "Battlefield Memories," 49.

42. Mar. 10, 1862, Holman Diary, SHSIIC; William H. Kinsman letter, Council Bluffs (Iowa) *Weekly Nonpareil*, Apr. 19, 1862.

43. Mar. 12 and 14, 1862, Holman Diary, SHSIIC; Apr. 27, 1862, Herrington Diary, USAMHI.

44. Curtis to Van Dorn, Mar. 9 and 21, and Van Dorn to Curtis, Mar. 14, 1862, *OR* 8:194, 195, 206–8, ser. 2, 3:398–99; Sigel letter, Chicago *Tribune*, Apr. 3, 1862.

45. Walter L. Brown, "Albert Pike and the Pea Ridge Atrocities"; Fayel, "Second Day at Pea Ridge"; Elias C. Boudinot letter, St. Louis *Missouri Republican*, Jan. 2, 1886.

46. Mar. 10, 1862, Bennett diary, Bennett Papers, UMR; Apr. 4, 1862, Herrington Diary, and Mar. 17, 1862, Seaman Diary, USAMHI; Mar. 9, 1862, Holman Diary, SHSIIC. A graphic description of this section of Pea Ridge as it appeared several months after the battle is in Britton, *Memoirs of the Rebellion*, 170.

47. Curtis to his brother, Mar. 13, 1862, Curtis Papers, HL.

48. Conrad to Sigel, Mar. 13, 1862, *OR* 8:278–79; Bek, "Civil War Diary," 319–20.

49. Sheridan to Curtis, Mar. 5, 1862, Letters Received, NARA.

50. Special Order No. 110, Mar. [10], 1862, General Orders, NARA; Curtis to Halleck, Mar. 10, and to Allen, Mar. 11, 1862, Curtis Papers, SHSIDM.

51. Curtis to Halleck, Mar. 10, 1862, Curtis Papers, SHSIDM; Curtis to Boyd and to English, Mar. 10, 1862, Letters Sent, NARA.

52. Curtis to English, Mar. 18 and 22, and to Halleck, Mar. 22, 1862, Letters Sent, NARA; Curtis to Halleck, Mar. 18, and Halleck to Curtis, Mar. 14 and 19, 1862, *OR* 8:624, 617, 626.

53. Curtis to English, Mar. 22, 1862, Letters Sent, NARA; Curtis to his wife, Mar. 21, 1862, Curtis Papers, SHSIDM.

54. "Union" letter, Davenport (Iowa) *Daily Democrat and News*, Apr. 2, 1862; Special Orders No. 109, Mar. 10, 1862, General Orders, NARA; Curtis to Sigel, Mar. 15, and to Davis, Mar. 20, 1862, Letters Sent, NARA; Curtis to Halleck, Mar. 24, 1862, *OR* 8:640; Davis to Curtis, Mar. 11, and Byron Carr to Curtis and Sigel to Curtis, Mar. 14, 1862, Letters Received, NARA.

55. Curtis to Halleck, Mar. 10, 1862, Curtis Papers, SHSIDM (original italics); Halleck to Curtis, Mar. 7, 1862, *OR* 8:596.

56. Halleck to Curtis, Mar. 19, 1862, *OR* 8:626.

57. Curtis to Halleck, Mar. 10, 1862, Curtis Papers, SHSIDM.

58. Fayel, "Second Day at Pea Ridge"; Voelkner to his parents, Mar. 18, 1862, Voelkner Papers, UMC; Jacob Kaercher letter, Belleville (Ill.) *Advocate*, Mar. 13, 1862; Marsh to his father, Mar. 21, 1862, Marsh Papers, ISHL. It is not known if Curtis did the same with Knox's account of the battle, which is less accurate than Fayel's version and somewhat more favorable to Sigel.

59. McKinney to Curtis, Mar. 15, and Dodge to Curtis, Apr. 5, 1862, Curtis Papers, SHSIDM; Sigel to Curtis, Mar. 24, 1862, and Curtis to Halleck, Apr. 11, 1862, Letters Sent, NARA.

60. Greusel to Fish, Mar. 21, 1862, Sigel Papers, NYHS.

61. Asboth to Sigel, May 27, 1862, ibid.; Apr. 4–6, 1862, Noble Diary, SHSIIC.

62. Curtis to Halleck, Apr. 11, 1862, Letters Sent, NARA.

63. Bussey to Curtis, Mar. 14, 1862, *OR* 8:233–34; Trimble to Edwin M. Stanton, Nov. 30, 1862, Trimble Letters, PRNMP; Byers, *Iowa in War Times*, 121; Bussey to N. B. Baker, Apr. 1, 1862, Civil War Reports, SHSIDM; Apr. 20, 1862, Boyle Journal, SHSIDM; Sept. 5, 1862, Dysart Diary, PRNMP. Bussey's sword is on display at the Iowa State Historical Society in Des Moines. After the war Trimble, a lawyer, specialized in cases involving insanity.

64. Byers, *Iowa in War Times*, 121; Dodge to A. P. Wood, [n.d.], 1866, Dodge Papers, SHSIDM; Dodge to Curtis, Mar. 21, 1862, Letters Received, NARA; Dodge to Williamson, Apr. 2 and 4, 1862, Williamson Papers, SHSIDM.

65. Halleck to McClellan and to Grant, Mar. 10, to Buell, Mar. 13, and to Curtis, Mar. 13, 14, and 19, 1862, *OR* 8:602, 611, 617, 626, 10:27, 33.

CHAPTER FIFTEEN

1. Van Dorn to Johnston and to Benjamin, Mar. 18, 1862, *OR* 8:789–90, 282–83.

2. Van Dorn to Cooper, Mar. 17, 1862, *OR* 8:786–87; Van Dorn to Cooper, Mar. 19, 1862, Letters and Telegrams Sent, and General Orders No. 27, Mar. 20, 1862, General and Division Orders, NARA. Van Dorn complained to his wife that "I have had to command an army almost disorganized and without discipline, staff departments defective, and supplies deficient, the enemy near and threatening, and with all this I have been suffering with chills and fevers again, as I did in Texas. . . . I expect to grow gray before the war is over. I never knew what care was before." Emily Van Dorn Miller, *Soldier's Honor*, 71.

3. Special Orders No. 24, Mar. 17, 1862, Special Orders, Van Dorn's Command, NARA; General Orders No. 27, Apr. 8, and Price to Benjamin, Mar. 19, 1862, *OR* 8:813, 792.

4. Special Orders No. 24, Mar. 17, 1862, Special Orders, Van Dorn's Command, NARA.

5. Fitzhugh, *Cannon Smoke*, 168, 181–82.

6. Van Dorn to Curtis, Mar. 15, 1862, Letters and Telegrams Sent; Curtis to Van Dorn, Mar. 20, 1862, Letters Sent; and Memoranda of an Agreement, Mar. 20, 1862,

Letters Received, NARA. Colonel Mitchell of the 14th Arkansas was not included in this exchange because he and about two dozen other officers had been sent to St. Louis with the bulk of the Confederate prisoners. M. G. Galloway letter, Little Rock *Arkansas True Democrat*, June 12, 1862.

7. Convention on Exchange of Prisoners, Mar. 26, 1862, *OR*, ser. 2, 3:405–6; St. Louis *Missouri Republican*, Apr. 5, 1862; Chicago *Tribune*, Apr. 8, 1862.

8. Van Dorn to Price, Mar. 18, 1862, Letters and Telegrams Sent, NARA.

9. Beauregard to Van Dorn, Feb. 21, 1862, *OR* 7:900–901.

10. Van Dorn to Beauregard, Mar. 16, and to Johnston, Mar. 17, 1862, ibid., 8:784, 787.

11. Van Dorn to Churchill, Mar. 19, 1862, ibid., 791–92; Calkin, "Elkhorn to Vicksburg," 14.

12. Van Dorn letter, Little Rock *Arkansas True Democrat*, Mar. 27, 1862; Van Dorn to Cabell, Mar. 17 and 22, 1862, Letters and Telegrams Sent, NARA; Beauregard to Van Dorn, Mar. 19, Van Dorn to Beauregard, Mar. 21, Van Dorn to Price, Mar. 22, and Special Orders No. 81, Mar. 19, 1862, *OR* 8:791, 796, 798, 793.

13. Connelly, *Army of the Heartland*, 126–42; McDonough, *Shiloh*, 64–70.

14. Johnston to Van Dorn, Mar. 23, and to Davis, Mar. 25, and Beauregard to Van Dorn, Mar. 23, 1862, *OR* 10(2):354, 361.

15. Van Dorn to Price, to Churchill, to Little, and to Cabell, Mar. 25, and to Johnston, Mar. 29, 1862, ibid., 8:802–4.

16. Emily Van Dorn Miller, *Soldier's Honor*, 71; Van Dorn to Price, Mar. 22, and to Frost, Apr. 9, 1862, *OR* 8:798, 816; Fitzhugh, *Cannon Smoke*, 170, 177; Worley, *War Memoirs*, 13.

17. Special Orders No. 39, Apr. 5, 1862, Special Orders, Van Dorn's Command, NARA; Petition to Davis, Apr. 15, 1862, *OR* 13:814–16.

18. Curtis to his daughter, Mar. 26, 1862, Curtis Papers, SHSIDM.

19. Mar. 27, 1862, Curtis Journal, ISHL; Jan. 10, 1862, Noble Diary, SHSIIC.

20. Curtis to his wife, Mar. 27 and 30, and Henry Curtis to his mother, Mar. 27, 1862, Curtis Papers, SHSIDM; Curtis to his brother, Apr. 11, 1862, Curtis Papers, HL.

21. Curtis to Halleck, Mar. 31 and Apr. 4, 1862, *OR* 8:650, 659.

22. Curtis to Davis and to Mills, Apr. 4, 1862, Letters Sent, NARA; Special Orders No. 134, Apr. 4, 1862, *OR* 8:659.

23. Halleck to Curtis and Curtis to Halleck, Apr. 5, and Halleck to Curtis and Curtis to Halleck, Apr. 6, 1862, *OR* 8:661, 662, 664, 665–66.

24. Curtis to Halleck, Apr. 6, 10, and 19, 1862, ibid., 665, 679, 13:363–64.

25. Steele to Halleck, Apr. 13, Halleck to Stanton, Apr. 8, 1862, ibid., 10(2):105, 98–99.

26. Halleck to Steele, Apr. 15, 1862, ibid., 13:362; Carlin to Curtis, Apr. 15, 1862, Letters Received, NARA; Apr. 24, 1862, Curtis Journal, ISHL.

27. Curtis to Winslow, Apr. 18, and to Small, Apr. 27, 1862, Letters Sent, and Allen to Curtis, Apr. 25, 1862, Letters Received, NARA.

28. Apr. 24, 1862, Curtis Journal, ISHL; Carr to Curtis, May 1, 1862, Letters Received, NARA; Curtis to Halleck, May 4, 1862, *OR* 13:64.

29. Curtis to Halleck, May 5 and 6, and Halleck to Curtis, May 2 and 6, 1862, *OR* 13:369–71.

30. Curtis to Halleck, May 10, and Special Orders No. 168, May 9, 1862, ibid., 374–75; Curtis, "Army of the South-West," 7:9–10; May 10, 1862, Curtis Journal, ISHL.

31. Special Orders No. 172, May 13, 1862, *OR* 13:381; Curtis, "Army of the Southwest," 7:10–12.

32. Halleck to Curtis, May 12, 1862, *OR* 13:378.

33. Rector proclamation, Little Rock *Arkansas True Democrat*, May 8, 1862; Roane to Beauregard, May 10, 1862, Roane Letters, AHC; Roane to Van Dorn, May 10, 1862, *OR* 13:827. Rector's flight from the capital prompted sharp criticism from both Little Rock newspapers, one of which sarcastically announced: "We would be glad if some patriotic gentleman would relieve the anxiety of the public by informing it of the locality of the State government." *Arkansas True Democrat*, May 22, 1862; *Arkansas State Gazette*, June 28, 1862.

34. Davis to Van Dorn, May 20, and Van Dorn to Davis and to Roane, May 19 and June 9, 1862, *OR* 13:827–29, 831–32.

35. Special Orders No. 100, May 27, Hindman to Pike, May 31, and to Cooper, June 9, 1862, and June 19, 1863, *OR* 13:829, 934, 832–33, 28–37. Two brief biographies are Roberts, "General Hindman," and Dougan, "Thomas Hindman."

36. General Orders No. 17, June 17, 1862, *OR* 13:835.

37. Curtis to Halleck, May 7 and 12, and to Steele, May 13, 1862, ibid., 371, 379, 380; Osterhaus to Curtis, May 12, 1862, Letters Received, NARA. A detailed inventory of the pontoon train is in an Iron Mountain Railroad receipt, Apr. 7, 1862, Steele Papers, SU.

38. Curtis to Osterhaus, May 13, 1862, Letters Sent, NARA; Curtis to Halleck, May 14 and 19, 1862, *OR* 13:384, 390.

39. Osterhaus to Curtis, May 17 and 18, 1862, Letters Received, NARA.

40. Osterhaus to Curtis, May 18, 1862, ibid.; Curtis to Halleck, May 19, 1862, *OR* 13:392; Curtis to Wood, July 1, 1862, Wood Papers, KSHS.

41. Curtis to Halleck, May 24, Osterhaus to Curtis, May 19, Hassendeuble to Osterhaus, June 1, Kielmansegge to Hassendeuble, May 20, Wilhelmi, Kaegi, Fischer, and Neun to Cramer, May 20 and 21, and affidavits by Schaub, Wurges, Ludwig, and Neun, May 20, 1862, *OR* 13:69–79, ser. 2, 3:558–59; E. W. Rogers and F. M. Chrisman letters, Little Rock *Arkansas True Democrat*, May 22 and 29, 1862; Curtis to Osterhaus, May 20, 1862, Letters Sent, NARA.

42. Winslow and Carr to Curtis, May 21, 1862, Letters Received, NARA.

43. May 20, 1862, Curtis Journal, ISHL (original italics); Carr and Osterhaus to Curtis, May 27, and Curtis to Halleck, May 27 and 30, 1862, *OR* 13:85–88, 399–400.

44. Curtis to Boyd, May 28, 1862, Letters Sent, NARA; Curtis to Halleck, June 5, Halleck to Schofield, June 21, and to Davis and Stanton, June 8, Davis to Welles, June 10, and Allen to Halleck, June 14, 1862, *OR* 13:417–18, 422, 440, 114, 116; Halleck letter, Little Rock *Arkansas State Gazette*, July 12, 1862.

45. Bearss, "White River Expedition," 305–62; Fitch to Quinby, June 19, Halleck to

Curtis, June 24, Curtis to Halleck, June 10, 13, and 25, and to Schofield, June 13 and 17, 1862, *OR* 13:104–5, 116–17, 428, 436, 448; Curtis to Schofield, June 26, 1862, Letters Sent, NARA.

46. Curtis to his brother, June 18, 1862, Curtis Papers, HL.

47. Shea, "Semi-Savage State," 325–26; F. O. W. letter, Aurora (Ill.) *Beacon*, June 12, 1862; Little Rock *Arkansas State Gazette*, July 28, 1862; "One of the People" letter, Little Rock *Arkansas True Democrat*, Sept. 10, 1862.

48. Shea, "Semi-Savage State," 323–24; Little Rock *Arkansas State Gazette*, July 28, 1862. Curtis developed an interesting rationale for his mass emancipations: "I give captured slaves their freedom on the ground that they became captured captives and therefore subject to my disposal instead of a former captor or assignee." May 21, 1862, Curtis Journal, ISHL.

49. Hindman proclamation, Little Rock *Arkansas State Gazette*, June 28, 1862; Hindman to Cooper, June 19, 1863, *OR* 13:37.

50. Steele to Curtis, July 20, Benton to Steele, July 18, Hovey to Steele, July 7, and Wood to Baker, July 15, 1862, *OR* 13:141–48; Metcalf letter of July 15, 1862, Quiner Papers, SHSW; C. E. Lippincott letter, Chicago *Tribune*, July 28, 1862. The Army of the Southwest crossed the Cache River at James Ferry in eastern Woodruff County. The site of the battle is about three miles southeast of the crossing, or three miles northwest of Cotton Plant.

51. Curtis to Halleck, July 14, 1862, Letters Sent, NARA; Hovey to Steele, July 7, 1862, *OR* 13:144–45; July 7, 1862, Curtis Journal, ISHL; Metcalf letter of July 15, 1862, Quiner Papers, SHSW; Wise, "Letters of Flavius Perry," 15. Approximately one hundred dead Confederates were buried in a single mass grave on the battlefield.

52. July 9, 1862, Curtis Journal, ISHL.

53. Love, *Wisconsin in the War*, 595; Curtis to Halleck, July 31, 1862, *OR* 13:525.

54. Snead, "With Price," 2:717–34; Rosecrans, "Corinth," 2:737–57; Hartje, *Van Dorn*, 214–46; Castel, *Sterling Price*, 84–127.

55. Record of Court of Inquiry, Nov. 1, 1862, *OR* 17:415, 459.

56. Hartje, *Van Dorn*, 247–327.

57. Castel, *Sterling Price*, 128–272.

58. Hess, "Confiscation," 56–75; General Order No. 135, Sept. 19, 1862, *OR* 13:653.

59. Markers denoting this reunion are located in the Bragg Reservation atop Missionary Ridge in Chickamauga and Chattanooga National Military Park.

60. Gallaher, "Curtis," 345–58.

61. Curtis, "Army of the Southwest," 7:220–22.

CONCLUSION

1. Frost, "Frost's State Secret."

2. Harwood, *Pea Ridge Campaign*, 6.

3. Dodge, *Battle of Atlanta*, 31, 33; Sheridan, *Personal Memoirs*, 1:132.

4. Clausewitz, *On War*, 119.

5. James F. Harris letter, New Orleans *Commercial Bulletin*, Apr. 16, 1862; Ross to D. R. Tinsley, Mar. 13, 1862, Ross Family Papers, BU.

6. Sigel, "Pea Ridge Campaign," 1:331; Fayel, "Curtis' Withdrawal."

7. Wangelin to [Greusel], [Mar. ?, 1862], *OR* 8:228–29.

8. Clark, "Battle of Pea Ridge," 364.

9. Dodge, *Fiftieth Anniversary*, 63–64.

APPENDIX 1

1. Warner, *Generals in Blue*, 70–71, 116, 353; Hess, "Asboth."

2. Warner, *Generals in Gray*, 118, 131, 189, 240.

3. Tuerck to Kircher, Sept. 30, 1870, Engelmann-Kircher Collection, ISHL.

4. Holmes, *52nd O.V.I.*, 162, 182.

5. Nevins and Thomas, *Diary of George Templeton Strong*, 3:214; Payne to his wife, Apr. 29, 1862, Payne Papers, LFC; Oliver H. P. Scott letter.

6. Curtis to Van Dorn, Mar. 9, 1862, *OR* 8:194; Curtis to Van Dorn, Mar. 21, 1862, in Moore, *Rebellion Record*, 4:264.

7. Curtis to Wade, May 21, 1862, *OR* 8:206; Walter L. Brown, "Albert Pike and the Pea Ridge Atrocities"; Boudinot, "Ross' Men."

8. John W. Noble, "Battle of Pea Ridge," 228.

9. Browne, *Four Years in Secessia*, 93–112; Chicago *Tribune*, Mar. 25, 1862; Curtis, "Army of the South-West," 4:152–54; Belleville (Ill.) *Advocate*, May 16, 1862; St. Louis *Daily Missouri Democrat*, Mar. 22, 1862.

10. Randolph, *Ozark Folksongs*, 2:247–50; "Battle of Pea Ridge," *Historical Review*; Stewart, "Battle of Pea Ridge"; "Battle of Pea Ridge," Folklore Project, UAF.

11. Russell, *Lives and Legends*, 5, 181; Buntline, *Buffalo Bill*, 3–7, 303–7.

12. Rosa, *They Called Him Wild Bill*, 55–57; Eisele, *Real Wild Bill*, 59–63; Wilstach, *Wild Bill Hickock*, 80–82; Russell, *Lives and Legends*, 58. A similar fictional treatment is Dunn, *Scout*, 306–44.

13. Knox, *Lost Army*.

14. Douglas C. Jones, *Elkhorn Tavern*. Another modern fictional treatment is Dee Brown, *Creek Mary's Blood*, 275–81. Pea Ridge plays only a minor part in the story, and Brown's description of the action is not entirely accurate. The plot does not deal much with scalpings despite the fact that the chief characters are Indians.

15. *Harper's Weekly*, Mar. 29, 1862, and Feb. 7, 1863; *Frank Leslie's Illustrated Weekly*, Mar. 29, 1862; Conningham, *Currier & Ives Prints*, 25.

16. Goodrich, "Robert Ormsby Sweeny," 147–54, 156. Sweeny accompanied the Army of the Southwest on the march to Helena and made several interesting sketches along the way.

17. *Oklahoma Passage* aired on the Oklahoma Educational Television Authority in April 1989.

18. Wilson's painting is in the Museum of the Confederacy in Richmond. The center panel is reproduced in Josephy, *War on the Frontier*, 144; the right panel, in

Catton, *American Heritage*, 121. Reasonably accurate prints of the center and left panels are in Sigel, "Pea Ridge Campaign," 1:328, 330. Poor painted copies of all three panels by Sidney King are in the Pea Ridge National Military Park visitor center.

19. The painting of the 37th Illinois is reproduced in Herr, *Episodes*.

20. Houston's painting is reproduced on the dust jacket of Fitzhugh, *Cannon Smoke*.

21. Bach, "Pea Ridge March," CHS.

22. Vincent, *Collected Poems*, 113. A crude poem by a Confederate veteran named W. H. Crawford is in a letter dated Mar. 9, 1862, Shahan Family Papers, TSLA.

23. Edsel Ford, "Return to Pea Ridge." Other modern poems on the battle include Riley, "Pea Ridge Battlefield," and Burrow, *Battle of Pea Ridge*.

24. Mar. 11, 1862, Bennett diary, Bennett Papers, UMR; Fithian to his wife, Mar. 29, 1862, Black Family Papers, ISHL; Nesbitt to his family, Oct. 23, 1862, Nesbitt-Raub Papers, USAMHI; Tilley, *Federals on the Frontier*, 42.

25. Prentis, *Kansas Miscellanies*, 7, 11, 12, 47, 52, 54.

26. Ibid., 53, 55, 60.

27. Ibid., 46–47; Logan, "Memories," 8; Plank, "Grim Reminders," 23.

28. Lemke, "Pea Ridge Dead," 27, 30; *History of the Confederated Memorial Associations of the South*, 66–67.

29. J. Dickson Black, *History of Benton County*, 93–94.

30. Hurley, "Blue and Gray Reunion."

31. Platt Memoir, PRNMP.

32. Payne, "Battle of Pea Ridge," PRNMP. Glasscock was killed by Payne's side in the final Confederate charge across Ruddick's field at dusk on March 7. See chapter 10.

33. Drury to Fulbright, Sept. 29, 1949, Fulbright Papers, UAF; *Congressional Record*, 102:15, 153–54.

34. Willett, "Development of Pea Ridge," 166; Vaught, "Memorial Associates."

35. Willett, "Development of Pea Ridge," 166; Gibbons, "Reestablishment of Prairie Vegetation," 1–3; Bond, "History of Elkhorn Tavern," 6, 15.

Bibliography

MANUSCRIPTS

Arkansas
  Arkansas History Commission, Little Rock
    A. L. Black Letter
    Calvin C. Bliss Papers
    Loughborough Letters
    John S. Roane Letters
    "The Spectator," Frank Horsfall Collection
  Pea Ridge National Military Park
    B. C. Childers Letter
    Henry M. Dysart Diary
    John Fenton Letters
    Asa M. Payne, "Story of the Battle of Pea Ridge"
    Jacob Platt Memoir
    Charles S. Squires Map
    Henry H. Trimble Letters
  University of Arkansas at Fayetteville, Special Collections
    "The Battle of Pea Ridge," Folklore Project
    William H. Cardwell Papers
    Josephine B. Crump Papers
    Clyde T. Ellis Papers
    J. William Fulbright Papers
    Albert O. McCollom Letters
    James S. Moose Papers
    Daniel H. Reynolds Papers
    William H. H. Shibley Letters
    Jacob M. J. Smith Journals
    Stirman-Davidson Papers
    John F. Walter, "Capsule Histories of Arkansas Military Units in the Civil War"
    Julius White Testimonial Letter
  University of Arkansas at Little Rock, Archives and Special Collections
    John R. H. Scott Collection
    Rowland B. Smith Letters
California
  Huntington Library, San Marino
    Samuel R. Curtis Papers
  Stanford University, Palo Alto
    Frederick Steele Papers

Colorado
  Denver Public Library, Western History Department
    Dodge Family Papers
Connecticut
  Yale University, New Haven
    Samuel R. Curtis Papers
Georgia
  University of Georgia, Athens, Hargrett Rare Book and Manuscript Library
    Frederick W. Benteen Collection
    Myron G. Love Papers
Illinois
  Belleville Public Library
    Peter J. Osterhaus, "What I Saw of the War"
  Chicago Historical Society
    Ch. Bach, "Pea Ridge March"
    Day Elmore Papers
    William Gale Papers
    Sterling Price Collection
    Logan U. Reavis Papers
  Illinois State Historical Library, Springfield
    Allen Buckner Memoirs
    John C. Black Family Papers
    Charles E. Calkins Papers
    Henry B. Coughenower Papers
    George A. Cummins Diary
    Samuel R. Curtis Journal
    Engelmann-Kircher Collection
    Edward R. Fielding Papers
    Herrick-Reasoner-Milnor-Sparks Family Papers
    John A. Higgins Papers
    Edward Ingraham Papers
    William H. Marsh Papers
    Thaddeus B. Packard Journal
    Lines L. Parker Diary
    Charles H. Peters Papers
    Edward M. Pike Papers
    James H. Roe Papers
    John H. Sackett Papers
  Illinois State University, Normal
    George P. Ela Papers
  Lake Forest College, Donnelly Library
    Eugene B. Payne Papers
  University of Illinois, Champaign-Urbana
    Order Book, 2nd Brigade, Missouri Infantry, 1861–1862

Indiana
  Indiana Historical Society, Indianapolis
    John S. Bryan Papers
    Elijah H. C. Cavins Collection
    Gilbert H. Denny Papers
    Fretageot Family Papers
    Stephen S. Harding Collection
    William Hendricks Collection
    Mike W. Jump Papers
    Thomas Marshall Collection
    Thomas Melick Letters, Jacob W. Bartness Collection
    John W. Prentiss Collection
  Indiana State Library, Indianapolis
    O. V. Brown Papers
    Jefferson C. Davis Papers
    Louis W. Knobe Memoir
Iowa
  State Historical Society of Iowa, Des Moines
    Alonzo Abernethy Papers
    James Boyle Journal
    Civil War Reports, Adjutant General's Collection
    Henry J. B. Cummings Papers
    Samuel R. Curtis Papers
    Grenville M. Dodge Papers
    William H. H. Rogers Journal
    James A. Williamson Papers
  State Historical Society of Iowa, Iowa City
    Vinson Holman Diary
    John W. Noble Diary
    David E. Rummel Papers
  University of Iowa Libraries, Iowa City
    Lot Abraham Papers
Kansas
  Kansas State Historical Society, Topeka
    William F. Creitz Diary
    George E. Flanders Letters
    Andrew J. Huntoon Collection
    Joseph H. Trego Diary
    Samuel N. Wood Papers
Louisiana
  Tulane University, New Orleans, Howard-Tilton Memorial Library, Louisiana Historical Association Collection
    Civil War Papers
    Correspondence of Major General Sterling Price, Johnston Collection

Pierson Family Papers, Rosemonde E. and Emile Kuntz Collection
Michigan
    University of Michigan, Ann Arbor, William L. Clements Library
        Eugene B. Payne Journal
Minnesota
    Minnesota Historical Society, Minneapolis
        Frederick N. Boyer Diary
Missouri
    Missouri Historical Society, St. Louis
        William Bull Memoirs
        Salem H. Ford Reminiscences
        William J. Hallook Reports
        Herman T. Hesse, "Battle of Pea Ridge"
        Richard M. Hubbell Reminiscences
        Mesker Collection
        John W. Noble Letter, William C. Breckenridge Papers
        John S. Phelps Letter, Hamilton R. Gamble Papers
        Thomas C. Reynolds, "Gen. Sterling Price and the Confederacy"
        Elizabeth J. White, "Sketch of Colonel B. A. Rives," B. A. Rives Material
    University of Missouri—Columbia, Western Historical Manuscript Collection
        R. C. Carter, "A Short Sketch of My Experiences During the First Stages of the
            Civil War"
        Coleman-Hayter Letters
        A. Loyd Collins, "The Battle of Pea Ridge, Arkansas"
        Company Orders of Captain Emmett MacDonald's Battery Flying Artillery C.S.A.
        Joseph Crider Letters
        Robert Gooding Letters
        William N. Hoskin Diary
        Waldo P. Johnson Letters
        Rowland S. Mantor Letters
        Robert P. Mathews, "Souvenir of the Holland Company Home Guards and Phelps'
            Regiment, Missouri Volunteer Infantry"
        Louis Riley Papers
        James S. Rogers Papers
        William Y. Slack Papers
        I. V. Smith Memoirs
        Henry Voelkner Papers
        Thomas W. Westlake Memoir, Watson-Westlake Papers
        John Wilson Memoir
    University of Missouri—Rolla, Western Historical Manuscript Collection
        Lyman G. Bennett Papers
        James S. Rogers Papers
        William A. Ruyle Memoir
    University of Missouri—St. Louis, Western Historical Manuscript Collection

Dyson–Bell–Sans Souci Papers
New Jersey
    Michael Mullins Collection, Wayne
        Herschel Felton Letter
        Henry Ketzle Memoir
New York
    Columbia University, New York
        Peter W. Alexander Papers
    New-York Historical Society, New York
        Francis J. Herron Papers
        Franz Sigel Papers
North Carolina
    Duke University, Durham, Special Collections Department
        S. S. Marrett Papers
        Abby E. Stafford Papers
    University of North Carolina at Chapel Hill, Southern Historical Collection
        David Garver Papers
        "An Autobiography of Louis Hebert," Louis Hébert Papers
Ohio
    Western Reserve Historical Society, Cleveland
        John N. Moulton Papers, William P. Palmer Collection
Pennsylvania
    U.S. Army Military History Institute, Carlisle Barracks
        Edward Anderson, "Battle of Pea Ridge"
        David L. Ash Papers
        Eugene A. Carr Papers
        Civil War Times Illustrated Collection
            Lyman D. Ames Papers
            W. H. H. Barker Memoir
            Henry Curtis, Jr., Papers
            Paul Dorweiler Diary
            Samuel J. McDaniel Memoir
            Henry J. Seaman Diary
        George Gordon Papers
        Samuel P. Herrington Diary, Rudolph Haerle Collection
        Nesbitt-Raub Papers
Tennessee
    Tennessee State Library and Archives, Nashville
        Joseph R. Mothershead Diary
        Shahan Family Papers
    Bruce Roberts Collection, Knoxville
        G. B. Kirkpatrick Letter
Texas
    Baylor University, Waco, Texas Collection

Jones Family Letters
Ross Family Papers
Texas State Library, Austin, Archives Division
Joseph M. Bailey, "The Story of a Confederate Soldier, 1861–5"
"Eleventh Texas Cavalry"
University of Texas at Arlington
Thomas S. Sutherland, Jr., Collection
University of Texas at Austin, Eugene C. Barker Texas History Center
William W. Black Family Papers
A. B. Blocker, "Personal Experiences of a Sixteen Year Old Boy in the War Between the States"
John H. Brown Papers
William C. Chambers Letters
Civil War Miscellany
Frazier Family Papers
L. H. Graves Diary
George L. Griscom Diary
Ben and Henry E. McCulloch Papers
Lawrence S. Ross Letters
Washington, D.C.
Library of Congress
E. E. Johnson Diary
Philip H. Sheridan Papers
Lyman Trumbull Papers
Earl Van Dorn Papers
National Archives and Records Administration
Compiled Service Records of Volunteer Union Soldiers Who Served in Organizations from the State of Missouri, Rolls 487–496
Records of the War Department, RG 94
Franz Sigel Papers
12th Missouri Regimental Papers
22nd Indiana Regimental Papers
Union Battle Reports
Records of the War Department, RG 393
General Orders, 1861–1862, Army of the Southwest
Letters Received, December 1861–June 1862, Army of the Southwest
Letters Sent, January–October 1862, Army of the Southwest
Special Orders, 1861–1862, Army of the Southwest
Records of the War Department, Collection of Confederate Records, RG 109
Endorsements, February–May 1862, General Earl Van Dorn's Command
General and Division Orders, October 1861–April 1862, Missouri State Guard
Letters and Telegrams Sent, January–June 1862, General Earl Van Dorn's Command
Special Orders, January–May 1862, General Earl Van Dorn's Command

Wisconsin
  State Historical Society of Wisconsin, Madison
    Calvin P. Alling, "Four Years With the Western Army in the Civil War of the United
      States, 1861 to 1865"
    Thomas Priestly Papers
    E. B. Quiner Papers
    Henry H. Twining Papers

NEWSPAPERS

Aurora (Ill.) *Beacon*
Belleville (Ill.) *Advocate*
Belleville (Ill.) *Democrat*
Belvidere (Ill.) *Standard*
Cassville (Mo.) *Democrat*
Chicago *Evening Journal*
Chicago *Tribune*
Cincinnati *Daily Gazette*
Cleveland *Daily Plain Dealer*
Council Bluffs (Iowa) *Weekly Nonpareil*
Davenport (Iowa) *Daily Democrat and
  News*
Fayetteville (Ark.) *War Bulletin*
Fort Smith (Ark.) *Tri-Weekly Bulletin*
Frank Leslie's Illustrated Weekly
Greenville (Ill.) *Advocate*
Harper's Weekly
Houston *Weekly Telegraph*
Indianapolis *Daily Journal*
Keokuk (Iowa) *Daily Gate City*
Lincoln (Ill.) *Herald*
Little Rock *Arkansas State Gazette*

Little Rock *Arkansas True Democrat*
Memphis *Daily Appeal*
Monmouth (Ill.) *Atlas*
Muncie (Ind.) *Delaware County Free
  Press*
New Orleans *Commercial Bulletin*
New Orleans *Times Picayune*
New York *Herald*
New York *Times*
New York *Tribune*
Peoria (Ill.) *Daily Transcript*
Richmond (Ind.) *Palladium*
Richmond (Va.) *Whig*
Rock Island (Ill.) *Weekly Argus*
Rolla (Mo.) *Express*
St. Louis *Daily Missouri Democrat*
St. Louis *Missouri Republican*
San Antonio *Weekly Herald*
Tyler (Tex.) *Reporter*
Washington (Ark.) *Telegraph*
Washington (D.C.) *National Tribune*
Waukegan (Ill.) *Weekly Gazette*

PUBLISHED WORKS

Abbott, John S. C. "Heroic Deeds of Heroic Men: The Wilds of Arkansas." *Harper's
  New Monthly Magazine*, Oct. 1866, 581–601.
Abbott, Othman A. *Recollections of a Pioneer Lawyer*. Lincoln, Neb., 1929.
Abel, Annie H. *The American Indian as Participant in the Civil War*. Cleveland,
  1919.
Abernethy, Alonzo. "Incidents of an Iowa Soldier's Life, or Four Years in Dixie."
  Annals of Iowa, 3rd ser., 12 (1920): 401–28.

Adair, W. A. "Missouri and the Confederacy." St. Louis *Missouri Republican*, Apr. 10, 1886.

Allen, William P. "Three Frontier Battles: Wilson's Creek, Pea Ridge, Prairie Grove." In *Glimpses of the Nation's Struggle: Papers Read Before the Minnesota Commandery of the Military Order of the Loyal Legion of the United States, 1897–1902*. St. Paul, 1897.

Allsop, Fred W. *Albert Pike: A Biography*. Little Rock, 1928.

Ambrose, Stephen E. *Halleck: Lincoln's Chief of Staff*. Baton Rouge, 1962.

Anderson, Ephraim M. *Memoirs: Historical and Personal; Including the Campaigns of the First Missouri Confederate Brigade*. St. Louis, 1868.

Anderson, John Q., ed. *Campaigning with Parson's Texas Cavalry Brigade, CSA: The War Journals and Letters of the Four Orr Brothers, 12th Texas Cavalry Regiment*. Hillsboro, Tex., 1967.

Anderson, Mabel W. *Life of General Stand Watie*. Pryor, Okla., 1915.

Anderson, Thomas F. "The Indian Territory, 1861 to 1865." *Confederate Veteran* 4 (1896): 85–87.

Asbury, A. Edgar. *My Experiences in the War 1861 to 1865; or, A Little Autobiography*. Kansas City, 1894.

Baber, I. M. "One Hundred and Fifty Missouri Dead." St. Louis *Missouri Republican*, Oct. 9, 1886.

Bailey, Anne J. *Between the Enemy and Texas: Parson's Texas Cavalry in the Civil War*. Fort Worth, 1989.

———. "Henry McCulloch's Texans and the Defense of Arkansas in 1862." *Arkansas Historical Quarterly* 44 (1987): 46–59.

Bailey, Joseph M. "The Death of General McCulloch." *Confederate Veteran* 36 (1928): 175.

Banes, Marian T. "Tebbetts Family History." Washington County (Ark.) Historical Society *Flashback* 21 (1971): 11–26.

Barnhart, John D., ed. "A Hoosier Invades the Confederacy: Letters and Diaries of Leroy S. Mayfield." *Indiana Magazine of History* 39 (1943): 144–91.

Barr, Alwyn. "Confederate Artillery in Arkansas." *Arkansas Historical Quarterly* 22 (1963): 238–72.

Barron, Samuel B. *The Lone Star Defenders: A Chronicle of the Third Texas Cavalry, Ross' Brigade*. New York, 1908.

Battlefield of Pea Ridge, Arkansas: Battlefield Folklore. Fayetteville, Ark., 1958.

"Battle of Pea Ridge." Pulaski County (Ark.) Historical Society *Historical Review* 14 (1966): 62–63.

The Battle of Pea Ridge. Rogers, Ark., 1963.

"The Battle of Whitney's Lane or the Battle of Searcy." White County (Ark.) Historical Society *Heritage* 1 (1963): 7–10.

Baxter, William. *Pea Ridge and Prairie Grove; or, Scenes and Incidents of the War in Arkansas*. Cincinnati, 1864.

Bearss, Edwin C. "The Battle of Pea Ridge." *Annals of Iowa*, 3rd ser., 36 (1963): 569–89; (1963–64): 9–41, 121–55, 207–39, 304–17.

————. "The Battle of Pea Ridge." *Arkansas Historical Quarterly* 20 (1961): 74–94.

————. *The Battle of Wilson's Creek*. Bozeman, Mont., 1985.

————. "The First Day at Pea Ridge, March 7, 1862." *Arkansas Historical Quarterly* 17 (1958): 132–54.

————. "Fort Smith Serves General McCulloch as a Supply Depot." *Arkansas Historical Quarterly* 24 (1965): 315–47.

————. "From Rolla to Fayetteville with General Curtis." *Arkansas Historical Quarterly* 19 (1960): 225–59.

————. "The White River Expedition, June 10–July 15, 1862." *Arkansas Historical Quarterly* 21 (1962): 305–62.

Behlendorf, Frederick. *The History of the Thirteenth Illinois Cavalry Regiment, Volunteers U.S. Army, From September, 1861 to September, 1865*. Grand Rapids, Mich., 1888.

Bek, William G., ed. "The Civil War Diary of John T. Buegel." *Missouri Historical Review*, 40 (1946): 307–29.

Benner, Judith A. *Sul Ross: Soldier, Statesman, Educator*. College Station, Tex., 1983.

Bennett, Lyman G., and William M. Haigh. *History of the Thirty-Sixth Regiment Illinois Volunteers, During the War of the Rebellion*. Aurora, Ill., 1876.

Benson, Wallace P. *A Soldier's Diary: Diary of Wallace P. Benson of Company H, 36th Illinois Volunteers*. [Algonquin, Ill.], 1919.

Berg, Richard. "Battles in the West: Wilson's Creek to Pea Ridge." *Strategy and Tactics* 80 (1980): 4–14.

Betts, Karl. "Pea Ridge Park Will Play Important Role in National Civil War Centennial." Benton County (Ark.) Historical Society *Pioneer* 5 (1960): 4–8.

Bevier, Robert S. *History of the First and Second Missouri Confederate Brigades, 1861–1865*. St. Louis, 1879.

Bigelow, James K. *Abridged History of the Eighth Indiana Volunteer Infantry*. Indianapolis, 1864.

Billingsley, William C., ed. "'Such Is War': The Confederate Memoirs of Newton Asbury Keen." *Texas Military History* 6 (1967): 238–52; 7 (1968): 44–47.

Bishop, Albert W. *Loyalty on the Frontier, or Sketches of Union Men of the South-West; with Incidents and Adventures in Rebellion on the Border*. St. Louis, 1863.

————. *An Oration Delivered at Fayetteville, Arkansas*. New York, 1865.

Black, J. Dickson. *History of Benton County*. Little Rock, 1975.

Black, John C. "Our Boys in the War." In *Military Essays and Recollections. Papers Read Before the Commandery of the State of Illinois, Military Order of the Loyal Legion of the United States*. Chicago, 1894.

Black, Sam. *A Soldier's Recollections of the Civil War*. Minco, Okla., 1912.

Blodgett, Edward A. "The Army of the Southwest and the Battle of Pea Ridge." In *Military Essays and Recollections. Papers Read Before the Commandery of the State of Illinois, Military Order of the Loyal Legion of the United States*.

Chicago, 1894.

Bond, John W. "The History of Elkhorn Tavern." *Arkansas Historical Quarterly* 21 (1962): 3–15.

Bondi, August. *Autobiography of August Bondi, 1833–1907*. Galesburg, Ill., 1910.

Boudinot, E. C. "Ross' Men Did the Scalping." St. Louis *Missouri Republican*, Jan. 2, 1886.

Brackett, Albert G. "A Memorable March." *United Service*, 2nd ser., 4 (1890): 336–41.

Bradley, James. *The Confederate Mail Carrier*. Mexico, Mo., 1894.

Bridges, Hal. "A Confederate Hero: General William Y. Slack." *Arkansas Historical Quarterly* 10 (1951): 233–37.

Britton, Wiley. *The Civil War on the Border*. 2 vols. New York, 1891–99.

———. *Memoirs of the Rebellion on the Border, 1863*. Chicago, 1882.

———. "Union and Confederate Indians in the Civil War." In *Battles and Leaders of the Civil War*, ed. Robert U. Johnson and Clarence C. Buel. 4 vols. New York, 1884–87.

Brown, Dee. "The Battle of Pea Ridge: Gettysburg of the West." *Civil War Times Illustrated* 6 (1967): 4–11.

———. *Creek Mary's Blood*. New York, 1970.

Brown, Walter L. "Albert Pike and the Pea Ridge Atrocities." *Arkansas Historical Quarterly* 38 (1979): 345–59.

———. "Albert Pike as Confederate General." *Confederate Historical Institute Journal* 1 (1980): 43–48.

———. "Pea Ridge: Gettysburg of the West." *Arkansas Historical Quarterly* 15 (1956): 3–16.

Browne, Junius H. *Four Years in Secessia*. New York, 1865.

Bunn, Henry G. "Early Days of the War in the West." *Confederate Veteran* 10 (1902): 449–53.

———. "Gen. Evander McNair." *Confederate Veteran* 11 (1903): 265–66.

Buntline, Ned. *Buffalo Bill and His Adventures in the West*. New York, 1886.

Burnham, John H. "The Thirty-Third Regiment Illinois Infantry in the War between the States." Illinois State Historical Society *Transactions* 17 (1912): 77–85.

Burns, William S. *Recollections of the 4th Missouri Cavalry*. Dayton, Ohio, 1988.

Burrow, Roy D. *The Battle of Pea Ridge*. Charleston, Ill., 1970.

Bussey, Cyrus. "The Pea Ridge Campaign Considered." In *Military Order of the Loyal Legion of the United States, Commandery of the District of Columbia*. Washington, D.C., 1905.

Byers, Samuel H. M. *Iowa in War Times*. Des Moines, 1888.

Cabell, William L. "Reminiscences from the Trans-Mississippi." *Confederate Veteran* 12 (1904): 173.

Calkin, Homer L., ed. "Elkhorn to Vicksburg." *Civil War History* 2 (1956): 7–43.

Campbell, William S. *One Hundred Years of Fayetteville*. Fayetteville, Ark., 1928.

Carlson, Gretchen. "Francis Jay Herron." *Palimpsest* 11 (1930): 141–50.

Carroll, John M., ed. *The Benteen-Goldin Letters on Custer and His Last Battle*.

Lincoln, Neb., 1991.

Castel, Albert. "Earl Van Dorn." *Civil War Times Illustrated* 6 (1967): 38–42.

———. *General Sterling Price and the Civil War in the West.* Baton Rouge, 1968.

———. "A New View of the Battle of Pea Ridge." *Missouri Historical Review* 62 (1968): 136–51.

Castle, John S., ed. *Grandfather Was a Drummer Boy: A Civil War Diary and Letters of Charles B. Stiles.* Solon, Ohio, 1986.

Cater, William D. *"As It Was": The Story of Douglas John Cater's Life.* [San Antonio], 1981.

Catton, Bruce. *American Heritage Picture History of the Civil War.* New York, 1960.

Civil War Medal of Honor Winners from Illinois. Springfield, 1962.

Clark, Leach. "The Battle of Pea Ridge." *Bivouac* 2 (1884): 362–66.

———. "Dreams That Came to Pass: A Thirty-Sixth Illinois Soldier's Dream and Its Strange Fulfillment." *Bivouac* 2 (1884): 330–32.

Clarke, Norman E., ed. *Warfare along the Mississippi: The Letters of Lieutenant Colonel George E. Currie.* Mount Pleasant, Mich., 1961.

Clausewitz, Carl. *On War,* trans. and ed. Michael Howard and Peter Paret. Princeton, 1976.

Clifford, Roy A. "The Indian Regiments in the Battle of Pea Ridge." *Chronicles of Oklahoma* 25 (1947): 314–22.

Coffman, Edward M., ed. "Ben McCulloch Letter." *Southwestern Historical Quarterly* 60 (1956): 118–22.

Coleman, R. B. "First Cherokee (Ind. T.) Cavalry, C.S.A." *Confederate Veteran* 21 (1913): 226.

Collins, Robert M. *Chapters From the Unwritten History of the War Between the States; Or, the Incidents in the Life of a Confederate Soldier in Camp, on the March, in the Great Battles, and in Prison.* St. Louis, 1893.

Colton, Kenneth E., ed. "Frontier War Problems: Letters of Samuel Ryan Curtis, Pioneer, Congressman, Engineer, Soldier." *Annals of Iowa,* 3rd ser., 24 (1943): 298–315.

Congressional Record. 84th Cong., 2nd sess. Vol. 102. Washington, D.C., 1956.

Conkling, Roscoe P., and Margaret B. Conkling. *The Butterfield Overland Mail, 1857–1869.* 3 vols. Glendale, Calif., 1947.

Connelley, William E. *Wild Bill and His Era: The Life and Adventures of James Butler Hickock.* New York, 1933.

Connelly, Thomas L. *Army of the Heartland: The Army of Tennessee, 1861–1862.* Baton Rouge, 1967.

Connelly, Thomas L., and Archer Jones. *The Politics of Command: Factions and Ideas in Confederate Strategy.* Baton Rouge, 1973.

Conningham, Frederick A. *Currier & Ives Prints: An Illustrated Check List.* New York, 1949.

Cook, Theodore M. *Boots and Saddles: Third Iowa Cavalry, 1861–1865.* N.p., 1974.

Cooper, J. W. "McCulloch at Pea Ridge." St. Louis *Missouri Republican*, Feb. 13, 1886.

Cooper, Paul R., and Ted R. Worley, eds. "Letters from a Veteran of Pea Ridge." *Arkansas Historical Quarterly* 6 (1947): 426–71.

Crabtree, John D. "Recollections of the Pea Ridge Campaign, and the Army of the Southwest, in 1862." In *Military Essays and Recollections. Papers Read Before the Commandery of the State of Illinois, Military Order of the Loyal Legion of the United States*. Chicago, 1897.

Cunningham, Frank. *General Stand Watie's Confederate Indians*. San Antonio, 1959.

Curtis, Samuel P. "The Army of the South-West, and the First Campaign in Arkansas." *Annals of Iowa*, 1st ser., 4 (1866): 625–45, 673–88, 721–37; 5 (1867): 769–85, 817–33, 865–76, 917–33; 6 (1868): 1–12, 69–84, 141–60, 249–70; 7 (1869): 1–20, 113–32, 209–25.

Dacus, Robert H. *Reminiscences of Company 'H,' First Arkansas Mounted Rifles*. Dardanelle, Ark., 1897.

Dale, Edward E. "The Cherokees in the Confederacy." *Journal of Southern History* 13 (1947): 159–68.

Davenport, Edward A. *History of the Ninth Regiment Illinois Cavalry Volunteers*. Chicago, 1888.

Delaney, Norman C., ed. "The Diary and Memoirs of Marshall Samuel Pierson, Company C, 17th Reg., Texas Cavalry." *Military History of Texas and the Southwest* 12 (1973): 23–38.

Dennet, Tyler, ed. *Lincoln and the Civil War in the Diaries and Letters of John Hay*. New York, 1939.

Depp, Thomas. "Personal Experience at Pea Ridge." *Confederate Veteran* 20 (1912): 17.

DeWolf, Izora. *A. L. Swap in the Civil War*. N.p., n.d.

Dilts, William G. *Record of the First Iowa Battery with the Autobiography of Captain W. H. Gay and Letters and Documents, 1861–1865*. N.p., [1905].

Dodge, Grenville M. *Address to Army Associations*. New York, 1904.

———. *The Battle of Atlanta and Other Campaigns, Addresses, Etc*. Council Bluffs, Iowa, 1911.

———. "Colonel William H. Kinsman." *Annals of Iowa*, 3rd ser., 5 (1902): 241–45.

———. *Fiftieth Anniversary: Fourth Iowa Veteran Infantry, Dodge's Second Iowa Battery, Dodge's Band*. Council Bluffs, Iowa, 1911.

———. "General James A. Williamson." *Annals of Iowa*, 3rd ser., 6 (1903): 161–84.

Donat, Pat, ed. "Diary of Joseph Sanders." Washington County (Ark.) Historical Society *Flashback* 34 (1984): 1–11.

Dougan, Michael B. *Confederate Arkansas: The People and Politics of a Frontier State in Wartime*. University, Ala., 1976.

———. "Thomas C. Hindman: Arkansas Politician and General." In *Rank and File: Civil War Essays in Honor of Bell Irvin Wiley*, ed. James I. Robertson, Jr., and Richard M. McMurray. San Rafael, Calif., 1976.

Douglas, Lucia R., ed. *Douglas's Texas Battery, CSA*. Waco, 1966.

Duncan, Robert L. *Reluctant General: The Life and Times of Albert Pike*. New York, 1961.

Dunn, Byron A. *The Scout of Pea Ridge*. Chicago, 1911.

Duyckinck, Evert A. *National History of the War for the Union, Civil, Military, and Naval*. 2 vols. New York, 1861.

Dyer, Frederick H. *A Compendium of the War of the Rebellion*. 3 vols. Des Moines, 1908.

Edwards, Dale. "Arkansas: Pea Ridge and State Division." *Journal of the West* 14 (1975): 167–84.

Edwards, John N. *Shelby and His Men; or, The War in the West*. Cincinnati, 1867.

Eisele, Wilbert E. *The Real Wild Bill Hickock: Famous Scout and Knight Chivalric of the Plains—A True Story of Pioneer Life in the Far West*. Denver, 1931.

Elliott, Isaac H., and Virgil G. Way. *History of the Thirty-Third Regiment Illinois Veteran Volunteer Infantry in the Civil War*. Gibson City, Ill., 1902.

Evans, Clarence, ed. "Memoirs, Letters, and Diary Entries of German Settlers in Northwest Arkansas, 1853–1863." *Arkansas Historical Quarterly* 6 (1947): 225–49.

Evans, Clement A., ed. *Confederate Military History*. 12 vols. Atlanta, 1899.

Fayel, William. "After Pea Ridge." St. Louis *Missouri Republican*, Jan. 22, 1887.

————. "Curtis' Advance From Springfield." St. Louis *Missouri Republican*, Dec. 12, 1885.

————. "Curtis' Withdrawal From Cross Hollows." St. Louis *Missouri Republican*, Dec. 19, 1885.

————. "From Rolla to Springfield." St. Louis *Missouri Republican*, Dec. 5, 1885.

————. "The Second Day at Pea Ridge." St. Louis *Missouri Republican*, Dec. 26, 1885.

Field, Charles D. *Three Years in the Saddle, From 1861 to 1865*. [Goldfield, Iowa, 1898].

"First Reunion at Pea Ridge." Benton County (Ark.) Historical Society *Pioneer* 7 (1962): 5–6.

First Reunion of the Ninth Iowa Infantry Regiment Veteran Volunteers Held at Independence on the Anniversary of the Battle of Pea Ridge, March 6th, 7th, and 8th, 1883. Independence, Iowa, 1883.

Fischer, Leroy H., and Jerry Gill. "Confederate Indian Forces outside of Indian Territory." *Chronicles of Oklahoma* 46 (1968): 249–84.

Fiske, John. *Mississippi Valley in the Civil War*. Boston, 1900.

Fitzhugh, Lester N., ed. *Cannon Smoke: The Letters of Captain John J. Good, Good-Douglas Texas Battery, CSA*. Hillsboro, Tex., 1971.

Flint, Mortimer R. "The War on the Border." In *Glimpses of the Nation's Struggle: Papers Read Before the Minnesota Commandery of the Military Order of the Loyal Legion of the United States, 1897–1902*. St. Paul, 1903.

Ford, Edsel. "Return to Pea Ridge." Benton County (Ark.) Historical Society *Pioneer* 5 (1959): 3.

————. "Winton Spring, With Fog." In *The Battle of Pea Ridge*. Rogers, Ark., 1963.

Ford, Harvey S. "Van Dorn and the Pea Ridge Campaign." *Journal of the American Military Institute* 3 (1939): 222–36.

Forman, Jacob G. *The Western Sanitary Commission; A Sketch of Its Organization, History, and Aid Given to Freedmen and Union Refugees, With Incidents of Hospital Life*. St. Louis, 1864.

Fox, William F. *Regimental Losses in the American Civil War*. Albany, N.Y., 1889.

Francis, John. "An Incident of the War in 1862." Kansas State Historical Society *Transactions* 7 (1902): 161–67.

Franks, Kenny A. "The Implementation of the Confederate Treaties with the Five Civilized Tribes." *Chronicles of Oklahoma* 51 (1973): 21–33.

————. *Stand Watie and the Agony of the Cherokee Nation*. Memphis, 1979.

Frémont, John C. "In Command in Missouri." In *Battles and Leaders of the Civil War*, ed. Robert U. Johnson and Clarence C. Buel. 4 vols. New York, 1884–87.

Frost, Daniel. "Gen. Frost's State Secret." St. Louis *Missouri Republican*, Feb. 20, 1886.

Funk, Erwin. "Twelve Corner Church Was a Pioneer." Benton County (Ark.) Historical Society *Pioneer* 12 (1967): 3–5.

Gaines, W. Craig. *The Confederate Cherokees: John Drew's Regiment of Mounted Rifles*. Baton Rouge, 1989.

Gallaher, Ruth C. "Samuel Ryan Curtis." *Iowa Journal of History and Politics* 25 (1927): 331–58.

Gallaway, B. P. *The Ragged Rebel: A Common Soldier in W. H. Parson's Texas Cavalry, 1861–1865*. Austin, 1988.

Gammage, Washington L. *The Camp, the Bivouac, and the Battle Field. Being a History of the Fourth Arkansas Regiment, From Its First Organization Down to the Present Day*. Selma, Ala., 1864.

Garner, Nell S. "A Pea Ridge Tale." Crawford County (Ark.) Historical Society *Heritage* 5 (1962): 24.

Gates, Arnold, ed. *The Rough Side of War: The Civil War Journal of Chesley A. Mosman, First Lieutenant, Company D, 59th Illinois Volunteer Infantry Regiment*. Garden City, N.J., 1987.

[Getzendamer, W. H., and A. M. Dechman]. *A Brief and Condensed History of Parson's Texas Cavalry Brigade*. Waxahachie, Tex., 1892.

Gill, Adelaide. "Frederick Steele." *Palimpsest* 11 (1930): 151–59.

Gilpin, Thomas C. *History of the 3rd Iowa Volunteer Cavalry, From August, 1861, to September, 1865*. Winterset, Iowa, n.d.

Goodrich, James W. "Robert Ormsby Sweeny: Some Civil War Sketches." *Missouri Historical Review* 77 (1983): 147–69.

Graves, L. H. "A Texas Soldier of the Confederacy Records His Experiences in Northwest Arkansas." Washington County (Ark.) Historical Society *Flashback* 3 (1953): 9–15.

Griffith, S. A. Letter in *Confederate Veteran* 4 (1896): 163.

Griffith, Paddy. *Battle Tactics in the Civil War*. New Haven, 1989.

Grigsby, Melvin. *The Smoked Yank*. Sioux Falls, S.D., 1888.

Gunn, Jack W. "Ben McCulloch: A Big Captain." *Texas Military History* 1 (1961): 24–40.

Guyer, Max H., ed. "The Journal and Letters of Corporal William O. Gulick." *Iowa Journal of History and Politics* 28 (1930): 194–267, 390–455, 543–603.

Hallum, John. *Reminiscences of the Civil War*. Little Rock, 1903.

Ham, Sharon. "End of Innocence." *Palimpsest* 60 (1979): 76–97.

Hanson, Maynard, Jr. "The Battle of Pea Ridge, Arkansas, March 6–8, 1862." *Journal of the West* 19 (1980): 39–50.

Harding, James. "Personal Reminiscences of Service With the Missouri State Guard." St. Louis *Missouri Republican*, July 18 and 25, 1885.

Hartje, Robert G. *Van Dorn: The Life and Times of a Confederate General*. Nashville, 1967.

Harwood, Nathan S. *The Pea Ridge Campaign, A Paper Read Before the Nebraska Commandery of the Military Order of the Loyal Legion of the United States*. Omaha, 1887.

Havins, Thomas R. *Beyond the Cimarron: Major Earl Van Dorn in Commanche Land*. Brownwood, Tex., 1968.

Herr, George W. *Episodes of the Civil War: Nine Campaigns in Nine States*. San Francisco, 1890.

Hess, Earl J. "Alexander Asboth: One of Lincoln's Hungarian Heroes?" *Lincoln Herald* 84 (1982): 181–91.

———. "Battle in the Brush." *Indiana Military History Journal* 8 (1983): 12–20.

———. "Confiscation and the Northern War Effort: The Army of the Southwest at Helena." *Arkansas Historical Quarterly* 44 (1985): 56–75.

———. "Osterhaus in Missouri: A Study in German-American Loyalty." *Missouri Historical Review* 78 (1984): 144–67.

———. "Sigel's Resignation: A Study in German-Americanism and the Civil War." *Civil War History* 26 (1980): 5–17.

———. "The 12th Missouri Infantry: A Socio-Military Profile of a Union Regiment." *Missouri Historical Review* 76 (1981): 53–77.

———, ed. *A German in the Yankee Fatherland: The Civil War Letters of Henry A. Kircher*. Kent, Ohio, 1983.

Hirshon, Stanley P. *Grenville M. Dodge: Soldier, Politician, Railroad Pioneer*. Bloomington, Ind., 1967.

History of the Confederate Memorial Associations of the South. New Orleans, 1904.

Hocker, P. S. "The Scalping at Pea Ridge." St. Louis *Missouri Republican*, Jan. 16, 1886.

Holcomb, R. I. "The Scalping at Pea Ridge." St. Louis *Missouri Republican*, Jan. 2, 1886.

———. "That 'State Secret.'" St. Louis *Missouri Republican*, Mar. 20, 1886.

Hollinsworth, B. P. "Battle of Elkhorn (Arkansas)." In *The New Texas School*

Reader, comp. J. R. Hutchison. Houston, 1864.

Holmes, James T. *52nd O.V.I., Then and Now*. Columbus, Ohio, 1898.

Hord, Benjamin M. "Gen. Ben M'Culloch." *Confederate Veteran* 36 (1928): 261–62.

Horton, Sam H. "We Left for Missouri." White River Valley (Mo.) Historical Society *Quarterly* 1 (1964): 15–17.

Hovey, Charles E. "Gen. Curtis's Army: The March Through Arkansas from Batesville to Helena." Washington (D.C.) *National Tribune*, Nov. 28, 1889.

Hughes, Michael A. "Pea Ridge, or Elkhorn Tavern, Arkansas, March 7–8, 1862." *Blue and Gray Magazine* 5 (1988): 8–36.

Hughes, William E. *The Journal of a Grandfather*. St. Louis, 1912.

Hurley, A. W. "The Blue and Gray Reunion at Pea Ridge, Sept., 1889." Benton County (Ark.) Historical Society *Pioneer* 2 (1957): 3–5.

Ingersoll, Lurton D. *Iowa and the Rebellion*. Philadelphia, 1866.

Ingram, Henry L., ed. *Civil War Letters of George W. and Martha F. Ingram, 1861–1865*. College Station, Tex., 1973.

Jines, Billie, ed. "Civil War Diary of Henderson P. Greene." Washington County (Ark.) Historical Society *Flashback* 17 (1967): 15–18.

Johnson, Robert E. "Fort Smith and the Civil War." Fort Smith Historical Society *Journal* 4 (1980): 2–10.

Jones, Douglas C. *Elkhorn Tavern*. New York, 1980.

Jones, James P., ed. "Campaigning in Missouri: Civil War Memoir of General Jefferson C. Davis." *Missouri Historical Review* 54 (1959): 39–45.

Josephy, Alvin M., Jr. *War on the Frontier: The Trans-Mississippi West*. Alexandria, Va., 1986.

Kennerly, William C. *Persimmon Hill: A Narrative of Old St. Louis and the Far West*. Norman, 1948.

Kerr, Homer L. "Battle of Elkhorn: The Gettysburg of the Trans-Mississippi West." In *Essays on the American Civil War*, ed. William F. Holmes and Harold M. Hollingsworth. Austin, 1968.

———, ed. *Fighting With Ross' Texas Cavalry Brigade, C.S.A.: The Diary of George L. Griscom, Adjutant, 9th Texas Cavalry Regiment*. Hillsboro, Tex., 1976.

King, James T. *War Eagle: A Life of General Eugene A. Carr*. Lincoln, Neb., 1963.

Kirkland, Frazar, comp. *The Pictorial Book of Anecdotes and Incidents of the War of the Rebellion*. Hartford, 1866.

Kirkpatrick, Arthur R. "The Admission of Missouri to the Confederacy." *Missouri Historical Review* 55 (1961): 366–86.

Knight, Wilfred. *Red Fox: Stand Watie and the Confederate Indian Nations during the Civil War Years in Indian Territory*. Glendale, Calif., 1988.

Knox, Thomas W. *Camp-Fire and Cotton-Field: Southern Adventure in Time of War*. New York, 1865.

———. *The Lost Army*. New York, 1894.

Lale, Max, ed. "The Boy Bugler of the Third Texas Cavalry: The A. B. Blocker Narrative." *Military History of Texas and the Southwest* 14 (1975): 71–92, 147–67, 215–27.

————, ed. *The Civil War Letters of David R. Garrett, Detailing the Adventures of the 6th Texas Cavalry, 1861–1865*. Marshall, Tex., [1964].

Lane, Walter P. *The Adventures and Recollections of General Walter P. Lane, a San Jacinto Veteran. Containing Sketches of the Texan, Mexican and Late Wars With Several Indian Fights Thrown In*. Marshall, Tex., 1928.

Lathrop, David. *The History of the Fifty-Ninth Regiment Illinois Volunteers*. Indianapolis, 1865.

Leeper, Wesley T. *Rebels Valiant: Second Arkansas Mounted Rifles*. Little Rock, 1964.

Lemke, Walter J., ed. *The Journals of James A. Walden*. Fayetteville, Ark., 1954.

————, ed. "The Paths of Glory: The War-Time Diary of Major John Henry Brown, C.S.A." *Arkansas Historical Quarterly* 15 (1956): 344–59.

————, comp. "Pea Ridge Dead in Fayetteville National Cemetery." Washington County (Ark.) Historical Society *Flashback* 12 (1962): 27–30.

————, ed. "Wartime Diary in Northwest Arkansas." Washington County (Ark.) Historical Society *Flashback* 6 (1956): 3–11.

Lemke, Walter J., and Ted R. Worley. *The Butterfield Overland Mail in Arkansas*. Little Rock, 1957.

Livermore, Mary A. *My Story of the War: A Woman's Narrative of Four Years Personal Experience*. Hartford, 1889.

Livermore, Thomas L. *Numbers and Losses in the Civil War in America, 1861–65*. Boston, 1900.

Logan, Robert R. "Memories of Pea Ridge and Prairie Grove." Washington County (Ark.) Historical Society *Flashback* 2 (1952): 7–8.

Lossing, Benson, Jr. *Pictorial History of the Civil War in the United States of America*. 3 vols. Hartford, 1866–70.

Lothrop, Charles H. *A History of the First Regiment Iowa Cavalry Veteran Volunteers*. Lyons, Iowa, 1890.

Love, William D. *Wisconsin in the War of the Rebellion; a History of All Regiments and Batteries the State Has Sent to the Field*. Chicago, 1866.

McDonough, James L. *Shiloh—In Hell before Night*. Knoxville, 1977.

McFarland, Bill. "John C. Black: Biography of a Medal of Honor Winner from Illinois." *Military Images* 8 (1987): 13–15.

McGugin, D. S. "Extracts from a Report on the Operations of the Medical Department during the Battle of Pea Ridge." In *The Medical and Surgical History of the War of the Rebellion, 1861–1865*. 6 vols. in 12. Washington, D.C., 1875–88.

McLoughlin, William C. *Cherokee Renascence in the New Republic*. Princeton, 1986.

McMyler, James J. *History of the 11th Wisconsin Veteran Volunteer Infantry, Giving a Reliable Account of Its Marches, Hardships and Battles*. New Orleans, 1865.

McWhiney, Grady. *Braxton Bragg and Confederate Defeat*. New York, 1969.

McWhiney, Grady, and Perry D. Jamieson. *Attack and Die: Civil War Military Tactics and the Southern Heritage*. University, Ala., 1982.

Marcoot, Maurice. *Five Years in the Sunny South*. N.p., n.d.

Marcus, Jacob R. *Memoirs of American Jews, 1775–1865*. 3 vols. Philadelphia, 1955.

Marsh, Lucy, ed. "The Confederate Letters of Bryan Marsh." Smith County (Tex.) Historical Society *Chronicles* 14 (1975): 9–30.

Marshall, Albert O. *Army Life; From a Soldier's Journal*. Joliet, Ill., 1884.

Marshall, Randolph V. *An Historical Sketch of the Twenty-Second Regiment Indiana Volunteers*. Madison, Ind., 1884.

Mathes, J. A. "Battles in Trans-Mississippi Department." *Confederate Veteran* 2 (1894): 79.

Mauck, Genevieve P. "Grenville Mellon Dodge, Soldier-Engineer." *Palimpsest* 47 (1966): 433–75.

Maury, Dabney H. "Recollections of General Earl Van Dorn." *Southern Historical Society Papers* 19 (1891): 191–201.

———. "Recollections of the Elkhorn Campaign." *Southern Historical Society Papers* 2 (1876): 180–92.

Medal of Honor Recipients, 1863–1878. Washington, D.C., 1979.

"Memorial Services at Pea Ridge, March 11, 1862." *Arkansas Historical Quarterly* 21 (1962): 158–65.

Mickey, Barry. "Whitfield's Cavalry: A Texas-Arkansas Battalion in the Western Confederacy." *Military Images* 7 (1986): 27–29.

Miller, Emily Van Dorn, ed. *A Soldier's Honor, With Reminiscences of Major-General Earl Van Dorn*. New York, 1902.

Miller, James M. *History of the Sixteenth Battery of Ohio Volunteer Light Artillery, U.S.A.* N.p., 1906.

Monaghan, Jay. *Civil War on the Western Border, 1861–1865*. Boston, 1955.

"Monument at Van Buren, Ark." *Confederate Veteran* 7 (1899): 155.

Moody, Claire N. *Battle of Pea Ridge or Elkhorn Tavern*. Little Rock, 1956.

Moore, Frank, comp. *Anecdotes, Poetry and Incidents of the War*. New York, 1866.

———, comp. *The Rebellion Record: A Diary of American Events, With Documents, Narratives, Illustrative Incidents, Poetry, Etc.* 10 vols. New York, 1861–67.

Morrison, James L., ed. *The Memoirs of Henry Heth*. Westport, Conn., 1974.

Morton, Ohland. "Confederate Government Relations with the Five Civilized Tribes." *Chronicles of Oklahoma* 31 (1953): 189–204, 299–32.

Moulton, Gary E. *The Papers of Chief John Ross*. 2 vols. Norman, 1985.

Mullins, Michael A. *The Fremont Rifles: A History of the 37th Illinois Veteran Volunteer Infantry*. Wilmington, N.C., 1990.

Musser, Richard H. "The Battle of Pea Ridge." St. Louis *Missouri Republican*, Nov. 21 and 28, 1885.

Neet, J. Frederick, Jr. "Stand Watie: Confederate General in the Cherokee Nation." *Great Plains Journal* 6 (1966): 36–51.

Nelson, Glenn T., and John D. Squier. "The Confederate Defense of Northeast Arkansas and the Battle of Cotton Plant, Arkansas, July 7, 1862." Woodruff

County (Ark.) Historical Society *Rivers and Roads and Points In Between* 16 (1989): 5–27.

Nevins, Allan, and Milton H. Thomas, eds. *The Diary of George Templeton Strong.* 4 vols. New York, 1952.

Noble, Henry T. *Military History and Reminiscences of the Thirteenth Regiment of Illinois Volunteer Infantry in the Civil War in the United States, 1861–1865.* Chicago, 1892.

Noble, John W. "The Battle of Pea Ridge, or Elk Horn Tavern." In *War Papers and Personal Reminiscences, 1861–1865. Read Before the Commandery of the State of Missouri, Military Order of the Loyal Legion of the United States.* St. Louis, 1892.

O'Connor, Richard. *Sheridan the Inevitable.* Indianapolis, 1953.

O'Flaherty, Daniel. *General Jo Shelby: Undefeated Rebel.* Chapel Hill, 1954.

Olpin, Larry. "Missouri and the American Civil War Novel." *Missouri Historical Review* 85 (1990): 1–20.

O'Neal, Bill, ed. "The Civil War Memoirs of Samuel Alonza Cooke." *Southwestern Historical Quarterly* 74 (1971): 535–48.

Ormsby, Waterman L. *The Butterfield Overland Mail.* San Marino, Calif., 1968.

Parrish, William E. "The Western Sanitary Commission." *Civil War History* 36 (1990): 17–35.

Payne, Eugene B. *The 37th Illinois Veteran Volunteer Infantry and the Battle of Pea Ridge, Arkansas.* Washington, D.C., 1903.

Payne, James E. "The Test of Missourians." *Confederate Veteran* 37 (1929): 101–3.

Pea Ridge March. N.p., 1862.

Pea Ridge Memorial Association. *Report on the Historic Marker Program, March 10, 1963.* Rogers, Ark., 1963.

"Pea Ridge National Military Park." *Civil War Times Illustrated* 20 (1981): 34–35.

Pease, Theodore C., and James G. Randall, eds. *The Diary of Orville Hickman Browning.* 2 vols. Springfield, Ill., 1925–33.

Perkins, J. R. *Trails, Rails and War: The Life of General G. M. Dodge.* Indianapolis, 1929.

Phillips, Christopher. *Damned Yankee: The Life of Nathaniel Lyon.* Columbia, Mo., 1990.

Plank, Will. "Grim Reminders of the Battle of Pea Ridge." Benton County (Ark.) Historical Society *Pioneer* 5 (1960): 23–25.

Pollard, Charleen P., ed. "Civil War Letters of George W. Allen." *Southwestern Historical Quarterly* 83 (1979): 47–52.

Prentis, Noble L. *Kansas Miscellanies.* Topeka, 1889.

Price, Celsus. "Gens. Price and Van Dorn." St. Louis *Missouri Republican*, June 5, 1886.

Quaife, Milo M., ed. *Absalom Grimes: Confederate Mail Runner.* New Haven, 1926.

Quiner, Edwin B. *The Military History of Wisconsin.* Chicago, 1866.

Randolph, Vance, comp. *Ozark Folksongs.* 4 vols. Columbia, Mo., 1946–50.

Ray, Johnette H., ed. "Civil War Letters from Parson's Texas Cavalry Brigade." *Southwestern Historical Quarterly* 69 (1965): 210–23.

Rea, Ralph R. *Sterling Price: The Lee of the West.* Little Rock, 1959.

"Reunion at Pea Ridge." St. Louis *Missouri Republican,* Aug. 20, 1887.

Riley, Amiel L. "Pea Ridge Battlefield, 1962." Benton County (Ark.) Historical Society *Pioneer* 7 (1962): 3.

Roberts, Bobby L. "General T. C. Hindman and the Trans-Mississippi District." *Arkansas Historical Quarterly* 32 (1973): 297–311.

Roland, Charles P. *Albert Sidney Johnston: Soldier of Three Republics.* Austin, 1964.

Roman, Alfred. *The Military Operations of General Beauregard in the War Between the States, 1861 to 1865.* 2 vols. New York, 1883.

Rosa, Joseph G. *They Called Him Wild Bill: The Life and Adventures of James Butler Hickock.* Norman, 1974.

Rose, Victor M. *The Life and Services of Gen. Ben McCulloch.* Philadelphia, 1888.

———. *Ross' Texas Brigade, Being A Narrative of Events Connected With Its Service in the Late War Between the States.* Louisville, 1881.

Rosecrans, William S. "The Battle of Corinth." In *Battles and Leaders of the Civil War,* ed. Robert U. Johnson and Clarence C. Buel. 4 vols. New York, 1884–87.

Ross, Frances M., ed. "'A Tie Between Us That Time Cannot Sever': Latta Family Letters, 1855–1872." *Arkansas Historical Quarterly* 40 (1981): 31–78.

Roth, Dave. "Battle of Pea Ridge." *Blue and Gray* 5 (1988): 48–60.

Russell, Don. *The Lives and Legends of Buffalo Bill.* Norman, 1970.

Schofield, John M. *Forty-Six Years in the Army.* New York, 1897.

Scott, Joe M. *Four Years' Service in the Southern Army.* Mulberry, Ark., 1897.

Scott, Kim A., ed. "Witness for the Prosecution: The Civil War Letter of Lieutenant George Taylor." *Arkansas Historical Quarterly* 48 (1989): 260–71.

Scott, Oliver H. P. Letter of March 10, 1862, in *Blue and Gray* 5 (1988): 4.

Scott, William F. *The Story of a Cavalry Regiment: The Career of the Fourth Iowa Veteran Volunteers From Kansas to Georgia, 1861–1865.* New York, 1893.

Seamster, Alvin. "Battlefield Memories." Benton County (Ark.) Historical Society *Pioneer* 17 (1972): 49.

———. "How the Plateau of Pea Ridge Got Its Name." Benton County (Ark.) Historical Society *Pioneer* 7 (1962): 4.

———. "Reunions of Blue and Gray." In *The Battle of Pea Ridge.* Rogers, Ark., 1963.

Shalhope, Robert E. *Sterling Price: Portrait of a Southerner.* Columbia, Mo., 1971.

Shea, William L. "A Semi-Savage State: The Image of Arkansas in the Civil War." *Arkansas Historical Quarterly* 48 (1989): 309–28.

Sheridan, Philip H. *Personal Memoirs of P. H. Sheridan.* 2 vols. New York, 1888.

Sigel, Franz. "The Pea Ridge Campaign." In *Battles and Leaders of the Civil War,* ed. Robert U. Johnson and Clarence C. Buel. 4 vols. New York, 1884–87.

Simpson, Harold B., ed. *The Bugle Softly Blows: The Confederate Diary of*

Benjamin M. Seaton. Waco, 1965.

Smith, Raymond A., Jr. "Yours in Haste, W. H. Kinsman." *Palimpsest* 66 (1985): 194–215.

Smith, W. Wayne. "An Experiment in Counterinsurgency: The Assessment of Confederate Sympathizers in Missouri." *Journal of Southern History* 35 (1969): 361–80.

Snead, Thomas L. "The Conquest of Arkansas." In *Battles and Leaders of the Civil War*, ed. Robert U. Johnson and Clarence C. Buel. 4 vols. New York, 1884–87.

———. "The First Year of the War in Missouri." In *Battles and Leaders of the Civil War*, ed. Robert U. Johnson and Clarence C. Buel. 4 vols. New York, 1884–87.

———. "With Price East of the Mississippi." In *Battles and Leaders of the Civil War*, ed. Robert U. Johnson and Clarence C. Buel. 4 vols. New York, 1884–87.

Snelling, Lois. "Leetown: It Stood When the Fury of Pea Ridge Broke; Now Only an Old House Remains." Little Rock *Arkansas Gazette Magazine*, July 9, 1961.

Sparks, Allison W. *The War Between the States, As I Saw It. Reminiscent, Historical and Personal.* Tyler, Tex., 1901.

Stewart, Faye L. "Battle of Pea Ridge." *Missouri Historical Review* 22 (1928): 187–92.

Stirman, E. I. "Career of Gen. Ben M'Culloch." *Confederate Veteran* 21 (1913): 172–73.

Stuart, Addison A. *Iowa Colonels and Regiments: Being a History of Iowa Regiments in the War of the Rebellion.* Des Moines, 1865.

Sunderland, Glenn W. *Five Days to Glory.* New York, 1970.

Taylor, Richard. *Destruction and Reconstruction: Personal Experiences of the Late War.* New York, 1879.

Thomas, David Y. *Arkansas in War and Reconstruction, 1861–1874.* Little Rock, 1926.

Thorndike, Rachel S., ed. *The Sherman Letters: Correspondence Between General and Senator Sherman from 1837 to 1891.* New York, 1894.

Tilley, Nannie M., ed. *Federals on the Frontier: The Diary of Benjamin F. McIntyre, 1862–1864.* Austin, 1963.

Travick, A. M. "Concerning the Death of Gen. McCulloch." *Confederate Veteran* 14 (1906): 62.

Truman, W. L. "Battle of Elk Horn." *Confederate Veteran* 11 (1903): 551–52.

———. "Battle of Elk Horn—Correction." *Confederate Veteran* 12 (1904): 27–28.

———. "The Battle of Elk Horn, or Pea Ridge, Arkansas." *Confederate Veteran* 36 (1928): 168–71.

Tunnard, W. H. *A Southern Record. The History of the Third Regiment Louisiana Infantry.* Baton Rouge, 1866.

Tyler, William N. *The Dispatch Carrier.* Port Byron, Ill., 1892.

The United States Biographical Dictionary and Portrait Gallery of Eminent and Self-Made Men. Iowa Volume. Chicago, 1878.

U.S. War Department. *The War of the Rebellion: A Compilation of the Official Records of the Union and Confederate Armies.* 70 vols. in 128. Washington, D.C., 1880–1901.

Vaught, Elsa, ed. "Diary of an Unknown Soldier." *Arkansas Historical Quarterly* 18 (1959): 50–89.

————. "The Memorial Associates." Benton County (Ark.) Historical Society *Pioneer* 6 (1961): 4–5.

Vincent, Howard P., ed. *Collected Poems of Herman Melville.* Chicago, 1947.

Ware, Eugene F. *The Indian War of 1864, Being a Fragment of the Early History of Kansas, Nebraska, Colorado, and Wyoming.* Topeka, 1911.

Waring, George E., Jr. *Whip and Spur.* New York, 1897.

Warner, Ezra J. *Generals in Blue: Lives of the Union Commanders.* Baton Rouge, 1964.

————. *Generals in Gray: Lives of the Confederate Commanders.* Baton Rouge, 1959.

"A War Time Letter from Thomas Green, September 3, 1862." Smith County (Tex.) Historical Society *Chronicles* 6 (1967): 37–39.

Watson, William. *Life in the Confederate Army, Being the Observations and Experiences of an Alien in the South During the American Civil War.* New York, 1888.

West, Emmet C. *History and Reminiscences of the Second Wisconsin Cavalry Regiment.* Portage, Wis., 1904.

Wiley, Bell I. *The Road to Appomattox.* New York, 1968.

Willett, John T. "Development of Pea Ridge National Military Park." *Arkansas Historical Quarterly* 21 (1962): 166–69.

Williams, T. Harry. *P. G. T. Beauregard: Napoleon in Gray.* Baton Rouge, 1955.

Wilson, Hunt P. "The Battle of Elkhorn." St. Louis *Missouri Republican*, July 4 and 11, 1885.

Wilson, James G. *Biographical Sketches of Illinois Officers Engaged in the War Against the Rebellion of 1861.* Chicago, 1862.

Wilstach, Frank J. *Wild Bill Hickock: Prince of Pistoleers.* New York, 1926.

Wise, Joe R., ed. "The Letters of Lt. Flavius W. Perry, 17th Texas Cavalry, 1862–1863." *Military History of Texas and the Southwest* 13 (1974): 11–30.

Woodruff, William E. *With the Light Guns in '61–'65: Reminiscences of Eleven Arkansas, Missouri and Texas Light Batteries, in the Civil War.* Little Rock, 1903.

Woodworth, Steven E. "'Dismembering the Confederacy': Jefferson Davis and the Trans-Mississippi West." *Military History of the Southwest* 20 (1990): 1–22.

————. *Jefferson Davis and His Generals: The Failure of Confederate Command in the West.* Lawrence, Kans., 1990.

Wooster, Ralph A., and Robert Wooster. "'Rarin for a Fight': Texans in the Confederate Army." *Southwestern Historical Quarterly* 84 (1981): 387–426.

Worley, Ted. R., ed. *At Home in Confederate Arkansas: Letters to and from Pulaski Countians, 1861–1865.* Little Rock, 1955.

————, ed. *The War Memoirs of Captain John W. Lavender, C.S.A.* Pine Bluff, Ark., 1956.

Wright, Marcus J. *Arkansas in the War, 1861–1865.* Batesville, Ark., 1963.

Yates, Paul C. "Incident from the Battle of Elkhorn." *Confederate Veteran* 36 (1928): 173.

————. "Incidents from Battle of Elkhorn." *Confederate Veteran* 14 (1906): 61–62.

Yeary, Mamie, comp. *Reminiscences of the Boys in Gray, 1861–1865.* McGregor, Tex., 1912.

Yeater, Sarah J. *Civil War Experiences of Sarah J. Yeater.* Sedalia, Mo., 1910.

Zuber, William P. *My Eighty Years in Texas.* Austin, 1971.

THESES AND DISSERTATIONS

Belser, Thomas A., Jr. "Military Operations in Missouri and Arkansas, 1861–1865." Ph.D. diss., Vanderbilt University, 1958.

Brown, Walter L. "Albert Pike, 1809–1891." Ph.D. diss., University of Texas, 1955.

Bullock, Neal T. "The Confederate Services of General Ben McCulloch." M.A. thesis, University of Arkansas at Fayetteville, 1957.

Burkard, Dick J. "The Edge of Glory: The Civil War Career of Samuel Ryan Curtis." M.A. thesis, Southern Illinois University, 1984.

Duffus, Gerald R. "A Study of the Military Career of Samuel R. Curtis, 1861–1865." M.A. thesis, Drake University, 1966.

Fortin, Maurice G., Jr. "Confederate Military Operations in Arkansas, 1861–1865." M.A. thesis, North Texas State University, 1978.

Geise, William R. "The Confederate Military Forces in the Trans-Mississippi West, 1861–1865: A Study in Command." Ph.D. diss., University of Texas, 1974.

Gibbons, James W. "Reestablishment of Prairie Vegetation at Pea Ridge National Military Park, Benton County, Arkansas." M.S. thesis, University of Arkansas at Fayetteville, 1977.

Gunn, Jack W. "Life of Ben McCulloch." M.A. thesis, University of Texas, 1947.

Hathaway, Worster M. "Brigadier General Stand Watie, Confederate Guerrilla." M.A. thesis, Oklahoma State University, 1966.

Holst, David L. "General Samuel Curtis and the Civil War in the West." M.A. thesis, Illinois State University, 1974.

Huff, Leo. "Confederate Arkansas." M.A. thesis, University of Arkansas at Fayetteville, 1964.

Smith, Thomas C. "Ecological Studies on Prairie Restoration at Pea Ridge National Military Park, Benton County, Arkansas." M.S. thesis, University of Arkansas at Fayetteville, 1979.

Sude, Barry R. "Federal Military Policy and Strategy in Missouri and Arkansas, 1861–1863: A Study of Command Level Conflict." Ph.D. diss., Temple University, 1987.

Index